RESEARCH METHODS IN
CRIMINAL JUSTICE

RESEARCH METHODS IN CRIMINAL JUSTICE

Ralph B. Taylor

Temple University

McGraw-Hill, Inc.

New York   St. Louis   San Francisco   Auckland   Bogotá   Caracas
Lisbon   London   Madrid   Mexico City   Milan   Montreal   New Delhi
San Juan   Singapore   Sydney   Tokyo   Toronto

This book was set in Palatino by Better Graphics, Inc.
The editor was Phillip A. Butcher;
the production supervisor was Richard A. Ausburn.
The cover was designed by Carla Bauer.
Project supervision was done by Tage Publishing Service, Inc.
R. R. Donnelley & Sons Company was printer and binder.

RESEARCH METHODS IN CRIMINAL JUSTICE

 This book is printed on recycled, acid-free paper containing a minimum of 50% total recycled fiber with 10% postconsumer de-inked fiber.

1 2 3 4 5 6 7 8 9 0 DOC DOC 9 0 9 8 7 6 5 4 3

ISBN 0-07-063001-1

Library of Congress Cataloging-in-Publication Data

Taylor, Ralph B.
    Research methods in criminal justice / Ralph B. Taylor.
        p.   cm.
    Includes bibliographical references and index.
    ISBN 0-07-063001-1
    1. Criminal justice, Administration of—Research—Methodology.
    2. Criminology—Research—Methodology.   3. Judicial statistics.
    4. Criminal statistics.   I. Title.
    HV7419.5.T39   1994
    364'.072—dc20   93-37861

ABOUT THE AUTHOR

RALPH B. TAYLOR is Professor of Criminal Justice at Temple University (Philadelphia, PA). He received his Ph.D. in Social Psychology from Johns Hopkins University in 1977. He has previously held positions at Virginia Polytechnic Institute and State University, and Johns Hopkins University (Center for Metropolitan Planning and Research, and Department of Psychology). He has been at Temple University since 1984. He served as Associate Dean for Graduate Studies, Research and External Funding in the College of Arts and Sciences at Temple University from 1989 to 1992. His research has appeared in a range of sociological, psychological, and criminal justice journals. He has received research funding from the National Science Foundation, the National Institute of Mental Health, the National Institute of Justice, and other agencies. He edited URBAN NEIGHBORHOODS (Praeger, 1986), and authored HUMAN TERRITORIAL FUNCTIONING (Cambridge University Press, 1988). He is a member of the American Psychological Association (Divisions 8, 27, and 34), the American Sociological Association, the American Society of Criminology, the Academy of Criminal Justice Sciences, the Eastern Psychological Association, and the Eastern Sociological Society. He has served as President of Division 34 (American Psychological Association), and was recently elected as a Fellow of that division.

PERMISSIONS ACKNOWLEDGMENTS

Page

35   Figure 2.4   "The Island of Research" from CANCER RESEARCH, December 1980. Reprinted by permission of the American Association for Cancer Research, Inc.

62   Table 4.1   From Warwick D.P. (1982). "Types of harm in social research." In T.L. Beauchamp, R.R. Feden, R.J. Wallace, Jr., and L. Walters (Eds.), ETHICAL ISSUES IN SOCIAL SCIENCE RESEARCH. Reprinted by permission of The Johns Hopkins University Press.

79   Table 5.1   Adapted from Wilkinson, L. (1988). SYGRAPH, Evanston, IL: SYSTAT, Inc., p. 66. Reprinted by permission.

124   Figure 6.6   From MAGNITUDE SCALING by M. Lodge. Copyright © 1981 Sage Publications, Inc. Reprinted by permission of Sage Publications, Inc.

147   Table 8.1   From STANDARDS FOR EDUCATIONAL AND PSYCHOLOGICAL TESTS. Copyright © 1974 by the American Psychological Association. Reprinted by permission.

169   Table 9.1   Dunford, F.W., Huizinga, D., and Elliott, D.S. (1990). The role of arrest in domestic assault: The Omaha police experiment. CRIMINOLOGY 28 (2): 183–206, Table 3. Reprinted by permission.

188   Figure 10.3   Blalock, H.M., Jr. (1979). SOCIAL STATISTICS (revised 2nd ed). New York: McGraw-Hill, Figure 7.7, p. 95. Reprinted by permission.

222   Table 11.4   From INTRODUCTION TO QUALITATIVE RESEARCH METHODS by R. Bogdan and S. J. Taylor. Copyright © 1975 by John Wiley & Sons, Inc. Reprinted by permission of John Wiley & Sons, Inc.

253   Box 12.4   Bradburn, N.M., & Miles, C. (1989) Vague quantifiers. In E. Singer and S. Press (Eds.) SURVEY RESEARCH METHODS. Chicago: University of Chicago Press. Adapted from Table 1, p. 159. Reprinted by permission.

280   Figure 13.4   Jones, P.R. (1990). "Community corrections in Kansas: Extending community-based corrections or widening the net?" in JOURNAL OF RESEARCH IN CRIME AND DELINQUENCY 27: 79–101. Reprinted by permission of Sage Publications, Inc.

287   Table 13.2   From EVALUATION: A SYSTEMATIC APPROACH, Third Edition by P.H. Rossi and H.E. Freeman. Copyright © 1985 by Sage Publications, Inc. Reprinted by permission of Sage Publications, Inc.

294   Figure 14.1   Knapp, K.A. (1984). What sentencing reform in Minnesota has and has not accomplished. JUDICATURE 68: 181–189, Figure 1. Reprinted by permission.

296   Table 14.1   Wolfgang, M., Figlio, R., and Sellin, T. (1972) DELINQUENCY IN A BIRTH COHORT. Chicago: University of Chicago Press. Table 6.1, p. 89. Reprinted by permission.

299   Figure 14.3   From Olweus, D. (1979): Stability of aggressive reaction patterns in males: A Review. PSYCHOLOGICAL BULLETIN (86): 852–875. Copyright © 1979 by the American Psychological Association. Reprinted by permission.

304   Figure 14.6   From Farrington, D.P. (1986): Stepping stones to adult criminal careers. In DEVELOPMENT OF ANTISOCIAL AND PROSOCIAL BEHAVIOR, edited by D. Olweus, J. Block, and M.R. Yarrow, 376. New York: Academic Press, Inc. Reprinted by permission.

327   Figure 15.1   Zahn, M.A. (1989). Homicide in the twentieth century: Trends, types and causes. In VIOLENCE IN AMERICA: THE HISTORY OF CRIME, Vol. 1, edited by T.R. Gurr. Copyright © 1984 Sage Publications, Inc. Reprinted by permission.

328   Figure 15.2   Gurr, T.R. (1989). Historical trends in violent crime: Europe and the United States. In VIOLENCE IN AMERICA: THE HISTORY OF CRIME, Vol. 1, edited by T.R. Gurr. Copyright © 1984 Sage Publications, Inc. Reprinted by permission.

339   Table 16.1   From Chiricos, T.G. (1987). Rates of crime and unemployment: An analysis of aggregate research evidence. © 1987 by the Society for the Study of Social Problems. Reprinted from SOCIAL PROBLEMS, Vol. 34, No. 2, 187–212 by permission.

At once a voice arose among
  The bleak twigs overhead
In full-hearted evensong
  Of joy illimited;
An aged thrush, frail, gaunt, and small,
  In blast-beruffled plume,
Had chosen thus to fling his soul
  Upon the growing gloom.

—Thomas Hardy, *The Darkling Thrush*

CONTENTS

PART FOUR

THE GALLERY OF RESEARCH TOOLS: DIFFERENT RESEARCH APPROACHES

PREFACE

It's hard to know how all this began. My interest in research methods. Maybe it was with the motorcycle rides.

Twenty years ago, fresh out of college, I was working with "pre" delinquents in a residential treatment center based on behavior modification principles. I am still not sure why the boys there merited the "pre" prefix. Some of them had already burned down schools, stolen cars, and burglarized stores by the time they got to the center. But they were good kids, and I liked many of them.

One boy, let's call him David Cone (no, he did not go on to become a pitcher) was smart but lazy in school, especially in math. The teachers were stumped; they had tried everything. But Dave liked my motorcycle, and was always teasing me about giving him a ride. Hmm, I thought. Dave and I worked out a deal where if he improved his behavior in class, he could earn rides on the motorcycle. I monitored his classroom behavior intermittently, using video cameras, and recording how much of his class time was "on task," working on math, and how much was "off task," throwing spitballs and such. We agreed that if he averaged over a certain portion of observed time "on task," for a specified length of time, he could earn a ride on the back of my motorcycle. I plotted the classroom behavior over a period of about two weeks. His behavior improved, as did his math grades. We went for a motorcycle ride or two, chugging up and down the hills on a beatup and underpowerd Honda. The administration of the center where I worked, however, decided that their insurance did not cover such situations. And, to our mutual regret, the deal was off and the spitballs resumed.

So that was my first admittedly crude research study. In graduate school I collaborated with researchers who used a wide range of techniques. Sidney Brower is a planner who used projective techniques with three-dimensional models, as well as behavioral observation techniques, sending observers around study blocks to count people and code activity. I assisted Clint De Soto, a social psychologist, on some lab experiments. I worked with Robert Hogan, a personality psychologist, developing standardized personality inventories. Roger Stough is a geographer by training. We did several studies of environmental cognition, using an obscure scaling technique adapted from personality research, the Kelly Repgrid technique. I collaborated with Lois Verbrugge, a sociologist and demographer, on a household sample survey. Working with a cadre of graduate students we developed the instrument, sampled households, fielded the survey, and coded and analyzed the results.

I absorbed an important lesson as a result of working with so many different scientists from varying backgrounds, each devoted to their own brand of tool. Each instrument told a different story, creating a perspective that was unique. Each one shed a different light on the behavior or attitude or sentiment of interest.

In the present volume I have tried to share my appreciation for the value of different types of research tools. In Part 4 I discuss specific methodologies. I attempt to provide you with a sense of the relative strengths and weaknesses of different approaches. I hope that, as a result, you, as a consumer of research, will better understand when a tool does or does not fit the problem or situation being investigated.

The field of criminal justice is made whole, in part, because it does rely on such diverse instruments. All of these approaches make equivalent contributions to the field. Unstructured studies of single individuals, such as *The Fence* by Karl Klockars, or of many groups, such as William Thrasher's *The Gang*, play as great a role in defining the field as Wolfgang's first study of a group of thousands of boys all born in Philadelphia during the same year, or an analysis of data from a nationwide victimization survey. The field is as strong as it is because it embraces all these styles of research.

Let me turn briefly to what you will find in this textbook that is new, and perhaps represents an advance in the treatment of criminal justice research methods.

I have woven into the text two approaches to scientific inquiry: Holmes's and Einstein's. With Holmes's approach, you focus largely on data from a specific situation. You want to understand why something happened in a specific instance. It is a grounded theorizing or discovery-oriented approach. With Einstein's approach you hope to find if your theory, which represents your ideas about how things work in a broad range of situations, is correct. It uses a hypothetico-deductive approach. Some tools are better suited to one approach than the other; some tools can be used with either approach. But these alternate pathways are equally valid, and in effect complement one another.

Some students have reported that they find Holmes's approach liberating. They can begin to generate theory just by looking at data they may have in hand. We do this all the time in everyday life anyway. For example, you observe that your roommate is grumpy on Thursday afternoons. You start to wonder why. You collect data and build a theory based on these data. The discussion in this volume of Holmes's and Einstein's approaches to scientific inquiry merely formalizes many of the steps we already follow in different parts of our lives.

A second distinctive feature of the text is my extensive use of three detailed, hypothetical scenarios. I describe three plausible situations, one in each of three different areas: community policing, electronic monitoring, and sentencing reform. I return to these scenarios several times in the volume to illustrate how a particular research tool might be used in a specific situation. Through these scenarios I hope that you develop a more detailed picture of how research can be applied to definite problems and questions.

Third, I introduce two new research tools that are becoming increasingly important in criminal justice. Meta-analysis allows researchers to *systematically* "add up" the results of several studies on a topic to obtain an overall "verdict." Simulation techniques allow you to mathematically model how different processes might affect one another. For example, what is the relationship between total prison costs, average length of stay, and number of prisoners admitted per some unit time? Simulations, which in simplified form can be carried out on a PC using a spreadsheet program, provide precise answers to such questions. Given the extraordinary pressures buffeting the criminal justice system, and the requirement that criminal justice policy makers be able to predict future directions in the system, simulations are extremely important. These two tools have not been covered in other criminal justice research methods texts.

Finally, I also devote a separate chapter to a method, related to prediction, that is perhaps the most important in criminal justice: longitudinal studies. Such studies can tell us about the likely course of an offender's career, or the probable effects of a sanction on the future behavior of an offender. I can think of no type of investigation more important for an enlightened criminal justice system.

A note on nonsexist language is in order. When first writing the volume I used the obligatory "s/he" or "he or she," but quickly grew tired of these clumsy terms. I tried different terms; in the wee hours of the morning phrases such as "hesh" or "hermself" exuded an odd appeal. Finally, I settled on sometimes using male pronouns, and other times using female pronouns. I have not totaled the number of times I used each, but I tried to make the usage balanced across the sexes.

Turning to acknowledgments, many people helped steer this project along. Initial discussions with Bill Laufer, and his willingness to put me in contact with the people at McGraw-Hill, were extremely helpful. My editor at McGraw-Hill, Phil Butcher, has been supportive but stimulating, patient but prodding, and enthusiastic but questioning. His firm belief in the vision of this volume, tempered with his understanding of the relevant practical constraints, have both been invaluable. His staff, especially Melissa Mashburn, were courteous, efficient and professional throughout. Production work was mastered by Tony and Maria Caruso at Tage Publishing Service, Inc. I appreciated their persistent good humor and attention to detail. The following conscientious reviewers provided invaluable criticism and suggestions, leading to a drastic overhaul of the first draft: Steven G. Brandl, Michigan State University; Bruce Bullington, Pennsylvania State University; Gary Copus, University of Alaska, Fairbanks; Roger Jarjoura, Northeastern University; Peter R. Jones, Temple University; Richard Lawrence, St. Cloud University; JoAnn Miller, Purdue University; R. Richard Ritti, Pennsylvania State University; Albert Roberts, Rutgers University; and Ralph A. Weisheit, Illinois State University. I owe a special debt to Dick Ritti and Peter Jones for their painstakingly careful and thoughtful remarks on several of the chapters.

I inflicted earlier versions of the volume on numerous students. They suffered the burden cheerfully. Comments and reactions from graduate students in my Spring 1992 Research Methods class were edifying in many respects. These students included Nick Goodwin, John Kinkead, Nafessah Miles, Chuck Rossel, and Barb Koons. Figure 3.1, which ties together theorizing, operationalization, and measurement, emerged from a stimulating conversation we had one evening. Undergraduates in my Summer 1992 Research Methods class also contributed substantially toward improving exposition, examples, and some of the exercises. Mr. Wallace, a student in that class and a security officer at the Philadelphia Zoo, explained how he had been misled in a security investigation because he used Einstein's approach rather than Holmes's. Thereafter he became an advocate of the latter logic of scientific inquiry.

Of course, all the remaining faults, outright mistakes, inaccuracies, and muddles persisting in the volume are solely my responsibility.

Last on this list, but certainly foremost in my Lewinian lifespace, I owe a debt that can never be repaid to Michele, Mara, and Nyssa.

They all forbore the hours I spent shackled to the computer table, and the vacation days I missed. At a time when her own career was making extensive demands on her, Michele, innumerable times, helped create needed blocks of time. Nyssa and Mara expressed interest in the project, and supported my goal of doing something other than a "boring textbook." You the reader will have to judge if I came close to that goal. All three accepted, always with grace, the pernicious, persistent mental preoccupation that accompanies a project of this scope. Now that I'm getting out of the study, I'll work on breaking the habit.

Ralph B. Taylor

RESEARCH METHODS IN
CRIMINAL JUSTICE

START HERE
OR
README NOW

Welcome. You are beginning your exploration of *Research Methods in Criminal Justice*. I would like to take this opportunity to provide you with a brief orienting overview of the material to come. I have organized the text into four different sections. Let me tell you a little about each one.

Part One deals with some lofty material: theory. Criminal justice is a social science. Therefore, criminal justice researchers interpret the findings they obtain in their different studies in the context of theories. Theories are their ideas about how things work in the "real world." Theories are always simpler than the real world, but at least they provide a means of predicting, explaining, and describing some of the events that happen there.

Part Two examines two different topics. You will read about charts and tables, the two most common means of presenting research information. You will see how these devices can summarize information but also sometimes hide information. You also will review general ethical guidelines for conducting social science research. Researchers have obligations to their colleagues, to the participants, and to the wider society. Every study has an ethical dimension.

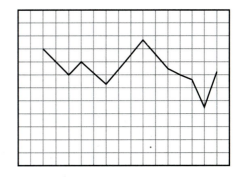

Part Three examines benchmarks of scientific quality. I have a cabinet full of research studies. In that cabinet I have some high-quality studies, many mediocre studies, and some poor-quality studies. Not all research studies are created equal. Some are better done than others. You will encounter three benchmarks of scientific quality: reliability, internal validity, and external validity. You will see how scientists take steps to improve the quality of their studies. Nevertheless, sometimes they must choose between maximizing one quality over another.

In Part Four you take a tour of the different research methods in criminal justice. You will see that social scientists use a broad range of methods to examine questions. The methods range from those requiring no more than a clipboard, pencil, and a sharp eye, to those generating massive quantities of computer printout. Each of these different tools has its own particular strengths and its own particular weaknesses. After reading this section you will understand what research tools best match particular research questions.

I began conducting funded research in 1975. I have been teaching research methods to undergraduate and graduate students in criminal justice since 1985. The planning and writing of this volume occupied me for about 4 years. I hope you find a few things in here to spark your interest in research.

THE CONTEXT OF RESEARCH METHODS

This first section of the volume addresses the context within which criminal justice research is conducted. In *Chapter 1* you learn about the steps involved in conducting social science research, and what it means for criminal justice to be a social science. I suggest that you, as a researcher, can adopt different orientations to social science problems and findings. Finally, I introduce three hypothetical scenarios. Each draws on a current problem confronting the field. I will refer to these situations throughout the volume. Each scenario asks you to imagine you are in a criminal justice agency, with responsibility for resolving a particular situation. As you progress through the volume, you will see how different research methods can be applied to these particular scenarios.

A fundamental concern of criminal justice research methods is to connect theory—our ideas about what is going on in a real-world situation—with data—our observations of the real world. But, there are *different ways* scientists connect theory and data. You can start either with the data or with the theory. In *Chapter 2* you will examine alternate pathways for making such connections. You also will explore implications of pursuing one pathway over another. I suggest that Sherlock Holmes's and Albert Einstein's approaches to scientific inquiry captured the essentials of each of these two pathways.

Nonetheless, whatever the route taken to connect theory and data, there are some rules or norms governing how scientists go about getting their information, thinking about and assessing their information, and reporting their information. Scientists generally agree these should be followed. You will review some of these norms and the reasons scientists generally follow them.

In *Chapter 3* you examine how scientists use *theory* to organize their ideas. Scientific theories make science different from accounting or newspaper reporting. You will appreciate why scientists need theory, and you will examine its building blocks.

In *Chapter 4* you investigate another set of "rules" followed by scientists: those concerned with ethics. In the past 20 years society has begun demanding that scientists of all types respect the rights of people participating in their studies, and also the rights of the larger society. I note the nature of these obligations, and the reasons for them. Unfortunately, as we shall see, despite mechanisms for protecting the rights of study participants and the larger society, it is not always clear to the scientist what is or isn't ethical. *Every* criminal justice research project has an ethical dimension.

After you have read Part One you should be prepared to discuss questions such as the following:

"What are some different ways of connecting theory and data?" "Why do scientists need theory?" "What are the basic building blocks of theory?" "How do I decide if one theory is better than another?" "When should I follow Holmes's method of scientific investigation? When should I follow Einstein's method?" "What are some of the most important 'rules' scientists follow, and why do they do so?"

Of course, there are some perennial questions that have puzzled philosophers for millenia. Part One will not address: "Why is there air?" "Why ask why?" Carry on, nevertheless.

CRIMINAL JUSTICE RESEARCH AND THE SOCIAL SCIENCE PROCESS

To set limits to speculation is treason to the future.
—ALFRED NORTH WHITEHEAD, *[1]*

OBJECTIVES

You will learn what it means for criminal justice to be a social science. You will examine the broad outlines of the social science investigation process. You will read three different hypothetical scenarios based on current problems confronting criminal justice practitioners.

You've done it. You've cracked open your research methods text. You might have done this for any number of reasons. Maybe you've got a quiz or a test coming up next week. (I hope it's not a midterm!) Maybe your class has been under way for a couple of weeks and you're beginning to get curious about what's in this tome that has been gathering dust on your desk under your CDs. Perhaps it's the first day of classes, and you've got some free time. Or possibly you're curious about a required course in your major you're going to be taking next term.

No matter how you got here, my guesses are that you are taking this course because it is a requirement for your major, and you have heard negative comments about the course. Other students may have said things like "It's a tough course," or "It requires a *lot* of work." If my guesses are correct, I expect you are deeply ambivalent about this course and concerned about whether you will do well in it.

WHAT IT REQUIRES OF YOU

If you're not ambivalent or concerned, great. But if you *do* have such feelings: relax. Don't think about *the whole book.* Just take it one step at a time. (You don't sit down to dinner and think about all the hamburgers (veggie burgers?) you are going to eat for the rest of your life, do you?) Read one chapter. Discuss it with your classmates. Try answering questions on the workdisk. Try some of the exercises you will find there. Discuss some of these with your friends. In short, be an empiricist. Gather data for yourself on what this course is about.

I can assure you that as you do gather data, you will find this text does not require the mathematical skills of the proverbial rocket scientist. Yes, some math is required. But it is no more complex than basic high school, prealgebra material. *Research methods are not so much concerned with math as they are with a way of thinking about research.* In short, this text requires no more of you than did the other texts you took in your other courses for the major: an inquiring mind and a willingness to explore different ways of solving some of society's most vexing social problems.

Helpful Hints

To speed your learning, use the different resources I have built into the text. I have divided the text into four sections. A prologue precedes each section and highlights the major features of the forthcoming material. Go over these prologues when you begin a section, and again when you *finish*. Each prologue concludes with a few questions. Try answering these after you have completed a section. You could discuss them with other students or practice making outlines of short answers.

Within each chapter you will find embedded features to help you. Each chapter concludes with a summary of main points and a list of key words that have appeared in the chapter. These key words are always **boldfaced** in the text. Go over these key words and recall for yourself the contexts in the chapter in which they appeared. It's as important to know how to use key words as it is to know their definition.

At the end of most chapters you will find a short list of *selected readings*. Most often these are books, but I do include some articles. Take a look at some.

Discussion questions and *exercises* can be found on the workdisk. Try writing outline answers to the questions. Better yet, discuss them with other classmates. Perhaps the best approach would be for you and another classmate to write answers to the questions, and then to discuss your answers and the differences between the two of you. You will find some exercises suitable for in-class purposes. Others can be done by an individual student or group of students. They allow you to "apply" the concepts covered to a variety of situations.

In short, if you are concerned or ambivalent about the material in this volume, that is a totally normal reaction. But don't let your anxiety overwhelm you. Take the material one chapter at a time, gather data for yourself about what the material requires, and use the text features to simplify your learning.

CRIMINAL JUSTICE AND THE SOCIAL SCIENCE PROCESS

Criminal justice is a social science. (For a simplified description of social scientists, see Figure 1.1.) As such it is an *empirical* enterprise.

FIGURE 1.1

"I'm a social scientist, Michael. That means I can't explain electricity or anything like that, but if you ever want to know about people I'm your man."

(*Source.* Drawing by Handelsman; © 1986. The New Yorker Magazine, Inc.)

It relies heavily on observed evidence or data; ideas about how things work are evaluated in the light of this evidence. These data come from investigations conducted by social scientists.

The Process of Social Science Investigation

Figure 1.2 describes the *process* of social science investigation in broad, outline form. These are the steps a social scientist will go through. The figure makes the process look much more orderly than it often is. Nevertheless, it does capture the steps underlying the enterprise.

Possible Starting Points

The social scientist may initiate the process for any number of reasons. The spur may be theoretical or speculative in origin. The scientist may have theoretically important questions about a setting or a behavior or a characteristic. These queries may arise from curiosity, observation, or works completed by others. Alternatively, the social scientist may simply have a hunch she wishes to pursue [2].

In contrast to these more speculative inducements to inquiry, the cause may be of an applied nature. Social scientists may be confronted with practical concerns or pressing problems requiring information. They may need to know the effects of intensive supervision on recidivism, for example. Or correctional administrators might ask how they can most safely reduce prison overcrowding. Or, finally, people may turn to the social scientist to evaluate a program and decide if it was effective. Whatever the impetus may be, the practical concern spurs the social scientist to collect relevant data systematically, or to analyze systematically data that are available.

Deciding What to Collect and How

Social scientists' first decision is to decide what data they will collect, and how to collect them. They will consider many factors in making these decisions. What data are available? What are the ethical constraints in the situation? What are the available resources for funding research? How much time do they have? In short, they must choose their research tool and develop the tool as needed. Their choices are shaped by ethical, practical, and theoretical elements. Personal factors also may play a role.

Independent and Dependent Variables In many research projects—but *not* all—researchers make distinctions between *independent variables* and *dependent variables*. A variable captures measurable scores on an attribute or feature. When you ask 10 people their age and write down the answers, you have measured a variable. If you ask 20 classmates if they have been a victim of a crime in the last 6 months, and write down their "yes" or "no" answers, you have measured a variable. You intend that the observed scores you have gathered reflect a concept. You will learn more about concepts and their roles in theory in Chapter 3.

You treat a variable as an **in**dependent **variable** when you focus more on its effects than on its causes. You are interested in what results *from* the variable. You treat a variable as a **de**pendent variable when you focus more on its causes than its consequences. You are interested in what *leads to* the variable.

I may ask you to complete a survey project on campus fear of crime. I may choose your methodology for you, and tell you to do in-person surveys. I also may define your dependent variable for you. For example, I may suggest you use an item such as: "How safe do you feel when walking alone on campus at

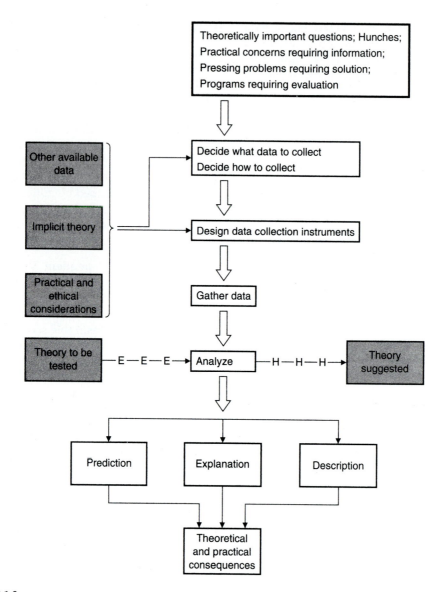

FIGURE 1.2
Shaded boxes represent other factors influencing or influenced by the process. The
main process begins at the top and proceeds to the bottom. The figure also captures
an important difference between Holmes's and Einstein's scientific method. With
Einstein's approach, the theory to be tested guides the scientific analysis. With
Holmes's approach, a theory is suggested by and emerges from the analysis of data.

night? Would you say you feel very safe? Safe? Unsafe? Or very unsafe?" This variable is your *dependent variable*. It is intended to measure a concept: fear of crime while on campus. You will try to explain why people give differing answers when asked this question.

In designing your survey you will decide what *independent* or *predictor* variables you will use. You hope these variables help you predict the level of fear your respondents report.

Theory Impinges on Variable Selection
Pull out a pencil and a piece of paper. Write down the independent variables you will use in your survey; think of the characteristics of individuals that make them more or less fearful for personal safety while on campus.

Really: please do this. I can wait.

Write down at least three predictors, but no more than six. If you have a list of more than six, cross off all but the six most important.

OK? I will bet you one simoleon that your list includes at least two of the following: sex, race, age, and victimization experiences.

You have chosen these independent variables because you have a *theory* about fear of crime—a set of ideas about what independent variables influence this dependent variable. You drew on this theory to generate your list of predictors.

Your theory may have been implicit, only vaguely formulated. You may think that older students will be more fearful because they have a better understanding of the campus environment. Or it may have been explicit. For example you may have learned in another course that victims have higher fear of crime levels than nonvictims. Whatever the form, you relied on *some* type of theory to focus your efforts.

Your theories about the causes of fear of crime also steered you *away* from certain

predictor variables: hair color, number of brothers, parents' occupation, whether ever arrested for a nontraffic violation, wattage of their dorm stereo, and so on. You did not use these variables because you did not have a theory suggesting how these variables could influence fear of crime, the dependent variable.

How I suggested above that you would use structured surveys to gather information about fear of crime. If you were actually beginning a research project, you could use any number of different research tools to investigate fear of crime. [3] You could look at records available from different sources: student use of campus escort services, sales at late night restaurants around the campus, or purchases of Mace in the student bookstore. Alternatively, you could examine essays in the campus newspaper on the topic. In short, you can use any one of several tools. As you progress through this volume, you will be learning more about these different tools, and the strengths and weaknesses of each.

Designing Collection Instruments, Collecting Information

Once social scientists have decided what information they want, they will try to learn if it is already available. If they learn that it is not available elsewhere, they must design their data collection instruments. Whether conducting a survey, retrieving information from historical documents, observing behaviors, or coding up the speeches of state legislators, they will need some type of form on which they or coworkers can note the relevant information.

Analysis

Once you have collected, checked, processed, and double-checked your data, you analyze them. Data analysis may conjure up images of behemoth mainframe computers with tape drives spinning and line printers spewing printout far into the night. You should bear in mind, however, that data analysis may involve activities far different from such a "high-tech" vision.

Instead, your analysis may follow a path that relies little on computers. You may pore over field notes, a tool in ethnographic research discussed in Chapter 11, and write memos to yourself for a few weeks. You may classify responses from open-ended surveys where respondents provided detailed, lengthy answers to questions. Or, you may follow a "medium-tech" avenue, sorting and classifying records on a database using a microcomputer. Analysis comes in many forms.

Further, I would advise you to guard against any prejudices you might have about the superiority of some types of analysis as compared to others. You might assume that the more numbers used in an analysis, and the more use made of computers, the more sophisticated and accurate the analysis. Your assumption might not be valid. There are no a priori reasons why an analysis based on field notes and using no numbers at all would be inferior to an analysis generated from 16 hours of computer analysis. The different analyses might have different strengths and weaknesses, but one will not be inherently inferior to the other.

Not only are there different ways to do analyses. There are also different ways you can link theory to data at this stage in the process. You can follow a method akin to Sherlock Holmes's and allow the data to suggest theories. (See the → H → H arrow in Figure 1.2.) Or, you can follow a method akin to Albert Einstein's, allow the theory to suggest what the data should say, and test that prediction. (See the → E → E arrow in Fig-

ure 1.2.) In Chapter 2 you will learn more about Holmes's and Einstein's approach to scientific inquiry. Holmes's method and Einstein's method represent two different logics of scientific investigation. Both are valid. They serve different purposes, and have different strengths and weaknesses. Again, neither is inherently inferior to the other.

Description, Explanation, and Prediction

From analyses may emerge **description**, **explanation**, **prediction**, or a combination of the three.

Description

Description may take two different forms. The social scientist may seek to *learn about the current or past level of a phenomenon in some group*. She might want to know: the rate at which African-American males between the ages of 18 and 24 were murdered in the year 1992 in Los Angeles, the proportion of homeless men in Newark, New Jersey who were the victims of a street crime in the last 6 months, the number of police officers in Great Britain killed in the line of duty in 1994 or 1894, total expenditures of all police departments in the state of Colorado for calendar year 1995, or the number of incarcerated offenders released on parole in Oklahoma in 1993 who remained arrest-free for at least one calendar year after their release. Stated more technically, in these examples she is trying to *estimate* a *parameter* for a *population*. **Parameter estimation** involves describing some aspect of an entire, defined group of units.

Alternatively, the description may focus on **describing linkages** between two or more factors. She may hope to clarify the processes at work or the factors influencing individuals, settings, or other units. She may focus on just one unit—one arrestee, one gang, or one prosecutor's office. Or, she may focus on many units: numerous arrestees, several gangs, or several prosecutors' offices.

Understanding or Explanation

When social scientists *describe*, some insight and understanding inevitably emerges from the description. *Understanding* or *explanation* derives from and provides insight into the processes at work among these individuals or in these situations. We begin to understand the *social regularities* underlying the behaviors or attitudes observed. " 'Understanding' . . . is grasping the *point* or *meaning* of what is being said or done." [4 p. 115]

Everyday Understanding All of us, whether social scientists or not, understand things. My neighbor tells me, "It is my understanding that the death penalty really does deter offenders." Your father may say, "I understand that people who jump bail are almost always guilty." Your roommate may affirm: "It is my understanding that the 1992 Los Angeles riots, the largest civil disorders in U.S. history, were caused by a criminal justice system that treats African-Americans unfairly." All these statements represent *everyday* understanding.

Social Scientific Understanding But **social scientific understanding** goes *beyond* this, as Max Weber, a German sociologist, and others, have pointed out. Social scientific understanding may have the same origins as everyday understanding. It may *originate* with hunches, intuition, conversations, observation, or other theories. [2] But social scientists do not stop there. Social scientists *weigh* their understanding in the light of empirical evidence—data gathered and pro-

cessed according to accepted rules of scientific conduct. Social scientific understanding, whatever its origins, is modified, rejected, or embraced based on *sound empirical evidence*. [5]

Social Scientific Understanding vs. Natural Scientific Understanding The understanding of social regularities is qualitatively different in two ways from the understanding of physical regularities held by natural scientists. [6] (1) Understandings of natural scientists are external to the physical phenomena themselves. You do not have to be a wave to understand the relationship between the moon and the tide. You do have to be a person to understand the effects of victimization experience on fear of crime. (2) Also, natural scientists' understandings *necessarily* imply certain predictions. If the tides no longer rise and fall as predicted by the position of the moon, then the natural scientist's understanding of the cause of tides is proven false. Social scientists' understandings will not always necessarily imply certain predictions.

Let me amplify the last point. I can understand the factors leading to a teenage boy's involvement in cocaine dealing. My understanding may lead me to *predict* that he will leave the business within X months. Nevertheless, if he does *not* leave the trade in X months, it does not mean my understanding was incorrect. My understanding may have been compatible with *more* than one outcome. [7] Failed prediction does not falsify understanding in the social sciences, but it does do so in the natural sciences.

Prediction

This leads us to the third goal of social scientists: **prediction**. What factors decide whether a person released on bail will appear at trial? What factors decide whether violent felony cases of Class C will be plea bargained? What factors predict if a parolee will commit a technical violation of her parole conditions?

These three purposes—describing, understanding, and predicting—are of necessity *complementary*. Of course, the complementarity of these three purposes does *not* mean social scientists have an equal interest in these three purposes in all situations. Sometimes social scientists will pursue one goal more hotly than another.

Criminal justice researchers and policy makers, as a group, have strong interests in prediction. The better criminal justice agencies can predict crime, offenders, prisoners, cases, potential offenders, parolees, and probationers, the more efficiently and equitably they can run.

Consequences

The three purposes of the social scientist have a range of both practical and theoretical consequences. A single investigation may simultaneously refute Theory A, support Theory B, suggest the outlines of a new Theory C, describe problem P, evaluate solution S to problem P, and offer guidance to policy makers in decision-making process D. It is also possible that a study has significant theoretical consequences and few practical consequences, or that it has significant practical import and little theoretical interest. In short, there is no necessary trade-off in a study between practical and theoretical implications.

THREE CURRENT CRIMINAL JUSTICE SCENARIOS: YOU ARE THERE

In this section I introduce three different issues currently confronting the criminal jus-

tice system. You have probably heard about or discussed some of these issues in your other criminal justice classes. I will then introduce three specific hypothetical situations related to each of these issues. (Any resemblance between these hypothetical scenarios, or the characters depicted therein, and any real situations or individuals, is purely coincidental.) Throughout the volume I will return to these running examples to illustrate and amplify various points of discussion. I will spin out different "endings" to these scenarios in the different chapters.

You will find each of these examples most instructive if you really "get into it." Think of it as a role-playing exercise where you imagine what you would do, your reasons, and how you would feel were you *actually* in such a situation. Feel free to elaborate the scenarios and add details, and to discuss them with your instructor and fellow students, or maybe even over dinner at home.

Community Policing

The National Scene   Over the last 20 years police departments throughout the country have carried out a variety of initiatives geared toward increasing their efficiency and, simultaneously, strengthening ties to the local communities they serve. Developments reflecting this trend include active support of citizen-based community crime-prevention programs, team policing arrangements with the same officers assigned to the same neighborhoods over time, emphases on problem-oriented policing, and the resurgence of patrol officers on foot in urban neighborhoods.

There has been widespread debate about the advantages and disadvantages of many of these initiatives. Foot patrol, in particular, has drawn the ire and praise of many. Numerous neighborhood groups and policing experts argue that the presence of the officer on foot creates a more salient law and order presence in the neighborhood. But others suggest that such initiatives reduce the effectiveness of the officers, making it more difficult for them to respond speedily and effectively to emergencies. These differences of opinion persist despite many evaluations of initiatives. [8]

Nonetheless, enthusiasm for this approach remains strong. For example, in August of 1990 the Commissioner of the New York City Police Department, Lee Brown, announced plans to train *all* new officers in foot patrol techniques. [9] As of this writing it seems likely that police departments around the country are going to continue with policing initiatives in urban areas that include a foot patrolling component.

The Specific Situation: YOU Are There
You are a career police officer in a large midwestern city with a population of around 400,000 residents. You currently direct operations in the department's Research and Development section. Most of your time is devoted to routine work such as filing Uniform Crime Reports for the FBI, keeping track of recorded crimes, officer and beat statistics, and so on.

In the past two years your department, in response to pressure from vocal citizen groups and some members of the City Council, carried out a foot patrolling initiative in one section of the city. Residents there had complained vociferously about open drug dealing on the streets. A special class of police recruits was trained in foot patrolling. They subsequently received assignments, along with some more seasoned officers, to this area. A local foundation provided funding for some additional training costs, but those funds will run out at the end of the year.

The neighborhood associations in the locations receiving the foot patrol officers are demanding that the initiative be continued. They claim it has dramatically improved "life on the street" in their neighborhoods, and reduced crime. Neighborhood leaders in adjoining areas are also calling for an expansion of the program to their communities. Members of City Council support the program but are reluctant to pick up the cost of continuing or expanding the program now that foundation funding is virtually exhausted. In short, there are significant pressures to keep the program going and make it larger, but no one is quite sure where the money will come from.

Within your department there are a variety of views on the issue. From what you have heard the majority of "seasoned" patrol officers who were reassigned to foot patrol expressed dissatisfaction with the assignment. You understand that, among the rookies assigned to foot patrol, some really enjoyed the work, whereas others were upset, complaining that the assignment kept them out of *real* crime fighting.

A small amount of the initial grant from the local foundation was put aside for evaluation of the initiative. These funds would support some modest data collection efforts and the hiring of an outside consultant from the local university's criminal justice department.

Your boss, the chief of police, has directed you to work with the consultant to design an evaluation of the foot patrol initiative and collect the appropriate data. He wants to know how effective the initiative was before deciding whether to advocate for including funds to keep the initiative going, or to expand it. Your boss, although a political animal, also believes in rational planning based on empirical evidence. Further, for future training purposes, he wants to know which officers served most successfully as community policing officers, and which were most satisfied with their roles as community policing officers.

Electronic Monitoring of Probationers

The National Scene Confronted with burgeoning prison populations, rising costs of prison construction and severely stressed state budgets, jurisdictions have turned to a variety of methods to divert prison-bound convicted criminals to intermediate punishments. Such nonincarcerative punishments must serve several sentencing purposes. For example the degree of punitiveness of the sanction must fit the crime, and the sanction also must protect the public from the sentenced offender. [10]

Electronic monitoring, also known as "house confinement with electronic monitoring," "electronic supervision," or "electronic jail," has emerged as an intermediate punishment option since the mid-1970s. [11, 12, 13] The option can take one of several forms. For instance, an electronic device hooked up to the offender's telephone can send a signal to a central computer, located in a police or a probation department, if it fails to detect a signal sent to it from the electronic bracelet or anklet worn by the offender. The device can continuously monitor the offender's presence. Or it can be activated only in the evening and on weekends so that the offender can go to work during the day. In this way agency personnel can know when the offender is away from home, and act accordingly. Although electronic monitoring was originally applied as a sentencing option to restricted classes of offenders such as those convicted of driving while intoxicated (DWI), over the past few years it has been applied to broader ranges of offenders, including those convicted of more serious offenses.

The Specific Situation: YOU Are There You are the chief of probation services in a southern state. Over the past decade in your state, as in many others, courts have ordered officials to reduce prison overcrowding. In response to that order the state has launched a massive prison construction program and provided funds to local jurisdictions to pay for jail construction.

Several factors have forced the state to slow its construction agenda dramatically: a worsening local economy resulting in less state revenue, contracting snafus, and decreased financial support from the federal government. To reduce the state's prison population safely, early release of low-risk offenders to parole was increased. In spite of these steps, however, the state was still looking for ways to reduce the numbers of offenders coming *into* the prison system.

In response the state courts, over the past 3 years, have sentenced more prison-bound, convicted offenders to probation with electronic monitoring. Offenders convicted of a range of offenses have received this intermediate punishment; white collar criminals, drug dealers, and burglars have all been put on probation with electronic monitoring. Sometimes the probation period has extended beyond 24 months. Judges have tailored to the severity of the crime not only the length of the probation period, but also the intrusiveness of the monitoring. For example, whereas some probationers are monitored only during the evenings, others are required also to be at home all weekend as well.

As you might expect, the public disagrees sharply about the costs and the benefits of the electronic monitoring program. An unexpected coalition of "far left" advocates of prisoners' rights and "far right" advocates of harsher punishments for all offenders has demanded an abolition of the program. Those advocating for the prisoners argue that the state is intruding too much into the lives of probationers when it monitors and unnecessarily restricts their activities for lengthy periods of time, such as 2 to 3 years. They suggest that, if a probationer can "stay clean" for

12 months on electronic monitoring, then he or she should be released from electronically monitored probation and placed on regular probation.

By contrast, those advocating harsher treatment of all offenders think the electronically monitored probation is too lenient for these offenders. They think diverted offenders should be sent to prison despite the overcrowding there. They claim that not to sentence these offenders to prison sends the wrong message to the public about the punitiveness of the criminal justice system. They also argue that reducing the pressure for new prison construction, by sentencing more offenders to forms of house arrest, ensures further delays in the procurement of these needed resources.

Actors within the criminal justice system in the state generally support the monitoring program, except for several rural county police chiefs. General support for the electronic monitoring of probationers seems to be strong, particularly in suburban areas where citizens heartily endorse the cost-saving features of the program.

Matters have come to a head because of two unfortunate incidents. One electronically monitored probationer had served 15 months of his term. He was originally convicted of selling drugs. While electronically monitored, and at work in an electroplating factory, he killed three coworkers, hurling them into a vat of molten copper. Security officers at the plant then shot and killed the probationer. The news stories on the event suggested that the mental strain of "being on a leash" contributed to the probationer's breakdown.

An unrelated incident occurred the same week and involved another offender sentenced to house arrest with electronic monitoring. He was serving his third sentence for burglary. He shot and killed a prominent local couple who came home to find him ransacking their house. At the time of the incident the burglar was supposed to be at home and under electronic surveillance. Problems with the computer equipment at the sheriff's office receiving probationers' signals, however, prevented enforcement personnel from learning the burglar's whereabouts at the time.

The governor has called your boss and demanded that your agency produce a report on the safety provided by, and amount of punishment meted out with, electronically monitored probation. He wants to know if it is safe and sufficiently punitive. You have a month to complete the work and write it up.

Sentencing Guidelines

The National Scene   In the last 20 years this country's court system has witnessed a remarkable change in sentencing practices. Most states, and the federal courts, have gone from a model of discretionary sentencing to a model of determinate or "flat" sentencing. The purpose of the new sentencing guidelines is to ensure that all convicted felons will receive sentences proportionate to the seriousness of their offense, and proportionate to the danger they represent to the community.

The sentencing guidelines used vary from state to state and are implemented in different ways in different locales. Evaluations of some new sentencing guidelines showed that they have been effective in reducing disparity in sentencing. [10]

The Specific Situation: YOU Are There You are the research assistant to a sentencing commission in a southeastern state. Your commission, created by the governor and the legislature, implemented presumptive sentencing guidelines 3 years ago. "Liberals" looking to reduce racial disparities in sentencing, and "conservatives" tired of seeing crim-

TANK McNAMARA MILLAR & HINDS

Proposal to revise Pete Rose's sentence. (*Source.* TANK McNAMARA © 1990 Millar/Hinds. Distributed by Universal Press Syndicate. Reprinted with permission. All rights reserved.)

inals punished too lightly, both welcomed the implementation of the presumptive sentencing guidelines.

The governor is in the midst of a tough fight for reelection. Her opponent is charging that the state's skyrocketing costs for new prison construction are due in large part to the implementation of the new sentencing guidelines. According to her opponent, were it not for those guidelines the state would not be going broke trying to pay for new prisons. Her opponent also has argued that the new guidelines have *not* served to reduce racial disparity and ensure that blacks and whites convicted of similar crimes receive similar sentences. The governor's opponent airs these and other charges during a statewide televised debate.

The morning after the debate the head of the sentencing commission comes storming into your office. He is clearly not happy. The following conversation takes place.

Boss: (Tersely) Did you see the debate last night?

You: (In a relaxed tone) Sure.

Boss: Did you see her get *creamed* on the guidelines issue?

You: Well, it wasn't that bad, I thought. . . .

Boss: (Voice rising) Like &%*@ it wasn't! She got wiped all over the place on that stuff. And I want to tell you, she is MIGHTY unhappy about it.

You: (Carefully) I see. . . .

Boss: (Emphatically) And furthermore, she wants some hard numbers, *fast*, on what has happened as a result of the guidelines. Are sentences longer or shorter? Has racial disparity increased or decreased? Is it contributing to the need for new prisons? The whole nine yards.

You: (Carefully) I see. . . . This will take time, I'll have to—

Boss: Like %&*+@ it will. I need that report in 5 days from right now, right this minute. (Boss turns to leave.)

You: Uh, just one thing. Do you want the straight numbers, or do you want the answer you want?

Boss: Give it to me straight. (Slams door)

You: (muttering) where was that application to law school . . . I know it's here somewhere . . . I just might have time to get my application in. . . .

SUMMARY OF MAIN POINTS

- Criminal justice is a social science, committed to empirical inquiry.
- Social scientists may seek any combination of the following three goals: description, understanding or explanation, and prediction.
- The nature of social scientific understanding is such that social scientists may be able to understand but not predict very well. Or they may be able to predict but not understand very well.
- Social scientists, to pursue these three goals, rely upon empirical evidence, gathered and analyzed according to norms shared by social scientists.
- Social scientific thinking relies upon theory to focus data collection and analysis, and uses the results of these efforts to evaluate and generate theories.

SUGGESTED READING

Peter Winch's *The Idea of a Social Science* (1958) clarifies the differences between social science, natural science, and philosophy. It is geared to those interested in the philosophy of science.

Michael Polanyi's (1966) *The Tacit Dimension* starts with the startling premise "We can know more than we can tell" (p. 4). He argues that this tacit knowing plays a vital and largely ignored role in scientific inquiry.

KEY WORDS

describing linkages
dependent (outcome) variable
description
explanation
independent (predictor) variable
parameter estimation

prediction
social scientific understanding
theory
understanding

REFERENCES

1. Whitehead, A. N. (1958) *The function of reason*, Beacon Press, Boston (Paperback edition; original publication 1929), p. 76.
2. Polanyi, M. (1966) *The tacit dimension*, Doubleday, New York.
3. Archer, D., and Erlich-Erfer, L. (1991) Fear and loading: Archival traces of the response to extraordinary violence. *Social Psychology Quarterly 54*, 343–352.
4. Winch, P. (1958) *The idea of a social science and its relation to philosophy*, Routledge & Kegan Paul, London.
5. Winch, P. (1958) *The idea of a social science and its relation to philosophy*, Routledge & Kegan Paul, London, p. 112.
6. Winch, P. (1958) *The idea of a social science and its relation to philosophy*, Routledge & Kegan Paul, London, p. 88.
7. Winch, P. (1958) *The idea of a social science and its relation to philosophy*, Routledge & Kegan Paul, London, p. 91.
8. Greene, J. R., and Taylor, R. B. (1988) Community-based policing and foot patrol: Issues of theory and evaluation. In Green, J. R., and Mastrofski, S. D. (eds.), *Community policing: Rhetoric or reality?* Praeger, New York, pp. 195–224.
9. McKinley, J. C., Jr. (1990) The best time to stop a crime is before it happens. *The New York Times*, 5E.
10. Morris, N., and Tonry, M. (1990) *Between prison and probation: Intermediate punishments in a rational sentencing system*, Oxford University Press, New York.
11. Berry, B. (1985) Electronic jails. *Justice Quarterly 2*, 1–22.

12. Baumer, T. L., and Mendelsohn, T. I. (in press) Electronically monitored home confinement: Does it work? In Byrne, J. M., and Lurigio, A. (eds.), *Smart sentencing?: An examination of the emergence of intermediate sanctions*, Newbury Park, CA: Sage Publications.

13. Renzema, M., and Skelton, D. T. (1990) Use of electronic monitoring in the United States: 1989 Update. *NIJ Reports 222* (November/December), 9–13.

CHAPTER 2

THE CONDUCT, LOGIC, AND PROCEDURES OF SOCIAL SCIENTIFIC INQUIRY: INTRODUCTION TO ALTERNATE PATHWAYS

'Data! Data! Data!' he cried impatiently. 'I can't make bricks without clay.'
—SHERLOCK HOLMES

'Then I would have been sorry for the dear Lord—the theory is correct.'
—ALBERT EINSTEIN

OBJECTIVES

You will learn about two approaches to scientific inquiry—theory testing and discovery. I call these, respectively, Einstein's method and Holmes's method. They represent two important variations on the social scientific method. You will discover how scientists working in each mode think and proceed.

ORGANIZATION OF THE CHAPTER

This chapter bridges the discussion in the last chapter on the general social scientific process, and the material on theory you will encounter in the next chapter. You will explore two different views on the *logic* and *conduct* of scientific inquiry.

Two dominant approaches to scientific inquiry—discovery and theory testing—are illustrated by the approaches of Sherlock Holmes and Albert Einstein to solving problems. They represent alternative views on a fundamental problem for scientists: what is the relationship between *scientific evidence* and my *ideas* about the evidence? Ideas about the evidence represent *theories*.

Which of these two perspectives you adopt in a particular situation has operational as well as conceptual consequences. It may influence the kind of research tool you choose, how you use the research tool, and how you analyze the resulting data.

You can adopt either of these perspectives at different points in time. Some scientists might be committed to a particular approach for their entire career. Other scientists might change the approach they use depending on the project they are pursuing. Still others might switch approaches while working on a particular research project. You can change from Einstein's to Holmes's approach or vice versa at any particular time during a scientific investigation. At any particular time, however, you are following one perspective or another.

I introduce each perspective with a specific case. I illustrate how you could apply these approaches to a particular problem related to the hypothetical scenario on community policing introduced in the last chapter.

These differences in approach operate *within* the general social scientific perspective on answering questions. They represent specific variations on this process but do not contradict it. Holmes's and Einstein's approaches both assume that understanding, description, and prediction must be grounded on, or evaluated in the light of, empirical evidence gathered and analyzed according to certain scientific rules of conduct. Both approaches also assume that methods and results should be aired openly, so that they can be scrutinized by others.

THE LOGIC OF SCIENTIFIC INQUIRY: INTRODUCING TWO APPROACHES

Theory comes in many varieties, and has several building blocks. In Chapter 3 you will explore theory in more detail. The important point to bear in mind now is that we constantly use theory in everyday living to support our everyday understandings.

In very general terms we regularly use two different kinds of theories. One variety helps us explain particular situations. If I want to help explain my own or someone else's behavior or feelings in a particular situation I will use a theory that considers features of the *particular* situation. Such theories provide **idiographic explanation**. The explanations relate to a particular situation. (Literally, an *idiograph* is a trademark or a personal signature.)

Criminal justice, as a field, has benefited over several decades from explanations based on studies of one individual. Eli Anderson, an urban ethnographer, recently told a story of one urban, African-American male, "John Turner." "Turner" was unable to eschew his involvement in illicit activities, despite "straight" career opportunities available to him. Anderson's explanation of this situation represents an example of idiographic explanation. [1] Holmes's approach, described below, most often focuses on exactly this type of explanation.

A second variety of theoretical explanation seeks to explain a *broad range* of situations.

Such explanations are **nomothetic** in orientation. (*Nomos* is the greek word for law.) They seek to lay bare the *laws* or *social regularities* relating different characteristics in a *class* of situations. A theoretical explanation of the factors distinguishing parolees who are re-arrested within a year of release, from those who are not, would be a nomothetic explanation. [e.g., 2] Einstein's approach, described below, usually focuses on nomothetic explanation.

Holmes's Approach

Sherlock Holmes was the fictional private detective created and later despised by the late Sir Arthur Conan Doyle. Doyle thought Holmes distracted him too much from his more serious work, writing historical novels. Holmes's exploits first appeared in *Strand* magazine in the 1890s. Holmes, with his reliance on the scientific analysis of clues and his commitment to sound theories to explain the clues, revealed the stunning feats possible by combining rationalism with scientific inquiry. He confronted one of the first fictional leaders of organized crime, Professor Moriarty, in several situations. He was only bested once, by the beautiful and brainy Irena Adler. Holmes's views about the relationship between theory and data are of particular interest, and are well illustrated in "The Adventure of the Copper Beeches."

A young governess, Miss Violet Hunter, comes to Holmes before accepting a position at a remote mansion near Winchester. She discusses with him the strange conditions of her employment. Her employer has asked her to cut her hair quite short—a painful task for a well-bred woman of late 19th-century, British society—and to wear a special dress. He has offered an unusually high salary. Although Holmes thinks there may be some danger, she accepts the position nonetheless.

PICTURE 2-1
Sherlock Holmes and Mr. Watson listen as Miss Violet Hunter explains the strange letter she has received from Mr. Rucastle, in "The Adventure of the Copper Beeches." (*Source:* Sir Arthur Conan Doyle, *Sherlock Holmes (Greenwich Unabridged Library Classics).* 1976 (1983 edition). New York: Chatham River Press (A Division of Arlington House, Inc., Distributed by Crown Publishers, Inc.)

A few days after her departure Watson asks Holmes what he thinks is going on. Holmes replies in great frustration. "'Data! Data! Data!' he cried impatiently. 'I can't make bricks without clay.'"

About a fortnight later Holmes and Watson receive a letter from Ms. Hunter asking them to come to her assistance. They catch the train and head out. On the train the two discuss the situation.

Holmes: Had this lady who appeals to us for help gone to live in Winchester, I should never have had a fear for her. It is the five miles of country which makes the danger. Still, it is clear that she is not personally threatened.

Watson: No. If she can come to Winchester to meet us, she can get away.

Holmes: Quite so. She has her freedom.

Watson: What *can* be the matter then? Can you suggest no explanation?

Holmes: I have devised seven separate explanations, each of which could cover the facts as far as we know them. But which of these is correct can only be determined by the fresh information which we shall no doubt find waiting for us.

Several features of Holmes's approach to crime solving are notable.

Facts Come First The most important preliminary task is to gather full information about the situation. *All* facts, regardless of how bizarre, should be considered. You do *not* ignore a fact because it does not agree with your notions of what is happening. As Holmes repeatedly warned Watson, theorizing with too little data was dangerous, because one could become overly committed to a theory that later might prove wrong.

The Goal Is to Understand the Situation Holmes was not seeking to come up with general laws of human behavior. His goal wasn't to devise general axioms of criminal behavior. Rather he was working toward developing an explanation of the particular events occurring in, and *only* in, a particular case. In other words, Holmes focused on *idiographic* explanations, the causal factors identified with that *particular* constellation of events.

In Holmes's view, then, the important part was gathering all the relevant facts and finding a theory that exactly fit those facts. In case after case he explored a situation thoroughly and then embraced the explanation that precisely corresponded to it. He sought to understand the dynamics of the situation in detail.

By the way: Want to find out what happened to Miss Hunter? Read the story!

Holmes's Approach to the Community-Policing Example

In the last chapter you encountered a hypothetical scenario concerning community policing. As a police R&D officer you are conducting an evaluation of the trial foot-patrolling/problem-policing initiative. As part of that evaluation you are exploring the differences between those officers satisfied with the assignment, and those dissatisfied with it. You could use Holmes's approach to understand the differences between police officers satisfied with a community-policing assignment, and those dissatisfied with such an assignment. Holmes's method advises that you begin with the data present in the situation, and do not begin with a theory.

Distinguishing Satisfied vs. Dissatisfied Community Police Officers For future training and selection purposes your department needs to be able to identify, not only those officers who are successful in such roles, but also officers who find job satisfaction in such roles. Satisfied community-policing officers are less likely to request job transfers than dissatisfied community-policing officers. You also expect that more satisfied officers might be more effective in the problem-policing assignment. In short, if you can identify those who are satisfied, you may be able to lower training and replacement-training costs, and to mount more effective programs.

How You Might Go About Constructing an Explanation You begin by talking with a couple of officers who expressed considerable satisfaction with the assignment. You discuss the features of the assignment they enjoyed, and the challenges of the work. One of these officers is a new recruit, the other a veteran with 10 years on the force. After your

conversations with each of these officers, you make notes about the main points coming up in your conversations.

The two officers found several sources of satisfaction in the community-policing assignment. They enjoyed the close contact they had with many neighborhood residents. They felt that they got to know a range of citizens and participated in a variety of affairs such as block club meetings, playground fairs, and the like. Each noted that the residents "felt they could trust us, that we could really help them, and that we *cared* about what happened in the neighborhood."

Later you discuss the assignment with two officers who had expressed considerable dissatisfaction with the assignment. You interview them individually. They express an initial reluctance to speak with you about their irritations. You assure them you will not be reporting individual responses back to anyone, and that all the data will be held in confidence.

The older officer, with 12 years of service as a uniformed officer, reported dissatisfaction stemming from the difficulties presented by the assignment. She felt that the demands of the community policing assignment were excessive and exposed the officer to too many conflicting constituent concerns. The community policing officer, she felt, always had to be ready to respond to things a regular patrol officer need not worry about. As she saw it, formal and informal leaders in the community were always trying to involve the community police officer in helping them solve "small time" problems. She had done her best, as she put it, "not to play partisan politics," but found it difficult.

The younger officer you interview, who also reported dissatisfaction, expressed a markedly different set of concerns. He became upset with the assignment because it involved much less "real crime fighting" than

Variables and predictions	How measured
Variable: Sociability	This is a personality characteristic that can be measured with standard questionnaires. Persons who are high on sociability are extroverted and enjoy interacting with others. Those who are low on sociability are introverted and do not enjoy interacting with others as much.
Prediction 1:	Those officers who like socializing with others, and score higher on sociability, reported more satisfaction with the community-policing assignment. It afforded them more opportunities to interact with an array of citizenry. Those officers who scored low on sociability found the interactions with citizenry less satisfying.
Variable: Age	Age at last birthday, measured in years
Prediction 2:	In general, older officers with more years in service will be more dissatisfied with a community-policing assignment. It represents a drastic change from the routines in which they have been trained and with which they are familiar. Older officers in general have learned how to be good officers and resent new approaches, seeing them as annoying "gimmicks." Younger officers, in contrast, have not yet wedded themselves to a particular style of policing. They are also generally more optimistic about the possibilities of changing the policing role and achieving better results.

he imagined a regular patrol officer encountered. He thought he could go running after drug dealers. Instead, he spent most of the time taking care of problems like getting city services to tow burned out cars out of a vacant lot.

From these initial interviews you generate an initial, provisional theory. Your theory has as the outcome or dependent variable *satisfaction vs. dissatisfaction with a community policing assignment*. It includes the following *predictors* or *independent variables*, and predictions linking independent variables to the dependent variable.

Each of these two predictions is stated as a **main effect**. A main effect says: Controlling

for other predictors, as scores on this predictor go up, scores on the outcome will go up. As scores on sociability increase, levels of satisfaction with community policing will increase. The main effect also can go the other way: As scores on the predictor increase, scores on the outcome will *de*crease. As age increases, satisfaction with community policing will *de*crease. But the effect links just one predictor with the outcome.

The third prediction of your theory, however, goes beyond the idea of a main effect. It says that the effect of one predictor on the outcome will be *contingent upon* the score on *another* predictor. It is your respondent's scores on *both* predictors that shape the out-

Variables and predictions	How measured
Age	Age at last birthday, measured in years
Crime-fighting views	Answers yes or no to the following: "Do you think that the most important job of a police officer, at all times, is to fight crime?" Respondents who agree think that the major and overriding purpose of police work is to stop criminals. Respondents disagreeing think that police at times have important service functions.
Prediction 3:	*Age x crimefighting views interaction.* You theorize that younger officers will be more dissatisfied with the community-policing assignment *if* they subscribe to the view that regular patrolling involves a significant amount of "real crime fighting." This prediction says that the effects of these two predictors, age and views of police officers as real crime fighters, have a *joint* effect on the outcome.

come. Such a prediction represents an **interaction effect**.

Here is why you predict such an interaction effect. In general your theory predicts that younger persons will be more satisfied with a community-policing assignment because they are less wedded to a traditional policing methodology. Yet you have noticed that one young officer expressed dissatisfaction, feeling he was "cheated" out of real crime fighting. The third prediction of an interaction effect emerges from this observation.

Each of these predictions can be expressed graphically. Figure 2.1 shows data results that would support these predictions.

Qualities of Your Theory   Note the following features of your theory.

First, your theory *is practical*. It provides you with clues about how to improve the situation. Satisfaction of officers assigned to community policing can be improved. You can select officers whom your theory predicts will be satisfied.

Second, your theory includes one or more *predictors* (independent variables) and one or more *outcomes* (dependent variables). It focuses on specific variables.

Third, your theory suggests the *directions of the connections* between the predictors and the outcome. Extroversion connects positively with satisfaction, and age is linked negatively, according to Predictions 1 and 2.

Fourth, your theory is *parsimonious*, or relatively simple. It has only three predictors, not a dozen or more. As theories become more cumbersome, with more predictors, they may become less practical, and more theoretically confused.

Fifth, your theory *directs you toward the situations that can be used to test it*. It suggests collecting information from *contrasting* situations. In more technical terms it suggests **theoretical sampling**. When you sample theoretically, you collect data from situations where scores on your outcome or predictor variables will be substantially different from the situations where you have already collected data. [3]

Further, the information from these contrasting situations can be used to *test* the theory. The test emerges from comparing two situations that are critically different from each other, or that differ from each other on key predictors used by your theory. For example, you can compare the satisfactions of a

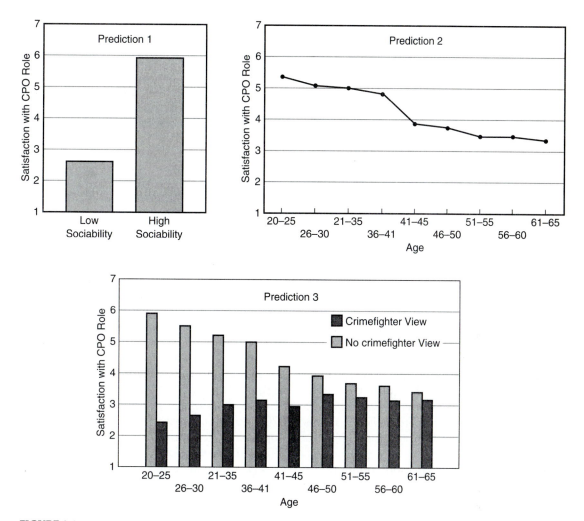

FIGURE 2.1

The three predictions emerging from your initial theorizing, based on the data gathered, can be portrayed graphically. You will learn more about constructing and reading graphs in Chapter 5.

group of older community-policing officers with a group of younger community-policing officers. You would predict the younger group would be more satisfied with a community-policing assignment. To state this point more elegantly, your theory is *verifiable*. It can be *empirically tested* and *falsified*. You will know, after you test it with data, if your theory is correct or incorrect.

Seeing How Well Your Theory Performs
To expand on this last point: Say you do decide to test your theory. You have a new cohort of community-policing officers complete several questionnaires *before* they begin their community-policing assignment. On the questionnaires you ask them to fill out standard measures tapping sociability and cynicism about police work. You ask them

TABLE 2.1
Results Testing Predictions from Initial Theory
(author-generated data)

	Scores on predictors suggest *low* level of satisfaction with CP role (older, less sociable, or younger *and* do hold crime-fighter views)	Scores on predictors suggest *high* level of satisfaction with CP role (younger, more sociable, or younger and do *not* hold crime-fighter views)
Actual satisfaction score was LOW	23	27
Actual satisfaction score was HIGH	3	47

about their age and number of years in the force. You query them on their crime-fighting views.

You then reinterview these officers 2 months after they have begun their assignments. You ask them how satisfied they are with the assignment now that it has begun. Based on their scores on the satisfaction item, you categorize them as having either *high* or *low* scores on *actual* satisfaction. These scores represent the dependent or outcome variable.

You can use the information you gathered initially to predict which officers will later express satisfaction with the assignment, and which will not. In short, you make a prediction based on information derived from the set of independent variables.

Table 2.1 provides results. The two columns separate people based on their scores on the predictor variables. The two rows separate people based on their scores on the outcome variable. If your theory had been completely correct, all those predicted to score low on satisfaction with community policing would have reported low satisfaction levels. All those predicted to score high on satisfaction would have reported high satisfaction levels. In short, all respondents

would have appeared either in the bottom right cell (predicted high satisfaction; reported high satisfaction) or the top left cell (predicted low satisfaction; reported low satisfaction).

Most officers scored as you had predicted. Their numbers are in the top left and bottom right cells. Your theory correctly predicted the satisfaction levels of 70 officers out of 100 (70% correct). Most people appeared in the top left and bottom right cells, as predicted. But it did not predict correctly for *everyone*. Thirty people did not score as predicted. Theories are never perfect.

Grounded Theorizing　Given your results, you can do one of several things to your theory.

Reject Theory Based on Results　Of course, if your results had turned out to be markedly different from what you had predicted, with most people not appearing in the upper left and bottom right cells, you could have chucked your theory altogether and started over with a new one. The data would have falsified the theory, at least for this group. In this author-generated example, however, the data do not suggest that you discard your theory.

Trim Theory Based on Results Although you might not discard your theory, you might use the data you have collected to modify your theory and make it better. One way you can adjust it is by trimming it. You can see if you need all your independent variables and all your predictions. A good theory is a relatively simple theory. If you can streamline your theory, that would be an improvement.

To simplify it, you might reexamine each of your three predictions. Reconstruct scores on your prediction measure so that you take account only of Predictions 1 and 2, and ignore the interaction effect in Prediction 3. You may find that you can predict the outcome just as well. In other words, the data may suggest that Prediction 3 was unnecessary. You can therefore remove this prediction from the theory. You now have a simpler theory.

Elaborate Theory Alternatively, instead of subtracting from your theory, you can add to it. A second way to modify your theory is to alter it so that it will make better predictions in the future. You use the *data* from the test to help you *generate more theory*.

This theoretical elaboration will concentrate on the cases your original theory failed to correctly predict (bottom left cell, top right cell). For these respondents, predicted scores on the outcome and actual scores on the outcome failed to match. Why?

You might examine questionnaires for those respondents whose results did not fit the theory. You can look for other factors to which your theory did not attend that may help explain the actual scores.

Your examination may suggest that you add another predictor and *progressively elaborate* your theory. You may find that those who were predicted to be satisfied with the community-policing role, but were not, had high scores on a *police cynicism* scale. [4] They held a generally cynical view of the role of

police work and the capabilities of police departments. You decide to add this predictor to your theory. You now have a fourth prediction.

Variable and prediction	How measured
Cynicism about police work	Scores on a police cynicism scale, based on several questionnaire items.
Prediction 4:	Respondents scoring higher on police cynicism will be less satisfied with their roles as community police officers.

The two steps you have taken here—trimming out unnecessary predictions, and adding new predictions—represent further steps in **grounded theorizing**. You have proposed improvements in your theory, and those improvements were grounded in data you had obtained.

Theories Can Always be Modified or Improved: Repeating the Process There is no such thing as perfect theory. Consequently, there is always room for improvement. You can improve your theory by repeating the process of grounded theorizing until your theory becomes "good enough" at approximating the data.

The improvements arise because theory modification is an *iterative* process. It can be repeated more than once. Theory is not created once and then left alone.

You would modify your theory as follows. Gather more data for your theory after you have completed this initial cycle of data collection and theory modification. Adding your new prediction (Prediction 4), and dropping one of your original predictions (Prediction 3), you can collect data from a new sample and see how well the theory, using just these predictions, estimates the new results.

If the predictions describe the obtained data well, then you will be satisfied. You can now start to use your theory for practical purposes such as selection or training. If the predictions do not describe the obtained data as well as you would like, you can explore the data for additional suggestions about how to modify your theory.

Here are the steps you are following:

Data → Theory → New → Adjust →
                Data   Theory

More → Adjust → Even
New   Theory   More
Data   New
                           Data

You can repeat the cycle as often as needed. You are "tuning" the theory, and with each iteration your theory improves. The actual outcomes observed agree more closely with the predicted outcomes. Of course, at some point you decide the theory is "good enough." You stop "tuning" the theory.

The Process of Theory Development

The example above illustrates several general points about Holmes's approach to scientific theorizing.

Dynamic Interchange Between Theory, Data, and Analysis

The unexpected results from the first systematic test of your theory led you to elaborate your theory. You added Prediction 4 on police cynicism. You also deleted Prediction 3. You then sought out new data with which to test the revised theory. This dynamic interchange between theory, data, and analysis is illustrated on Figure 2.2. What happens in one area influences what you do in the other two. This dynamic interchange is a key feature of *all* scientific theorizing.

Explanation and Prediction

The theory serves to explain or describe the situation, also to make predictions for what will happen in future situations. Your scientific theorizing has served two purposes. First, it has helped to both explain and describe the results you obtained on officer satisfaction with community policing. You used your theory to link satisfaction or dissatisfaction with the community police officer role to a set of causal factors or predictors. Your theory explained the observed scores of individuals on the outcome variable.

But your theory did more than provide insight. It helped you *predict*. You forecasted how satisfied specific people would be with the assignment. Your theory performed adequately in this role, and you modified it a little to make it even better. Given this predictive power, you might begin to wonder about the reach of your theory.

Using the Theory in Other Situations

You might ask: "How far can my theory go?" "Does it help predict how satisfied CP officers will be in the future?" "Does it predict satisfaction with the role after 12 months on the job, as well as after 2 months?" You are asking: "How *generalizable* is the theory across *time*?"

You also might wonder if it helps predict how satisfied *other* community policing officers are. You are asking "How *generalizable* is the theory across *persons*? Does it apply to different folks than the ones who have been tested?"

You also might wonder if it applies to different situations, such as community policing officers in different *departments*. You are asking: "Does it apply to different *settings*?"

In general terms you are asking: "Is my theory valid—does it hold? Does it work? Can I use it to predict—in situations beyond

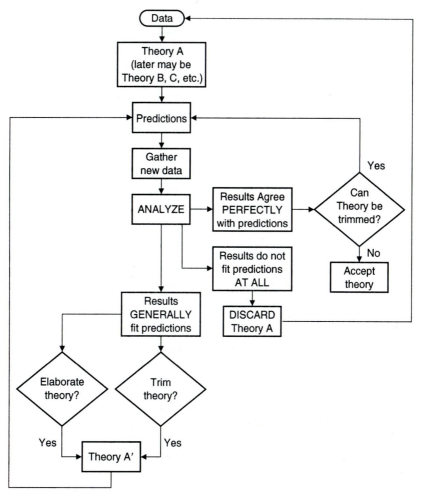

FIGURE 2.2 **Dynamic interchange between theory, data, and analysis**

those where it was developed?" This is the essence of the question of *external validity: generalizability* across *settings, times,* and *persons.* You will be learning more about it in Chapter 9.

So far, you have learned the following points about Holmes's scientific method. First, it describes the *specific* situation and predicts. Second, data, analysis, and theory interact dynamically. These two features also apply to Einstein's approach to scientific

inquiry. We will be examining Einstein's approach momentarily. Before we leave Holmes's approach, however, I want to emphasize an important way it is different from Einstein's outlook on scientific inquiry.

With Holmes's method, *the specific situation is the starting point* for inquiry, and the fundamental focus. (See Figure 2.3.) The goal is to understand the dynamics operating in (i.e., the facts of) a *particular* situation. The theory developed leads to suggestions for collecting information from different, contrasting situations.

You will see, by contrast, in Einstein's approach the *theory* is the starting point. Although the theory is, of course, based on prior theories and prior evidence, the key focus of the scientific enterprise is to *test propositions* of the theory.

From a logical point of view Holmes's approach uses **inductive reasoning**. Induction involves "the process of reasoning or drawing a conclusion from particular facts or individual cases" [5]. It also is called **grounded theorizing** or **substantive theorizing**. [3] By contrast Einstein uses **deductive reasoning**, which involves "reasoning from a known principle to an unknown, from the general to the specific, or from a premise to the logical conclusion" [5]. The general expectation based on the theory leads to a specific expectation about what to observe in a particular situation.

Einstein's Approach

Excitement on Principe Island: Will Sir Arthur Eddington Go Mad? Albert Einstein developed his theory of relativity during the first quarter of the 20th century. The first papers on Special Relativity appeared in 1905. Subsequently he worked on incorporating the force of gravity and developing his more "general" theory of relativity. Much of his theory, although it relied partly on the experimental results of other physicists at the time, was based on hunches and intuition.

Einstein's ideas were *not* tailored to specific patterns of scientific observations. He did not seek to explain particular findings. Rather he sought to explain how nature worked. "Einstein thus believed that theories into which facts were later seen to fit were more likely to stand the test of time than theories constructed entirely from experimental evidence." [6] It is not surprising, therefore, that many scientists were reluctant

to accept his theories, since they seemed without empirical support.

Einstein's theory predicted that light had mass, and that gravity could bend light. He threw down the gauntlet to experimental scientists in a paper published in 1911. He predicted specifically how much light from stars would be bent as it passed near the sun, and showed how his ideas could be tested during a solar eclipse. Scientists would have to wait for 8 years for the test.

On May 29, 1919, British astronomical observation teams off West Africa and Brazil, organized under the leadership of Sir Arthur Eddington, photographed a solar eclipse to see if the shift of starlight passing near the sun occurred as Einstein had predicted.

Earlier, a colleague had told Eddington's coworker, Cottingham, "'Eddington will go mad and you will have to come home alone'" if the results do not come out as predicted. [7] Eddington and Cottingham were on Principe Island, off West Africa, during the eclipse. After the event, while they were making measurements from the developed photographic plates, Eddington turned to Cottingham and remarked: "'Cottingham, you won't have to go home alone.'" [8]

The results exactly supported the predictions made by General Relativity theory. As results from these observations were later confirmed and news spread throughout the world, Einstein, previously known only to his scientific colleagues, became world-renowned. Asked what he would have done if the observations did not support his theory, Einstein is said to have remarked: " 'Then I would have been sorry for the dear Lord— the theory *is* correct.' " [9]

The Basics of the
Hypothesis-Testing Approach

Einstein's views represent a markedly different approach to the connections between theory, data, and analysis. With this approach *the primary purpose of the scientific enterprise is to develop general theories and to test the hypotheses that are part of these theories. Scientists discover if hypotheses have empirical support.*

This mode of scientific inquiry, shown on the right hand side of Figure 2.3, represents a different approach from the discovery or grounded theory approach of Holmes. *Most importantly, the development of the theory comes before the gathering of data.* Theory is *prior*. Theory testing and development, not examination of data, is the starting point for inquiry. Einstein's theory about gravity and light led to the specific prediction of what would be observed during a solar eclipse. The researchers did not gather the data and then try to fit a theory to it. Instead they set out to test a specific *hypothesis* or *prediction* emerging from the theory.

A second feature of this mode of inquiry is that the theory *specifies explicitly what type of data to collect.* It points toward the features of the situation most critical to the theory. In other words Einstein's deductive approach is more "closed" to the situation, whereas the inductive approach of Holmes is more "open." The astronomers in 1919 did not

seek to measure many different things, such as brightness of the starlight, shifts in wavelength, or other features. They focused on one specific type of measurement—the amount the starlight was bent.[1]

A third distinctive feature of this mode of inquiry is that there are two major results: (1) An understanding of certain features of the situation emerges. (2) More importantly, examination of theoretically relevant data suggests either that you retain the proposed hypothesis, or that you reject it. In other words the data 'fit' the hypothesis or prediction, or they don't. If the data fit the prediction, the theory can be accepted, as happened with Einstein's General Relativity theory. If they do not fit the observations, the theory can be rejected or modified. Despite Einstein's confidence in his theory and his unwillingness to modify it, most scientists *do* modify their theories if data fail to fit.

A final and fourth difference: the deductive approach is more *nomothetic* in nature

---

[1] The inductive approach is not *completely* open to the situation. Implicit theories restrict to some degree the range of factors considered by the scientist.

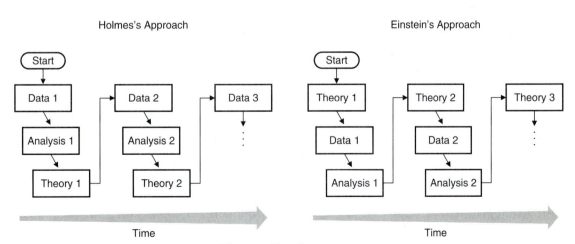

FIGURE 2.3 **The Dynamic Interchange: Holmes vs. Einstein**

than the inductive approach. It starts out with general propositions, and seek to explain a broad class of situations, individuals, or behaviors.

How You Might Use Einstein's Approach for Predicting Community Police Officer Satisfaction

Suppose you were to adopt Einstein's approach to explaining why some officers report more satisfaction with their community-policing roles than others. How would you proceed? You might begin by digesting relevant research completed on the topic. You could read appropriate books, journal articles, book chapters, and research reports. *Or* you could think hard about the matter and *not* rely on other work in the field. From your reading or your own thoughts you will develop a specific theory. Your theory will suggest certain predictions; it will link independent variables with an outcome variable. Each of these linkages represents a *hypothesis*. You then test these predictions by gathering relevant data. You analyze the data to see if they support or fail to support your predictions.

For the sake of brevity in exposition, imagine that the theory you develop, based on your examination of others' research, or on original thinking, contains the exact same propositions as those emerging from the initial grounded theory based on Holmes's approach. Let's focus on Prediction 1 (high sociability $\rightarrow$ more satisfaction with CPO role). The following reasoning underlies Einsteinian hypothesis testing.

Every hypothesis in some way is about a difference. Varying scores on the predictor variable (e.g., sociability) lead to different scores on the outcome variable (e.g., satisfaction with CPO role). If the hypothesis was not true, different scores on the predictor would not lead to different scores on the outcome. Those with high scores and those with low scores on the predictor would have

equivalent scores on the outcome. There would be *no difference* among them on the outcome. Thus, each hypothesis is linked to a **null hypothesis** predicting no difference; that is, that high scorers on sociability and low scorers on sociability are equally satisfied. In hypothesis testing we seek to *reject the null hypothesis of no difference*. But if your data do show a difference and allow you to reject the null hypothesis, you are still not sure if your data support the hypothesis you are testing, or an **alternate hypothesis** that also would fit the data.

For example, research suggests a positive correlation between police cynicism and years in service. [10] The data may support Prediction 2, linking age and satisfaction in a negative direction (more age, less satisfaction). At the same time the data also could support an alternate hypothesis linking cynicism and satisfaction in a negative direction (more cynicism—less satisfaction). The data might support this alternate hypothesis as well or even better than they support Prediction 2. So we cannot be sure if hypothesis 2, or an alternate hypothesis, is correct. Therefore, with Einstein's approach, you *do not* use the data in hand to further elaborate the theory. If you were using this approach you would *not* explore the cases in the upper right cell of Table 2.1 to develop the theory.

Comparing and Contrasting the Inductive and Deductive Modes of Inquiry

The example we have been developing with community police officers illustrates key differences between these two modes of scientific inquiry. First, with Einstein's approach theory development preceded data collection. By contrast, with Holmes's approach you *discovered* the theory from the initial data—the informal interviews with four officers.

Second, with Einstein's approach the theory pointed *more explicitly* toward the key features of the situation for you to assess. You did not consider the role of other, theoretically irrelevant factors. Holmes's approach was more open to different features of the situation.

Third, with Einstein's approach, the results of the data collection and analyses provided formal tests of hypotheses. Based on these tests you either reject or fail to reject the null hypotheses connected with your theory. The entire purpose of the analysis is formally to evaluate theory by means of hypothesis testing.

There is also a final, perhaps more subtle difference in the two approaches. Einstein's approach begins with a *general* focus, potentially applicable to many individuals or situations. Holmes's approach begins with a focus on the situation at hand.

Of course, despite these four differences, you will note several similarities between Holmes's and Einstein's approaches. With each you tested your ideas against data. The empirical findings decided if the theory you were examining was adequate. That is why

both inductive and deductive approaches represent modes of *scientific* inquiry. You use what the data tell you to assess your theoretical notions, not your own feelings or Jay Leno's opinion on the matter.

Further, both modes of inquiry are *iterative* processes. In the inductive example you modified the theory based on analysis of the data; you added Prediction 4 and dropped Prediction 3. If the results in the deductive example had not come out as hoped, you would have questioned one or more hypotheses. This also would have led to modifications in your theory.

Perhaps most importantly, in both modes of inquiry, discovery and hypothesis testing, the theory is as essential as the data. Theory focuses data collection and analysis, and provides the groundwork for interpreting patterns of results. Facts *by themselves* do not provide answers to the question "Why did it come out this way?"

Table 2.2 summarizes the main differences between these two modes of inquiry.

TABLE 2.2

Contrasting Two Approaches to Scientific Inquiry

	Holmes's approach	Einstein's approach
Alternate names:	Discovery; Grounded Theory Development; Substantive Theorizing	Hypothesis Testing; Theory Testing; Hypothetico-Deductive model
In the theory–data-analysis interchange this approach begins with:	Data from a particular situation	A general theory relevant to a broad class of situations
The main purpose of approach is to:	Understand what is going on in a particular situation	Test a theoretically derived hypothesis and see if facts fit the prediction
The type of logic usually associated with this approach is:	Induction: going from particular to the general	Deduction: applying general ideas to a particular situation and seeing if they work there
Concerned more with understanding or prediction?	Usually more concerned with understanding	Usually more concerned with prediction
Types of linkages in resulting theory:	Idiographic	Nomothetic

Understanding the Two Modes Within the Broader Context of Agreement

Holmes's and Einstein's modes of inquiry represent two different approaches for linking theory, data, and analysis. Much has been made in discussions of research methods about the relative merits of these different approaches to social science. Some feel that the inductive approach is superior, others favor the deductive approach. [11] In addition, and further complicating matters, different types of scientific methodologies have become generally linked with particular methodologies. Many scholars link ethnography, field work, open-ended interviewing, and historical research with Holmes's discovery-oriented mode of inquiry, and surveys, secondary analysis, field experiments, and quasi-experiments with Einstein's hypothesis-testing approach. Furthermore, Einstein's approach has been linked to "big science" projects: research investigations that collect large amounts of quantitative data, and gain substantial financial support from government grants and contracts. Figure 2.4 lampoons the process behind these projects.

My own opinion is as follows. Each logic of inquiry can be used with a variety of specific methodologies. Certainly, a few of the research tools you will be reading about work better for scientists using Holmes's approach, and a few work better for scientists using Einstein's approach. Nevertheless, you profitably can use most tools discussed in this volume for either Einstein's approach or Holmes's approach to scientific inquiry. In each chapter devoted to a specific research tool, I discuss the suitability of the tool for each mode of inquiry.

I further believe that neither Holmes's nor Einstein's approach is inherently superior. Each serves different purposes, calls for different approaches to data, and yields different types of insights. They represent equally viable *alternate pathways* of scientific inquiry.

But please, don't accept my opinions on the matter. Develop your own opinions on the relative merits of the two approaches. With many students, the choice is a personal one.

IMPLICATIONS OF ALTERNATE PATHWAYS

You Choose How to Investigate

The existence of these alternate pathways to scientific investigation "liberates" you, as a criminal justice researcher, in several respects. For one thing, there is no one right "way" to get started on a research topic. Let's say you are interested in the topic of electronic monitoring. You might think that the most "scientific" way to get started would be to go to the library and read all the scholarly articles written by experts on the topic—or at least as many as you can stand. Then you would know what *they* say, and could develop your theory from there.

Going to the library is one way to begin. Yet it *may* not be the best way and it certainly is not the *only* way. An alternate approach would be to contact a local probation, parole, or prerelease agency, and find out if they are using electronic monitoring, and, if so, for what kinds of cases. You could talk to the people who monitor the equipment about the problems. You could talk to the offenders coming into the office about what it's like to be on an electronic monitor. You could talk to the people who make and sell the equipment, and find out their concerns and goals. You could talk to judges to find out what they consider when placing someone on an electronic monitoring sentence. In other words you could start by doing *field work*, exploring a particular situation firsthand.

Would field work be a better way to start than going to the library? Not necessarily; which approach you will want to follow will

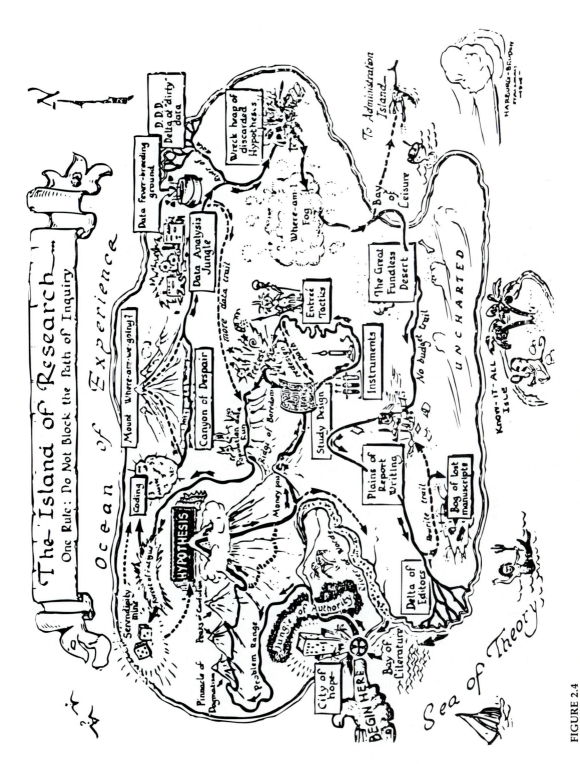

FIGURE 2.4
A satirical view of "big science." (*Source. Cancer Research,* December 1980.)

depend upon your own personal orientation to research, and your goals in this particular project. If your goal is to gain insight into the situation, the field work approach may be superior to the library approach. You can proceed most successfully if you adopt an orientation that you find personally compatible, and that is also appropriate to the research situation.

Changing Perspectives

You might wonder: Can I change from one perspective to another? Can I switch from Einstein's approach to Holmes's approach, or the reverse?

You are free to adopt one or the other approach, depending upon your research project. You can even switch approaches in the middle of a research project.

You might start your research project seeking formally to test hypotheses with data you have collected. You may find that your data support none of your predictions. If this happens, you may switch modes, adopt Holmes's approach, and begin searching through your data in an open-ended fashion for clues. Such shifts in mode of inquiry occur often in social science research. But at any one point in time you *are* following one mode or another.

SUMMARY OF MAIN POINTS

- Key elements of scientific inquiry are the interconnections that exist between theory, data, and analysis.
- There are two different approaches to making such connections: Holmes's approach and Einstein's.
- Holmes's approach is concerned with collecting data that allow an understanding of what has happened in a very particular situation.
- Einstein's approach is concerned with predicting what will happen in a broad class of

situations, and whether general theoretical propositions receive empirical support.
- Holmes's approach starts with data from the particular situation; Einstein's approach starts with a general theory.
- On the basis of data theories can be accepted, modified, or rejected altogether.
- There is no one correct approach to scientific inquiry, nor is there one correct approach to beginning a scientific study of a topic.

SUGGESTED READINGS

Clarke, R. W. (1971). *Einstein: The Life and Times.* New York: World Publishing. The volume carefully considers the relationship between the development of Einstein's ideas and the surrounding scientific climate. From reading this book you will better understand how Einstein's ideas integrated and extended the scientific work of other physicists at the time, and why the general climate in physics was so "ripe" for Einstein's radical approach.

Watson, J. D. (1969) *The Double Helix.* New York: New American Library. This slim volume is a delightful read about Watson and Crick's drive to discover the structure of DNA. Watson lays bare the hurly-burly and messiness of leading-edge science. Although we have become somewhat inured to the idea of corrupt science in the last few years, this book was a "shocker" when it appeared; scientists were upset that all the dirty wash had been hung out.

GLOSSARY OF KEY WORDS

alternate hypothesis
deductive reasoning
grounded theorizing
idiographic explanation
inductive reasoning
interaction effect
main effect
nomothetic explanation
null hypothesis
substantive theorizing
theoretical sampling

REFERENCES

1. Anderson, E. (1992) The story of John Turner. In Peterson, G. E., and Harrell, A. (eds.), *Crime, drugs and social isolation: Barriers to urban opportunity*, Urban Institute Press, Washington, pp. 147–180.

2. Burgess, E. W. (1928) Factors determining success or failure on parole. In Bruce, A. A. (ed.), *The Workings of the indeterminate sentence law and the parole system in Illinois*, Illinois State Board of Parole, Springfield, Il.

3. Glaser, B. G., and Strauss, A. L. (1967) *The Discovery of grounded theory: Strategies for qualitative research*, Aldine, Chicago.

4. Niederhoffer, A. (1967) *Behind the shield: The police in urban society*, Anchor Books, New York.

5. *Webster's New Universal Unabridged Dictionary, Second Edition.*

6. Clark, R. W. (1971) *Einstein: The life and times*, World Publishing Company, New York, p. 63.

7. Clark, R. W. (1971) *Einstein: The life and times*, World Publishing Company, New York, p. 228.

8. Clark, R. W. (1971) *Einstein: The life and times*, World Publishing Company, New York, p. 229.

9. Clark, R. W. (1971) *Einstein: The life and times*, World Publishing Company, New York, p. 230.

10. Niederhoffer, A. (1967) *Behind the shield: The police in urban society*, Anchor Books, New York, p. 239.

11. Glaser, B. G., and Strauss, A. L. (1967) *The discovery of grounded theory: Strategies for qualitative research*, Aldine, Chicago, p. 223.

CHAPTER 3

THEORIES

There is nothing so practical as a good theory.
—KURT LEWIN
*Regardless of whether it is called basic or evaluative, research that neglects theory
has little long-run impact.*
—DANIEL GLASER
Nothing can justify a theory except its explaining observed facts.
—C.S. PEIRCE

OBJECTIVES

Without theory, scientists would be no different from newspaper reporters or accountants. Criminal justice would not be a respected social science discipline. In this chapter you will examine the building blocks of theories, and how theories connect to the real world and the world of data. You also will consider a difficult issue: What is the relationship between theory and reality?

WHO NEEDS THEORY

Theories sound fancy and useless. You may think scientists who make up theory are just big "eggheads" or "nerds," like Fred Mac-Murray in *The Absent-Minded Professor*, who couldn't even remember his wedding date. You may envision **theorizing**, the process of constructing theories, to be marginally less exciting than watching paint dry. You may have chosen a criminal justice major because you thought you could *do* something with it, perhaps as a police officer, a correctional worker, and administrator, or a reformer in the criminal justice system. You might not view your future career as exciting as Jamie

Lee Curtis's in *Blue Steel*, or Danny Glover's in *Lethal Weapon*. Nevertheless, you probably did not think that activities like "theory building" or "theory testing" would play a big part.

Have I correctly anticipated your reactions to the topic of theory? If so, I want you to change your mind or to at least *think* about changing your mind. I will suggest that, without theory, you, and the entire field of criminal justice, are lost. Researchers investigating the criminal justice system and evaluating correctional programs have been led astray when they have failed to use theory to guide their investigations. [1]

ORGANIZATION OF THE CHAPTER

In the last chapter I continued the scenario in which you were an R&D officer in a police department. You were investigating why some police officers expressed more satisfaction with a community-policing assignment than others. In this chapter I revisit the scenario. Returning to the theory I suggested you might have developed, we inspect its details more closely. You will explore the *components* of theory and the *steps of theory construction*. Finally, you will examine the relationship between scientific theories and the nature of reality.

THE PROCESS OF THEORIZING AND THE ELEMENTS OF THEORY

The Theory of Community-Policing Satisfaction

In Chapter 2 the theory I suggested you might have developed, using Holmes's method of scientific inquiry, contained the following initial predictions:

1. More sociable officers found the community police officer role more satisfying.
2. Older officers found the community police officer role less satisfying; younger officers found it more satisfying.
3. Younger officers, believing that crime fighting is always the most important job of a police officer, were less satisfied with the community-policing role than younger officers not holding this view.

The empirical evidence you gathered subsequently supported Predictions 1 and 2, but did not support Prediction 3. Close inspection of the data suggested a fourth prediction:

4. Officers who were more cynical about police work were less satisfied with the community police officer role.

The Elements of the Theory and Theory Testing

Level Your theory focuses on dynamics occurring at a particular *level of analysis*. It concerns *individuals*, not organizations or groups or counties or states or countries. Theories can focus on *different* levels of analysis. (See Box 3.1.)

BOX 3.1

LEVELS OF EXPLANATION IN CRIMINAL JUSTICE AND CRIMINOLOGICAL THEORY

Theorists can frame their ideas at a general and abstract level. Such theories represent **macrotheories**, concerned with societal or systemwide dynamics. [2] A criminal justice macrotheory, for example, might explain how the criminal justice system protects the vested interests of the higher classes of society. A criminological macrotheory might explain the different rates of juvenile delinquency across different social classes. Such theories focus on societal or structural concepts. They are sociological in spirit.

By contrast, **microtheories** focus on specific cases, or groups of people, or individuals. [2] The component ideas are more concrete. A criminological theory might explain why certain youths in a neighborhood become delinquent whereas others do not. A criminal justice microtheory might explain why some cases are plea bargained, while other comparable cases are not.

Between these two levels of explanation you will find **bridging theories**. They concentrate *both* on structural factors and individual-level or small-group-level factors. [2] They also can be called *structural–contextual* theories. They consider both social structure, and the specific context in which events are occurring. [1] In criminology such theories consider both the societal and individual factors leading to criminality. In criminal justice such theories consider the social and political milieu of the criminal justice system and its subsystems, as well as subsystem characteristics and connections.

Where Do Theories Come From? In this section I portray the development and testing of theory using Einstein's approach to scien-

For a very brief period, medieval scientists were known to have dabbled in the merits of cardboard armor.

An example of a theory that did *not* fit reality.
(*Source*. THE FAR SIDE © 1989 FarWorks, Inc. Distributed by Universal Press Syndicate. Reprinted with permission. All rights reserved.)

tific inquiry. Then I will explain how to follow the process using Holmes's scientific approach.

Theories arise from many sources. We observe, directly and through media and conversation, what happens in the "real world." We absorb ideas and attitudes from the surrounding political, social, and intellectual context. Theories often start with a concern about things that occur in, or could occur in, the real world.

Look at Figure 3.1. It represents a schematic for guiding our discussion on theories and theorizing. Following Einstein's approach, we will move from the top to the bottom of the figure.

Theories have their origin in **features** and *dynamics* in the *real world*. Features, as I use

the term here, refer to **attributes** or facets of units or groups of units in the real world. All of the following qualify as features of the real world:

attitudes toward the death penalty for persons convicted of killing police officers;

burglary clearance rates in midwestern towns during calendar year 1993; and

the levels of satisfaction held by the community-policing officers in our running scenario.

Dynamics describe connections between features. We often presume that these connections are *causal* in nature. Something happened, and this caused something else to happen. For example, your mother's good high school friend had a police officer for a husband who was killed in the line of duty. Consequently, your mother holds the belief that all convicted killers of police officers deserve the death penalty. In our running scenario, because certain officers had more sociable personalities, they enjoyed their community-policing role more.

The dynamics and features happening and observed in the real world, or that could happen, are *not* theory. They represent one possible origin of a theory.

In Your Head: Building Blocks and Glue
Concepts Through several different channels, the features and dynamics occurring in the real world, or that could occur in the real world, produce notions in our own heads. We observe, we read, we imagine, we reflect, we discuss, and sometimes we argue with others about a range of topics of interest. During and after these activities we develop **concepts**. These also can be called **constructs**. *These make up the basic building blocks of theory.*

Concepts refer to features of real or possible worlds. But the concepts themselves *do not exist* "out there" in the real world. They are *ideas* about things that exist or could exist.

DOMAIN	Features	Dynamic Linking Features
"REAL" WORLD	Events Charactericstics Attitudes of: People, organizations, other units	Process or dynamics whereby one thing leads to another F1 $\longrightarrow$ F2
IN YOUR HEAD: THEORY BEFORE OPERATIONALIZATION	Concept of x (Cx) Concept of y (Cy)	Propositions link concepts e.g.; Cx $\longrightarrow$ Cy Causal logic assumed
	⬇ Op. G.T. ⬆	
IN YOUR HEAD: THEORY AFTER OPERATIONALIZATION	Variables reflecting concepts e.g.; $V_{x1'}, V_{x2'}$ e.g.; $V_{y1'}, V_{y2'}$ ("True" scores)	Hypotheses express links between variables e.g.; $V_{x1} \longrightarrow V_{y1}$ Causal logic assumed
	⬇ Meas; E added G.T. ⬆	
DATA WORLD: WHAT YOU OBSERVE WITH YOUR DATA	Variables as measured e.g.; $V_{x1obs'}, V_{x2obs'}$ e.g.; $V_{y1obs'}, V_{y2obs'}$ (Observed scores)	Correlations between two or more observed variables e.g.; $V_{x1obs} \longleftrightarrow V_{y1obs}$ Associational logic observed

(left margin: Einstein's Mode of Inquiry; right margin: Holmes's Mode of Inquiry)

Note: E = error, G.T. = grounded theorizing, Meas. = measurement process; Op. = operationalization

FIGURE 3.1

Although they are based on features of the real world, *they exist only in your head.*

In the case of the running scenario, you developed the concept of satisfaction with the community-policing role based on your conversations with officers, observations of officer–citizen interactions, and perhaps readings about the topic. Your *concept* of officer satisfaction with the community-policing role *relates* to these real world features, but is *separate* and distinct from it.

Propositions You connect the different conceptual building blocks—concepts—to each other through *propositions*.[1] **Propositions** are statements about the linkages between concepts. These statements often assume a **causal logic**. Something has caused something

----

[1] It is possible for a theory to have one building block and no glue. For example, your theory may simply state that over half of all community-policing officers will be more satisfied than dissatisfied with their role as community-policing officers. You can translate this theory into a testable hypothesis, and verify or falsify it. Most theories of interest to criminal justice researchers, however, have two or more concepts.

else. For example, in the running scenario your fourth prediction says that officers who were more cynical about police work would be, as a result, less satisfied with a community-policing role. Graphically, you could express this proposition as follows:

$$C_{\text{Police Cynicism}} \xrightarrow{(-)} C_{\substack{\text{Satisfaction with} \\ \text{Community Officer} \\ \text{Role}}}$$

Propositions Classify Concepts   Once you have connected concepts with propositions, you have divided your concepts into two classes. First, you have **predictor concepts**. Their role in your theory is to cause other concepts. These also can be called *exogenous* concepts, or *independent* concepts. They are exogenous, because their origins are *external* to the theory. They are independent because your theory does not anticipate that they are dependent upon, or caused by, any other concepts.

Second, you have **outcome concepts**. Their role in the theory is to be caused by other concepts. They also can be called *dependent* concepts, because they are influenced, according to your theory, by other concepts. You also can call them *endogenous* if you wish. They are endogenous because their origins are internal to the theory.

Theories often contain more than one proposition. Your theory of community-policing satisfaction is a case in point. Graphically, you could portray the theory, after its first empirical test, as follows:

Predictors   *Outcome*

$$C_{\text{Sociability}} \xrightarrow{(+)} \Big\} \quad \text{(Pred. 1)}$$
$$C_{\text{Age}} \xrightarrow{(-)} \Big\} \to C_{\substack{\text{Satisfaction} \\ \text{with CPO} \\ \text{Role}}} \quad \text{(Pred. 2)}$$
$$C_{\text{Police Cynicism}} \xrightarrow{(-)} \Big\} \quad \text{(Pred. 4)}$$

Although a proposition necessarily separates two concepts into predictor and out-

come concepts, it also can create a third class of concept if the theory included three or more concepts. A proposition can classify a concept as a **mediating concept**. A mediating concept connects the predictor and outcome concepts by "carrying" or "channeling" the impact of the predictor to the outcome.

For example, after collecting your data on CPO satisfaction and examining them closely, you might conclude that the concept of police cynicism *mediates* the connection between age and satisfaction. You may propose that older officers exhibit less satisfaction with the community police officer role *because* their years of service have led them to develop cynical attitudes about police work. Age affects satisfaction because older officers become more cynical. It is this higher level of cynicism, not age per se, that results in less satisfaction with the CPO role. So now you would connect these three concepts so:

$$C_{\text{Age}} \xrightarrow{(+)} C_{\text{Police Cynicism}} \xrightarrow{(-)} C_{\substack{\text{Satisfaction} \\ \text{with CPO Role}}}$$

You can express your entire theory as follows:

$$\left. \begin{array}{l} C_{\text{Sociability}} \xrightarrow{(+)} \\ C_{\text{Age}} \xrightarrow{(+)} C_{\text{Police Cynicism}} \xrightarrow{(-)} \end{array} \right\} \to C_{\substack{\text{Satisfaction} \\ \text{with CPO} \\ \text{Role}}}$$

In sum: concepts are connected by theoretical propositions that are usually causal in nature. The independent concept (C_x) or predictor causes the dependent concept (C_y) or outcome. Sometimes theories may position mediating constructs (C_m) between the independent and dependent constructs.

Different Causal Logics   Propositions can assume several different causal logics. Here are the possibilities:

1. More of a predictor concept leads to more of an outcome concept. The outcome does not in turn influence the predictor. The

proposition posits a **positive, unidirectional** causal logic:[2]

$$C_x \xrightarrow{\quad(+)\quad} C_y$$

In the officer satisfaction model, more sociability leads to more satisfaction.

2. More of a predictor concept leads to less of an outcome concept. The outcome does not in turn influence the predictor. The proposition posits a **negative, unidirectional** causal logic:

$$C_x \xrightarrow{\quad(-)\quad} C_y$$

In the officer satisfaction model, more cynicism leads to less satisfaction.

3. More of a predictor concept leads to more of an outcome concept, which in turn leads to more of the predictor concept. The proposition posits a **positive feedback, bidirectional** causal logic.[3] This causal logic consists of two distinct propositions.

$$C_x \begin{array}{c} \xrightarrow{\quad(+)\quad} \\ \xleftarrow{\quad(+)\quad} \end{array} C_y$$

For example, you might modify the satisfaction theory as follows. It not only predicts that more sociable officers will find the CPO role more satisfying. It also predicts that the more satisfied they are with the role, the more sociable they become. Over time such connections lead to more of each concept.

4. Your proposition can be *bidirectional* but posit **negative feedback** between the two concepts. More of the predictor leads to less of the outcome, which in turn leads to more of the predictor. Graphically:

$$C_x \begin{array}{c} \xrightarrow{\quad(-)\quad} \\ \xleftarrow{\quad(-)\quad} \end{array} C_y$$

For example, the satisfaction theory might be modified to state the following: Not only do more cynical officers exhibit less satisfaction with the CPO role; in addition, the less satisfied they are with the role, the more cynical they become. Over time such a bidirectional proposition leads to less and less of the outcome.

5. Finally, your proposition may contain a **bidirectional homeostatic** logic. More of the predictor concept leads to less of the outcome concept, which in turn, leads to less of the predictor concept.

$$C_x \begin{array}{c} \xrightarrow{\quad(-)\quad} \\ \xleftarrow{\quad(+)\quad} \end{array} C_y$$

Or, the relationship could work in the opposite way:

$$C_x \begin{array}{c} \xrightarrow{\quad(+)\quad} \\ \xleftarrow{\quad(-)\quad} \end{array} C_y$$

Both relationships are *homeostatic* because the predictor concept and the outcome concept tend to balance each other. Thus the two concepts remain at relatively stable levels over time. It is not unlike the connection between the thermostat and the furnace in your house. The temperature drops, leading the thermostat to kick

---

[2] A fancier term sometimes used for a unidirectional causal logic is *recursive*.

[3] A fancier term sometimes used for a bidirectional relationship is *nonrecursive*.

the heater on. The temperature rises again, shutting off the thermostat and the heater. Over time the temperature stays relatively constant.

All the Constructs Must Be Linked Together by One or More Propositions Constructs take their meaning in part from the propositions linking them to other constructs in the theory. [3] These connections represent the **constitutive definition** of the constructs. [4] If a theory has three constructs, and the third construct does not link to the other two constructs by any propositions, that third construct is superfluous. It has no constitutive definition.

Still in Your Head But in the Realm of Operational Definitions and Hypotheses The theory you have developed now contains concepts and propositions. Nevertheless, it is still vague. You have not specified how you intend to *operationalize* each concept in the theory. You do not yet know what you would *do* to collect data for each concept.

To guide your data collection efforts you must provide **operational definitions** of the concepts. The operational definition of a concept tells you *how to assess it empirically— how to gather data on the concept*. The process of operationalization—attaching operational definitions to each concept—takes us from the second to the third row of Figure 3.1. Operationalization leads us to a vital intermediate stage in the theorizing process, a stage connecting actual scientific data with theoretical constructs.

Through the process of operationalization we translate concepts into **variables**. Variables, before they are measured, represent the observable and measurable portions of concepts that you have defined operationally. They provide a specific direction for measuring the concepts in your theory.

Killer bees are generally described as starting out as larvae delinquents.

A developmental theory of delinquency before operationalization. (*Source.* THE FAR SIDE © 1989 FarWorks, Inc. Distributed by Universal Press Syndicate. Reprinted with permission. All rights reserved.)

Concepts $\xrightarrow{\text{(operationalization)}}$ Variables

In the running scenario predicting CPO satisfaction, you could operationalize the construct of "satisfaction with the CPO role" in several different ways. You could ask officers directly how satisfied they are with the role. You could ask them about several specific facets of the role, and the levels of satisfaction associated with each. You could ask fellow officers about the target officer's satisfaction with the job. You could look at supervisors' assessments of CPO job commitment.

No one potential variable or set of potential variables is more appropriate than another. To bring the point closer to home: "There is no correct recipe for a white cake. Similarly there is no one correct operational definition for a concept." [5]

A social science theory will have an operational definition for most of its concepts, but it need not necessarily have an operational definition for *all* of its concepts. The theory may have a concept defined solely in terms of other concepts, such as a mediating construct. "It is only necessary that a sufficient number [of constructs] in any system be operationally defined." [4, 6]

In short, you need at least one operational definition for most, and preferably all, of the constructs in your theory. These operational definitions suggest potential variables. You may wish to use more than one operational definition, and thus several variables, for one construct in your theory, or for several constructs.

Operationalization Translates Propositions Into Hypotheses The process of attaching operational definitions to most of the constructs in your theory permits you to translate your general propositions into specific hypotheses.

$$\text{Propositions} \xrightarrow{\text{(operationalization)}} \text{Hypotheses}$$

A **hypothesis** states the expected relationship between two or more variables; the statement embodies a causal logic framed so that it can be empirically tested.[4] *Hypotheses state specifically what you expect to observe with your data.* Each prediction (1, 2, and 4) stated in your revised theory of CPO satisfaction can be stated as a specific hypothesis. So the proposition that stated:

> Officers who are more cynical about police work will consequently be less satisfied with their jobs of community-policing officers

can be translated into a hypothesis stating the connection between two variables:

> Those officers who receive higher scores on the Police Cynicism Scale, compared to those officers with lower scores on the form, will provide a lower score on an item asking about satisfaction with the assignment as a community-policing officer.

Your hypotheses must be both *empirically verifiable* and *falsifiable*. A hypothesis is falsifiable if you can state before you examine your data what specific pattern of results would not support your hypothesis.

Moving From Your Head to the Data World
You are ready to move from your head to the world of data collection (row 4, Figure 3.1). You have operationalized the constructs in your theory, translating them into specific variables. You have stated the propositions linking your concepts in terms of specific, empirically testable, and falsifiable hypotheses. You are ready to *measure* and collect data. **Measurement** will move you from the conceptual realm to the empirical. The process achieves two results. It will generate observed scores on specific variables for the cases actually studied. It also introduces measurement error.

$$\text{Variables} \xrightarrow{\text{(measurement)}} \begin{array}{c}\text{Observed Scores}\\ \text{on Variables}\end{array}$$

$$\text{Hypotheses} \xrightarrow{\text{(measurement)}} \begin{array}{c}\text{Observed}\\ \text{Associations}\\ \text{Between Variables}\end{array}$$

What Gets Lost in the Translation Process In the data world you have **observed scores** on specific variables. Officer 1 checked the box "1"–"extremely dissatisfied" when responding to the question on overall satisfaction as a CPO. Officer 2's total score on the cynicism scale you used was 56. Officer 3's score on the sociability scale you used was 38.

---

[4] Again, it is possible to have a hypothesis about just one variable. Such a hypothesis would specify the expected level of the variable.

As you proceeded from your *idea* of specific variables to the actual *observed scores* on specific variables, measurement error crept in. People may have misread questions. People may have not wanted to report their true feelings. You will be learning more about measurement error in Chapter 6. The only point you need remember here is to make an important distinction between *potential scores on potential variables as conceptualized* and *observed scores on variables actually measured*.

Similarly, the causal logic connecting variables loses something as it too is translated from the conceptual realm to the empirical realm. You framed your hypotheses using a causal logic. All that you can observe empirically, however, are *associations* between measured variables. You might have hypothesized that higher cynicism scores caused lower levels of satisfaction with the CPO role. But the data may show you only that observed scores on the two variables correlate in a negative fashion; they reveal only an *associational* logic. More cynical officers were less satisfied, and less satisfied officers were more cynical. Data do not reveal a causal logic. From the simple association you cannot be sure which variable caused which other variable if both were measured simultaneously.[5] This point underscores an oft-quoted social science maxim: Correlation does not imply causation. For example, a high volume of ice cream sales does not cause high temperatures, although the two measures are correlated.

---

[5] You can attempt, through complex statistical techniques such as partial correlation, regression analysis, and modeling of simultaneous equations, to make inferences about causality by examining complex patterns of associations between variables. The observed data, nevertheless, do not directly support a causal logic. You are still making causal inferences based on empirical patterns of association.

You also can try to get more directly at causes by using research designs that measure the predictor at an earlier time frame than they measure the outcome. See Chapter 14 on longitudinal research.

Of course, when you are operating in Einstein's mode of inquiry you interpret the associations you observe *in light* of your hypotheses. If the associations revealed by the observed scores on the variables support your hypothesis, you may be justified in inferring that the causal logic embedded within your hypothesis is at work. But then again this justification may not be warranted. (See Box 3.2)

Einstein, Holmes, and the Theorizing Process

The description I have presented above moves from the real world, to your head, and ends up in the world of data. As such it represents Einstein's logic of scientific inquiry. You move from the general to the particular, and from general expectations, to specific hypotheses, to actual data to test hypotheses. You proceed from the top of Figure 3.1 to the bottom.

It is possible, and perhaps even desirable, however, to approach the process of theorizing in exactly the opposite manner. You can use Holmes's grounded-theory approach and proceed from the bottom up. In this process you move from the world of data, to your head, to the real world.

You would begin at the bottom of Figure 3.1, with data that have been collected. You examine particular measured variables and the data collection process. You scrutinize the observed correlations between variables. Based on the measured variables and observed correlations, you make estimations about the variables before measurement. You may use procedures to try to remove error introduced through the process of measurement. The associations you observe permit you to derive hypotheses about how the variables relate to one another. You have moved from the fourth row in the figure up to the third row, and are ready to generate theory.

BOX 3.2

SOME PROBLEMS WITH SOCIAL SCIENCE THEORY

Social science theory encounters several problems arising from the fact that it attempts to model complex societal matters. [7] These real-world complexities have several impacts on social science enterprises, including criminal justice. First, our theories about the aspects of society we investigate always represent simplifications of the features and dynamics present out there. No model of plea bargaining, for example, will ever capture all the intricacies of real-life events.

Second, often the variables we label as "independent" are partially influenced by the variables we have labeled as "outcomes." Modeling such bidirectional causal logics can be a daunting task.

Third, social scientists confront serious measurement problems that, in effect, introduce a host of "unknowns" into our hypothesis testing. [8] You will learn more about these in Chapter 6.

Fourth, sometimes social scientists have an interest in a phenomenon that is changing. To investigate such a matter is troublesome. The phenomenon may be changing too slowly; much important data may have been lost to history. Or, alternatively, the phenomenon of interest may be changing while several other phenomena are *also* changing. You will learn how criminal justice researchers cope with this problem in Chapter 15 on historical criminology.

Fifth, the social reality confronting researchers is "often fuzzy or imprecise." [9] For example, *recidivism* can be defined as rearrest, or as conviction of a new crime after release. Which measure we choose is to some extent arbitrary. This situation places limits on the level of accuracy researchers can achieve in predicting or understanding a phenomenon.

All these problems make the process of social science theorizing and theory testing extremely challenging.

To construct theory you move from the third row up to the second row. You develop concepts based on the variables, and propositions based on the hypotheses that appear to be supported by the correlations between the variables. You decide what theoretical constructs underlie the variables, and what propositions underlie the connections between variables.

Finally, in the last stage of grounded theorizing, you move from the second row to the first row. You make guesses about how features, and dynamics linking features, operate in the real world.

With grounded theorizing you proceed from associations, to hypotheses, to propositions; and from measured variables, to conceptualized variables, to concepts. You conclude with data-based theory describing how features connect in the real world.

Which approach to theorizing is better? Neither one. The relative appropriateness of Einstein's 'top-down' vs. Holmes's 'bottom-up' approach depends on your purposes and the nature of the research project. It may even be desirable to switch from Einstein's approach to Holmes's approach partway through a research project. You may want to stop trying to test ideas on the data and instead look closely at the data themselves to see what *they* tell you.

THEORIES PROVIDE UNDERSTANDING, PREDICTION, AND PLANS

Understanding

By clarifying how dynamics link different features in a situation, theories afford insight and understanding. Descriptions of classes of phenomena help us penetrate the connections between different aspects of the phenomena examined. This understanding is *probabilistic* in nature. It does not describe the dynamics linking features for *all* the cases investigated, just—hopefully—*most* of them. Your theory of CPO satisfaction does not allow us to understand completely the satisfaction levels of *all* the CPOs. Yet it does help us to understand much about the satisfaction levels of many officers assigned to community policing. It tells us why some officers report more satisfaction than others.

Prediction

Theories afford prediction because they allow us to estimate an outcome. **Prediction** concerns itself with foretelling the "condition or state of a system as a whole." [10]

A weather forecaster uses information from several sources to predict the chance of rain tomorrow. Similarly, parole boards use information from several sources to predict the chance that an offender can avoid recidivism in the outside world.

Nonetheless, the nature of social science prediction has its limits. No theory predicts perfectly. As long as you have fewer predictors than cases it is impossible to develop a theory that correctly estimates every outcome. There is always slippage between what the theory expects—the expected or predicted outcome—and the actual outcome. As you saw in Chapter 2 when you tested the initial theory predicting officer satisfaction with the community-policing role, everyone did not report the satisfaction level predicted by the theory.

Therefore, theories state predictions in probabilistic terms. The theory tells us what is likely to be the case *in the long term*—over a large number of individuals or occurrences or units. An everyday example of probabilistic prediction is the weather forecast. It tells us that, on days where the conditions are like the current situation, in the long run, rain follows within 24 hours in 60 out of 100 cases. Therefore, there is a 60% chance of rain tomorrow.

Since a prediction is probabilistic, it does *not* apply to *each* specific case. That is why your mother is always going to win arguments like the one in Box 3.3.

BOX 3.3

WHY YOUR MOTHER WILL *ALWAYS* WIN

A former colleague of mine used to have many arguments with his mother that went like this. He'd be explaining some theory, such as a delinquency theory, and would say something like the following: "Those having more delinquent friends are more likely to become juvenile delinquents or adult criminals."

His mother would immediately counter, "Well, that theory just *can't* be right. Mrs. McGillicutty's son Willy hung out with the worst delinquents in the town of Mayfield for years when he was a teenager. They all ended up in jail. *He* went on to finish high school and college, do graduate work, and now he's an astrophysicist at a university in New Zealand." His mother would then flash an "I told you so" smile. The "hidden message": How can anyone believe any theory so stupid!

What my colleague's mother and many adults fail to appreciate is that social science theory is probabilistic in nature. It describes what happens to *lots* of juveniles, not just Mrs. McGillicutty's marvelous boy, who do or don't associate with mostly delinquent peers. Since it focuses on what happens, on average, to many youths, it is *nomothetic* and *probabilistic*.

One counterexample does not refute the theory; it just shows that the theory does not always perfectly predict what happens. The theory was not *intended* to do this in the first place.

Of course, if I find out that Willy McGillicutty was working for an international drug cartel when he went on many trips to attend scientific conferences, and he is currently being pursued by the authorities, I wouldn't be too surprised either.

Plans

Every time policymakers implement a social program or a policy change, theory, in some form, guides their actions. Their theory may be vague and may not include operational definitions of concepts and specific hypotheses, but it steers their actions nonetheless.

For example, James Finckenauer has evaluated a "Scared Straight" program in New Jersey. [11] Youths thought to be at risk of delinquency met inmates at a state institution and learned what it was like "inside." Such exposure, program planners thought, would reduce subsequent delinquency. Finckenauer has shown that this program was based on a vague version of deterrence theory.

Often, policymakers either will assume that certain theories hold true when this has not yet been proven, or they will embrace theories too vague to be empirically tested. The policies *allude* to theory but are not *solidly grounded* in theory. Researchers have suggested that this insufficient theoretical grounding represents a major shortcoming in delinquency prevention programs. [12]

Brief Comment on Some Other Functions of Theory

Theory does some other things for us too beside explain, predict, and guide policy. [13] For example, theories contribute to the advance of an academic, scientific discipline. A social science discipline advances as its theories do a better job of providing insight into situations, and better predictions of attitudes and behaviors. If the theories of the discipline failed to predict or explain, the discipline would not be viewed as "scientific" by other social science disciplines.

And finally, as discussed in Chapter 2, theory "drives" data collection. It can tell us what kinds of information to consider or collect or calculate. When we examine this point in a general way, we can see how theory "drives" a whole discipline. For example, in

juvenile delinquency research, Hirshi's control theory, first published in 1969 [14], has stimulated an enormous volume of research and articles. It has played a major role in shaping this domain of criminological research over the last 20 years.

SOME FINAL QUESTIONS ABOUT THEORY

In this closing section I touch on several questions about theories that often arise. What is good theory? What is the relationship between theory and reality?

What Makes for a Good Theory?

A "good" theory has several characteristics.

1. It is not too complicated. Theorists value **parsimony** in their models—an ability to explain a range of phenomena with a few constructs or concepts.

You might think that scientists like simple theories so that they won't get themselves too confused by their own models, and you're partly correct. But there is also more to it. Theories that are complex are extremely difficult to test empirically. [7] A complex theory produces a large number of hypotheses. Getting empirical support for each of these hypotheses can be a long and laborious process.

Thus, if two theories are equally matched in terms of their abilities to predict actual outcomes and provide insight, all else equal, scientists will prefer the more parsimonious theory.

2. Its range and limitations are specified.

Those creating or using the theory suggest the range of phenomena to which it can be applied. For example, a model developed to explain juvenile delinquency does not explain adult criminality. Subsequent empirical research may show that a model has a broader range of application than the researcher originally intended. If so, the researcher can then redraw the specified boundaries of the model to make it more inclusive.

A good theory, however, should not start out by trying to explain a lot. As the popular wisdom puts it: "A theory that purports to explain everything ends up explaining nothing."

3. A good theory focuses on a problem that is important. It concerns itself with nontrivial aspects of a situation.

4. A good theory is stated so that empirical data can support or refute it. A researcher can easily learn what types of information will support the specified hypothesis.

5. Finally, a good theory *gets* empirical support; it is successful at predicting certain features of situations and providing insight into those situations. As the American philosopher C. S. Peirce insisted: "nothing can justify a theory except its explaining observed facts." [15]

Values: The Relationship Between Theory and Reality?

Over the last two decades scientists and philosophers have argued at length about several features of scientific theorizing.

Values One topic generating many papers has been the question: Can a particular social science be "value free?" Can criminal justice theory and research directions be uncontaminated by the values and morals of the researchers themselves?

Most recently, researchers have recognized that our values and biases creep into the theories we develop in untold ways. We can have different personal orientations to developing theory. It is much easier to believe that the theories developed in this discipline *are* influenced by our prejudices and biases than it is to believe the opposite.

Even if values do play a role in the models developed and the concepts used, however, these theories still undergo rigorous empirical tests. The resulting publications receive careful reviews by peers who are also scientists. I see nothing wrong with admitting that our biases influence the models we create. What I would find frightening is the possibility that these same values would result in my "cheating" when it came to testing the models I developed. In Chapter 4 we'll look into ethics.

Theory and Reality Let's admit that our values and biases influence the shape of the theories we develop. Do these influences result in theories that describe real-world dynamics less accurately? This concern leads to an even broader question: Do theories accurately describe what happens out there in the "real world" at all? If they do, over time do they get increasingly accurate? As a discipline moves along and rejects inferior theories in favor of those that work better, is the field coming any closer to understanding the real world? In short, what is the relationship between theory and reality, and how does it change as a discipline progresses?

In thinking about such questions, keep in mind several limitations of theories that scientists generally accept. They have recognized that their theories always *simplify* reality, focusing on some aspects and leaving out others. To be empirically testable, theories must simplify matters.

A second limitation accepted by scientists is that their constructs or concepts are *hypothetical*. They are simply convenient labels with no existence outside the scientific models in which they are used. Although theories try to reflect and capture features of the real world, the theoretical explanation they offer do not necessarily correctly describe the events. Theory A might provide hypotheses that fit the data. This does not mean that

Theory A is the *only* model providing hypotheses that fit the data. Theory XY6 might do just as well.

You might be troubled by this last limitation. You might wonder: if the constructs in theories do not really exist "out there," how do we know if our models are getting better or worse, over time, at describing, predicting, or affording insight into what is happening out there in the real world?

Are you seated?

The answer is: We don't know with certainty if our theories are getting closer to reality or not, over time. This insight has led to sobering views about the idea of scientific "progress."

Thomas Kuhn, a historian of science, proclaimed in his 1962 book *The Structure of Scientific Revolutions* that scientists traded scientific models like teenagers change loyalties to top bands. Scientists would work in a special type of framework, called a **paradigm**, until that framework became unworkable. A paradigm includes a particular world view of a set of scientific matters.

When the paradigm becomes too cumbersome, scientists "jump ship," adopting a new paradigm for investigating a particular problem. The switch from Newtonian views to Einsteinian views in the world of physics in the first quarter of this century is an example of just such a paradigm shift. According to Kuhn the new paradigm adopted would not necessarily be any closer to "truth" than the one abandoned, although it would solve some problems better than the old one. [16]

The paradigm-based view of the history of science suggests that scientists, over time, adopt and abandon frameworks for a variety of reasons. They do not necessarily switch to an alternate theory because that theory better approximates reality.

Markedly different from, and more optimistic than, Kuhn's view, is Donald Campbell's approach, called **hypothetical realism**.

[17] His approach contains the following elements.

1. There IS an objective reality out there; we're not just asleep and dreaming.
2. But we can never know this objective truth with certitude. No scientist in an area of research will ever get to the point where he or she, and all others working in an area, will proclaim *with complete certainty* that the theory they are using perfectly reflects the truth.
3. Theories get at truth by providing "fit" or "correspondence" between the theoretical ideas and the data gathered. The data gathered behave *as if* the theory correctly described reality.
4. Scientists who are rejecting old models, embracing new models, and elaborating those new models are slowly moving toward a closer approximation of the real world with their theories. Theories survive and are adopted widely if they help achieve a closer correspondence.
5. Thus, if, over time, scientists working in one area progressively adopt a particular theory, it is probably because that theory more closely approximates the real world or "truth." In this painfully slow manner scientists make progress.

In short, Campbell suggests that: The job of theories is to mimic reality; over time theories that do this better than other theories, and are parsimonious, will be adopted and will flourish. Theories that don't do this as well become weeded out. Due to this selection process, scientists are getting closer to the "truth."

Personally, I find Campbell's model of modest scientific progress more palatable than Kuhn's notions of paradigm shifts. I readily admit my self-serving motives in embracing Campbell's approach. His approach justifies what I do as a theorist and leads me to believe that the field of criminal justice is farther along now than it was 80 years ago. It leads me to hope that, 80 years from now, theories in the field will be much advanced over those of today.

SUMMARY OF MAIN POINTS

- Features in the real world, and dynamics linking those features, can inspire theoretical notions in our heads.
- In the initial stages of theory development we develop constructs or concepts, and propositions connecting the concepts.
- Our propositions often assume a causal logic.
- Propositions classify concepts into independent or predictor constructs, dependent or outcome constructs, and mediating constructs.
- A concept is defined in two ways. Its constitutive definition reflects how it is defined within the theory in terms of other concepts. Its operational definition suggests how it can be operationalized using specific potential variables. Each concept must have a constitutive definition, because it must be connected to at least one other concept in the theory. Most concepts in the theory, but not all, need to have operational definitions.
- After a concept has been operationalized, you can discuss the concept in terms of specific, potentially measurable variables.
- After operationalization you can discuss propositions in terms of specific, testable hypotheses.
- A hypothesis states the connection you expect to observe between two variables.
- Hypotheses are empirically testable, falsifiable statements.
- The causal logic of propositions and hypotheses becomes translated into a logic of associations in actual data. The data do not inform us about causes; they merely inform us about how closely observed scores on different variables are associated with one another.
- You can use Einstein's approach while theorizing, moving from observation, to theory, to specific hypotheses, and to tests of those hypotheses in the data world. You also can use Holmes's approach, and work backwards from data, to hypotheses, to theory.
- Theories generate understanding and prediction.
- Theoretical predictions are by definition probabilistic and nomothetic; they tell us about what will happen, in general, in the long run.
- Theories in one form or another provide the basis for all social programs.
- One view of scientific progress holds that scientists use a theoretical perspective until it becomes unwieldy, and then discard it for another. The new theory may or may not provide a better representation of reality.
- Another view of scientific progress—hypothetical realism—holds that, over time, scientists discard models that represent reality less satisfactorily for models that provide closer approximations of reality.

SUGGESTED READINGS

Thomas Kuhn's (1962) *The Structure of Scientific Revolutions* presents a disconcerting view of how scientists go about developing and discarding theory. A "must" for those with a historical or philosophical bent. Although scientists labeled much of his thesis as "radical" at the time of its appearance, his views are currently accepted by many.

Hubert M. Blalock's *Basic Dilemmas in the Social Sciences* (1984) provides a frank, nontechnical discussion of current problems in social science theorizing and research. He clarifies how theo-retical and measurement limitations conspire to impede social scientific investigations. He provides some suggestions for improving things. With chapter subheadings like "Limitations imposed by a fuzzy reality," how can you resist?

GLOSSARY OF KEY WORDS

attributes
bidirectional homeostatic logic
bridging theories
causal logic
concepts
constitutive definition
constructs
dynamics
features
hypothesis
hypothetical realism
macrotheories
measurement
mediating concept
microtheories
negative feedback
negative unidirectional causal logic
observed scores
operational definitions
outcome concepts
paradigm
parsimony
positive feedback, bidirectional causal logic
prediction
predictor concepts
propositions
theorizing
variables

REFERENCES

1. Hagan, D. (1990) Why is there so little criminal justice theory? *Journal of Research in Crime and Delinquency 26*, 116–135.
2. Williams, F. P., and McShane, M. D. (1988) *Criminological theory*, Prentice Hall, Englewood Cliffs, NJ, p. 4.
3. Torgerson, W. S. (1958) *Theories and methods of scaling*, John Wiley and Sons, New York, p. 4.
4. Torgerson, W. S. (1958) *Theories and methods of scaling*, John Wiley and Sons, New York, p. 5.
5. Katzer, J., Cook, K. H., and Crouch, W. W. (1982) *Evaluating information: A guide for social science research*, Second ed., Random House, New York, p. 76.
6. Hull, S. C. (1943) *Principles of behavior*, Appleton-Century Crofts, New York.
7. Blalock, H. M., Jr. (1984) *Basic dilemmas in the social sciences*, Sage Publications, Beverly Hills, CA.
8. Blalock, H. M., Jr. (1984) *Basic dilemmas in the social sciences*, Sage Publications, Beverly Hills, CA, p. 18.
9. Blalock, H. M., Jr. (1984) *Basic dilemmas in the social sciences*, Sage Publications, Beverly Hills, CA, p. 20.
10. Dubin, R. (1978) *Theory building*, Revised ed., The Free Press, New York, p. 19.
11. Finckenauer, J. O. (1982) *Scared straight! and the panacea phenomenon*, Prentice Hall, Englewood Cliffs, NJ.
12. Waegel, W. B. (1989) *Delinquency and juvenile control: A Sociological perspective*, Prentice Hall, Englewood Cliffs, NJ, p. 250.
13. Glaser, B. G., and Strauss, A. L. (1967) *The discovery of grounded theory: Strategies for qualitative research*, Aldine, Chicago, p. 3.
14. Hirschi, T. (1969) *Causes of delinquency*, University of California Press, Berkeley, CA.
15. Peirce, C. S. (1931) Notes on scientific philosophy. In Hartshorne, C., and Weiss, P. (eds.), *Collected papers of Charles Sanders Peirce*, Vol. 1, Harvard University Press, Cambridge, MA, Original manuscript 1897.
16. Kuhn, T. S. (1962) *The Structure of scientific revolution*, University of Chicago Press, Chicago.
17. Brewer, M. B., and Collins, B. E., eds. (1981) *Scientific inquiry and the social sciences (A volume in honor of Donald T. Campbell)*, Jossey-Bass, San Fransisco.

CHAPTER 4

ETHICAL ISSUES IN CRIMINAL JUSTICE RESEARCH

OBJECTIVES

Social scientists have ethical obligations to their colleagues, study participants, and the wider society. You will review these obligations, the reasoning behind them, the procedures used to help assure that scientists follow these guidelines, and the limitations that have resulted from these checks.

You will consider two ethical dilemmas particularly troublesome for criminal justice and criminological research. After reading this chapter, you will possess the basic tools needed for evaluating studies from an ethical perspective.

ORGANIZATION OF THE CHAPTER

You will learn in this chapter about an extremely important dimension of criminal justice research: its moral and ethical basis. Every research study, even if its methodology and topic seem innocuous, has an ethical dimension. In some studies these dimensions can be obvious, as in situations where scientists invade the privacy of jury deliberations. But even studies involving routine surveys raise ethical questions.

I begin by considering the ethical obligations that scientists have to other scientists. Violations of these obligations play havoc with the central concern of scientific inquiry—linking theories and data. I describe the ethical obligations of social scientists to their study participants and the general society, and the institutional structures assuring that those obligations are honored. Finally, I discuss ethical issues for two particular types

of criminal justice research—violence predictions and fieldwork.

Scientists have obligations to their scientific colleagues, the larger society, and the individuals whom they interview or who participate in their studies. We need to attend to these requirements, because scientists are human. Some scientists may commit **scientific fraud**. This occurs whenever a scientist misrepresents or withholds any important aspect of method, data sources, analyses, or results. Sometimes scientists may not treat study participants with the full respect that one human owes another. Although most scientists conduct themselves ethically in all aspects of their work, misconduct by even a few investigators can influence societal views of, and support for, the scientific enterprise.

You are a consumer of research. As a consumer you need to be able to tell if a scientific study followed proper procedures for ethical scientific conduct. Studies that do not follow these policies probably contain ethical flaws and may represent inferior work.

SCIENTISTS' OBLIGATIONS AS SCIENTISTS

Scientists have held a respected position in Western societies for much of this century. But in the last 20 years exposés of scientific fraud have snowballed. A scientist admitted faking data in a biomedical lab at Emory University in Atlanta. The president of the Harvard School of Public Health stepped down because repeated instances of his plagiarism had been discovered. A dean in Arizona maintained, despite considerable contrary evidence, that his book on "Muzak" did not copy extensively from an unpublished dissertation of a sociology graduate student. Because of this trend new reports of academic fraud have less "shock value;" calls for monitoring or "policing" science seem on the increase.

Nevertheless, scientific fraud has been around for several centuries. Apparently, even Erasmus (1466–1536) did it. [1] On a more recent note, one of the most eminent social scientists of this century was probably guilty of deliberate fraud.

The Case of Sir Cyril Burt

Sir Cyril Burt was an extremely eminent psychologist whose research spanned the second and third quarters of this century. He is the only psychologist to have been knighted. His research covered such topics as the relationship between social class and delinquency, and the relationship between social class and IQ, as well as the inherited basis of IQ. He was an enormously powerful and intimidating figure in British social scientific circles.

Doubts about Burt's work began to surface in the early 1970s. Investigators turned up oddities such as a fictitious female coauthor. As questions about the accuracy of his work spread, scientists questioned the source of the inaccuracies. Were they just the results of carelessness? Or were they the result of something more deliberate?

An important paper by Burt published in 1961, "Intelligence and social mobility," has been scrutinized carefully. This paper demonstrated, ostensibly, that the IQ of children was closely related to the IQ of their fathers. It was based on a large study of over 40,000 persons, and had influenced the discussion on IQ, social class, and inheritability of intelligence.

Professor D. D. Dorfman published a paper in the prestigious journal *Science* analyzing Burt's 1961 paper. [2] He argued, based on extensive statistical analyses of Burt's numbers, that the data reported had been fabricated. When Dorfman compared Burt's results to numbers from other IQ studies, the chances that Burt's numbers were *not* made up were less than one in a million. According to Dorfman, Burt had made the numbers conform precisely to what he sought to prove.

In short, problems of scientific fraud afflict more than desperately struggling graduate students or fly-by-night market research firms. Researchers at all levels, from the highest to the humblest, may fall prey to the lure of misrepresentation, and have been doing so for some time.

Any student who has ever worried about getting a bad grade in a course should find the temptation to commit academic fraud easy to understand. Although I think scientists who commit academic fraud should be held accountable for their actions, I also think it is important to recognize the enormous pressures confronting academic researchers who must "publish or perish." In most social sciences, assistant professors seeking tenure are expected to publish many research articles in refereed journals, as well as to teach conscientiously.

Obligations to Scientific Peers

These pressures notwithstanding, academic researchers are expected to adhere to extremely high standards of scientific conduct. Failure to follow these guidelines is counter to the entire spirit of the scientific enterprise, which is to "seek truth." It also damages the relationship between society and the scientific community.

Don't Lie About the Data or the Procedures, and Report Fully   Researchers, in keeping with norms of academic integrity and the openness of scientific inquiry, need to report their study procedures and their findings fully and accurately. The details provided allow other scientists to independently verify the results should they wish to do so. Scientists attempt to verify another study by conducting a replication effort. In a **replication** a scientist tries to re-create the original investigation, hoping to obtain results nearly identical to the original.

Treat Collected Data Carefully   Once data are in hand, social scientists need to prevent such data from being accidentally altered. It is possible in a study for small changes in data entries to result in noticeable changes in the pattern of results. Of course there will always be some level of coding and data entry error, but researchers are obligated to check the data after these operations to be sure, insofar as it is practicable, that the final numbers and text are as correct as they can be.

Never Change the Original Data   Intentional changes in data, so that they accord more closely with the hypothesis under investigation, or for any other reason, are, of course, completely unacceptable.

Make as Much Available as Possible   If a study represents an extensive data collection effort, such as a national survey, there is little chance that another scientist will try to replicate the original study. It is simply too costly. But another researcher can do **secondary analysis** of an original dataset if that information is made available. In secondary analysis a second researcher reanalyzes the original researcher's data, examining questions that may be the same as, or different from, those addressed by the original researcher.

The National Institute of Justice and the Inter-University Consortium on Political and Social Research at the University of Michigan (ICPSR) have played leading roles in efforts to make large scale datasets available to the broader scientific community. NIJ requires that grant awardees supply tapes with their file data on them at the conclusion of a research project. Such availability allows for more extensive secondary analyses of data. The arrival of large capacity microcomputer-based storage devices such as CD-rom drives, hard drives, and high-capacity floppy disks make it easier and cheaper to share datasets widely.

Acknowledge Sources   When using the ideas or information originally created by others, researchers are expected to say from what place the ideas or information came. Such admissions are fully in keeping with the cumulative nature of scientific inquiry. Even Newton admitted: "If I have seen far it is because I have stood on the shoulders of giants."

SCIENTISTS' OBLIGATIONS AS MEMBERS OF SOCIETY

Perhaps less easily agreed upon are the scientists' obligations to act ethically vis-à-vis the participants in research, and the wider public. Further, these broader ethical obligations may conflict with the researcher's goals as a scientist.

The Wichita Jury Study

The following case may give you a better sense of the conflict between *scientific goals* and *social responsibility*. Juries represent a hallowed and central feature of the American criminal justice system. Although only a modest portion of cases do go to trial, all defendants in the Federal court system, and all defendants accused of serious crimes in local court systems, have the right to a trial by jury.

In the early 1950s some well-respected researchers at the University of Chicago Law School decided that it would be important to investigate closely the dynamics of jury deliberation. [3, 4, p. 170] Without the jury members' knowledge the researchers recorded their conversations. The researchers were especially interested in how interaction patterns and other features of the process influenced the outcome. The study did lead to some important findings about juries.

But when the larger public caught wind of this investigation, they were shocked. Congressional inquiry followed, spearheaded by an indignant Senator Eastland. Later, in 1956, legislation was passed declaring such investigations out of bounds. The public had decided that the topic, even if of considerable scientific interest for a variety of sound scientific reasons, was not permissible. The institution was simply too "sacred." "Such taboos

PICTURE 4.1
In the film "Twelve Angry Men" Henry Fonda (left) persuades other jurors, including Lee J. Cobb (right), to reconsider evidence in a murder trial. Nominated for "Best Picture" Oscar in 1957. The study of jury deliberations, like those taking place in the film, is "off limits" to social scientists. (*Source.* © 1957 Orion-Nova Twelve Angry Men. All rights reserved.)

express a society's desire to maintain the sacred quality of certain social arrangements and conventions." [4, p. 170]

The *goals* of the researchers were acceptable—understanding what happens in jury deliberations—but the *means*—invading the privacy of a hallowed institution—were not. Oversight of the ethics of scientists has arisen in response to this tension between ends and means.

Since this decision prohibiting research with real juries, investigations have focused on "mock" jury deliberations. In these studies, groups of people discuss and vote on real or fictitious cases as if they were real juries. Some scientists feel that such studies provide little insight into the dynamics at work in real juries. Observing society's respect for the institution of the jury may have limited our understanding of it.

Concern about social science has been spurred not only by worries about scientists invading the privacy of individuals and institutions. Social scientists' treatment of study participants has also been questioned. For example, in the mid-1960s the late Stanley Milgram, a social psychologist, conducted a series of experiments on obedience. An experimenter instructed participants to deliver increasingly painful electric shocks to a loudly complaining subject in another room. In fact the shocks were not delivered, the other subject was a confederate acting as if he were shocked, and the researcher informed participants of this after the experiment. Milgram cogently defended the ethics of his procedures. [5] Nonetheless, evidence suggested that some participants experienced trauma from the experience. Guidelines have arisen, in part, as a response to such situations.

A Framework for Understanding These Obligations

Historical Background The modern concern with ethical issues in social research originated in the Nuremberg trials following World War II. The atrocities reported as part of the "scientific" experiments carried out in concentration camps led to the adoption of a set of principles, the Nuremberg Code, which provided guidelines for research involving human subjects. [6] Later, in 1966, the Public Health Service began to require that research done with human subjects be reviewed for ethical issues by the local institution. In 1971 the American Sociological Association and the American Anthropological Association adopted new ethical standards for their members, as did the American Psychological Association in 1977. Federal guidelines currently exist specifying ethical guidelines for research with humans.

The Current Mechanics of How it Works
Current federal guidelines require all institutions of higher learning receiving federal support to review study procedures and decide if the rights of human subjects—the participants in the research—are adequately protected. Researchers proposing projects involving humans submit documentation about key aspects of their proposed study to an institutional review board (IRB). This review board includes scientists from different disciplines. I have been a member of such a review board. In addition to including academics of varying backgrounds and some retired professors, it also included a local minister. It met monthly and carefully considered the ethical implications of the research proposals brought to its attention. Such boards decide whether the proposed projects are ethical.

Making such decisions is a complex task. Nonetheless, it is doable because the federal government has said specifically what a study must do to be ethical. You will consider these ethical guidelines below.

The General Issues Four general ethical principles underlie the specific guidelines currently used in human subjects research. [6]

1. **Autonomy**. Social scientists need to respect the rights of individuals to make their own decisions and hold their own values. As long as people are not hurting others, they have a right to behave as they wish. This principle requires that social scientists obtain the *voluntary* informed consent of individuals before their participation in a study begins. When participants voluntarily provide their **informed consent**, they are stating that they understand key features of the study, and with

this understanding willingly and freely agree to take part. We explore the specifics of informed consent shortly.

2. **Nonmaleficence**. Social scientists should avoid intentionally harming individuals who are participating in research. This principle prohibits knowingly inflicting physical or psychological damage. It also requires scientists to take steps to prevent possible harm to individuals, and to minimize the diffuse harm the research may cause to the wider society or to participant–researcher relationships. For example, according to this principle a researcher interviewing probationers and gathering evidence about actions that could be grounds for revocation ought not return to the office of the courts and transmit these details to the relevant probation officers. You will return to reconsider this and related issues when you examine the special ethical issues emerging in field research.

3. **Beneficence**. This principle is the reverse of the preceding one. Social scientists have an obligation not only to alleviate or minimize harms where feasible, but also to confer benefits where feasible. If it is reasonable for them to stop the hurt their study participants are experiencing, or make things significantly better for those participants, then they ought to do it.

4. **Justice or equity**. This last ethical principle enjoins researchers to treat equally everyone who is similar. This idea relates to the principle that everyone accused stands equally before the law. Personal factors irrelevant to the situation at hand ought not influence how the participant is treated.

The principle does not mean that the ethical guidelines we use when dealing with "good" people are different from those guiding our interactions with "bad" people. We should be as unwilling to lie to a prostitute or drug dealer as we are to a police officer (or vice versa). This principle is embedded within a broader ethical assumption: that the researcher has a fundamental respect for those persons and groups she studies.[1]

A hypothetical research example with electronic monitoring provides an example application of this principle. Serving a sentence of home confinement with electronic monitoring (HCEM) usually requires a phone in the offender's home. You are a researcher examining the effects of HCEM on burglars receiving probation. You want to compare the effects of receiving probation with HCEM vs. the effects of receiving probation with frequent visits from a probation officer. You decide, on a random basis, using a flip of a coin, whether each participant receives probation with frequent visits or probation with HCEM. But what should you do when you assign probationers from households without a phone? Should they all simply be assigned to the "frequent visits" condition? The principle under discussion here suggests that these individuals should be provided with phones. That way they have the same chances of receiving a condition as do study participants from houses with telephones.

These four general principles provide the underlying basis for the specific guidelines adopted to protect participants in social science research.

---

[1] I am indebted to Ralph Weisheit for statements on this broader ethical framework.

The Specific Ethical Considerations

Potential Benefits of the Research Should Outweigh the Potential Harms   The main framework used to carry out a normative moral evaluation of a proposed study is a risk–benefit analysis. What is the potential good that can come out of the proposed investigation? What is the potential harm? How do the two compare? If the potential benefits outweigh the potential risks, then the research is permissible from an ethical standpoint. In addition, *none* of the potential risks must be of an extremely serious nature. No IRB would condone a study, no matter how great its benefits, if there were any chance at all of participants being killed or seriously disabled, physically or psychologically, because of their participation. So in the end an IRB may approve a project because the potential benefits outweigh the risks, disapprove it because they do not, or disapprove it because some potential risks are too serious (see Figure 4.1).

Possible Benefits   Researchers usually invoke a variety of benefits, some tangible, some more speculative, to justify their research ethically. The benefits can apply to the

FIGURE 4.1   Three possible outcomes when benefits and harms of a study are weighed by an IRB.

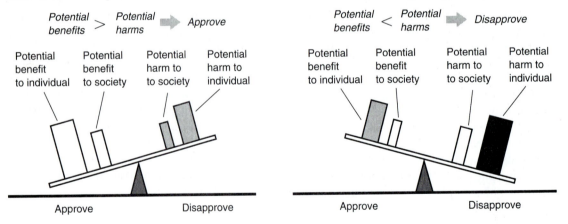

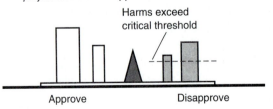

individuals participating or to society as a whole.

Specific and highly plausible benefits include several outcomes. Participants can get paid. If the project is well funded, these payments can be considerable. If participants are completing a test or assessment, they may receive their results, along with an interpretation of their own individual scores. A specific but perhaps less desirable benefit is that subjects have a chance to learn about the findings produced by the study. Besides the cold cash, it is difficult to gauge how much participants might value these other benefits.

Beyond the benefits conferred on individuals, IRBs also consider benefits to the wider society. Biomedical research, and social science investigations evaluating major programs, provide results that are certainly beneficial to society. As an example of the latter, consider an evaluation of DARE programs. As of this writing DARE (Drug Awareness Resistance Education) programs are being implemented in school systems in 49 states. Typically, uniformed police officers are trained in a DARE curriculum and give 17 1-hour lessons to one class. DARE seeks not only to educate young teens and preteens about the effects of drugs, but also to improve the problem solving and coping skills of these youths. A study evaluating the effects of such programs benefits society considerably. If the evaluation shows that the programs cause the wanted changes—improving self concept or delaying the onset of drug usage—society at least knows what it is getting for its money. If evaluation shows the program does not work then policy makers can consider alternate ways to combat the problem. You will read more about evaluation research in Chapter 13.

Aside from evaluations of major programs where the societal benefits of getting an answer are sizable, however, the societal utility of most social science studies remains hazy. Typically investigators claim that knowing if X influences Y by itself benefits society. IRBs do take this into account. Unless the proposed investigation contains serious methodological flaws, they are willing to accept that society may benefit *somehow* from the proposed investigation, even if the path leading to these benefits is not clear.

Possible Harms and Related Concerns

There are more of these than you might think. Table 4.1 organizes the major concerns.

The most obvious potential harms are those reflecting clear-cut injury of a psychological or physical nature to the participants.

Theoretically, participation in a research project may have the potential for causing *death* or *physical abuse or injury*. Luckily the former possibility is nil in nearly all social science research conducted in this country. Zimbardo's mock prison experiment of the early 1970s represents a clear-cut example of the latter. [7] It is extremely *unlikely* that a study like this would be permitted today by any IRB in the U.S.

High school students, randomly assigned to roles, acted as guards or prisoners in a "mock" prison. The "experiment" was ended after 6 days because the volunteer "prisoners" had suffered some physical abuse from the "guards." Zimbardo's experiment also inflicted *psychological abuse or injury* on the study participants. Prisoners were maltreated by the guards, yet they endured the treatment. Certainly this made them anxious and lowered their self-respect. The guards themselves may have felt similarly after the experiment, upset with the knowledge they could be bullies. Such intense role-playing situations may cause stress, guilt, anxiety, lessened self-confidence, lowered self-re-

TABLE 4.1
Some Potential Harms Inherent in Social Science Studies

Type of Harm	Effect on: Individual Participants	Wider Society
Physical or Psychological Injury	Death Physical abuse or injury	
	Psychological abuse or injury Damaged interpersonal relations as a result of participating	Certain groups in society may be scapegoated, stereotyped, blamed, or vilified as a result of research findings
Related to Loss of Privacy and Confidentiality	Legal jeopardy Reduced control over self-presentation	
	Loss of privacy and confidentiality resulting in public exposure of actions or attitudes that could have psychological, social, or legal consequences	Reduction of "private space" of society; increased concern about surveillance
Deception	Deception resulting in impaired capacity for decision making	Deception results in increased cynicism about, and mistrust of, others in society
Social Control		Information gathered can be used by authorities for manipulation and control of certain groups in society

Note: Items from Warwick, D. P. (1982). Types of harm in social research. In T. L. Beauchamp, R. R. Faden, R. J. Wallace, Jr., and L. Walters (Eds.), *Ethical issues in social science research.* Baltimore: Johns Hopkins University Press.

spect, or other psychological reactions. [8, p. 105]

If such research were widely permitted, societal views toward the scientific enterprise would worsen dramatically. The public would become more hostile toward research, demand tighter controls on research activities, and be less willing to fund social science investigators.

A very different type of *societal* harm may emerge from social research. Research may reveal or assume undesirable features about a particular grouping of society. Consequently, the members of that group may experience

social injury in the form of denigration or scapegoating. For example, in the early part of this century social researchers such as E.A. Ross compiled "findings" specifically geared to making U.S. immigration policy more exclusionary. Box 4.1 discusses a current research situation where some claim that societal harm also may occur.

Study participants may experience *damaged interpersonal relations* as a result of participating. Studies may be done in natural settings using naturalistic techniques such as open-ended interviews and unstructured observations. (Chapter 11 discusses these stud-

BOX 4.1

VIOLENCE INITIATIVE AT THE NATIONAL INSTITUTES OF HEALTH SPARKS CONCERNS

In the spring of 1992 a citizens group, the National Committee to Stop the Federal Violence Initiative, formed to oppose plans for federally funded violence research. Several factors sparked citizens' concerns including plans for a federally funded conference on genetics and crime and statements by federal administrators that observers labeled racist.

In early 1992 Frederick Goodwin, MD, an administrator at ADAMHA, the Alcohol, Drug Abuse and Mental Health Administration, discussed the possibility of identifying children who are likely to become violent at later ages, and intervening to avert the predicted-to-emerge violent behavior. Critics charged that the proposed research "will involve giving drugs to children who have been identified as potentially violent." [9, p. 18] Critics also charged that such research "tries to 'locate the problem in the person rather than in the social system and its failure to provide social services.'"

In the fall of 1992 Health and Human Services Secretary Louis Sullivan, MD, addressed the Congressional Black Caucus on the matter. He reassured them: "I will not tolerate racism under the guise of science." He also denied critics' claims about plans to drug segments of the African-American population. He stated there was not "any truth to claims that HHS proposed administering drugs to inner-city black youth to control violent behavior."

Citizens continue to be sensitive to research assumptions that may be damaging to disadvantaged populations. They express concern when they perceive that proposed research activities may harm a particular segment of society. Such expressions of concern, and the obligation of federal research agencies to respond, represent part of the public discourse surrounding science in an open, democratic society.

---

ies.) If done with probationers, parolees, offenders, or ex-offenders, participants may become suspect in the eyes of their "colleagues." Their colleagues may worry about them having said too much.

Less obvious but equally important are damages associated with a *loss of privacy or confidentiality*. Clearly, a criminal justice research project investigating illegal activities, such as one on white-collar crime, places participants in jeopardy. If information is released to authorities or just becomes widely known, legal action against the participants seems possible. Unintended distribution of

confidential information, even if the information does *not* touch on illegal activities or publicly embarrassing attitudes, can be damaging and anxiety arousing for the participant.

Marvin Wolfgang, a well-known criminologist, suggested researchers recognize such concerns and shape their data collection procedures accordingly. He recommends obtaining only the information that is directly relevant to study purposes. Specific information that may create liabilities for the participant or researcher should be avoided. [10]

The participant loses control over self-presentation if confidential data should be divulged. Erving Goffman has argued that a key element of an individual's mental health is his or her ability to present publicly certain features of his or her person, and to withhold other features. [11] The disclosure of confidential data threatens this selective disclosure and thus an individual's mental health.

Perhaps Laud Humphreys's study of anonymous homosexual encounters in public bathrooms represents the most dramatic recent example of this potential risk. As a participant observer he acted as "watchqueen" guard at the entrance to the public restrooms where the encounters took place. A **participant observer** is a researcher who enters a natural setting to conduct research; while observing people and events in the setting he also may take on a "role" or a position in the setting, and thus participate in activities.

Humphreys recorded license numbers and later tracked down his participants, interviewing them in their homes some months later—after he had altered his appearance. The main 'finding' of his study was that many people involved were respectable citizens. They had good jobs, families and homes in the suburbs. He was working in a small midwestern town, and in accordance with Murphy's law—anything that can go wrong will—the newspapers got hold of the story. Participants called him up to be sure their identities were not in danger. Humphreys burned tapes, shredded transcripts and assured the participants their identities were safe. Nonetheless the idea of authorities in a small town obtaining documents about 100 local homosexuals presents a chilling, Orwellian prospect.

At a societal level, possible losses of privacy may result in elevated concerns about government intrusion into private lives. I think the volume of U.S. citizens refusing to fill out the 1990 Census reflects this concern about government intrusion. I have heard people worry that the information they provide could somehow be used against them.

History suggests such worries have some basis. In World War I the Census Bureau provided names of young men to government agencies trying to track down people for the draft. At the beginning of World War II, 1940 Census information on the location of Japanese-Americans was released to the Army and used to quickly round up members of this group in California and other locations. [12, pp. 20–36] These events occurred even though the charter for the Census Bureau specifically prohibits releasing information that might be detrimental.

More troubling than inadvertent or unplanned disclosure of confidential information is intentional *deception* by social science researchers. Such deception is in direct conflict with the principle of autonomy. Individuals cannot make fully informed decisions about how to act or what to say if full knowledge of the situation is withheld from them. Their ability to make their own decisions is impaired.

Luckily, very little deception is involved in current social science research. It was more prevalent 20 years ago. Milgram's experiment on obedience to authority, noted earlier, represents such an example. In another example a research confederate staged a theft from a beer store after the owner had gone into the back. The researchers wanted to know if the customer—the participant—would report the theft to the owner. [13] Many did not.

You can imagine how the participants in such a study felt after they were *debriefed*. A **debriefing session** occurs at the end of an experiment, when the researcher tells the participant what really went on. If an experiment involved deceiving participants, the experimenter also would explain in these sessions the reason for deception. In the beer store shoplifting field experiment I imagine that many participants were outraged at the experimenter for 'duping' them, and angry at themselves, regardless of whether or not they had chased the 'thief.' If they had gone after the thief, they had been taken in by a hoax. If they had not pursued, they might wonder if they would act appropriately in a *real* emergency.

You can envision easily the consequences for the whole society were such chicanery to increase substantially. More widespread deception in research probably would result in more extensive and deeper cynicism about scientific research. How individual researchers manage ethical issues such as deception has implications for the broader ties between the public and the scientific community.

I think current surveys by researchers and private corporations conducting telephone interviews are in many cases guilty of deception by not informing the participant who their sponsor is. Market researchers will announce the name of their company, but will not divulge the name of their sponsor. Most of the market research interviewers who have contacted me have either refused to do so or have pleaded ignorance. I have taken to refusing to answer any question on a market survey unless they tell me the name of their specific client, and what their client is trying to find out. I'm willing to be a participant, but only if I know who will use the information and how.

Lastly we come to issues of *social control.* Research exploring the attitudes and behaviors of a group in society always has the potential to be used by those in power against that group, or perhaps to control it. For one current area that is a concern to some, see Box 4.1.

A related concern is the *integrity* of research and nonresearch information once it

has been collected. The criminal justice establishment in this country has amassed a wealth of information about offenders. These files, such as centralized fingerprint databases at the FBI, are an essential ingredient of society's efficient response to crime and wrongdoers. But they also can create problems.

The FBI maintains computerized databases at the National Crime Information Center for all criminals formally charged. Local police departments can obtain information on local suspects via telecommunications. In the early 1970s, however, Senator John Tunney made a disturbing discovery. The FBI, from 1971 to 1974, had included in these files persons who were "politically suspect," although they had not been charged with a crime. [14] The FBI was using the files to "track" citizens. In short, centralized, computerized information files can be seriously misused.

Don't misunderstand me: I am not attacking the need for, or societal benefits of, computerized information in centralized files. This information is vitally important for a variety of reasons. Nonetheless, I think we need to be concerned about the uses to which this information can be put. We ought not underestimate the potential for abuse of this information, and the need to be vigilant against such abuses. Current "watchdog" groups seeking to protect privacy rights of citizens may play important roles in preventing or limiting possible abuses.

In a different arena, market research scientists have used census information to compile detailed information about the neighborhood in which you live. [15] The information is used to profile political attitudes and consumer preferences. Researchers often sell the information to companies seeking to identify potential customers. This represents another way information files can provide revelations about you based on available information.

CURRENT PRACTICES FOR PROTECTING THE RIGHTS OF SUBJECTS

Because of ethical concerns, social science researchers currently are required to follow several procedures when collecting information from human subjects. Here are some steps researchers are obliged to follow.

1. Researchers are required to obtain **informed consent** from the study participants. Participants read or have explained to them an informed consent form. The form explains several points.

    (a) It describes the general nature of the research. The researcher points out in general terms what he hopes to achieve from the study, and what problems or issues are being addressed.

    (b) The participant is told what the study procedures involve, and whether any of the study procedures are "experimental." This latter point is most relevant to biomedical research, where a new procedure or drug might be tried.

    (c) The form assures the participant of the steps that the researcher will take to prevent inadvertent disclosure of information. For example, in surveys results are usually coded by identification number, and not by subject name. **Linked identifiers** may be present. These permit people to trace the numbers back to individual names. Investigators usually promise to keep linked identifiers securely locked away. Further, the form usually reassures the participant that results will only be reported in aggregate, and that the researcher will not publish or distribute any text or tables that allow others to identify particular individuals.

    (d) The form assures the participant that participation is totally voluntary; he need not participate, and if he chooses not to participate, he will not suffer any adverse consequences. If he does choose to participate, he may withdraw at any time or refuse to answer some questions.

    (e) The form says that the participant understands all of this, has been free to answer questions, has received satisfactory answers, and, by signing the form, *voluntarily* agrees to participate.

    No coercion must be used in these procedures. After the explanation the participant *freely* consents to participate in the research project.

As you can well imagine, such a form, with its legalistic tenor, can put a damper on a participant's willingness to contribute to a study. Such detailed procedures are fully appropriate in situations where participation presents a real risk for the participant. But many types of research, such as routine surveys or behavioral observations of public life, do not present such risks. Thus, the 1981 Health and Human Services regulations on informed consent allow consent requirements to be waived if the risk of harm to the participant is remote. "Where the risk of harm is remote, the need for consent diminishes." [16, p. 122] What this boils down to is whether the researcher can make the case that the potential risks are "minimal and no more than would be experienced in everyday life." Everyday risks include things like saying the wrong thing, being embarrassed, walking under ladders with paint cans on them, and so forth. If the researcher can make the case that the risks in the research to the participant are similarly small, then consent requirements may be loosened or waived altogether.

Some criminal justice researchers have argued that even in situations where the risks are *not* minimal, informed consent procedures should *not* be used. [10] They argue that the oral request for participation is sufficient in sociological research, and well understood. People understand that they can refuse to answer questions if they wish. To use informed consent procedures when interviewing ex-offenders may disturb the rapport between the interviewer and the respondent, and may result in lower participation rates.

I think such critics are correct. In field research settings, formal informed consent procedures might interfere with the research process and the researcher–participant relationship. In some situations informal consent may be sufficient. But whatever the level of formality, it is important that the researcher communicate fully and openly with participants regarding her goals and procedures, and subsequently obtain informed consent.

2. As noted above the researcher is obligated to protect against *potential loss of confidentiality*—some outsider finding what an individual's responses were on a questionnaire or test, for example. Thus, as mentioned above, the researcher is expected to guard closely files that could be used to learn who is linked to which survey form.

You may find it hard to imagine why it is so important to be so careful about such information. Who could care? Admittedly, most surveys are innocuous. But bear two points in mind. The participant wanted to tell these matters to *the researcher*, not the evening papers. Second, it is not too hard to imagine cases where inadvertent disclosure can create serious problems. In the late 1970s Steve Gottfredson and I conducted a study of correctional reform in Maryland, and interviewed dozens of high-ranking offi-

cials. [17] Many of those interviewed were extremely critical of then-Governor Hughes's correctional policies. Had the local papers gotten hold of some of those uncensored comments and been able to match them up with particular individuals, serious damage to several politicians' careers could have resulted.

3. Related to the problem of the potential loss of confidentiality is the problem of **statistical disclosure**. [18, p. 250] If information about an individual can be more accurately known after some statistics are released, then statistical disclosure has occurred. See Figure 4.2. The left part of the figure shows a situation where no statistical disclosure can occur. In the situation depicted the Census Bureau reports, for a *large* group of households, such as several hundred, the number of households living below the poverty line. In this situation a person obtaining this information is going to be unable to make a guess about the poverty status of a *particular* household in which he might be interested. He has no reasonable basis on which to make a guess. But the right part shows a different situation. The Census reports the number of households living below the poverty line among a *much smaller* group of households. In this situation it is easier for an observer to make a reasonable guess about the poverty status of a particular household. The information released has improved the observer's ability to estimate the characteristics of a particular household.

Protections against such disclosures exist in the U.S. Census, which *suppresses*—i.e., does not show—block-level information if there is a possibility of identification. **Data suppression** is a common practice when the number of cases in a group is quite small.

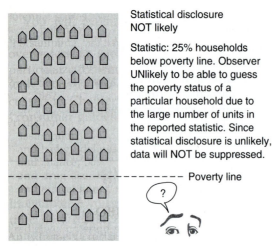

FIGURE 4.2   Statistical Disclosure.

SOME ETHICAL ISSUES PARTICULAR TO CRIMINAL JUSTICE CONCERNS

The topics criminal justice researchers investigate raise special ethical concerns. You will consider here two classes of ethical problems pertinent to criminal justice.

The Prediction of Violence

The Practical Issue   The criminal justice system bases many decisions on predictions of whether an individual will be violent in the future. [19] For example, predictions of violence come into play in the following decisions:

If the person is convicted, should he be eligible for probation in the community? If so, what level of supervision should be required?

If the felon is incarcerated, should he be eligible for work release? Should the felon be paroled or allowed other kinds of conditional releases?

Do you remember the firestorm of publicity surrounding the stabbing of a pregnant worker in Bellevue Hospital in New York City in the winter of 1989 by a probationer

classified as low risk? How about the infamous Willy Horton ads during George Bush's second presidential campaign in 1988? Serious damage can result when criminal justice predictions about who will and who will not be violent, and the decisions based on those predictions, are just plain wrong.

Criminal justice researchers and administrators use **risk prediction devices** to help make these predictions. These devices use background information about offenders and their criminal history. They also consider how, among a large group of offenders, scores on those background factors connect to violence or criminality.

For example, you are a prisoner eligible for parole. I am a parole officer trying to predict parole success. I define success as not being rearrested within the parole period and not testing positive for drug use during the same period. I know from other statistical work I have done that, for prisoners like yourself, those who have a juvenile record are more likely to be arrested for a violent crime while on parole, as compared to those who do not have a juvenile record. If you have a juvenile record I will predict that *you* will be more likely to commit a violent crime while on parole.

My risk prediction instrument would examine several factors that I know, based on research with other offenders, predict rearrest for violent crimes while on parole. I then examine *your* score on these factors and decide if you are a "good risk" or a "bad risk" for release on parole. Using tools like these, researchers can predict correctly, for 10% to 40% of cases, whether future violence will occur in a specified period. [20] For more details on risk prediction, see Box 8.1.

The Ethical Problems   Two ethical problems accompany these prediction activities. First, there are bound to be a substantial number of people who *are* predicted to be violent, who turn out *not* to be violent. These are called **false positives**. If, on the basis of the prediction of violence, which turns out to be incorrect, they are incarcerated or in other ways denied a less restrictive punishment, then the research has inflicted a harm on them. As a result of incorrect prediction they have experienced, unjustly some prisoner-advocates might claim, severely reduced autonomy.

Citizens also can complain about the process. Parole officers might release an offender because it is predicted that he will not be violent. Yet, the releasee subsequently commits a violent crime. Such a case is called a **false negative**. Victim and public safety advocates argue that *their* rights have been diminished in these cases. For further discussion of these issues see Chapter 14.

A second ethical concern centers around the items used to make these predictions of dangerousness. To put it bluntly: the factors most predictive of future violence may be exactly those factors society does *not* wish us to consider. These factors can be one of two classes.

One class may include items reflecting the individual's offense history, such as age at first arrest, total number of arrests, most serious offense ever arrested for, and so on. If the researcher uses these to predict future violence, and then bases release decisions on these factors, the individual in question is being punished for *past* acts. These are acts for which he may already have paid.

A second class of factors may be features of the individual over which he had no control, such has his social class, income level, or ethnicity. To base release decisions on such factors is, some would argue, to victimize further those who are already victims of social injustice. On the other hand, others argue that to leave such items out of instruments predicting future violence "is to doom the effort from the start." [20, p. 91]

Predictions of dangerousness raise ongoing, difficult ethical dilemmas for criminal justice researchers and practitioners. Current ethical guidelines provide scant guidance on these issues.

Fieldwork

You'll be learning more about fieldwork later in the volume (see Chapter 11). It represents a range of naturalistic techniques where the researcher, at some level, becomes involved in the situation she is studying and the people who live or work in that situation. For example, a researcher examining police work may ride along in patrol cars for a few months, and talk with officers about their duties, responsibilities, and attitudes. A main advantage of field work is that it allows the researcher to see the situation from the inside.

Preserving Confidentiality   One problem that may arise is that the *confidentiality of the researcher–participant relationship can be jeopardized if the information collected is subsequently demanded for legal purposes and released to the courts.* The precursor to the National Institute of Justice, the Law Enforcement Assistance Administration, has safeguarded this confidentiality. Research information cannot be dragged into any court or administrative process unless the person who originally provided the information agrees to such a step. This **immunity provision** safeguards the confidentiality of the research information from legal pressures. The Omnibus Crime Control and Safe Streets Act reauthorized this protection in 1979. So if you're interviewing a defendant just after arrest, and he tells you he's going to plead the insanity defense because it's his best shot, lawyers for the prosecution cannot have access to your questionnaires, field notes, or even ask you to remember what the defendant said. This provision seems to safeguard confidentiality of data adequately in most cases. Nonetheless, field researchers strongly caution their field contacts that legal difficulties may arise. [21]

When to Deceive and How Much? The problem of *deception* often troubles field researchers. Although they usually tell their collaborators something about their purposes, much is left unsaid. There are three levels at which collaborators in the setting can be deceived. [22, p. 53]

1. The researcher can seek to hide completely the fact that research is being conducted. Humphreys's research, and studies employing hidden observations of public behavior in public settings, represent examples of this level of deception.
2. A second level of deception occurs when participants know they are involved in a research situation, but some key features of it are kept from them. A fieldworker, for example, might misrepresent the purposes of his study, or his affiliations.
3. A third level of deception can occur when the fieldworker seeks to check the accuracy of information provided to him by a participant in the setting, without the participant knowing he

is being check on. A researcher might ask a participant the same question a few months later to see if he gets the same response. The participant knows he is in a study and what the topic is, but does not know exactly the researcher's purpose.

These levels of deception represent increasing awareness by the participant that he is in a study, and increasing awareness of what the study is about. Therefore, as we go from the first stage to the third stage, *the participants have more autonomy in deciding how to act.* This increased autonomy may serve also to protect the researcher from subsequent legal claims brought against him by field participants.

Levels of Deception in Fieldwork

MORE DECEPTION <————>		LESS DECEPTION
LESS PARTICIPANT <————> AUTONOMY		MORE PARTICIPANT AUTONOMY
1	2	3
Researcher hides *both* status as a researcher and ongoing research project	Researcher reveals role as researcher and ongoing research project, but is vague about both	Researcher fully informs participants about role and project, but masks efforts to check information

In fieldwork and in some other types of research, the individuals with whom one is working are not subjects. Rather they are collaborators. The researcher may have a relationship with participants that is coequal in some respects. [23] Given the researcher's basic respect for the autonomy of all study participants, in fieldwork the researcher should *only* engage in the third type of deception noted above—checking participants' responses. This level of deception should occur only when it is absolutely needed. [22] Other types of deception, according to this view, are not permissible.

In sum, some argue that the complex relationships that develop between researcher and participants in fieldwork demand a different, more exacting standard of conduct. Minor deception can be used only in a few circumstances, and major deceptions are not permissible, according to this view.

Furthermore, criminal justice fieldwork often brings the researcher into contact with individuals labeled by the society as deviant: crooks, fences, dealers, con men, and so on. In working with these individuals, some feel it is important for the researcher not only to be honest with study participants, but to "honor" the roles she may be encouraged to adopt in these situations. See Box 4.2.

FINAL COMMENT ON ETHICAL GUIDELINES

Criminal justice researchers cannot know what it means to act ethically in all the research situations they encounter. Existing guidelines for the protection of human subjects provide some directions on how to proceed but are of necessity general. They cannot provide a sense of how researchers should act in specific situations. [25] In short, the guidelines may just not be helpful for all researchers in all situations.

Leslie Wilkins has gone even further. He suggested that ethical guidelines may be harmful. They may force researchers to avoid important and interesting research topics. [26] If a researcher knows that she leaves herself open to certain liabilities by doing certain research, she is likely to avoid it altogether. In this way ethical guidelines may be helpful to administrators and policy makers, because they may prevent information being generated that would challenge their beliefs. I do not know how widely shared Wilkins's

DEMANDS OF FIELD RELATIONSHIPS

Carl Klockars argues that the role that develops between a fieldworker and his "deviant" subjects demands, in some situations, that the researcher get his hands dirty. He calls this the "dirty hands problem." Honoring that role is a "good end" by itself, he suggests, despite the situations into which it may lead the researcher. The researcher may have to use "bad means"—such as lying—so as to uphold that role. "This good end is the fieldworker's responsibility to the deviant . . . subjects who have placed their confidence in him and given him firsthand access to their deviance based upon that confidence . . . Explicitly or implicitly the fieldworker and his deviant subjects must agree upon a field role for the fieldworker, and, what is more, the fieldworker must agree to stick to it and play it competently. If his deviant subjects are shoplifters and they agree to let him watch their work from the role of "shopper," he is obliged to play that role well and maintain it even if store security guards grab him and accuse him of being a lookout for his subjects." [24, p. 275]

views on this are, but they bring up an intriguing perspective.

Regardless of the flaws or limitations, ethical guidelines for human-subject research are likely to remain with us. They do not help the researcher resolve every ethical issue confronted, but they do certainly result in decreased chances of abuse in many research situations. Further, by following these guidelines researchers can reduce their own vulnerability to legal problems that may develop later.

SUMMARY OF MAIN POINTS

- Scientists have a range of obligations to the community of scientists.
- These obligations place boundaries on how scientists may collect, handle, discuss, and publicly represent information.
- Scientific fraud is not a new problem; it has been problematic in humanities and social science research for some time.
- Scientists, as members of society, also have obligations to that larger society to act ethically in their research involving other humans.
- Many ethical problems arise because of the conflict between the scientific goals of researchers and their responsibilities, as members of society, to treat others decently.
- Concerns about the potential for the unethical use of human study participants, and some controversial studies, have produced ethical guidelines governing research with humans.
- Every research study has a moral or ethical component.
- Research guidelines may indicate that some topics, such as jury deliberations, are simply too "sacred" to be investigated by certain means.
- Current ethical guidelines are meant to honor certain ethical principles such as autonomy, avoiding harm, doing good where feasible, and promoting equity.
- Local institutional review boards (IRBs) consider whether a proposed study will follow these principles.
- In social science research the most prominent ethical concerns are usually fully informing the participants about the study before they decide to take part, and taking steps to prevent others from gaining access to the information gathered.

- IRBs weigh the potential risks of a study against the potential benefits.
- Some "routine" research is exempted from IRB review.
- Criminal justice research presents several ethical problems for which we do *not* have clear-cut guidelines about how to act.
- Two examples of such problems are the morality of the factors used to predict violence, and the problems inherent in fieldwork with "deviants" in naturalistic settings.

SUGGESTED READINGS

Sissela Bok's *Lying: Moral choice in public and private life* (Pantheon, 1978) explores the reasons for and against using deception in a variety of practical situations, such as with doctors and their patients, politicians, and so on. If you think deception in research is justified or are just wondering about the issue, put this one on the top of your "To Read During January or Spring Break" list. You of course, already have such a list. (Don't you?)

David Burnham's *The Rise of the computer state* (Vintage, 1984) will chill you or at least entertain you. Discusses the threats posed by centralized information and interfile connections. Not scholarly, but provocative.

Bortner, M. A. (1983). Research within the juvenile courts: The Dilemma of human subjects regulations. *Sociological Methods and Research, 11,* 519-533.

Breger, M. J. (1983). Randomized social experiments and the law. In R. F. Boruch & J. S. Cecil (Eds.), *Solutions to ethical and legal problems in social research* (pp. 97-117). New York: Academic Press.

Broad, W., & Wade, N. (1982). *Betrayers of the truth: Fraud and deceit in the halls of science.* New York: Touchstone. An excellent "popular" history of academic fraud.

Bernard Gert's *The Moral rules* (Harper and Row, 1966) is for those interested in understanding the reasoning behind ethical principles, but who don't want a bunch of mumbo-jumbo. Even though Gert's work is now somewhat dated, his writing is such a model of clarity you might consider this a timeless book. I do. Highly recommended for all of those with a philosophical or legal interest.

Laud Humphreys's *Tearoom trade* (Aldine, 1975) is the most hotly debated field study of deviance ever. So if you're interested in field work or have an anthropological bent, read it.

Polsky, N. (1967). *Hustlers, beats, and others.* Chicago: Aldine.

Weppner, R. S. (Ed.). (1977). *Street enthnography.* Beverly Hills: Sage.

Zimbardo, P. G., Haney, C., Banks, W. C., & Jaffe, D. (1973, April 8). The Mind is a formidable jailer: A Pirandellian prison. *New York Times Magazine, 122*(Section 6), 38-60. A gripping recounting of the "mock prison" experiment using high schoolers that was cut short due to its dramatic impact on "prisoners" and "guards."

GLOSSARY OF KEY WORDS

autonomy
beneficence
data suppression
debriefing session
equity
false negative
false positive
immunity provision
informed consent
justice
linked identifiers
nonmaleficence
participant observer
replication
risk prediction devices
scientific fraud
secondary analysis
statistical disclosure

REFERENCES

1. Grafton, A. (1990) *Forgers and critics: Creativity and duplicity in Western scholarship,* Princeton University Press, Princeton, NJ.
2. Dorfman, D. D. (1978) The Cyril Burt question: New findings. *Science 201,* 1177–1186.
3. Katz, J., ed. (1972) *Experimentation with human beings,* Russell Sage Foundation, New York, pp. 67–109.
4. Nelkin D. (1982) Forbidden research: Limits to inquiry in the social sciences. In Beauchamp, T. L., Faden, R. R., Wallace, R. J., Jr., and Walters, L. (eds.), *Ethical issues in social science research,* Johns Hopkins University Press, Baltimore, pp. 163–174.
5. Milgram, S. (1971) *Leadership and obedience,* Harper Colophon, New York.
6. Beauchamp, T. L., Faden, R. R., Wallace, R. J., Jr., and Walters, L. (1982) Introduction. In Beauchamp, T. L., Faden, R. R., Wallace, R. J., Jr., and Walters, L. (eds.), *Ethical issues in social science research,* Johns Hopkins University Press, Baltimore, pp. 3–39.
7. Zimbardo, P. G., Haney, C., Banks, W. C., and Jaffe, D. (1973) The mind is a formidable jailer: A Pirandellian prison. *New York Times Magazine 122*(Section 6,8 April), 38–60.
8. Warwick, D. P. (1982) Types of harm in social research. In Beauchamp, T. L., Faden, R. R., Wallace, R. J., Jr., and Walters, L. (eds.), *Ethical issues in social science research,* Johns Hopkins University Press, Baltimore, pp. 101–124.
9. Adler, T. (1992) Violence research comes under attack. *The APA Monitor 23*(12, December), 1, 18.
10. Wolfgang, M. (1981) Confidentiality in criminological research and other ethical issues. *Journal of Criminal Law and Criminology 72,* 345–361.
11. Goffman, E. (1959) *The Presentation of self in everyday life,* Doubleday, Garden City, NY.
12. Burnham, D. (1984) *The Rise of the computer state,* Vintage Books, New York.
13. Piliavin, I. M., and Rodin, J. (1969) Good samaritanism: An underground phenomenon? *Journal of Personality and Social Psychology 13,* 289–299.

14. Burnham, D. (1984) *The Rise of the computer state*, Vintage Books, New York, p. 84.

15. Weiss, M. (1988) *The Clustering of America*, Harper and Row, New York.

16. Breger, M. J. (1983) Randomized social experiments and the law. In Boruch, R. F., and Cecil, J. S. (eds.), *Solutions to ethical and legal problems in social research*, Academic Press, New York, pp. 97–117.

17. Gottfredson, S. D., and Taylor R. B. (1987) Attitudes of correctional policymakers and the public. In Gottfredson, S. D., and McConville, S. (eds.), *America's correctional crisis*, Greenwood Press, New York.

18. Steinberg, J. (1983) Social research use of archival records: Procedural solutions to privacy problems. In Boruch, R. F., and Cecil, J. (eds.), *Solutions to ethical and legal problems in social research*, Academic Press, New York, pp. 249–262.

19. Shah, S. A. (1978) Dangerousness: A paradigm for exploring some issues in law and psychology. *American Psychologist 33*, 224–238.

20. Monahan, J. (1983) Ethical issues in the prediction of criminal violence. In Boruch, R. F., and Cecil, J. S. (eds.), *Solutions to ethical and legal problems in social research*, Academic Press, New York, pp. 83–96.

21. Sullivan, M. (1989) *Getting paid: Youth crime and work in the inner city*, Cornell University Press, Ithaca, NY.

22. Reiman, J. H. (1979) Research subjects, political subjects, and human subjects. In Klockars, C. B., and O'Connor, F. W. (eds.), *Deviance and decency: The Ethics of research with human subjects*, Sage Publications, Beverly Hills, CA, pp. 35–60.

23. Douglas, J. D. (1979) Living morality versus bureaucratic fiat. In Klockars, C. B., and O'Connor, F. W. (eds.), *Deviance and decency: The Ethics of research with human subjects*, Sage Publications, Beverly Hills, CA, pp. 13–34.

24. Klockars, C. B. (1979) Dirty hands and deviant subjects. In Klockars, C. B., and O'Connor, F. W. (eds.), *Deviance and decency: The Ethics of research with human subjects*, Sage Publications, Beverly Hills, CA, pp. 261–282.

25. Manning, P. K., and Redlinger, L. J. (1979) The political economy of fieldwork ethics. In Klockars, C. B., and O'Connor, F. W. (eds.), *Deviance and decency: The ethics of research with human subjects*, Sage Publications, Beverly Hills, CA, pp. 125–150.

26. Wilkins, L. T. (1979) Human subjects—whose subject? In Klockars, C. B., and O'Connor, F. W. (eds.), *Deviance and decency: The Ethics of research with human subjects*, Sage Publications, Beverly Hills, CA. pp. 99–124.

PART TWO

ORGANIZING AND PRESENTING DATA

These two chapters examine some common means of presenting findings and collecting information. The material provides a bridge between the discussions of theory and ethics in the previous chapters, and Part III, which discusses the benchmarks of scientific quality.

Chapter 5 examines graphs and tables. These are two common ways of summarizing social science information. You will encounter five types of graphs: bar charts, line charts, pie charts, histograms, and scatterplots. You will learn about the situations where each type of chart is most appropriate. You will view cross-tabulations, tables summarizing the relationship between two or three variables.

Chapter 6 reviews the process of measurement. You will examine what it is that social scientists measure when they collect data. (Be prepared: you may be surprised by the answer!) You will review the different types of data social scientists can collect, how they classify the data they obtain, ways of eliciting data, and ways they can organize data once they have been obtained.

After completing this section you should be able to: explain when to use different types of graphs, interpret two-way and three-way cross-tabulation tables, understand the meaning of different levels of measurement, and comprehend scaling procedures and index construction.

CHAPTER 5

GRAPHS
AND
TABLES

OBJECTIVES

You will learn how to read graphs and tables presenting information. Science articles report most information in tabular and graphic formats. If you understand the basics of tabular and graphic construction you can grasp more effectively the information presented, and gauge more speedily the information hidden or downplayed.

It is a truism that we live in an information society. At times, we seem awash in factoids. Graphs and tables convey much of the information pumped at us by the media. They also are especially important for scientific communication. Researchers use them extensively in reports, journal articles, and presentations. In this chapter you examine the logic behind the construction of these items, and the rules of "good form."

ORGANIZATION OF THE CHAPTER

You examine five types of graphs: pie charts, bar charts, line charts, histograms, and scatterplots. You will encounter good and bad examples of each. You will learn rules for deciding which type of chart to use in different situations. You will go on to consider data tables. They report scores on one, two, or three variables. They can show relationships between scores on two or three variables.

Graphs and tables both represent excellent tools for a variety of purposes. They can summarize data, providing descriptive overviews of scores on one or more variables. They can be used in hypothesis testing, following Einstein's logic of scientific inquiry, to examine how scores on an independent variable link to scores on a dependent variable. You also can use them to explore relationships among variables, following Holmes's logic of scientific inquiry.

We continue in this chapter with our hypothetical scenario concerning community policing in an urban neighborhood. You find that a local researcher recently has surveyed households in this locale on a range of topics related to community policing and victimization. You also examine national level data on some of these same topics, for the purposes of comparison. Furthermore, you have available information from 100 officers who have been trained recently as community police officers (CPOs) and are beginning work in that capacity. The information you have about them relates directly to the theory you developed to explain satisfaction with community policing assignments. (See Chapter 3.) You use two-way and three-way tables to examine key hypotheses in your theory.

On the workdisk you will find the datafiles used to construct most of the charts and graphs appearing in this chapter. I also have placed there suggestions for exercises. I have included additional datafiles on drunk-driving arrests, and on government spending on drug control strategies. Exercises on the workdisk encourage you to engage in grounded theorizing, and to test hypotheses, using graphs constructed from these datafiles. I hope you actively explore these materials. The more you do, the more you will understand the process.

Graphs can be poorly presented or even misleading. Cognitive psychology has learned a considerable amount in the last 20 years about how we organize and perceive visual information. This knowledge suggests how to construct graphs so they communicate effectively. [1, 2, 3] I combine the general implications of work in this area, with comments on deception in graphical presentation, to offer a list of "do's" and "don'ts" to follow when constructing graphs. [4]

CHARTS AND GRAPHS

The Type of Data and Number of Variables Suggest the Recommended Graph

You decide what type of graph to use based, in part, on the kind of data you have. First, you consider how many variables you will examine at a time. Do you just want to look at how people score on one variable? Or are you interested in two? Or three? Second, you con-sider the *type* of data. For graphical purposes, data are of two different types: *categorical* and *continuous*.

> Continuous data come from a scale of values that can be any real number from minus to plus infinity. Categorical data may be numerals or characters but their distinguishing feature is that they fall into a few unordered discrete categories. [5]

Sex, race, political party affiliation, region of the country, suburban vs. rural vs. urban, convicted vs. not convicted, or incarcerated vs. not incarcerated represent categorical variables. Age, scores on a satisfaction scale, scores on a personality inventory measuring sociability, or scores on a scale measuring police cynicism represent continuous variables.

Once you have answered these two questions—the type or types of data examined, and the number of variables—you can decide the type of graph best suited to your purpose. Table 5.1 shows recommended graph types once you have answered these two questions.

You will note from the table that, for some data situations, more than one of the graphs discussed here are recommended. You have choices. You also will see that, in some situations, I comment on the number of possible response categories. A variable may be continuous but allow only a few response categories. For example, in a survey you may ask about the level of officer satisfaction with the community-policing role but only allow responses ranging from 1 (not at all satisfied) to 10 (completely satisfied). Some kinds of graphs are "messy" and difficult to interpret if the variables contain a large number of response categories. I suggest that pie charts should be avoided if the number of categories exceeds 5, and bar charts should be avoided if the number of categories exceed 15. These represent arbitrary cutoff points, and you

TABLE 5.1
Types of Data, N of Variables, and Recommended Graph Types[1]

Type(s) of Data	Number of Response Categories	Number of Variables		
		One	Two	Three
Categorical	< 5	Pie	Multiple Pie Charts	Multiple Pie Charts
	< 15	Bar	Bar	Bar
Continuous	Any	Histogram (Density)	Scatterplot Line	Line
	< 5	Pie	Multiple Pie Charts	Multiple Pie Charts
	< 15	Bar	Bar	Bar
Mixed			Bar	Bar Scatterplot

Note: Adapted from Wilkinson, L. (1988). *SYGRAPH.* Evanston, IL: SYSTAT, Inc. p. 66.

[1] The types of graphs examined here represent just a small portion of those currently available for displaying numerical information. Additional types include: box-and-whiskers plots, stem-and-leaf plots, polar plots, Chernoff faces, quantile plots, density traces, and more. I discuss in this chapter the types of graphs that are most commonly used in scientific literature as well as in the general press.

may not agree with them. Personal tastes vary widely in this area.

Pie Charts

Purposes You use pie charts to display the portions of a whole in different individual categories. When people make judgements about portions or proportions, pie charts can be as effective as other types of charts. [6]

Scenario You have learned that a criminal justice professor at a local university recently surveyed 1,000 households in the neighborhood which was the site of your community-policing initiative. In a 1989 survey interviewers asked household members: "How fearful are you of being a victim of violent crime in the 1990s?" People could reply "very fearful," "somewhat fearful," or "not at all fearful." The professor has supplied you with the results for this question. You want to learn how the concerns about victimization expressed by household members compared

to the concerns expressed by household members across the country. You come across data from a national survey conducted at the same time [7]. Figure 5.1 provides two depictions of answers to this question on the national survey.

Bad Form The top pie is misleading for several reasons.

- First, it presents the pie floating in *three dimensions*. In general, three-dimensional charts are more difficult to interpret than two-dimensional charts.
- Second, a piece of the pie has *exploded*; it has been separated from the rest of the pie. This makes it more difficult to make judgements about proportions.
- Third, *data have been collapsed*. "Very fearful" and "Somewhat fearful" responses have been collapsed into one piece of pie, rather than appearing as two separate pieces.
- Fourth, the *pieces are not labeled*. You do not

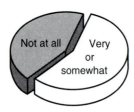

How fearful are you of being a victim of violent crime in the 1990s?

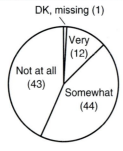

How fearful are you of being a victim of violent crime in the 1990s?

FIGURE 5.1
Pie charts showing fear of violent victimization, based on a national survey conducted in 1989. Top pie is *less* informative; bottom pie is *more* informative. (*Source:* Bennack, F. A., Jr. (1989). *The American public's hopes and fears for the 1990s.* New York: Hearst Corporation. Table 58 (p. 38). Reprinted in Flanagan, T. J., and Maguire, K., eds. (1992). *Sourcebook of criminal justice statistics 1991.* Washington: USGPO. Table 2.24 (p. 191)).

know the actual percentage or count associated with each piece.

- Fifth, one of the pieces has been shaded. *Shading* that differs across pieces interferes with judgements about proportions.
- Finally, *missing data have been excluded.* You do not know it from the chart, but 1 percent of the sample did not answer this question.

Good Form The bottom pie chart is correctly displayed. It is presented in two di-

mensions. Each portion has a clearly labeled percentage. The data are not collapsed across categories. There is no different shading across pieces. Missing data are included and labeled. No pieces are "exploding" out of the pie. I guess this is not a high energy food (tic).

Different Interpretations The two different pie charts suggest different pictures. The top chart suggests that Americans are extremely fearful of violent victimization. The bottom chart provides a different depiction. It suggests that only a small portion of Americans, about 12 percent, are extremely fearful of being a victim of a violent crime. But at the same time, a roughly equal portion of Americans are not at all fearful (43%) or only somewhat fearful (44%).

Bar Charts

Purposes *One variable* When displaying one variable, a bar chart depicts the percentage, count, or proportion of cases, or average, for each category or level of a variable. The height of each bar reflects the count, proportion or percentage of cases; or the average for cases in that category. Figure 5.2 presents information from the pie chart in Figure 5.1 in the form of a bar graph.

Two or More Variables With two variables, bar charts depict relationships between scores on one independent variable, and scores on a dependent variable. Each bar represents one category or range of the independent variable. The height of each bar reflects how cases in that category of the independent variable, or in that range of the independent variable, score on the dependent variable. The score on the dependent variable may be a percentage, a proportion, a count, an average, or some other statistic.

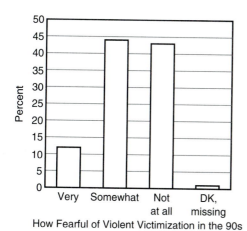

FIGURE 5.2
Bar chart of responses to the question "How fearful are you of becoming a victim of violent crime in the 1990s?" (*Source*: See Figure 5.1).

Scenario You learn that the local researcher who surveyed households in the neighborhood where your community-policing initiative took place also asked respondents about places to avoid while walking the streets. He asked them: "Is there any area right around here—that is, within a mile—where you would be afraid to walk alone at night?" You find in the data that women express higher avoidance than men. You seek a context in which to interpret these data. You find that the same question was asked of a national sample of respondents in 1991. Figure 5.3 shows two bar charts constructed from that national sample.

In the top figure, the left-hand pair of bars indicates the percentages of men and women in the sample who said "yes" in response to the question; the right-hand pair of bars shows the percentages of men and women saying "no" in response to the question. Dark bars represent women; light bars represent men.

Bad Form The top bar graph is inadequate in several respects.

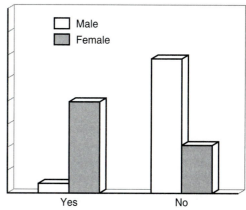

Night-time fear close to home

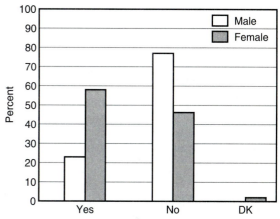

1991 responses to the question: "Is there any area right around here—that is, within a mile—where you would be afraid to walk alone at night?"

FIGURE 5.3
Bar chart of sex differences in places to avoid while walking alone at night. Top graph represents *bad* form; bottom graph represents *good* form. (*Source*: 1991 General Social Survey, conducted by the National Opinion Research Center. From tabulations in Flanagan, T. J., and Maguire, K, eds. (1992). *Sourcebook of criminal justice statistics 1991*. Washington: USGPO. Table 2.28 (p. 197)).

- Most importantly, the Y or *vertical axis is not labeled*; you do not know that the different heights correspond to.
- Second, the Y axis *does not start at 0*, but instead starts at 20. You would not learn

this unless you had the bottom chart to compare with the top one.

- Third, the graph is again presented in *three dimensions*, making the bars blocky. With such bars it is even more difficult to gauge height exactly than it is in the two dimensional case. [8]
- Difficulty in gauging bar height is compounded by the *lack of a horizontal grid* running along the back.
- Finally, *missing data are excluded*.

Good Form   The bottom bar graph avoids the above mistakes. The Y axis is clearly labeled and begins at 0. Missing data are included. The graph appears in two rather than three dimensions. A horizontal grid is provided.

Different Interpretations   Both graphs depict the same general picture. Women, as compared to men, are more likely to report avoiding a place while walking alone at night. But the graphs also reveal differences. In the top graph men look more fearless than in the bottom graph. The bottom graph reveals that almost a quarter of men report a place to avoid while walking alone at night. The bottom graph also reveals a small proportion of respondents who were unable or unwilling to answer this question.

Histograms

Purpose and Construction   Histograms look like bar charts. And, like bar charts, they can be used to represent scores on one continuous variable. Nevertheless, they are different from bar charts in their construction and in their purpose. Whereas bar charts provide information about scores or counts at specific values of the variable, or at specific ranges of the variable, histograms provide general information about the *shape* of the distribution. They display the sample density for a contin-

uous variable. [9] They tell you where, along the range of the variable, most of the data appear. The height of each bar tells you how many cases score at that value of the variable, or at that range of the variable. Thus, they have a more specialized purpose than bar charts. They show how *scores* are *distributed* along a variable.

There are also important differences in construction. Most programs that construct histograms, like MYSTAT or SPSS-PC, will "automatically" select an interval for each bar in order to best show the distribution of the data. A second important difference is that the bars are shown touching each other, rather than separate. The bars are contiguous because they represent a continuous variable. Third, with a histogram, each bar should represent an equal range of scores on the variable. The bars should be of equal width.

Scenario   The survey conducted by a local researcher in the neighborhood where your department initiated community policing included 1,000 households. They reported how many years they had lived in the neighborhood. The histogram in Figure 5.4 displays the results. Each bar represents an interval of five years.

Interpretation   The bulk of respondents are newcomers to the neighborhood, with about 70 percent of the respondents reporting a length of residence of 5 years or less. Fewer respondents report longer stays in the neighborhood. Most of the data are at the lower end of the variable.

Line Graphs

Purposes   Line graphs depict relationships between two continuous variables. They are often used effectively when the independent variable is time and the purpose is to show changes on the dependent variable over

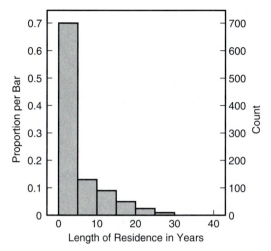

FIGURE 5.4

Histogram of 1,000 responses to the question: "How many years have you lived in this neighborhood?" Artificial data. Right-hand *Y* axis shows count. Left-hand *Y* axis shows proportion of all cases per bar.

some unit of time. Scores on the dependent variable, or percentages, or proportions, or counts, appear on the *Y* or vertical axis. Scores on the independent variable, often some unit of time, appear on the *X* or horizontal axis.

Scenario A local neighborhood leader has been complaining vociferously about "increasing rates of street crime in this neighborhood and across the country." Her comments have prompted you to investigate recent trends in robbery and assault victimizations. You turned to data from the *National Crime Survey*. It is a national survey that asks people about recent victimization experiences. You will learn more about it in Chapter 12. Researchers have constructed *victimization rates* from these data. A victimization rate divides the number of victimization incidents by the number of people, and generates a rate of victimization incidents per 1,000 persons or households. You have obtained information about national victimization rates and

graphed them. The results appear in Figure 5.5.

Bad Form The top graph is inadequate in several respects.

- The three-dimensional perspective turns each line into a "ribbon." But the three-dimensional perspective makes it difficult to connect the ribbon with actual scores on the *Y* axis.
- Although the units on the *Y* axis are numbered, the axis itself is not labeled.
- The lines representing different scores on the *Y* axis do not extend across the back, making it harder to interpret scores.
- The figure lacks a legend clearly stating that the "solid" ribbon represents the assault rate, and the "dotted" ribbon the robbery rate.

Good Form The bottom figure corrects these problems.

- The figure appears in two dimensions rather than three.
- The units on the *Y* axis are now labeled as well as numbered.
- Lines for different *Y* values extend across the figure, making it easier to interpret *Y* scores at different points on the line.
- A legend is provided.

Different Interpretations The top graph suggests that assault rates have perhaps declined slightly over the period, while the robbery rate has stayed steady. The bottom graph suggests a slightly different and more precise interpretation. Assault rates have declined about 10 percent from the beginning of the period to the end. Robbery rates have declined by roughly a third. When assault rates increased in the late 1970s, robbery rates did not show a corresponding increase. But when assault rates increased in the early 1980s, from 1981 to 1984, robbery rates also increased.

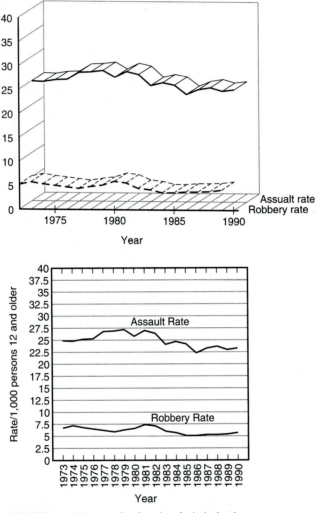

FIGURE 5.5 Line graph of national victimization rates: Assault and robbery. Top graph depicts *bad* form. Bottom graph depicts *good* form. (*Source.* Flanagan, T. J., and Maguire, K., eds. (1992). *Sourcebook of criminal justice statistics 1991.* Washington: USGPO. Table 3.2 (p. 257)).

Line Graphs of Change Researchers and policy makers have strong interests in reporting and interpreting yearly changes in victimization or crime rates. Every January rings in not only the new year, but also a spate of reports from police departments in major cit- ies describing changes in the crime rate for the preceding year. Sometimes agencies also report longer term trends. Agencies can re- port changes in different ways. The way they choose to report these changes can result in widely different interpretations. Two choices you make in constructing line graphs of change are particularly important.

One way to report change is to compare subsequent years, or months, or quarters to a fixed period. In the top panel of Figure 5.6, one line graph of changes in assault uses 1973 as the rate against which the assault rates for subsequent years, 1980 through 1990, are compared (solid line). The other graph uses 1979 as the base year (dotted line). Since the assault rate in 1979 was higher than in 1973, the dotted line reveals a more substantial drop over the decade of the 1980s (about 14%) than does the solid line (about a 6% drop).

A second way to report change is to compare each period to the immediately preceding period. The solid line graph in the bottom panel of Figure 5.6 compares the assault victimization rate for each year to the preceding year. The dotted line graph in the panel is the same in the top panel: assault rates in 1980 through 1990 are compared to 1979. The two line graphs suggest markedly different trends in assault over the decade of the 1980s. The yearly change line suggests no net change; the line based on comparisons with 1979 suggests a sizable decline.

Scatterplots

Purposes Scatterplots display relationships between two continuous variables. They show a **bivariate distribution**—how scores on *two* variables are arrayed or *distributed* vis-à-vis one another. Each data point is positioned in the plot depending on its exact score on each variable. Scores on the predictor or independent variable are arrayed along the horizontal or *X* axis. Cases scoring low on *X* appear on the left; cases scoring high on *X* appear on the right. Scores on the dependent or outcome variable are arrayed vertically along the *Y* axis. Cases scoring low on *Y* appear in the lower part of the plot; cases

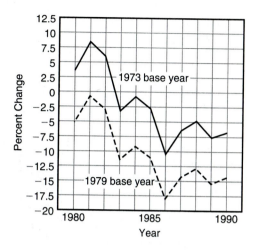

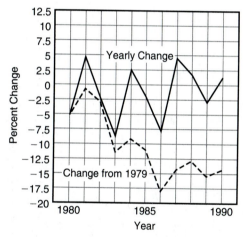

FIGURE 5.6 Different line graphs showing changes in the national assault victimization rate. In the top panel rates are compared to a specific base year, either 1973 or 1979. Although the *shape* of each trend is similar, using 1979 as a base year produces a more significant drop than using 1973 does. The bottom panel contrasts yearly changes (solid line), with changes based on one base year (1979—dotted line). The yearly change graph (solid line) shows no net change over the period, whereas the comparisons with 1979 show a substantial drop over the period (dotted line). (*Source:* Data from Flanagan, T. J., and Maguire, K., eds. (1992). *Sourcebook of criminal justice statistics 1991.* Washington: USGPO. Table 3.2 (p. 257)).

High *Y*	Low *X*, High *Y*	Medium *X*, High *Y*	High *X*, High *Y*
Medium *Y*	Low *X*, Medium *Y*	Medium *X*, Medium *Y*	High *X*, Medium *Y*
Low *Y*	Low *X*, Low *Y*	Medium *X*, Low *Y*	High *X*, Low *Y*
	Low *X*	Medium *X*	High *X*

scoring high on *Y* appear in the upper part of the plot.

If a case scores low on *both X* and *Y*, it appears in the *lower left* portion of the plot. If a case scores high on both *X* and *Y*, it appears in the *upper right* portion of the plot. In short, where a case appears in the plot depends on its position on *both* variables. The figure above shows how data points are positioned within the scatterplot depending on their *X* and *Y* scores.

Scenario   In preparation for a possible expansion of department community-policing activities, a total of 100 officers has received extensive training in community-policing techniques. During their training they completed a battery of inventories, including a sociability scale and a police cynicism scale. They also answered a question about policing, saying whether crime fighting was always the most important part of the job of policing. They also rated, on a 10-point scale, how satisfied they were with their role as a community-policing officer. Lower scores represented dissatisfaction; higher scores represented satisfaction. You can use this information to assess empirically the hypotheses you developed in Chapter 3 about factors associated with high levels of satisfaction as a community-policing officer.

The artificial data shown in these scatterplots were generated by me, and do *not* represent results from an actual study.

Positive Correlation   Your theory predicts a positive association between sociability and satisfaction with community policing. Those

officers scoring higher on the sociability inventory should anticipate more satisfaction with the community-policing assignment. Thus, those who score low on sociability should score low on satisfaction, appearing in the lower left hand portion of the scatterplot. Those scoring high on sociability also should report high satisfaction, appearing in the upper right portion of the plot.

Figure 5.7 displays the results. The top plot displays just the data points. There tend to be more points in the upper right and lower left portions of the plot than there are in the upper left and bottom right portions. Thus, there is a weak tendency for scores on *Y* (satisfaction) to increase as scores on *X* (sociability) increase. There is a positive albeit weak correlation between *X* and *Y*.

The bottom plot displays the same data points as the top plot but also adds the **regression line**. This line shows the linear relationship between the *X* and *Y* variables. The line is made up of points that would be generated if scores on *Y* (satisfaction) could be predicted perfectly from scores on *X* (sociability). These data points along the line are not actual data points but are rather $Y_{predicted}$ data points. The points making up such a line could be generated from an equation of the form:

$$Y_{predicted} = A + (B * X)$$

A represents the score on *Y* (satisfaction) when *X* (sociability) = 0. It is called the **intercept** because it is the predicted score on *Y*, on the line, when *X* = 0. *B* represents the **slope** of the line. It tells you how many units on the *Y* variable you increase, when you increase

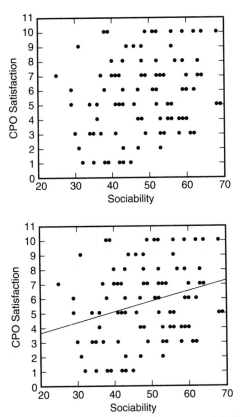

FIGURE 5.7 Positive correlation between sociability and satisfaction with community policing role: 100 community-policing officers.

scores on satisfaction range from 1 to 10, whereas scores on the sociability scale range from 20 to about 70.)

When you look at the top plot, you might feel that it is hard to judge if there is a positive association, or no association, between the two variables. This is because the correlation, albeit positive, is a weak one. The connection between the two variables is not strong. The weakness of the correlation also is reflected in the fact that the data points do not cluster strongly about the regression line; many of them are quite distant from it.

Figure 5.8 displays a stronger positive correlation. It shows the association between age and cynicism about police work among the 100 officers. Again, the top panel shows the data points themselves; the bottom panel displays the data along with the regression line. Research has shown that older officers tend to be more cynical about the effectiveness of police work. [10] The data here support the same conclusion. You also can see that the correlation is stronger than the one between sociability and satisfaction, as the data points cluster more strongly about the regression line. You do not "need" the regression line to decide that there is a positive correlation between the two variables. The correlation between these two variables is described by the equation:

$$\text{Cynicism}_{\text{predicted}} = 41.50 + (.21 * \text{Age})$$

Thus, an officer aged 40 would be predicted to have a cynicism score of 49.9 (41.50 + (.21 * 40)). A 50-year-old officer would have a predicted cynicism score of 52.0. For every single-year increase, cynicism is predicted to increase by .21 units; for every ten-year increase in age, cynicism is predicted to increase 2.1 units.

Negative Correlation Your theory predicts a *negative* correlation between age (*X*) and

one unit on the *X* variable. For these 100 officers the actual equation describing the regression line is:

$$\text{Satisfaction}_{\text{predicted}} =$$
$$2.51 + (.06 * \text{Sociability})$$

The line rises from left to right, supporting your hypothesized positive relationship between sociability and satisfaction. Those who are more sociable report a higher level of satisfaction. For every one unit increase on the sociability scale, scores on satisfaction are predicted to increase .06 of a point. (If this slope strikes you as small, just remember that

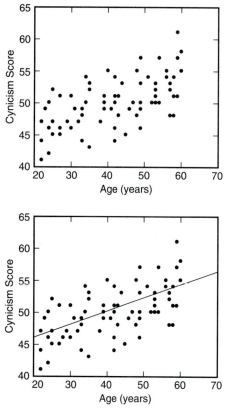

FIGURE 5.8   **Strong, positive correlation between age and cynicism about police work: 100 community-policing officers.** The top panel contains just the data points; the bottom panel also shows the regression line.

satisfaction with a community policing assignment (*Y*). As age increases, satisfaction with community policing should decrease. With a negative correlation, as scores *increase* on the *X* or horizontal axis they *decrease* on the vertical of *Y* axis.

Figure 5.9 displays the relevant data for the 100 officers. The negative relationship is evident in both the top panel, displaying just the data, and the bottom panel, which also

includes the regression line. That line is defined by the equation:

$$\text{Satisfaction}_{\text{predicted}} = 13.31 + (-.19 * \text{Age})$$

For every additional year, satisfaction, on average, decreases by 1/5 of a point. Thus the predicted satisfaction score for an officer of 30 years of age would be 7.61 (13.31 + ((−.19)*(30))), whereas the predicted satisfaction score for a 50-year-old officer would be 3.81 (13.31 + ((−.19)*50))).

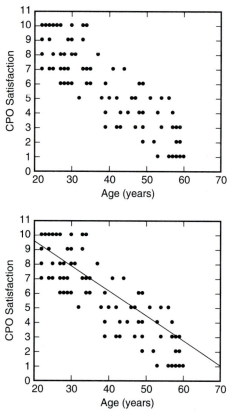

FIGURE 5.9   **Strong, negative correlation between age and satisfaction with police work: 100 community-policing officers.** The top panel contains just the data points; the bottom panel also shows the regression line.

No Correlation If there is no correlation between scores on two variables, data points will be distributed evenly within the scatterplot. As scores on *X* increase, scores on *Y* will neither increase nor decrease.

Figure 5.10 contains an example. Your theory predicts no relationship between age and sociability. Although you predict older officers will be more cynical, you do not predict that they will be more sociable, or less sociable, than younger officers. The data support this expectation. Note that the regression line in the bottom panel is almost perfectly flat. Sociability$_{predicted}$ neither increases nor decreases as age increases.

Good Form and Scatterplots All of the scatterplots presented have followed these basic rules of good form in construction of scatterplots.

- Mention if missing data are not included in the plot, stating how many cases have been excluded.
- Extend the *X* and *Y* axes so that no data points are located on the "frame" surrounding the scatterplot. Depending on the plotting symbol used, it may be difficult to "pick up" a data point if it "touches" an edge of the plot.
- Attend to the relationship between the cluster of data and the total size of the plot. Ideally, the data points should extend 70 percent to 90 percent of both the *X* and *Y* axes. Perception of the degree of relationship can be influenced by the size of the frame around the data points. The correlation looks stronger between two variables if the surrounding frame is larger because the data points contrast more strongly with the background. [2]
- Clearly label *X* and *Y* axes.

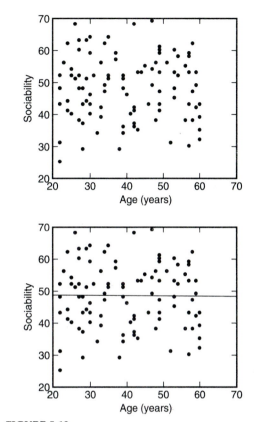

FIGURE 5.10
No correlation between age and sociability. The top panel contains just the data points; the bottom panel also shows the regression line.

SUMMARY

Graphs can inform or mislead. They can confuse or embody effective communication. Table 5.2 summarizes the "do's and don'ts" discussed above.

TABLES

We turn now to the *tabular* as compared to the graphical presentation of data. You will examine data tables containing one, two, and

T A B L E 5.2
"Do's and Don'ts" for Graph Construction

Type of Graph	Do	Don't
Pie Chart	Label percentage or count associated with each portion. Include missing data.	Shade pieces differently. Present in 3 dimensions. Collapse data.
Bar Graph	Include missing data. Start Y axis at 0. Clearly label units on the Y axis. Provide horizontal grid.	Present in 3 dimensions.
Line graph	Start Y axis at 0. Clearly label units on the X and Y axes. Provide horizontal grid. Provide legend for each series.	Present in 3 dimensions.
Scatterplot	Maintain proper relationship between data and frame. Clearly label axes. Mention excluded data.	Have data points touching the frame.

three variables. When you have more than one variable, these tables are also called **cross-tabulations** or **contingency tables**.

When do you use tabular rather than graphical presentation of your data? Tabular presentation is warranted if you are examining two or three variables, and all the variables are categorical rather than continuous. You also can use tabular presentation if you have a continuous variable but wish to recode it into a smaller number of categories.

One Variable

Single variables are presented in **frequency distributions**. Recall that Figure 5.4 presented a histogram displaying the length of residence for 1,000 households residing in the neighborhood where your initial community policing initiative took place. Table 5.3 presents the same information in a frequency distribution.

The first two columns show the categories into which the data have been grouped. These categories are of equal width. They are also *mutually exclusive*. A data point can appear in only one category. Finally, they are *exhaustive*. All scores on the variable have been included in at least one category. No scores are too high or too low to fit into a category.

As in the histogram, each category represents a 5-year time span. These are the *apparent limits*. More precise boundaries for the data categories are provided in columns 3 and 4. These represent the *real limits*. To decide how to categorize specific cases, you refer to the real limits, not the apparent limits. Column 5 shows the number of cases that score within each interval. For example, 90 households reported a length of residence between 9.5 years and 14.5 years. These numbers are converted into percentages of the total in Column 6. These 90 households represented 9 percent of the total sample.

TABLE 5.3
Frequency Distribution:
Length of Residence in Neighborhood for 1,000 Households

1		2	3		4	5	6	7
Apparent Limits (in years)			Real Limits (in years)			N of Cases Within Interval	Percentage of Cases Within Interval	Cumulative Percentage of Cases Within Interval
From		To	From		To			
0		5	−.5		4.5	696	69.6	69.6
5		10	4.5		9.5	133	13.3	82.9
10		15	9.5		14.5	90	9	91.9
15		20	14.5		19.5	51	5.1	97
20		25	19.5		24.5	22	2.2	99.2
25		30	24.5		29.5	7	.1	99.9
30		35	29.5		34.5	1	.1	100
			TOTAL			1,000	100	

Column 7 reports the *cumulative percentage*—the percentage of cases scoring at that value of the variable or lower. 91.9 percent of the sample reported a length of residence of 9.5–14.5 years or less.

Frequency distributions present the same information as histograms, but for a different purpose. The histogram provides you with a rough estimate of where your data appear. By contrast, the frequency distribution shows exactly how many cases appear at each segment of the variable.

Two Variables

The purpose of two-way or bivariate contingency tables is the same as the purpose of scatterplots: to see how scores on one variable relate to scores on another variable. We first examine a two-variable contingency table where both variables are categorical. In a second example we inspect two continuous variables that each have been recoded into a small number of categories.

Categorical Variables

Scenario The 100 police officers trained in community policing were asked to answer a question about their views on police as "crime fighters." The question was: "A police officer's most important job at all times is to be a crime fighter." You are interested in seeing if men and women officers answer this question similarly.

Frequencies Table 5.4 displays the association between the two variables. In a cross-tabulation you typically use the categories of the independent variable to create the columns, and the categories of the dependent variable to create the rows. Here you treat sex of the officer as the independent variable, and agreement or disagreement with the "crime fighter" question as the dependent variable.

Appearing *outside* the table, in the margins, are the **marginal frequencies**. These are the frequency distributions for each variable.

TABLE 5.4
Sex by Crime-Fighting Views:
Frequencies

		Sex		
		F	M	
Crime Fighting Most Important?	N	6	31	37
	Y	16	47	63
		22	78	100

TABLE 5.5
Sex by Crime-Fighting Views:
Column Percentages

		Sex		
		F	M
Crime Fighting Most Important?	N	27%	40%
	Y	73%	60%
		100%	100%

You can see that 22 of the 100 officers trained in community policing were women. Sixty-three of the 100 officers felt that crime fighting was the police officer's most important job at all times.

Appearing *inside* the table are the **cell frequencies**, telling you exactly how many people appear in each of the four possible cells. You see, for example, that 16 of the 22 women officers agreed that crime fighting was the police officer's most important job. Forty-seven of the 78 men felt similarly.

You want to know if women officers, as compared to men, are more likely to feel that crime fighting is an officer's most important job. It is hard to compare directly the responses of men and women in this table because there are unequal numbers of each. Is 16/22 a greater fraction than 47/78?

You can control for the different number of cases in each category of the independent variable by computing **column percentages**. If the cases in each column add to 100%, what percentage of those cases appear in each cell? In other words, you percentage *down*. Table 5.5 displays the column percentages.

Here is a general formula for interpreting two-way tables when column percentages have been computed:

Whereas ____ percent of the [READ FIRST CATEGORY OF THE INDEPEN-

DENT VARIABLE] [READ MOST IMPORTANT CATEGORY OF THE DEPENDENT VARIABLE], ____ percent of the [READ NEXT CATEGORY OF THE INDEPENDENT VARIABLE] [READ *SAME* MOST IMPORTANT CATEGORY OF THE DEPENDENT VARIABLE].

This suggests the following interpretation for Table 5.6:

Whereas 73 percent of the female officers felt that crime fighting was an officer's most important job, 60 percent of the male officers felt that crime fighting was an officer's most important job.

In short, in this sample of 100 cases, women were somewhat more likely than men to endorse crime fighting as an officer's primary responsibility. To learn if this relationship was significant beyond this sample, you would conduct statistical analyses.

Continuous Variables You might examine the relationship between two continuous variables using a cross-tabulation. To do this you would first need to **recode** the scores on the continuous variables into a smaller number of categories. Say you want to examine the relationship between age and satisfaction with community policing using a cross-tab table. You want to examine satisfaction scores by decade of age. You could recode

TABLE 5.6
Age by Satisfaction with Community Policing:
Frequencies and Column Percentages

		Age (decades) 20s	30s	40s	50s	TOTAL
Satisfaction	Low	0 **0%**	6 **24%**	19 **79%**	25 **100%**	50
	High	26 **100%**	19 **76%**	5 **21%**	0 **0%**	50
		26 **100%**	25 **100%**	24 **100%**	25 **100%**	100

Note. Column percentages in bold.

actual age into the relevant decade (20s, 30s, and so on). You could recode scores on satisfaction into halves (lower half, upper half), thirds (lower third, middle third, upper third), fourths, or fifths.

Table 5.6 shows the relationship between age and satisfaction with being a community police officer. Satisfaction scores have been recoded into halves: those scoring 1–5 have been recoded into a "Low" group; those scoring 6–10 have been recoded into a "High" group. Age has been recoded into decades. The table shows marginal frequencies, cell frequencies, and column percentages in bold. The table allows you to make statements such as the following:

> Whereas 100 percent of those officers in their 20s express a high level of satisfaction with the community-policing role, 76 percent of those in their 30s express similar satisfaction, and 21 percent of those in their 40s express similar satisfaction. No officers in their 50s express a high level of satisfaction with the role.

Therefore, as age increases, satisfaction with the community-policing role decreases.

Independent and Dependent Variables Not Clear There may be situations where you

are *un*able to identify clearly your independent and dependent variables. In these situations your decision about which variable to use for the columns, and which variable to use for the rows, is somewhat arbitrary. In these situations **row percentages** or **total percentages** may be useful in a table. With row percentages all the cases in a single row of a table sum to 100 percent. If you are using row percentages you compare up and down. With total percentages all the cases in all the cells in the table add to 100 percent.

You may be interested in the relationship between age and sex of the 100 officers receiving community policing training. The table can be organized in different ways. For example, Table 5.7 shows the frequencies and, in bold, the row percentages. You can see that, whereas 63 percent (31% + 32%) of the men are in their 40s and 50s, none of the women officers fall into this age group.

Rules of Tabular Construction The bulk of the examples discussed above assume that you can identify clearly your independent variable and your dependent variable. In these cases:

• Categories of your independent variable become your columns.

TABLE 5.7
Age by Sex of 100 Community Police Officers:
Frequencies and Row Percentages

			Age (decades)				
			20s	30s	40s	50s	TOTAL
Sex	F	N	13	9	0	0	22
		Row %	**59%**	**41%**	**0%**	**0%**	**100%**
	M	N	13	16	24	25	78
		Row %	**17%**	**20%**	**31%**	**32%**	**100%**
			26	25	24	25	100

Note. Row percentages in bold.

- Categories of your dependent variable become your rows.
- You percentage down, calculating the percentage of cases in a column that are in each cell, such that the percentages in each column sum to 100 percent. This step standardizes for the different number of cases in each column. You are percentaging *within* each category of the independent variable.
- You compare percentages across, focusing on the *same* row of interest.

Three Variables

The tables you have examined so far have focused on two variables. Usually one variable functions as an independent variable (*X*), and the other as a dependent variable (*Y*). For example, you examined the relationship between age (*X*) and satisfaction (*Y*) with the community-policing role.

Cross-tab tables also can be used to look at three variables simultaneously: these show **trivariate** relationships. Why might you want to look at three variables simultaneously?

Reasons for Examining Three Variables Simultaneously   When you examine trivariate

relationships, you are looking at how a relationship between two variables may be influenced by a third variable. The nature of this influence can vary. This amounts to, in effect, further elaborating, specifying, delimiting, or testing the hypothesis of central interest. In general terms you think of these reasons for including a third variable as ways of *elaborating* the hypothesis in question. Not surprisingly the use of three-way tables has been called the *elaboration model*. [11, 12] The theorist is elaborating the conditions and processes surrounding the central relationship of interest. The third variable is also sometimes called a **test variable**—it allows the researcher to test under which conditions the relationship of central interest holds or doesn't hold.

The Third Variable Is an Intervening Variable
First, you might hypothesize that a third variable, *Z*, *intervenes* between *X* and *Y*. In other words *X* leads to *Y* because *X* leads to *Z*, which in turns leads to *Y*. Graphically:

$$X \longrightarrow Z \longrightarrow Y$$

You may recall that, in Chapter 3, you hypothesized that age (*X*) led to decreased satisfaction with community policing (*Y*) *because* increasing age led to increasing cynicism about police work (Z). Graphically you hypothesized that:

$$C_{Age} \xrightarrow{(+)} C_{Police\ Cynicism} \xrightarrow{(-)}$$
$$C_{Satisfaction\ with\ CPO\ Role}$$

Here, Z would be called an **intervening or mediating variable**. The effects of X on Y are carried by or mediated by Z.

The Third Variable Is a Moderating Variable
Alternatively you might hypothesize that a third variable *conditions* or *moderates* the effects of X on Y. For example, the effects of X on Y may only be present when a third variable, Z, is also present. Or the effects of X on Y may be increased, or decreased, when Z is present or when scores on Z are high. In these situations Z would be called a **moderator variable**.

Graphically, it is the *combination* of X and Z that leads to Y:

$$(X \times Z) \longrightarrow Y$$

You have seen in the above tables that more age leads to less satisfaction with the CPO role. You also have examined the connections between "police as crime fighter" attitudes and sex. You might hypothesize that the relationship between age (X) and satisfaction (Y) is moderated or influenced by the officer's crime-fighting views (Z). For example, a young officer may be *less* satisfied with the CPO role if he or she agrees that crime fighting is the most important job of police officers. Younger officers express more satisfaction with the CPO role if they do not view crime fighting as a police officer's most important job.

The Relationship Between X and Y Is Spurious
Third, you might hypothesize that a third variable *causes* both X and Y; thus X and Y

just seem related because they both stem from a third cause. If this is the case, the relationship we observe between X and Y is **spurious**, or false, because X does not cause Y; instead, Z causes *both* X and Y. Graphically, spuriousness can be shown as follows:

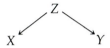

For example, you might ignore age (Z), and concentrate on the relationship between cynicism about police work (X) and satisfaction with the CPO role (Y). But, it may not be the increasing cynicism that is causing the decreasing satisfaction. Both variables may be jointly caused by increasing age. Graphically:

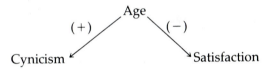

Although this example uses the same three variables as discussed above under intervening variables, the two examples are different theoretically. Here, when age is ignored, cynicism rather than age is treated as the independent variable.

An Example: Crime-fighting Views Moderate the Age–Satisfaction Connection You have seen that older officers express less satisfaction with being a CPO (Table 5.6). You want to investigate the possibility that crime-fighting views *condition* the relationship between age and CPO satisfaction. More specifically, you expect the relationship between age and satisfaction will be weaker among those officers who think crime fighting is an officer's most important job. Age is the independent variable (X), satisfaction is the dependent variable (Y), and crime-fighting view is the moderating variable (Z).

To examine this possibility, you construct a two-way cross-tab table for age and satisfaction *at each level of the moderating (Z) variable.* These tables constructed for each level of the moderating variable are called **subtables**. Each subtable presents just a portion of all the cases. You construct the first subtable focusing on those who do *not* think crime fighting is the most important job (Table 5.8). You construct a separate subtable focusing on those who *do* think crime fighting is the officer's most important job (Table 5.9). Each subtable includes cell frequencies, marginal frequencies, and column percentages.

To interpret the role of the moderating variable, focus on the particular cell in the two subtables where you see the largest difference in column percentages between the two subtables. The largest difference between the two tables appears for those officers in their 30s.

Whereas 100 percent of the officers who were in their 30s and *not* focused on crime fighting expressed high satisfaction with the CPO role, among the officers in their 30s who placed crime fighting foremost, only 70 percent expressed high satisfaction with the role. In other words, among the officers in their 30s, a focus

on crime fighting dampened somewhat their enthusiasm for the CPO role.

At the same time, regardless of the level of the moderating variable, i.e., in both subtables, there was still a significant negative relationship between age and satisfaction.

Two-Way Tables, Three-Way Tables, and Theory

Holmes's Approach Two-way tables can play key roles in discovering hypotheses; three-way tables can play key roles in refining hypotheses. You start with a **core concept**: the construct of central theoretical interest to you. In the examples examined here you have focused on satisfaction with the community policing role. You have examined how scores on satisfaction link to several other factors: age, sociability, cynicism about police work, and crime-fighting views. From a grounded theory perspective *it is perfectly acceptable to explore as many cross-tab tables as you want without any fixed expectations of what may emerge.* You are looking for hypotheses, not testing them. "The analyst may take his core concepts and run them with literally *every* other questionnaire item in the survey

TABLE 5.8
Age by Satisfaction with Community Policing
Subtable for Officers NOT FOCUSED on Crime Fighting

		Age (decades)				
		20s	30s	40s	50s	TOTAL
Satisfaction	Low	0 **0%**	0 **0%**	9 **82%**	13 **100%**	22
	High	8 **100%**	5 **100%**	2 **18%**	0 **0%**	15
		8 **100%**	5 **100%**	11 **100%**	13 **100%**	37

Note. Column percentages in bold.

T A B L E 5.9
Age by Satisfaction with Community Policing
Subtable for Officers FOCUSED on Crime Fighting

		20s	30s	40s	50s	TOTAL
		Age (decades)				
Satisfaction	Low	0 **0%**	6 **30%**	10 **77%**	12 **100%**	28
	High	18 **100%**	14 **70%**	3 **23%**	0 **0%**	35
		18 **100%**	20 **100%**	13 **100%**	12 **100%**	63

Note. Column percentages in bold.

that seems remotely relevant to his area of interest." [13] You are making comparisons. The patterns you observe are helping you to refine and elaborate the general idea with which you began.

Three-way tables also play important roles in this process; they help you be more specific about the associations you observe. You can explore roles of moderating or intervening variables, or examine the possibility of spurious correlations. What you find tells you if the central association in your theory does or does not depend on other, additional variables.

Einstein's Approach Two-way tables, of course, can be used to verify hypotheses generated before the data were gathered. Many of the two-way tables you examined here allowed you to examine hypotheses formulated in Chapter 3. With Einstein's approach you use two-way tables in a much more focused fashion than with Holmes's approach.

You would know beforehand specifically which variables you wished to cross-classify with which other variables, which were the independent and dependent variables, and how you expected each pair of variables to be linked. You also would apply a statistical test to each table, to decide if the relationship observed was due to "chance" or not. Each table examined would either support or fail to support the preformulated hypothesis.

The three-way tables provide you with more precise information concerning your hypotheses. For example, you observed, in accord with your hypothesis, that increasing age led to decreasing satisfaction with the CPO role. Yet you went on to see that this relationship between age and satisfaction was only slightly influenced by crime-fighting views. This finding that emerged from the three-way tables helped you understand the relevance of other factors to your main hypothesis.

SUMMARY OF MAIN POINTS

- Pie charts are best used for presenting proportions of cases within various categories of a variable when the number of categories is small.

- Bar charts can represent proportions, counts, or other statistics, for one or two variables.
- Histograms show the relative density of data at different points along one variable.
- Line charts are best used to show how scores on one or more variables fluctuate over time. Scores for one or more groups may be depicted.
- Scatterplots depict the relationship between two continuous variables. They show bivariate distributions.
- Frequency distributions show the precise distribution of scores on one variable.
- Cross-tab tables or contingency tables show associations between two or more variables where the variables are categorical.
- Cross-tab tables also can be used with continuous variables, but the scores must be coded or recoded into a small number of intervals.
- When you construct a cross-tab, you should include the name of each variable, its response categories, cell frequencies, column percentages, and the marginal frequencies.
- In two-way tables where you have a clear idea about the independent variable and the dependent variable, the categories of the independent variable should make up the columns, and the categories of the dependent variable should make up the rows.
- Two-way and three-way tables can be used either to generate hypotheses or to rigorously test them.
- Three-way tables show how a relationship between two variables (X and Y) is influenced, or not influenced, by a third variable (Z).
- Three-way tables *control* for a third variable by considering the X–Y relationship at each level of this third variable (Z).

SUGGESTED READINGS

D. Huff's *How to lie with statistics* (New York: Norton, 1954) will delight you. He explains how graphs can mislead without lying. Although some of his examples are dated, the volume is slim and highly recommended.

E. R. Tufte's *Envisioning information* (Cheshire, CT: Graphics Press, 1990) provides many contemporary and historical examples of graphics that convey significant amounts of information. You will find this a fascinating volume.

T. Hirschi and H. C. Selvin's *Principles of survey analysis* (New York: Free Press, 1973) and M. Rosenberg's *The Logic of survey analysis* (New York: Basic, 1968) both provide detailed explanations about constructing contingency tables from survey data. They explain the connections between two-way tables, three-way tables, and theory. Recommended only for the motivated, advanced undergraduate.

GLOSSARY OF KEY WORDS

apparent limits
bivariate distribution
bivariate relationship
cell frequencies
column percentages
contingency tables
core concept
cross-tabulations
cumulative percentage
frequency distribution
intercept
intervening variable
marginal frequencies
mediating variable
moderator variable
real limits
recode
regression line
row percentages
slope
spurious relationship

subtables
test variable
total percentages
trivariate relationship

REFERENCES

1. Chambers, J. M., Cleveland, W. S., Kleiner, B., and Tukey, P. A. (1983) *Graphical methods for data analysis*, Wadsworth, Duxbury; Belmont, Boston.

2. Cleveland, W. S., Diaconis, P., and McGill, R. (1982) Variables on scatterplots look more highly correlated when the scales are increased. *Science 216*, 1138–1141.

3. Cleveland, W. S., and McGill, R. (1984) The many faces of a scatterplot. *Journal of the American Statistical Association 79*, 807–822.

4. Huff, D. (1954) *How to lie with statistics*, W. W. Norton Co., New York.

5. Wilkinson, L. (1990) *SYGRAPH*, SYSTAT, Inc., Evanston, IL, p. 66.

6. Simkin, D., and Hastie, R. (1987) An information processing analysis of graph perception. *Journal of the American Statistical Association 82*, 545–565.

7. Bennack, F. A., Jr. (1989) *The American public's hopes and fears for the decade of the 1990s*, Hearst Corporation, New York.

8. Wilkinson, L. (1990) *SYGRAPH*, SYSTAT, Inc., Evanston, IL, p. 76.

9. Wilkinson, L. (1990) *SYGRAPH*, SYSTAT, Inc., Evanston, IL, p. 175.

10. Niederhoffer, A. (1967) *Behind the shield: The police in urban society*, Anchor Books, New York.

11. Hyman, H. H. (1955) *Survey design and analysis*, Free Press, Glencoe, IL.

12. Glaser, B. G., and Strauss, A. L. (1967) *The Discovery of grounded theory: Strategies for qualitative research*, Aldine, Chicago, p. 207.

13. Glaser, B. G., and Strauss, A. L. (1967) *The Discovery of grounded theory: Strategies for qualitative research*, Aldine, Chicago, p. 194.

CHAPTER 6

MEASUREMENT AND INQUIRY

Measurement enables the tool of mathematics to be applied to science.[1]

OBJECTIVES

An extremely crucial part of scientific inquiry is *measuring*. This process allows researchers to cross over from the safe territory of speculation to the harsh land of empirical verification. In this chapter you will master some fundamentals of how social scientists measure, what they measure, and the logic behind their actions.

Imagine you wake up one morning and find that none of the clocks in your house tells the usual time. Their faces simply have the message "It is now daytime." You look at the thermometer outside your window to check on the weather. All the numbers are gone. It has a message: "The temperature is not like it was yesterday." Suspecting that something has gone seriously awry somewhere, and regretting the *Twilight Zone* marathon you watched on cable the night before, you do not listen to the morning news or read the morning paper. You dress hurriedly, get in your car, and drive to work. The gas gauge in your car has no needle, no "E" or "F," but it does display the message "Yes, you do have some gas in the tank. Not sure how much." As you drive along to work, your speedometer simply displays the word "Moving" when you are moving, and "Stopped" when you are stopped. There are no numbers or needle. When you get to work and put

money in a parking meter, it tells you "Not expired." But it does not tell you how much time you have.

PURPOSE AND ORGANIZATION OF THE PRESENT CHAPTER

The scenario above depicts what life would be like if measurement did not exist.

> The purpose of the measurement process is to assign observed scores on variables for particular objects, and to understand the mathematical properties of those observed scores. The observed scores assigned describe the relative amounts of a variable or attribute possessed by specific objects. [2]

Without measurement we would be unable to learn how much of something this or that object had; we would not know how much gas there was in the tank, or how much time we had in the parking meter.

In everyday life we take the results of measurement for granted: time, speed, temperature, cost, and so on. If we did not have reports available to us on these matters, our days would be full of much more uncertainty than they already are!

The position of criminal justice researchers, and other social scientists, is similar to that in the above scenario. They are stranded in a land where the time, temperature, and speed of the cars are not known.

They must create, often from scratch, various measurements of the indicators of concepts of interest to them. The process of deciding what and how to measure represents an integral part of the scientific enterprise.

Measurement is *not* simply concerned with the "nuts and bolts" or "engineering" side of criminal justice research. The process of measurement intertwines with the processes of theoretical elaboration, hypothesis testing, and grounded theorizing. [3] Without measurement processes we cannot connect the constructs in a theory to observable data.

In Chapter 3 you learned about the importance of *operationalizing* concepts and choosing *empirical indicators* for constructs. In the last row of Figure 3.1 you obtained measurements, in the form of observed scores, on the variables of interest to you for specific objects. This chapter explains in more detail the process and consequences of moving from the third to the fourth row of Figure 3.1.

In this chapter you begin by reflecting on the transition from variables that exist in our head to variables that exist in the world of observed data. You then consider what we measure when we measure. You may be surprised to discover that criminal justice researchers do not measure what you might have expected. Next you will explore the properties and consequences of different levels of measurement. You will find that, from a mathematical point of view, not all variables are created equal. Then you will explore the properties of scales and indexes, and examine some indexes and scales widely used in criminal justice.

Return to the Electronic Monitoring Scenario

In many examples here I will refer to the running scenario, introduced in Chapter 1, concerning offenders sentenced to home confinement with electronic monitoring

(HCEM). You may recall that, after two embarrassing incidents, your boss ordered you to investigate the cases sentenced to home confinement with electronic monitoring.

You decide that one way to approach the project is to gather, from court records, information about the offenders sentenced to HCEM. You also collect information from the state police. The latter records report if the offender was arrested for a subsequent offense.

TEST THEORY

Your understanding of the measurement process will benefit from a short introduction to *classical test theory*. It is an area of measurement psychology that explains the different components making up the observed score of one individual on one variable.

Take another look at Figure 3.1 on page 41. Note that, going from the third row of the figure to the fourth row, you pass from variables as operationalized to variables as measured. With measured variables you obtain **observed scores** for particular cases studied. You go from thinking about specific variables to obtaining actual data for them.

Your variables as operationalized are different in important ways from your variables as measured. The process of measuring variables introduces **measurement error**. Measurement error arises from many sources, including the measuring instruments used, the measuring situation, the cases studied, and other factors. It results in nonsystematic discrepancies between how a case should have scored on a variable if the variable had been perfectly measured, and how it actually did score. Measurement error is unavoidable in social scientific research.

Think back to the time you took your SAT or ACT exams for college. Recall the first time you took the test. Think of all the factors leading up to the test that may have made you do less well than you thought you could: not enough sleep the night before, too much talking about it with classmates making you "psyched out" about the whole endeavor, or anxious parents deepening your own insecurities. Think also of the factors during the actual testing situation that may have made you do more poorly than you thought you should have done: someone sitting next to you nervously tapping a pencil, or a confused proctor who failed to give you the correct amount of time on a section of the test. All these factors added up to produce "measurement error"—a score that did not perfectly agree with your actual level of knowledge.

In short, in the third row of Figure 3.1 you are dealing with hypothesized **true scores** on variables. These true scores are hypothetical, unobserved constructs that exist only in your head, or in the head of others envisioning the same operationalized variables. As you proceed from the third row to the fourth row, the process of measuring these variables—obtaining actual scores on actual variables for studied cases using measuring instruments—introduces measurement error and results in observed scores.

This formulation linking true scores and observed scores has been called **classical test theory** [4]. It can be stated in the following equation:

Observed Score = True Score
+ Measurement Error

Turn your attention back to the offenders sentenced to HCEM. Imagine that, in your jurisdiction, all arrestees receive mandatory drug testing through urinalysis. The test used in this scenario detects drug use within the last 48 hours. One observed score produced by the urinalysis tells whether the arrestee tests positive for recent cocaine or crack-cocaine use. A range of factors could produce a discrepancy between the urinalysis results and the arrestee's actual behavior.

Samples may have been mislabeled. Instruments at the testing lab may have needed recalibration. Chemicals used in the process may have been past the expiration date. These and other factors may have resulted in disparities between what happened—cocaine or crack was or was not used by the arrestee in the 48 hours before the testing—and the results of the urinalysis test. The discrepancy may occur for one arrestee or for several.

The amount of measurement error may vary across cases studied. One worker in a lab may be much more careful with testing procedures for Cases 1–10 than is a second worker, who is testing samples for Cases 11–20. In addition, the amount of measurement error also can vary across different observed variables.

Imagine that all arrestees in your jurisdiction not only undergo urinalysis, but also are interviewed about their drug usage habits. You might imagine that many arrestees who used cocaine or crack-cocaine in the 48 hours before arrest would not report it. The discrepancy between observed scores and true scores would be greater for these observed scores based on self-report than it would for the observed scores based on urinalysis. [5] In sum, measurement error varies across cases studied, variables examined, and time.

WHAT DO WE MEASURE WHEN WE MEASURE?

An Argument

Several years ago, some work colleagues and I were dining at a restaurant. The conversation became merry as the beer and wine bottles were emptied. At one end of the table the conversation took up the following topic. One colleague maintained that "Anything worthwhile can be measured scientifically, i.e., quantified." Another colleague countered that this was not so, and proceeded to propose items defying quantification. Concepts such as "love" and "hate" and "justice" were bandied about. Lively discussion followed about whether indicators of such concepts could be assigned numbers, and the meaning of numbers that would be assigned. Others around the table took sides with one colleague or the other. Take a minute or so and consider the matter. Which side do you think was correct?

Defining Terms

To be as clear as possible about what our empirical indicators do and do not measure, we need to define our terms. [3]

1. **Objects** or **cases** refer to things that carry or possess properties. These include events, individuals, and items in the world about us: a crime, an arrest, a police officer, a judge, several judges, trials, bail hearings, a parole board, or a prison facility are all examples of objects. In our running scenario, the offenders sentenced to HCEM are objects. The dataset, introduced in Chapter 5, contains 100 officers trained in community policing; we call these objects.

2. **Attributes** or **variables** refer to potentially measurable properties of objects or cases. You can grade amounts of these properties; varying amounts can be arranged relative to one another. These are *features (Figure 3.1) that can be measured.*

   The offenders sentenced to HCEM in our running scenario have many attributes that might be of interest to you as you investigate why some offenders succeed on HCEM while others recidivate. The particular variables or indicators you choose will derive from or refer to concepts embodied in the theory you are testing or developing. Possible variables include: number of prior arrests, number of prior convictions, age, drug problems, age at first arrest, years of education completed, extent of prior criminal career, rehabilitation potential, and so on.

3. **Magnitudes** refer to *possible scores* reflecting "particular amounts of an attribute."[1] Three previous arrests, or an age of 24 years, or 8.5 years of school completed would all be examples of specific magnitudes. These are specific points or locations on different attributes. Magnitudes represent the *range of possible scores* on a variable, as well as *specific* scores within that range. These scores, however, have not yet been assigned to particular objects. In the police officer dataset used in Chapter 5, magnitudes for the variable "Satisfaction with the CPO Role" range from 1 to 10.

4. When a possible score on a variable (a magnitude) does apply to a specific object, we have a **quantity** of an attribute. It is a *particular* observed score on a *specific* variable for a *particular* case. In the dataset for the 100 officers trained in community policing, Case 1 reports a satisfaction score of "1"—this is a quantity. Quantities are the outputs produced by the empirical indicators used by the criminal justice researcher. These quantities allow the researcher to sort the objects investigated, whether that be people or institutions, on the underlying dimension. The dataset for 100 officers is sorted based on their satisfaction scores, with the lowest-scoring officers appearing first.

Observed scores on particular variables, such as satisfaction with the CPO role, for specific cases, are the end point of the measurement process and provide the basic "inputs" for many types of research analyses.

---

[1] Do not confuse the term *magnitude*, defined here, with a procedure called *magnitude scaling*, defined later in the chapter.

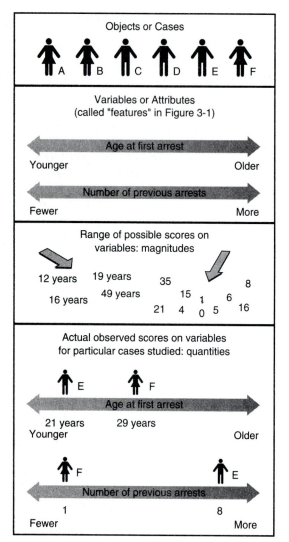

FIGURE 6.1 Terms used in measurement process.

Figure 6.1 provides a graphical explanation for the definitions of these different components of the measurement process.

Thinking of the Measurement Process in These Terms

Thus, the measurement tasks confronting the researcher involve:

- Selecting cases (objects) to be studied.
- Identifying measurable features or variables (attributes) of those objects. Each variable represents an underlying continuum or dimension along which the objects can be sorted or scored.
- Developing measuring instruments to assess possible scores (magnitudes of attributes) on these variables.
- Collecting information on actual observed scores of actual objects on the variables selected. These are the actual quantities of the attributes assigned to particular objects.
- Understanding the mathematical properties of these observed scores.

Let me try to sum up an answer to the question "What do we measure when we measure?" *The process of measuring involves generating numbers (quantities) that describe the relative amounts of an observed attribute (an observed variable) possessed by specific objects.* [2]

Let's go back to our restaurant party question. Can we scientifically measure any thing?

In simple terms: no. We can never measure criminals or crimes or institutions or courts or parole boards or parole officers or judges; or love or justice or equity or due process. Measurement refers to measuring *attributes* or features of objects. Measurement results in assigning observed scores on particular variables to particular cases. The cases *themselves* are not measured. We focus on specific features of these objects, and operationalize indicators of concepts as variables. The operational variables we define will pay attention to some features of these objects, and ignore others.

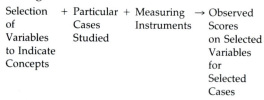

It might help you to think of a person connected to a special device that only allows for listening to certain features of a piece of music. If listening to a classical symphony, for instance, the device allows the listener to attend to the tempo of the tympani, or the pitch of the notes played by the first violins, or the rhythm of the notes played by the flutes. But when using this device, the listener cannot hear the whole symphony at once. Only certain features can be heard at one time.

The measurement process proceeds like this device. It transmits to the researcher just observed scores on certain variables for the cases being studied. As a result, the researcher does not attend to all possible variables of the cases he is examining, and is not examining the cases themselves.

CLASSIFICATION AND LEVELS OF MEASUREMENT

Levels of Measurement

Returning to our scenario, you now have observed scores on a range of variables for these offenders sentenced to HCEM under your jurisdiction's current program. These different scores not only represent different indicators of concepts. They also possess different mathematical properties. The different mathematical properties limit what you can and cannot do with observed scores. The *difference* between the four levels of measurement you will examine is as follows: *they vary in the amount of information they provide about the quantities of the attribute they reflect.* [6] These distinctions may arise from one of two sources: the nature of the attribute itself, or the nature of the measuring instrument.

We can never know empirically the "true" quantity of an attribute possessed by an object, or the "true" quantities of an attribute possessed by a series of objects. We can theorize about these "true scores." As shown in Figure 3.1, these "true scores" exist in your head after you have decided how you will operationalize an indicator of a concept. When you actually *measure*, you cross over to the data world and you obtain *observed scores*

on variables for those particular cases.

Consider, for example, that you are interested in how *serious* or *severe* the crimes are for which your offenders sentenced to HCEM were convicted. You hypothesize that each crime possesses a certain "true" quantity of the attribute of *seriousness* or *severity*. You could obtain *measured* quantities of seriousness in several different ways. You could ask a friend to order the crimes, ranging from most serious to least serious. You could ask 10 police officers to do the same and take the middlemost ranking for each crime as the measured quantity for each crime. Or you could have several thousand people across the nation rate them on a severity scale, as researchers did in a project to be described below. These are all different ways of coming up with *measured* quantities that do, you hope, correspond with the *true* quantities of seriousness. All measures, whatever their "level," are trying to achieve a correspondence between observed scores and "true" scores. What varies across the levels of measurement is the degree and type of correspondence.

Let's discuss those four different levels of measurement.[2]

Nominal Level of Measurement Nominal measures are really *classifications* of objects into one category or another.[3] The other

---

[2] There are more than the levels of measurement discussed here. For example, there are also partial orderings, and orderings with natural origins. I do not discuss those and other levels of measurement here, simply because they are not widely noted.

[3] There are strong differences of opinion among measurement experts on whether nominal measures are really measurements at all. S. S. Stevens says they are. Warren Torgerson says they are not. Stevens says they are because you can assign scores to variables measured at the nominal level. Torgerson says they are not because the scores you assign are arbitrary. Personally, I agree with Torgerson on this matter. In deference to the traditional pedagogical approach in this matter, however, I include nominal scales as one of the four levels of measurement.

three levels of measurement, which you will encounter shortly, include variables signifying *how much* of an attribute the object possesses. Nominal measures simply report to which category an object belongs.

In categorizing or classifying objects, nominal measures are both exhaustive and mutually exclusive. They are exhaustive because all objects are sorted into one category or another. They are exclusive because an object cannot simultaneously have two categories of the attribute.

The information you have collected on offenders sentenced to HCEM contains several variables measured at the nominal level. For example, you might have information from a presentence investigation (PSI) reporting if the offender has a drug problem. From this information you can construct a variable "Has a drug problem." If the PSI does not mention a drug problem, the case scores 0 on this variable. If the PSI does mention a drug problem, the case scores 1 on the variable. The cases scoring 1 on this variable are not *higher* on the attribute than the cases scoring 0. They are simply in a different category; they have the attribute, and those scoring 0 do not.

Your attribute "Has a drug problem" has been coded as a **dummy variable**. Nominal measures coded 0 or 1 are dummy variables. Criminal justice and sociological researchers use them often. In the example here you measure the attribute in question with one dummy variable. Sometimes, however, you need more than one dummy variable to measure an attribute. Ethnicity is a case in point.

The files of offenders on HCEM may include members of three racial groups: Hispanics, African Americans, and Whites. If you are particularly interested in Hispanics as compared to others, and African Americans as compared to others, you can construct two dummy variables for each case. Hispanics are coded 1 on the "Hispanic" dummy variable and 0 on the "African American" dummy variable. African Americans are coded 0 on the "Hispanic" dummy variable and 1 on the "African American" dummy variable. Whites are coded 0 on both variables. See Table 6.1.

Nominal measures and classifications, despite being simpler than the other levels of measurement, can play important roles in theory construction. Classifying cases into different "types"—groups that are qualitatively different from each other—and describing the factors associated with each type is a legitimate and important theoretical enterprise. For example, in the scenario here you may attempt to describe three "types" of offenders on HCEM: those who fail by committing a new crime and are rearrested, those who fail only because they violate the technical conditions of the sentence and consequently get sentenced to incarceration, and those who succeed. You might argue that there are fundamental *qualitative* differences between the three groups.

Ordinal Level of Measurement *An Ordinal Scaling Process Ranks or Orders Cases (a Set of Objects) on a Variable (an Attribute)* The magnitudes or observed scores assigned are: the object ranked 1 has more of variable A than the object ranked 2, the object 2 has more of variable A than the object ranked 3, and so on. The rankings show which object, relative only to the other objects in the series, has more of variable A.

For example, with your offenders sentenced to HCEM you might be interested in characterizing the *level of prior criminal activity*. You want to know how court personnel who prepare PSIs *perceive* this attribute. You could select 20 offenders sentenced to HCEM

T A B L E 6.1
Scores on Dummy Variables Capturing Ethnicity
for Different Offenders

Case Number	Ethnicity	Dummy Variables and Observed Scores	
		Hispanic	African American
27	African American	0	1
47	Hispanic	1	0
63	White	0	0

and ask several court personnel to review the files and *rank order* the cases on the variable: "Level of prior criminal activity." The observed scores on the variable generated by this process will be **ranks**. Each court worker, acting as a rater, will assign a ranking of 1 (highest level of prior criminal activity) to 20 (lowest level of prior criminal activity) to the 20 cases.

Variables measured at the ordinal level have the following measurement properties:

- Only the *relative* quantities of the variable (attribute) possessed by the objects are indicated (**ordering property**).
- Since you only know about relative observed scores or quantities, you have no information about the *specific absolute level* of an observed score.
- Thus you don't know if the difference in level of prior criminal activity between the offender ranked sixth and the offender ranked seventh is miniscule or gigantic compared to the difference between the offender ranked eighth and the offender ranked ninth. Therefore, you cannot compare differences in ranks.
- Since ordinal scales are crude, there may be

true differences in the quantities of an attribute possessed by two objects, but the ordinal scale may not reflect that. For example, Rater R-1 may rank the level of prior criminal activity of offenders A and G as equally high. He may say they are tied for first place, and assign both the rank of 1. But this tied observed score may not reflect actual differences on the dimension of interest.

Summary   With ordinal measurement we can order or rank objects on an underlying dimension or attribute. The observed scores on the variable merely sort the objects on the variable. You cannot compare differences in ranks.

Interval Level of Measurement   If quantities of an attribute are measured on an interval scale, then we know, besides the ordering of the objects on the attribute, two more points.

First, observed scores measured at the interval level of measurement have a linear relationship with the "true scores" on the variable. For each unit increase of "true scores," observed scores increase a constant amount. Because of this relationship we also

"Now! *That* **should clear up a few things around here!"**

PICTURE 6.1   What level of measurement is represented here? (*Source.* THE FAR SIDE © 1989 FarWorks, Inc. Distributed by Universal Press Syndicate. Reprinted with permission. All rights reserved.)

know something else about interval-level measures.

You can interpret the *differences* between the observed scores of different objects. The difference between any pair of observed quantities, when measured on an interval scale, can be calculated, and compared to the difference observed between any other pair of observed quantities. The difference between every pair of scores will be equal to, less than, or greater than the difference between every other pair of observed scores. This measurement property is called the **distance property**.

Consequently, mathematical operations can be meaningfully applied to differences between observed scores on a variable measured at the interval level. The differences between pairs of observed scores can be dis-

cussed as statements about differences in the underlying "true scores."

For example, in the jursidiction in which you work, information from all arrestees is used to complete an inventory. Its purpose is to predict the chances that an arrestee will commit a serious crime if released on bail. The inventory has been extensively tested on many arrestees. Scores on the inventory range from 0 to 100 and have been standardized, so that scores of 50 have the same meaning in different groups of arrestees, scores of 75 have the same meaning in different groups of arrestees, and so on. It is a standardized, widely used inventory.

Since observed scores on this variable represent interval level measurement, you can meaningfully discuss differences between pairs of scores. In your sample of offenders sentenced to HCEM you may find that Case A scores 10 on the inventory, Case B scores 30, Case C scores 30 and Case D scores 50. The difference between the scores of A and B is equal to the difference between the scores of C and D.

Ratio Level of Measurement   Variables measured at the ratio level of measurement possess all the features of ordinal measures (ordering) and interval measures (ordering and distance), plus one additional characteristic. *The variable has a unique zero point or natural origin.* Consequently there is an even closer relationship between measured quantities and true quantities of an attribute. Not only do observed scores increase linearly as true scores increase. You also know that, when the observed score = 0, barring problems of measurement error, the "true score" = 0.

Thus, we can now apply mathematical operations to the *measured quantities directly.* For example, if Case A has six prior felony convictions and Case B has two prior felony convictions, you can meaningfully say that A has three times more prior felony convictions than B.

Criminal justice abounds with a range of ratio scaled quantities. To cite just a few: number of victimization incidents in the last 12 months, number of previous arrests, length of incarceration in months, number of technical parole violations, length of probation in months, number of cases handled by a district attorney's office in a month, and so on. As a very rough rule of thumb, if a measured quantity refers to a *count* of criminal justice events, or the *length of time* of a criminal justice event, it is probably measured at the ratio level of measurement.

Summary Figure 6.2 summarizes what we know about the types of possible relationships between "true scores" on a variable and observed scores on a variable, at the three highest levels of measurement. Each panel displays two possible relationships between true scores and observed scores at that level of measurement. Each graph assumes that observed scores include only a modest amount of measurement error. Figure 6.3 summarizes the properties of observed scores for variables at all four different levels of measurement. You need to be able to identify the level at which a quantity is measured, so that you can know whether the operations the researcher is applying to the numbers in hand are correct or not.

You are undoubtedly wondering if a researcher can *change* the level at which an attribute is measured, after collecting the data. For example, if you have observed scores on a variable measured at the ordinal level, can you change observed scores on the variable into an interval level of measurement? Or, can observed scores measured at the interval level be transformed into observed scores measured at the ordinal level?

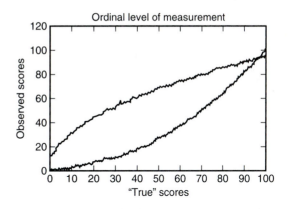

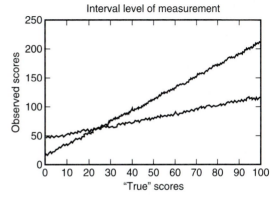

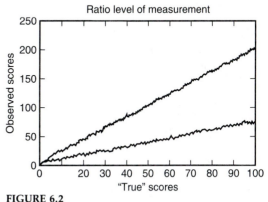

FIGURE 6.2

Possible relationships between observed scores on a variable, and "true scores" on a variable, under three levels of measurement: ordinal (top), interval (middle), and ratio (bottom). Each panel graphs two possible different relationships at that level of measurement. Measurement error, for each set of observed scores, is assumed to be minimal.

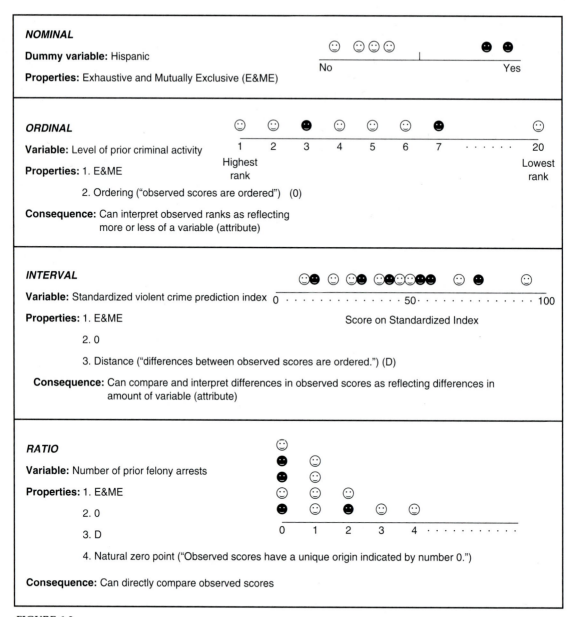

FIGURE 6.3
Properties of observed scores of variables at different levels of measurement. Quotes from [1].

Yes, such transformations are permissible, but only in one direction. You can convert observed scores on a variable from higher levels of measurement into lower levels (e.g., ratio to ordinal). You cannot, however, do the reverse. The information required for the latter treatment is simply not in the data.

INDEXES AND SCALING

In the remainder of the chapter you will examine two specific *types* of operational indicators—indexes and scales. **Indexes** are summary indicators, comprised of more than one variable. As a researcher you do not make distinctions between the different variables that make up the index. Most often, each variable you use in the index contributes about equally to the index summary score. Scores on an index represent a theoretical construct more general than scores on a single observed variable. After you construct an index you can array cases along the general variable or attribute tapped by the index.

The goal of **scale construction** is also to sort out the people being studied on the variable or attribute of interest. But the process involves two steps. First, the researcher learns the relationship of different items to one another. Then, based on their responses to particular items, people or items or both can be sorted on the variable. In short, with scales the researcher has to first *order* or *organize* the items being used before beginning to collect people's responses to the items. You will examine this process more closely later in the chapter.

Test Theory and Multiple Variables

Your insight into the conceptual foundations of scale and index construction will benefit if we spend more time with test theory. The equation on p. 102 showed that an observed score on one item reflected both a true score and measurement error. You can expand this equation to a situation where you have more than one variable.

As noted above, in the HCEM scenario, arrestees in your jurisdiction receive mandatory drug testing. Tests examine for four different substances: cocaine or crack-cocaine, heroin, amphetamines ("speed"), and marijuana. Each arrestee's urine sample is tested for each of these drugs, resulting in four different test results. Arrestees could test positive for any one of the four drugs.

You want to examine the drug-testing scores of convicted offenders assigned to HCEM. You want to develop one overall variable for the offenders showing the extent of their drug problem. You conceive of a construct: general involvement in drug abuse. You expect that you could operationalize this indicator of a concept by adding up the results of the different drug-testing results to produce one general drug test score.

Operationally, this is easy. You have four different drug test results for each offender. Each observed score is a dummy variable at the nominal level of measurement, showing drug positive or not (1 or 0), for each drug type, for each case. You add the observed scores on each case to obtain scores on an index "General Drug Involvement."

When you construct this index you are making some assumptions about each variable contributing to the index. By postulating the concept "General Drug Involvement" and choosing each of these four variables to contribute to an indicator of it, you assume that the true score of each variable has two portions. One portion is specific to the drug tested. The other emerges from a tendency toward or against general drug involvement; the first represents the *specificity* of the item, the second reflects what is *shared* between the specific concept (e.g., cocaine use) and the more general concept (general drug involvement). Therefore, if you are thinking of spe-

Creating a "General Drug Involvement" Index: Sample Cases

	Scores on Variables				Score on Summary Index
Case	Cocaine	Heroin	Speed	Marijuana	
A	0	0	0	0	0
B	0	0	0	1	1
C	0	1	0	0	1
D	1	1	1	0	3
E	1	0	0	1	2

cific variables in the light of a more general index, reflecting a more general concept, we can elaborate our equation for classical test theory as follows [7]:

Observed Score
on variable = True Score + Measurement Error

$$\text{Observed Score} = \left(\begin{array}{c} \text{Portion of} \\ \text{True Score} \\ \text{Specific to} \\ \text{Variable} \end{array} + \begin{array}{c} \text{Portion of} \\ \text{True Score} \\ \text{Shared with} \\ \text{General Index} \end{array} \right) + \begin{array}{c} \text{Measurement} \\ \text{Error} \end{array}$$

Observed Score = (Specificity + Communality) + Error

The portion of the item's true score that is unique to the item is called **specificity**. The portion of its true score that it shares with other items, and the more general concept indicated in the set of items, is called **communality**.

If the scores on each of the four specific drug tests are substantially influenced by general drug involvement, you will see positive associations between the four different drug results. This is because the true score of each item contains a large amount of communality. Offenders who tested positive for one drug will be likely also to test positive for a second, or third, or fourth drug. You will see cross-tabulation tables such as the following:

		Test Positive for Cocaine/Crack-Cocaine?	
		No	Yes
Test Positive for Amphetamines?	No	30 (60%)	10 (7%)
	Yes	20 (40%)	140 (93%)

Note. N and Column percentages shown. Artificial data.

Those who tested negative for cocaine or crack-cocaine were most likely also to test negative for amphetamines; 60% of those testing negative for crack or cocaine were also negative for amphetamines. Those who tested positive for cocaine or crack-cocaine were most likely also to test positive for am- phetamines; 93% of those testing positive for cocaine or crack also tested positive for amphetamines. Scores on these two variables correlate with each other because each variable reflects not only specific drug usage, but also a more general tendency toward or away from general drug use.

In sum, scores from different variables may correlate with one another if they tap into the same, more general construct. Indexes are variables providing summary observed scores referring to these more general concepts. Given this background, you can consider more closely the reasons researchers use scales and indexes.

Why Do Researchers Resort to Scales and Indexes?

There are three reasons. [8]

Items Are Noisy Each individual variable you use includes some error, introduced by the measuring process. When you focus on an indicator of a general concept, the error associated with each specific variable, and the specificity of each variable, operate like so much "noise," interfering with your measurement goal. If you use several different variables to make such a judgement, however, it is likely that the "noise" involved in the responses to the different items will partially cancel each other out.[4] The categorization or score you assign to the case using an index score will be closer to the case's "true score" on the general concept than the categorization or score based on one item. You gain this precision, however, if and only if the index is based on several specific variables that correlate positively with one another.

Parsimony In Chapter 3 you learned about theoretical model building, and the criminal justice researchers' goal of building *parsimonious* or *simple* models. They also like to have simple *tests* of their models as well. The use of scales and indexes allows them to

achieve this goal. A multifaceted or complex attribute can be represented with one summary score. In the example above, use of a summary "General Drug Involvement" index allows you to use just one concept in your theory, and one variable to reflect that concept.

Indexes Permit Discrimination By adding or averaging several variables, you can gauge scores on attributes with more precision than if you simply use one variable. If I have a variable showing a positive vs. a negative drug test result for one substance, then I can classify offenders into only two groups based on their results—those who tested positive, and those who did not. If I have four dummy variables, my general index will have scores ranging from 0 to 4; five different scores are possible. If I use the latter, the resulting ordering of offenders on the dimension will be more finely tuned to the true differences that exist.

Index Construction

An **index** is a summary indicator, based on several variables that correlate with one another and tap into the same general construct, where each component variable is treated as more or less equal.[5] You can use the *total* score based on the items in the index, or the *average* score. You want to verify that the different items reflect the *same* general attribute. You do so by verifying that scores on one variable correlate positively with scores from other variables referring to the same general concept. You can use cross-

---

[4] This is the case only if certain assumptions about the nature of the errors in each item, and across items, are valid.

[5] Depending upon the level of measurement and the range of possible scores for each variable, researchers may need to follow particular steps to ensure that each variable counts equally to the index. Typically, researchers standardize scores on each variable by converting scores to standard scores, also known as Z scores. See Chapter 10.

tab tables, as above, or scatterplots, for these examinations. If the different variables reflect the same general attribute, observed scores on the different variables will be generally consistent with one another. You will learn more about the mechanics of these procedures in Chapter 7 on Reliability.

Some Well-Known Criminal Justice Indexes
Several indexes are widely used in criminal justice research.

UCR Index of Reported Crimes   Police in almost all U.S. jurisdictions file monthly reports of crimes with the FBI. The FBI then totals these crimes in an index. The **Part 1 Crime Index** reports the total number of reported crimes occurring within a calendar year. The eight serious crimes added up to get the total number of serious crimes are: murder and nonnegligent manslaughter, forcible rape, robbery, aggravated assault; burglary; larceny–theft, motor vehicle theft, and, since October of 1978, arson. The index also can be expressed as a rate.[6] The Part 1 Index Crime Rate is calculated as follows:

$$\frac{\text{number of Part 1 index crimes in an area}}{\text{population in an area}} \times 100,000$$

The FBI provides further detail by separating out Part 1 crimes into a reported **Violent Crime Index** (murder, rape, robbery, aggravated assault), and a reported **Property**

Crime Index (burglary, larceny, and motor vehicle theft). Of course, violence can occur during a property crime and property damage, or theft, can occur during a violent crime.

Victimization Indexes from the National Crime Survey   The National Institute of Justice compiles the results of the *National Crime Survey*, a national survey conducted on an ongoing basis that asks people about victimization experiences. You will get a more detailed description of the NCS in Chapter 12. The Department of Justice constructs indexes from this survey.

The NCS asks about the following types of victimization incidents: rape, robbery, assault, burglary, personal and household larceny, and motor vehicle theft. [12] **Victimization counts** are calculated by adding up the number of victims of one or more crimes. Since a single crime incident can have more than one victim, victimization counts will be higher than victim incident counts. If a husband and wife both get robbed while walking home together one night, there is one victimization incident, but two victimization counts.

All victimizations are added up to get an index of **overall victimization counts** and generalizations are made *from* the surveyed population *to* the population of the country as a whole. For example, in 1988 there were approximately 35.8 million victimizations in the U.S. [13]

These victimization counts are then used to compute **victimization rates**. For personal crimes of rape, robbery, assault, and theft, *people* are used as the denominator to construct victimization rates of *personal* crimes.

More specifically:

$$\text{Personal victimization rate} = \frac{\text{number of personal crime victimizations}}{\text{total population 12 and over}} \times 1,000$$

---

[6] There has been considerable discussion for several years about the inappropriateness of the denominator used to construct the Part 1 Index Crime Rate. [9, 10, 11] Although population may be the appropriate denominator for constructing a murder rate, it may not be appropriate when constructing a burglary rate, where occupied housing units should be used instead, or a forcible rape rate, where the number of women should be used. Of course, on the practical side it would be extremely difficult for law enforcement officials to collect information for the appropriate denominators for each of the eight Part 1 index crimes on a routine basis.

For household crimes—burglary, household larceny, motor vehicle theft—the number of *households* is used to as the denominator.

$$\text{Household victimization rate} = \frac{\text{number of household victimizations reported}}{\text{total number of households}} \times 1,000$$

Because of the way the survey sample is constructed, the researchers are able to extrapolate from the survey respondents to the entire U.S. population, and develop estimated victimization rates for the entire country.[7] How do they perform this magic? You'll see in Chapter 10.

These rates we have been discussing so far—the UCR reported crime rates for personal and property crimes, the household victimization rate, and the personal victimization rate—are all indicators of the *incidence* of victimization. An **incidence-based rate** divides the number of *incidents* by *a population count*, whether that be individuals or households. (As a mental exercise, you may wish to estimate the level of measurement of these indexes.) Thus, for the household victimization rate, one household being burgled 10 times during a year contributes the same amount to the property victimization rate as 10 households each being burgled once during the year.

The Department of Justice researchers also generate an overall index of the *prevalence* of crime that includes both personal and household crimes. A **prevalence-based rate** divides the *number of persons (or households) experiencing* the event by the *total number of persons (or households)*. Note that, conceptually, this is very different from an incidence-based index rate. If a particular household experiences 1

burglary during a year, or 10 different burglaries, that household contributes the same amount to the prevalence-based indicator.

One prevalence-based rate developed from the NCS is an index of **households touched by crime**: the proportion of households in the country that have experienced one or more victimizations during a calendar year. A household is counted as "touched by crime" during a year if one or more of its members experience one or more of the following victimization experiences: rape, personal robbery, assault, personal theft, or motor vehicle theft; or if the household is burglarized or victimized by a theft. [14] Homicide is not included. Researchers extrapolate from the results of the National Crime Survey to estimate, nationwide, the number of households touched by crime.

Figure 6.4 shows the proportion of households, nationwide, "touched by crime" during the period 1975 through 1988, by race of household. Whereas the proportion has dropped consistently for White households during the period, it has dropped less among African American households. In 1988 nearly $1/4$ of U.S. households (24.6%) had been touched by a crime.

Problems with These Indexes Critics have pointed out shortcomings of these indexes. [15] (1) The general measures count attempted and completed crimes as equivalent. The proportion of attempted vs. successful crimes varies widely. Whereas roughly 90% of the household larcenies reported in the NCS were successfully completed, only about 35% of robberies reported in the NCS were successfully completed. (2) All these indexes add together "apples and oranges"— crimes that vary enormously in their severity, and in the type of victimization experience. In the personal victimization rate constructed from the NCS, a victimization incident of an attempted bicycle theft contributes the same

---

[7] Because of the way this extrapolation works the resulting estimates have some built-in imprecision. This built-in imprecision of the extrapolated rates is due to *sampling error*, which you will learn more about in Chapter 10.

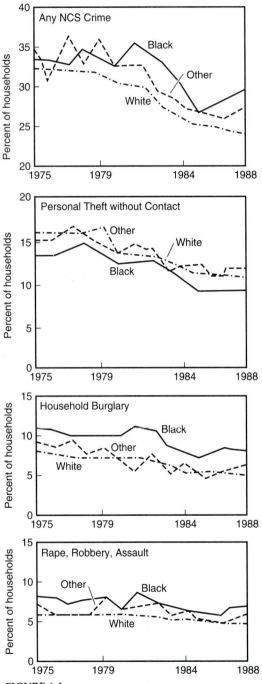

FIGURE 6.4
Source: Rand, M. (1989) Households touched by crime. Bureau of Justice Statistics Bulletin. Washington, DC: U.S. Department of Justice. Figure 2, p. 2.

amount to the rate as does a completed rape. The households touched by crime index, and the overall "Crime Index" calculated by the FBI from the UCR, are the two indexes that combine the broadest range of incidents.

This latter problem is inherent, somewhat, in every index. An index *always* adds variables that are, to some extent, unlike one another, to arrive at a more general variable. Thus, some blurring is inevitable. Such are the costs of seeking parsimony. In recognition of such costs, researchers have pursued the development of *scales*, to which we now turn.

Scale Construction

Scales are distinct from indexes. Scales consider the relationship *between items*. The items are ordered on an underlying attribute of interest. Numbers or categories are then assigned to the items based on their position on the variable. Psychologists over the decades have developed many procedures for scaling a wide variety of stimuli.

A scaling exercise may have one of three purposes: (1) to find the position of the item or stimulus itself on an underlying attribute or dimension, (2) to classify or position persons on an underlying attribute or dimension, or (3) to classify or position both persons and stimuli on an underlying attribute or dimension. [17] When the persons or items have been positioned on the underlying attribute of interest, they have been *scaled*.

Consider, for example, the scaling of crimes on a seriousness dimension. I may be interested in this simply to learn how serious people think heroin smuggling is compared to bicycle theft (scaling the items). Or I may be interested in finding how people differ in the perceived seriousness of a set of crimes, and then understanding those differences. Some may think that people convicted of bicycle theft should go to prison, whereas

BOX 6.1

A SAFETY INDEX FOR PHILADELPHIA'S SUBURBAN NEIGHBORHOODS
Who Decides Item Weights?

In December 1989 *Philadelphia* magazine published a guide to the safest suburban neighborhoods in the region. [16] They developed a "safety index" for each of the 251 locales surrounding Philadelphia.[8] Readers were encouraged to "find out . . . Just how safe is your town?"

The magazine developed their safety index in the following fashion. For each of the eight Part 1 UCR crimes they computed countywide rates. Then they calculated the UCR crime rates for each township within the larger counties. To get the relative safety of each township vis-à-vis its surrounding county, they divided each township's rate for each crime by its county rate. Thus, if the aggravated assault rate in a township was the same as in the larger county, the result would be 1.0; if it was half of the county rate, the result would be 0.5.

Each of these ratios was added up to calculate an "overall safety index." (Murder, rape and arson were excluded from the overall index.) In adding the crimes up, they weighted "the various crimes according to a 'worry factor'." Here is how their weighting went:

Crime	Index Weight According to "Worry" Factor
Robbery + Assault (combined)	50
Burglary	25
Auto Theft	15
Larceny or Theft	10

So according to the author of the study, a robbery is twice as worrisome as a burglary, and five times as worrisome as a larceny. But a burglary is only 67 percent more worrisome than an auto theft. Why were these relative weights chosen? Why not other weights? The use of a different weighting scheme would result in a different ordering of the communities on the index. You can try this out for yourself and see. The actual dataset appears in the file PHILASUB.WKS. The workdisk contains some suggested exercises that suggest ways you can test this out.

The main point is this: beware an index where the contributing variables have been assigned different weights, and a sound justification for those different weights is lacking. If the weights are arbitrary, so too are the resulting scores on the index.

---

[8] The area around the city of Philadelphia is divided up into seven large counties—three in New Jersey, and four in Pennsylvania. Each county is then further divided into townships. The units analyzed were these townships.

others may not (scaling persons). Or I may be interested in finding out how the crimes are arrayed along an underlying seriousness dimension, and what crime each person views as the most serious (scaling both items and people).

Suppose You Wanted to Measure Crime Seriousness Imagine you want to know about the seriousness of different offenses. This has been a topic of considerable interest to social scientists for some time. The great measurement psychologist Louis Thurstone published a paper on this in the 1920s [18, 19]. The most noted publication for criminologists in this area was Sellin and Wolfgang's seminal work on the topic, *The Measurement of Delinquency*, published in 1964. The 15 crimes in which you are interested appear in Table 6.2. You want to arrange these crimes so that you know which is more serious than the other, and by how much. What are the different ways you might want to go about this?

What I will do below is to describe different techniques that researchers might use to scale these 15 stimuli. For each technique I will discuss its advantages and its disadvantages.

Equal-Appearing Intervals *The Underlying Rationale* Louis Thurstone invented several different scaling procedures. The most

widely used was the method of *equal-appearing intervals*. Underlying this procedure is a presumption called **the law of comparative judgements**. This law assumes that, for each stimulus, there exists a **modal** or **typical response**. In crime seriousness a modal-judged level of seriousness is assumed to exist for each crime. It is *not* assumed that everyone judging the stimulus provides the modal judgement. People can vary in how seriously they judge the crime. But those variations will center on that modal judgement, disperse evenly on either side, and taper off as you move away from the modal judgement. Most judgements for a crime will be close to the modal judgement for that crime.

In technical terms he assumed that judgements formed a *normal distribution* around the modal judgement. You can learn more about

TABLE 6.2
Fifteen Crimes in Which You Are Interested

A. A person using force, robs a victim of $10. The victim struggles and is shot to death.

B. A person disturbs the neighborhood with loud, noisy behavior.

C. A person steals property worth $1,000 from outside a building.

D. A father beats his young child with his fists. The child requires hospitalization.

E. A man forcibly rapes a woman. Her physical injuries require hospitalization.

F. A person steals property worth $10 from outside a building.

G. A person, using force, robs a victim of $10. No physical harm occurs.

H. A person plants a bomb in a public building. The bomb explodes, and 20 people are killed.

I. A person steals property worth $10,000 from outside a building.

J. A person smuggles heroin into the country.

K. A person steals property worth $50 from outside a building.

L. A factory knowingly gets rid of its wastes in a way that pollutes the water supply of a city. As a result 20 people become ill, but none require medical treatment.

M. A person steals an unlocked car and later abandons it.

N. A person steals property worth $100 from outside a building.

O. A person, using force, robs a victim of $10. The victim is hurt and requires hospitalization.

the normal distribution in Chapter 10. Normal distributions are a family of hypothetical curves that describe how a series of scores is arranged: most scores appear in the middle, scores taper off evenly on either side, and you can describe how many scores will appear at different areas under the curve.

Furthermore, different stimuli may vary in terms of the degree to which people agree on the modal response. For example, across persons, the agreement about the seriousness of a white-collar crime (e.g., "several large companies illegally fix the retail prices of their products") may be much lower than the agreement about the seriousness of a violent crime (e.g., "a person robs a victim of $10 at gunpoint. No physical harm occurs."). This may occur though the *average* seriousness of each item is the same. These points are illustrated in Figure 6.5.

The Method   You would proceed in the following fashion. First you would select a large number of stimuli (crimes), say around a hundred or so. (In other words, the 15 crimes you are ultimately interested in start out merely as a subset of a much larger number of crimes.) The crimes chosen should span the full range of the attribute in question (seriousness). Judges—raters—would then be asked to place each stimulus in one of 11 categories that range from 1 (not at all seri-

FIGURE 6.5
Steps in creating a seriousness scale with Thurstonian equal intervals scaling procedures.

I. Assume that, for each crime, there is a *Modal* or *Typical* Response.

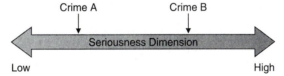

II. Not everyone, when asked about the seriousness of Crime A or Crime B, provides an answer that is the modal one. Individuals vary in where they place the stimulus on the seriousness dimension. Nonetheless, these variations *center around* the modal response.

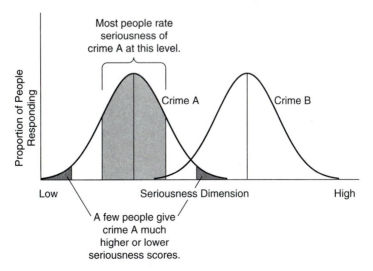

FIGURE 6.5   (continued)
III. Items also differ in terms of how much people agree about where each item should be placed on the seriousness dimension.

There may be low agreement with regard to seriousness (e.g., price fixing)

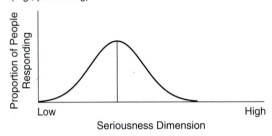

Or people may agree strongly about the seriousness of an item (e.g., armed robbery, $10 taken, no injury)

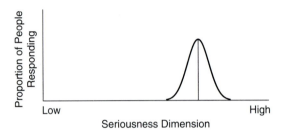

IV. In the resulting seriousness scale, a series of items will be chosen. For most of the items people will agree about seriousness. And the items will cover the range of the seriousness dimension.

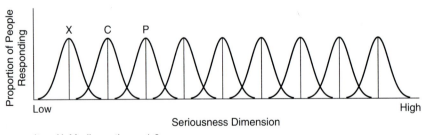

Item X, Median rating = 1.6
Item C, Median rating = 2.5
Item P, Median rating = 3.7

ous) to 11 (extremely serious), with the 11 categories positioned at equal points along the seriousness dimension. The judges are not asked to give their personal opinion, but instead to evaluate the items in terms of the seriousness dimension. You would use many raters for this task, preferably several dozen. The more heterogeneous the group of raters the better.

After the judges have rated the stimuli, you will examine, for each crime, its typical placement.[9] You also will examine the items to find those where subjects generally agreed on placement. In other words, you will look for items where the responses (judged seriousness) clustered strongly about the typical or modal response. Using these criteria, you can then select a few items, say around 15–20, (a) evenly spread along the seriousness dimension, and (b) with judges' ratings that agree closely with the modal response. (See Figure 6.5, panel IV.)

Now that you have scaled the items, you can use the scale to assess people. These people must be different from your original judges. Suppose you want to examine differences among voters in punitiveness. You decide to explore the seriousness of crimes for which voters think convicted offenders should be imprisoned, or jailed. You might ask: "Suppose that a person was convicted of crime_____. If jail or prison space was available, do you think such persons should spend some time in jail or prison?" The average seriousness value of the crimes for which the respondent *does* think jail or prison time should be served indicates the voter's punitiveness. Those saying "yes" only to high seriousness crimes are much less punitive than those saying "yes" to high *and* low seri-

ousness crimes. You can measure differences in levels of punitiveness.

Advantages and Disadvantages The advantages to Thurstonian scaling include the following. (1) You develop a scale with interval level properties. You can feel secure using sophisticated statistical techniques that assume such properties in the data. (2) You have relied upon many judges to decide scale values and have not arbitrarily assigned those values. (3) At least with respect to crime seriousness, such scales may remain relatively constant over a long span of time, even 40 years! [18]

Unfortunately, however, several disadvantages accompany the Thurstonian procedure. [20] (1) As you may have already noticed, the process is labor intensive. You need many raters to rate the stimuli before the scale can be constructed and used with the real subjects of interest. This requires a commitment in time and finances. You may be attracted to alternate, less time-consuming, less expensive scaling methods. (2) The judges who provide the initial information on items may be influenced by personal factors in making their judgments. Thus, if one group of judges was composed of extremely conservative college students from rural Pennsylvania, and another group of judges was composed of liberal Hispanic and African American students from southern California, the resulting items used in the scale, and the positions of particular items on the scale, might be quite different. (3) The subjects who are actually *using* the scaled items may be thinking about matters *other* than seriousness. For example, if a particular type of crime is a problem in a region, voters may be strongly in favor of incarcerating convicted offenders, even though the crime is not rated as that serious. (4) Finally, the Thurstonian procedure assumes but does not verify that the underlying attribute has *one* dimension. It

---

[9] The "typical" position is the median, a number which is the "middlemost" one; half the numbers are above the median, and half are below.

is possible that the attributes could have several dimensions or facets. Research suggests crime severity does have several dimensions. [21]

Likert Scaling[10] *The Underlying Rationale* The purpose of a Likert scale is to array *respondents* in terms of their agreement vs. disagreement with a particular attitude or opinion. The assumption is that, to measure an attitude or opinion, several different items can be used. It is further assumed that the items are almost interchangeable with each other, and that each person's response to an item reflects the position of that respondent on the issue. A Likert scale is different from an index because of the structure of how people respond to each item.

The Method Most typically with Likert-scaled items people are asked to state their degree of agreement or disagreement. So to get at the seriousness of the 15 crimes introduced earlier in the chapter, respondents might be asked: "The following is an *extremely serious* crime: A person using force, robs a victim of $10. The victim struggles and is shot to death." Following the item would be response categories:

Response	Score
Strongly agree	4
Agree	3
Neither agree nor disagree	2
Disagree	1
Strongly Disagree	0

The person would check the response representing her feelings. Across the 15 crimes the ratings of each respondent can then be added

---

[10] Technically, Likert scales are simply indexes made up from Likert-scaled items. Thus they could be discussed along with other indexes. I bow to current practice and discuss them here as scales.

up to come up with an overall scale score indicating how serious, in general, each respondent thinks crimes are. Those with higher scores view the 15 crimes as more serious than those with lower scores.

The qualities of the summative scale scores can then be examined. For example, you might see how well scores on each item correlate with the total score based on all the items. Further, you might then research the factors, such as age or previous victimization experiences, that lead some people to view crimes as more serious than others.

As in Thurstonian scaling, with Likert scaling you can begin with a larger number of items than you intend to keep. Then, once you have information on all the items, you can drop items that do not correlate with the total score based on all the items.

Advantages and Disadvantages Likert-scaled items summed to yield Likert summative scales have gained popularity among researchers for a variety of reasons. (1) Most notably, as you can gather from the straightforward procedure, the methods are relatively effortless and uncomplicated. You require no separate scaling procedure. You just ask people whether they agree or disagree with a series of items, then sum their responses. The ease of this procedure is probably the main factor accounting for its popularity. (2) You do not worry about the relationship between the items, as long as they all intercorrelate highly or "hang together." Aside from this concern, the different items used in a summative scale are treated as relatively interchangeable.

Nonetheless this approach has limitations. (1) Most notably, a respondent's score on the summative scale can be interpreted only in relative terms. People are spread out based on their scale scores. This dispersion is only with respect to *other respondents*. There is no external framework, based on item characteristics, within which respondent scores can be considered. By contrast, the judging procedure with Thurstonian scaling *does* yield such an external referent. (2) Given the relative nature of summated scales based on Likert-scored items, these total scores probably should be treated as ordinal-level, or quasi-interval-level, rather than interval-level measures. (3) The unidimensionality of the underlying dimension on which respondents differ is assumed, not shown. It could well be that a summative scale based on 15 items really contains three relative distinct subsets of items, suggesting three different dimensions along which respondents differed, rather than one.

Magnitude Scaling *Rationale* The two above scaling procedures use a limited number of possible scores or *categories* for each item, and thus they are **category scaling approaches**. Researchers have pointed out that in judging some items category scaling procedures may be too limiting. [22] Respondents may want to express differences that are greater than can be fitted into the categories.

For example, in the 15 crimes introduced earlier in the chapter a respondent might think that a person smuggling heroin into the country (crime J) is about 1,000 times more serious than a person stealing property worth $10 from outside a building (crime F). If the respondent is using a Thurstonian equal-appearing intervals procedure, how is he to express this 1,000-fold difference in perceived seriousness when he only has 11 categories to express these differences?

Magnitude scaling procedures can accommodate such differences. The only assumption is that people can say how much more of an attribute is present in one item than another. *In a magnitude scaling procedure, respondents provide numeric estimates of how many times a stimulus differs from a benchmark stimulus on some attribute.* It was developed originally to

learn how people perceived psychophysical stimuli such as brightness, weight, loudness, and so on. [23] More recently the technique also has been applied to social stimuli such as crimes and adjectives.

Magnitude scaling arises from dissatisfaction with several aspects of category scaling. [22, 24] (1) In category scaling the limited number of available categories results in *details* about judgements being lost. Respondents may place two stimuli in the same category although they view them as slightly different. (2) Category scaling often results in ordinal-level or quasi-level information (e.g., Likert summary scales). The subsequent application of statistics intended for interval-level data to these numbers may not be fully appropriate. (3) Category scaling procedures can significantly distort responses because the format artificially limits responses.

The Procedure The procedure used in the crime severity scaling supplement to the 1977 NCS was a typical magnitude scaling procedure, except for its size. There were 60,000 respondents and 204 items. Each respondent judged 25 items. Each respondent received a "benchmark" crime: "A person steals a bicycle parked on the street." They were told that the seriousness of this crime was "10." "They were then given a list of other crimes and told to compare them in seriousness to the bicycle theft. If a crime seemed to be twice as serious they were to rate it at 20. If it was four times as serious, they were to rate it 40 and so on." [25] If they thought something was *not* a crime they were to rate it "0."

Advantages and Disadvantages The greatest advantage of the magnitude scaling approach is that people's responses can have an extremely broad range. There are no restrictions. The seriousness scores generated from the national study for the 15 crimes described

FIGURE 6.6   Estimates of crime seriousness provided by a national sample.

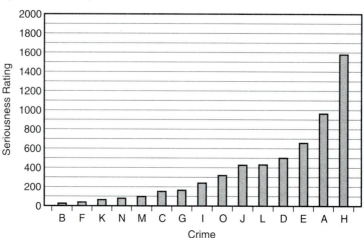

A. A person using force, robs a victim of $10. The victim struggles and is shot to death.

B. A person disturbs the neighborhood with loud, noisy behavior.

C. A person steals property worth $1,000 from outside a building.

D. A parent beats his young child with his fists. The child requires hospitalization.

E. A man forcibly rapes a woman. Her physical injuries require hospitalization.

F. A person steals property worth $10 from outside a building.

G. A person, using force. robs a victim of $10. No physical harm occurs.

H. A person plants a bomb in a public building. The bomb explodes and 20 people are killed.

I. A person steals property worth $10,000 from outside a building.

J. A person smuggles heroin into the country.

K. A person steals property worth $50 from outside a building.

L. A factory knowingly gets rid of its wastes in a way that pollutes the water supply of a city. As a result 20 people become ill but none requires medical treatment.

M. A person steals an unlocked car and later abandons it.

N. A person steals property worth $100 from outside a building.

O. A person, using force, robs a victim of $10. The victim is hurt and requires hospitalization.

Source. Lodge, M (1981). *Magnitude scaling.* Beverly Hills, CA: Sage Publications, p. 20.

earlier in the chapter appear in Fig. 6.6. As you can see, the response for H (planting a bomb that kills people) is rated as almost 158 times more serious than the bicycle theft. A second advantage is that the resulting scale values have interval-level measurement properties. Thus, precise relationships between the values of different items can be determined. Third, if the stimuli have some measurable attribute, the relationship between the attribute and the judgements can be examined. For example, in the work on offense seriousness scaling researchers have been able to discover how the amount of dollar loss involved in a crime influences perceived seriousness of the crime. [26, 27, but compare 28]

There are, of course, disadvantages. Such a scaling procedure can sometimes result in seemingly inconsistent patterns, particularly if not all respondents rate all stimuli. For example, in the NCS supplement, one crime where a bomb was planted and no one killed was rated as more serious than one where a bomb killed 20 people. [29] These inconsistencies can be resolved if all respondents rate all items, and if more detailed rating instructions are provided. [e.g., 23] Such detailed instructions, however, use up valuable time in an interview situation.

Multidimensional Scaling In the last 40 years procedures have been developed permitting stimuli to be scaled simultaneously on several dimensions. [30] Respondents judge pairs of stimuli, rating, for each pair, how similar the two are to each other. From these ratings the position of the stimuli in a multidimensional space can be recovered. Fancier versions of these programs even allow the researcher to see if different types of respondents place the stimuli differently in the resulting multidimensional space. So you *can* scale stimuli on more than one dimension.

OTHER SCALING
AND INDEXING PROCEDURES

There are a range of additional scaling procedures, and index construction techniques, beyond those you have begun to learn about here. For example:

- Guttman Scalogram procedures attempt simultaneously to order items and people;

- Coombs's unfolding technique attempts to uncover a common scale used by people when they supply preference orderings;
- the Bogardus social distance scale attempts to find the desired intimacy vs. distance people prefer vis-à-vis particular social stimuli such as persons of different races;
- the Kelly Rep grid technique uses triads of stimuli to elicit from the respondents the attributes they use to discriminate the stimuli;
- the semantic differential technique focuses on a number of adjective pairs, on which stimuli are rated, and assumes that indexes based on ratings across sets of adjective pairs representing three independent underlying dimensions of assessment.

I could go on, but I think you are beginning to get the idea. There are many techniques available. [23, 31] The techniques I have discussed here are simply widely used and general purpose. The techniques not discussed here have more of a "specialty" flavor or may have assumptions that have proven problematic in recent years (e.g., semantic differential, Bogardus social distance).

BUT WHAT SHOULD I USE?

Now comes the hard question: Which technique should I use? Should I use a scale or an index? If a scale, what type of procedure should I use?

Now comes the easy answer: It all depends. (I am practicing in case I ever want to become an economist.)

Do you have a lot of cheap labor available to help you with your task? If so, you may want to consider a magnitude scaling procedure that allows you to generate measures with interval level properties.

Is your research being done on a shoestring budget, and are your friends tired of helping you out with bizarre questionnaires? If so, consider constructing an index. If the items in which you are interested lend themselves to an "agree vs. disagree" response, consider using Likert-scaled items, and a Likert-summated scale.

Do you have time? Then experiment with different types of scaling procedures. Test things out for yourself. (Don't trust an author of a text; be empirical!)

There is no one technique you *should* use. But you should know about the measurement properties resulting from the technique that you use, and you should use a technique that fits the task.

SUMMARY OF MAIN POINTS

- Measurement is the process of assigning numbers (observed scores) to represent the actual magnitudes of a variable or attribute possessed by a series of objects.
- When you measure you translate conceptualized variables, which exist in your head, into actual scores on variables for cases studied.
- While measuring you introduce measurement error, resulting in a discrepancy between observed scores and true scores.
- Classical test theory states that:

  Observed Score = True Score + Error

- Different levels of measurement describe different relationships between observed scores and true scores.
- Variables measured at the nominal level of measurement classify objects into categories that are exhaustive and mutually exclusive.
- At the ordinal level of measurement, observed scores have the property of order, with higher-ranked objects possessing more of the attribute in question than lower-ranked objects.
- At the interval level of measurement, observed scores have the properties of order and distance.
- Given the distance property, you can interpret differences between pairs of observed scores measured at the interval level of measurement.

- At the ratio level of measurement, observed scores have the properties of order, distance, and origin.
- Given the property of origin, variables have a unique or natural zero point or origin.
- You can directly compare observed scores if they are measured at the ratio level of measurement.
- You apply to observed scores the mathematical and statistical tools that are appropriate to that level of measurement, or to a lower level of measurement.
- You use indexes to achieve theoretical parsimony, differentiation, and reliability.
- An index is a summary indicator, based on responses to several items that correlate with one another, where each item is treated as roughly equal.
- Some well-known criminal justice indexes include the Part 1 Crime Index based on the UCR, the personal and household victimization rates based on the NCS, and the Households Touched by Crime Index based on the NCS.
- An index that is an incidence rate reports the number of events, summed across several subtypes of events, occurring per unit of population (e.g., NCS-based personal victimization rate).
- An index that is a prevalence rate reports the proportion of the population affected by one or more events (e.g., NCS-based "Households Touched by Crime" Index).

- All indexes are somewhat problematic in that they add or average different items, each of which is somewhat specific.
- An index is useful to the extent that the component variables making up the index have something in common.
- Scales are summary indicators taking into account the relationship between the different constituent items.
- Scaling can be used to organize items, people, or both items and people.
- Scaling items with the equal-appearing intervals method requires that raters or judges provide a category scaling of the items to be used *before* subjects respond to the items.
- Likert-scaled items ask respondents to report how much they disagree or agree with various items. Likert-scaled items can be summed to yield a Likert-summated scale that organizes people in terms of their agreement vs. disagreement with a set of items.
- Magnitude scaling asks respondents to report "How many times more *something* (e.g., serious) is Item I" as compared to a benchmark item.

GLOSSARY OF KEY WORDS

attributes
cases
category scaling approaches
classical test theory
communality
distance property
dummy variable
equal-appearing intervals
households touched by crime
incidence-based rate
index(es)
law of comparative judgements
magnitudes
measurement error
modal (typical) response
natural origin

objects
observed scores
ordering property
overall victimization counts
Part I Crime Index
prevalence-based rate
Property crime Index
quantity
ranks
scale construction
specificity
true scores
variables
victimization counts
victimization rates
Violent Crime Index

REFERENCES

1. McIver, J. P., and Carmines, E. G. (1981) *Unidimensional scaling*, Sage Publications, Beverly Hills, CA, p. 9.
2. Torgerson, W. S. (1958) *Theories and methods of scaling*, John Wiley and Sons, New York, p. 17.
3. Torgerson, W. S. (1958) *Theories and methods of scaling*, John Wiley and Sons, New York, p. 25.
4. Green, B. F. (1981) A primer of testing. *American Psychologist 36*, 1001–1011.
5. Mieczkowski, T., Barzeley, D., Gropper, B., and Wish, E. (1990) Tripartite concordance of self-reported cocaine use and three immunoassay techniques in the arrestee population. Paper presented at the annual meeting of the American Society of Criminology, November, Baltimore.
6. Torgerson, W. S. (1958) *Theories and methods of scaling*, John Wiley and Sons, New York, p. 21.
7. Thurstone, L. I. (1947) *Multiple factor analysis and the expansion of the vector model*, University of Chicago Press, Chicago, p. 75.
8. McIver, J. P., and Carmines, E. G. (1981) *Unidimensional scaling*, Sage Publications, Beverly Hills, CA, p. 15.
9. Boggs, S. (1965) Urban crime patterns. *American Sociological Review 30*, 899–908.
10. Harries, K. D. Local crime rates. Department of Geography, Oklahoma State University (unpublished final report).

11. Harries, K. D. (1981) Alternative denominators in conventional crime rates. In Brantingham, P. J. and Brantingham, P. L. (eds.), *Environmental criminology*, Sage, Beverly Hills, CA, pp. 147–166.

12. Bureau of Justice Statistics. (1990) *Criminal victimization in the United States, 1988.* U.S. Department of Justice, Washington, DC (A National Crime Survey Report NCJ-122024), p. 1.

13. Bureau of Justice Statistics. (1990) *Criminal victimization in the United States, 1988,* U.S. Department of Justice, Washington, DC (A National Crime Survey Report NCJ-122024), p. 2.

14. Karmen, A. (1990) *Introduction to victimology*, Second ed., Brooks/Cole, Monterey, CA, p. 6.

15. Karmen, A. (1990) *Introduction to victimology*, Second ed., Brooks/Cole, Monterey, CA.

16. Hooper L. (1989) The safest places to live. *Philadelphia 80*, 142–149, 197–200.

17. McIver, J. P., and Carmines, E. G. (1981) *Unidimensional scaling*, Sage Publications, Beverly Hills, CA, p. 9.

18. Coombs, C. H. (1967) Thurstone's measurement of social values revisited forty years later. *Journal of Personality and Social Psychology 6*, 85–91.

19. Thurstone, L. (1927) The Method of paired comparisons for social values. *Journal of Abnormal and Social Psychology 21*, 384–400.

20. McIver, J. P., and Carmines, E. G. (1981) *Uni dimensional scaling*, Sage Publications, Beverly Hills, CA, p. 21.

21. Gottfredson, S. D., and Taylor, R. B. (1987) Attitudes of correctional policymakers and the public. In Gottfredson, S. D., and McConville, S. (eds.), *America's correctional crisis*, Greenwood Press, New York.

22. Lodge, M. (1981) *Magnitude scaling: Quantitative measurement of opinions*, Sage Publications, Beverly Hills, CA, p. 5.

23. Lodge, M. (1981) *Magnitude scaling: Quantitative measurement of opinions*, Sage Publications, Beverly Hills, CA.

24. Walker, M. (1978) Measuring the seriousness of crimes. *British Journal of Criminology 18*, 348–364.

25. Klaus, P., and Kalish, C. B. (1984) *The severity of crime*, Bureau of Justice Statistics, Washington, DC, p. 2.

26. Sellin, T., and Wolfgang, M. F. (1964) *The Measurement of delinquency*, John Wiley, New York.

27. Figlio, R. M. (1976) The seriousness of offenses: An Evaluation by offenders and nonoffenders. *Journal of Criminal Law and Criminology 66*, 189–200.

28. Gottfredson, S. D., Young, K. L., and Laufer, W. S. (1980) Additivity and interactions in offense seriousness scales. *Journal of Research in Crime and Delinquency 17*, 26–41.

29. Klaus, P., and Kalish, C. B. (1984) *The severity of crime*, Bureau of Justice Statistics, Washington, DC.

30. Kruskal, J., and Wish, M. (1978) *Multidimensional scaling*, Sage Publications, Beverly Hills, CA.

31. McIver, J. P., and Carmines, E. G. (1981) *Unidimensional scaling*, Sage Publications, Beverly Hills, CA.

PART THREE

BENCHMARKS OF SCIENTIFIC QUALITY

All criminal justice research studies are not created equal. Researchers use different types of research tools. You will learn about these different tools in Part IV. If you focus on studies using one kind of tool, however, important differences in *study quality* are likely. In this section you will learn about the three major benchmarks of scientific quality.

In *Chapter 7* you explore reliability. Social scientists want to use measurement procedures that do not generate wildly fluctuating readings when repeated on similar occasions. They can examine the stability of their measurement procedures over time, over items, and over raters.

In *Chapter 8* you investigate internal validity. This topic addresses both the meaning of the specific measures used in a study, as well as the soundness of the conclusions reached in a study.

In *Chapter 9* you consider external validity, the likelihood that results of a specific study also will apply to other populations, other places, and other times. You will see that, although researchers can take steps to make it more likely that their results will generalize, they do not know about generalizability until they actually conduct an additional study. In this chapter you also will contemplate the relationship between the three different benchmarks of scientific quality. Researchers cannot always maximize all three but must sometimes make trade-offs between them. I suggest that, for criminal justice researchers, the most important benchmark is internal validity.

After reading this section you should be able to describe each of the three benchmarks of scientific quality, and to discuss methods that researchers use to learn how their studies and measures score on these benchmarks.

CHAPTER 7

RELIABILITY

*Reliability is the agreement between two efforts to measure the same trait
[or construct] through maximally similar measures.* [1]

OBJECTIVES

This chapter opens a trio of chapters on the benchmarks of scientific quality: reliability, internal validity, and external validity. You can decide how much causal inference or discovery a particular study provides only after you have examined these three issues. In this chapter you examine the reliability of measures used to generate observed scores on variables.

In his film *Sleeper* Woody Allen portrays a jazz clarinetist turned health food store entrepreneur. Freeze dried in the 20th century, scientists thaw him a few hundred years in the future. Fleeing authorities with Diane Keaton, he discovers a dust-covered VW "Bug" in a cave. They get in and turn the key. It starts promptly.

Since I once owned a "Bug" I find this scenario plausible. Mine was similarly reliable. I knew it would start—always. I knew what would happen going uphill with a headwind, or downhill with a tailwind, or on snow. It was consistent, predictable, and trustworthy. It never surprised me.

We use the terms *reliable* and *unreliable* to describe many elements in everyday life besides cars: friends and hard disks, for example. Social scientists use the terms in roughly

the same way, to describe the measures and procedures they use to generate observed scores on variables.

ORGANIZATION

Three different aspects of reliability interest criminal justice researchers: over items, over time, and over raters or observers. Although the specific meaning of reliability varies across these three areas, the three meanings all have the same core idea as our everyday usage of the term *reliable*: consistency and predictability.

What does it mean specifically to have a high level of reliability? If a measurement procedure has a high level of reliability, the observed score for a variable that you assign to a case based on information from

{ one item }
{ an assessment at one point in time }
{ one rater or observer }

will be maximally similar to the observed score for the same variable that you assign to the same case based on information from

{ a second or subsequent items. }
{an assessment at a subsequent point in time.}
{ additional raters or observers. }

You will explore each of these areas of reliability in turn: over items, over time, and over raters. In each area you will examine a particular problem, inspect the connections with some of the measurement theory discussed in Chapter 6, and encounter specific "consumer guidelines."

CONSISTENCY OVER ITEMS

The Problem

In Chapter 6 you read about index construction: how researchers may combine specific variables reflecting specific concepts into a more general index variable reflecting a more general concept. In the running scenario concerned with probationers assigned to HCEM, you encountered an example combining four measures of specific drug use, based on urinalysis, into a more general index you called Overall Drug Involvement. In a wide range of situations, criminal justice researchers think about combining items into more general index variables. The items that researchers may want to combine into indexes can tap three types of attributes.

Types of Attributes *Behaviors* Items can report on past behaviors. The items may come from several possible sources: court records, police records, questionnaires, or other persons who know the subject. In the urinalysis example you assumed that scores on the different tests reflected actual drug-using behavior.

Attitudes or perceptions or cognitions Items in a questionnaire, or a face-to-face interview, for example, can reveal how a person thinks about different topics or particular events: capital punishment, funding for police departments, unethical behavior of judges, support for new prison construction, the causes of the riots in south-central Los Angeles in May 1992, and so on.

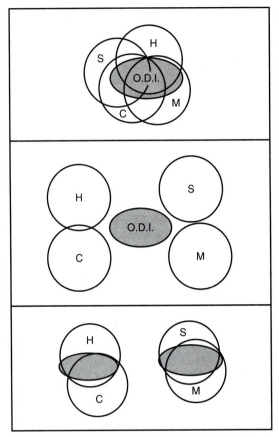

FIGURE 7.1
Possible patterns connecting specific items on specific drug use with a more general index reflecting a more general concept of Overall Drug Involvement. O.D.I. = Overall Drug Index. C = cocaine and crack cocaine. S = Speed and other amphetamines. H = heroin. M = marijuana. **Top panel.** Correlations suggest one general concept. Scores on all four urinalyses correlate strongly with one another. **Middle panel.** Correlations between the four items are low, suggesting no general concept. **Bottom panel.** Pattern of correlations suggests two somewhat general concepts. Heroin and crack-cocaine scores correlate with one another; marijuana and speed scores correlate with one another.

Abilities Criminal justice researchers may express an interest in how well a respondent can do something. For example, a researcher might take convicted burglars past 50 different houses in a suburban area. Half the houses may have been burglarized in the last year. The researcher might ask the burglars to guess which houses were burglarized. Burglars whose responses match more closely what happened score higher on a concept the researcher labels "Ability to Detect Burglarized Households." In general, criminal justice researchers have less interest in measuring abilities than do some other social scientists, such as psychologists.

How Do the Specific Items Connect to the General Concept?   For all these types of attributes, of course, the researcher cannot directly examine the general concept she is proposing. All she knows about the general concept is revealed by the index variable intended to reflect it. Her only source of information about the general concept is what she observes about the specific items making up the index variable. She can examine how the different items correlate with each other. With the Overall Drug Involvement Index introduced in the last chapter, three types of correlation patterns among specific items are possible. (See Figure 7.1.)

All Items Have a Lot in Common with General Index   Recall from the last chapter the discussion of "true scores." Thurstone's model of multiple items suggests that each item's true score reflects two components: features specific to the item, and features it shares in common with other items reflecting the same general concept. [2]

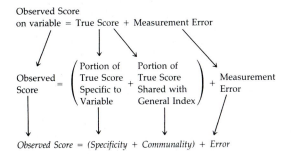

Observed Score
on variable = True Score + Measurement Error

$$\text{Observed Score} = \left(\begin{array}{c} \text{Portion of} \\ \text{True Score} \\ \text{Specific to} \\ \text{Variable} \end{array} + \begin{array}{c} \text{Portion of} \\ \text{True Score} \\ \text{Shared with} \\ \text{General Index} \end{array} \right) + \begin{array}{c} \text{Measurement} \\ \text{Error} \end{array}$$

Observed Score = (Specificity + Communality) + Error

With the four urinalysis variables, the true score of each item could be based largely upon what it shares with the general index of Overall Drug Involvement. The specificity of each item may contribute little to the true score. Thus the true score may derive largely from what the item shares with other items, or its communality. (See top panel in Figure 7.1.) In this case, if an arrestee scores positively on one drug, he is likely to score positively on the other three drug tests; if he scores negatively on one test, he is likely to score negatively on the other tests. Therefore, scores are consistent across items.

Two consequences follow. First, if your purpose is to measure general drug involvement, any of the four items are generally interchangeable with one another; one serves as well as another. Second, the pattern of positive association provides empirical support for your proposed general concept of Overall Drug Involvement. You conclude the positive associations emerge *because* each of these variables reflects your proposed general concept.

All Items Are Largely Specific: Have Little in Common with General Index.   The true score of each item could be based largely on what is specific to the item and the concept reflected by the item. Scores on the specific drug tests in the urinalysis may not reflect Overall Drug Involvement; they may reflect only involvement with the specific drug. They may not tap into or reflect the proposed more general concept (See middle panel in Figure 7.1.) If so, two consequences follow. First, on the mechanical level, if your purpose is to measure general drug involvement, scores are *not* consistent across the specific items. Thus scores on one item are not interchangeable with scores from another item. Second, on the conceptual level the low association between scores on the different items suggests that the proposed general concept of

Overall Drug Involvement may not exist. Or if it does exist, these four items have not reflected it.

Some Communality Across Some Items. True scores of subgroups of items may have something in common with one another, but the communality may not extend across all the items assessed, only some of them. (See bottom panel in Figure 7.1.) For example, scores on the urinalysis for heroin and the urinalysis for crack-cocaine and cocaine may correlate with one another. At the same time, scores for speed and marijuana may correlate with one another. Scores on the former pair of variables may not correlate with scores on the latter pair of variables. Such a pattern of correlation would suggest that a general concept of Overall Drug Involvement may not be warranted. Nevertheless, less general concepts may be justified. You might combine scores on heroin and crack to obtain a "Serious Drug Involvement" index score. You also might sum scores on speed and marijuana to gain scores on an "Entertainment Drug Involvement" Index. In this situation you have consistency across *some* items. Two consequences follow. For the purposes of assessing more general drug use concepts, you can only substitute scores on some items (e.g., crack-cocaine) for scores on some other items (e.g., heroin). Conceptually, you have obtained support for concepts that are more general than the specific items, but the concepts are not as general as originally envisioned.

An Example from Delinquency Research

To pursue the question of consistency across items in more detail, we turn to a study of delinquency done in the late 1970s by three well-known criminal justice researchers: the late Michael Hindelang, Travis Hirschi, and Joe Weis. [3] Box 7.1 outlines the project.

B O X 7.1

Outline of the Seattle Delinquency Study

Males and females enrolled in public school in Seattle, aged 15 to 18, were selected from three different groups: official nondelinquents, those delinquents with only a police record, and those delinquents with a police and a court record. Participants included both African Americans and Whites, and had backgrounds of varying income levels. They were assigned, using a random procedure, to one of four testing conditions. The different testing conditions allowed researchers to explore different aspects of the reliability and validity of delinquency self-report scales. The final participants included about 3,000 males and about 3,000 females.

The basic delinquency self-report questionnaire the participants completed under different conditions included 69 items that covered five categories of activity: official contacts with the criminal justice system (e.g., "Have you ever been questioned as a suspect by the police about some crime?"), serious crimes (e.g., "Have you ever broken into a locked car to get something from it?"), general delinquency (e.g., "Have you ever broken the windows of a school building?"), drug offenses (e.g., "Have you ever gone to school when you were drunk or high on some drugs?"), and school and family offenses (e.g., "Have you ever been suspended or expelled from school?").

The conditions under which the participants completed the self-reports varied, but in all cases an interviewer elicited responses. Some participants answered 22 of the self-report items a second time after a delay of about 45 minutes.

Besides reporting their own delinquency, participants provided information about the delinquency of friends and siblings. The researchers were able to compare the responses of the participants on the self-report questionnaires with police and court records.

They examined *delinquency self-report indexes.* These indexes allow researchers to learn about delinquent involvement by just questioning youth. Researchers have argued extensively about the reliability and validity of scores based on delinquency self-report forms.

The researchers expected that, if delinquency is really *one* underlying construct, not several, individuals who answer positively on some items should answer positively on others. If delinquency is a general tendency, and not something of which there are specific types, then answers to the various items should be generally consistent (as in top panel in Figure 7.1). If it's the other way around, however, and delinquency is *not* a unitary construct, but several different constructs, then you would not expect consistency across items in how people respond. People might give "delinquency" answers for the items concerned with school and parental delinquency, but not give "delinquency" answers to items concerned with drug and alcohol abuse for example (bottom panel in Figure 7.1).

Researchers may assess interitem consistency by examining **split half reliability.** You split the items making up the index into two random halves. You might use a coin toss to assign each item to one group or another. Each group of items is called a split half. You then examine how well total scores from one split half correlate with total scores from the second split half. The average reliability coefficient produced if you split the items into all possible split-halves is indicated by a statistic called **Cronbach's alpha.** It is somewhat like a correlation. A high positive score on Cronbach's alpha suggests that the total based on half the items on a test agrees with the total based on the other half of the items on the test. In short, it suggests that responses across the different items are consistent with one another. Cronbach's alpha is probably the most widely used measure of internal

consistency for data measured at the interval or ratio level of measurement.[1]

Hindelang et al. assessed the consistency of the total delinquency score based on 63 items in their study. They observed alphas above .80, suggesting that responses to the different items were quite consistent. These results suggest one underlying, general dimension of delinquency.

Consumer Guide

As a consumer of research you should look for an internal consistency coefficient if the researcher uses a variable that is a total score based on several items. If the items were measured with an interval level of measurement or better, the consistency coefficient will probably be Cronbach's alpha. The internal consistency coefficient should be at least $+.60$, and preferably above $+.70$. If it is not, the researcher may not have acted appropriately in adding up scores from the different items to get one total index score.

CONSISTENCY OVER TIME

The Problem

When people answer items on a questionnaire or a test researchers want to know how stable or consistent those answers are over time. The **test-retest reliability** of a questionnaire item, set of items, or a test, refers to the consistency or stability of the observed scores provided by persons when asked the same things twice. Unless a long interval has passed between test and retest, researchers should report strong positive correlations between the scores from the test and retest sessions. If they do, they can convince other researchers that their instruments are reliable over time.

---

[1] Other consistency statistics must be used for nominal and ordinal data.

Researchers generally expect that all the items or indexes or tests they use will possess at least a moderate level of test-retest reliability. The specific amount of consistency that the researcher expects depends upon the type of item, and the amount of time that passes between the first and second assessment. Items assessing abilities or personality should be highly reliable if the time passing between the first and second assessment is less than a few years. Personality researchers have reported substantial test-retest correlations between scores on personality inventories taken several decades apart. [4] Items assessing behaviors or attitudes should be highly reliable if a short period passes between testing and retesting. Researchers would expect lower levels of consistency as the period between testing and retesting increases. (See Figure 7.2.)

In terms of measurement theory, when the interval between testing and retesting is short, measurement error alone lowers test-retest correlations. But as the interval increases, measurement errors combine with changes in true scores to lower test-retest correlations.

An Example from Delinquency Research

Delinquency self-report indexes ask about past behavior. If only a short time passes between a testing and retesting occasion, then the major source of unreliability in self-reported delinquency may be problems with the instrument itself. Questions may be unclear or confusing. Response formats, the options available to the person for answering the questions, may be vague or inappropriate. These and related problems contribute to measurement error in the observed scores.

But suppose a longer period passes between the first and second testing session? Then the changes in the individual participants may be a more substantial source of

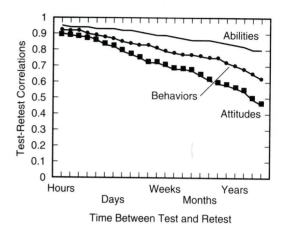

FIGURE 7.2

Examples of some acceptable test-retest reliability coefficients. You expect the coefficients to decrease the longer the period between test and retest sessions. You also expect, all else equal, that measures of attitudes will be less reliable than measures of behaviors, and that measures of behaviors will be less reliable than measures of abilities.

unreliability. "It becomes increasingly likely that actual changes in behavior rather than changes in reporting account for the discrepancies between test and retest results." [5] Measurement errors combine with changes in true scores to cause discrepancies between observed scores at testing and at retesting.

For example, Dave Farrington followed up London boys 2 years after conducting an initial delinquency assessment. He found moderately strong, positive test-retest correlations, around +.60, between the delinquency scores taken 2 years apart. Had he obtained a correlation between test and retest scores that was positive and nearly perfect it would have suggested that the research instrument was invalid. The measuring instrument would have failed to register the changes in delinquency that undoubtedly would have occurred during this period. [6]

In Hindelang et al.'s study they found test-retest correlations of around .90—a very strong positive correlation—for the total score based on 22 delinquency questions that respondents answered twice. Less than a couple of hours passed between testing and retesting.

Consumer Guide

When a researcher uses scales or tests or other paper-and-pencil diagnostics, look for the test-retest correlations to convince yourself that the measuring instruments used provided stable readings. If the items or indexes are tapping reports of past behaviors or attitudes, test-retest correlations of less than .80 should be a source of concern if only a brief interval of a few hours or a few days has passed between testing and retesting. If several days, weeks, or months have passed, test-retest correlations of less than .60 should be a source of concern. Measures of ability should yield high levels of test-retest reliability, above .70, unless an extremely long period has passed between testing and retesting.

CONSISTENCY OVER RATERS

The Problem

Sometimes the variables of interest to you are not readily available from paper-and-pencil forms, archival records, or other easily accessed forms. Sometimes you must *extract variables* from a setting or a set of records or another source. You might be interested in how often the theme of mercy arises in transcripts of mock jury deliberations. You would need to have people rate these transcripts for this theme, or count occurrences of specified phrases. We will discuss this process of content analysis in Chapter 15. Or, alternatively, you might want people to observe and rate the behaviors of inmates in a crowded jail. We will discuss the process of behavioral observation in Chapter 15. As a general rule,

whenever you have raters or coders working with research materials, and those raters or coders are making *judgments*, and not simply transcribing, you want to know about inter-rater reliability: the extent to which different raters rate the same materials similarly.

Discrepancies between observed scores generated by different raters can arise from individual differences in how raters do their work. Some raters may work more carefully than others. Some raters may just give higher ratings on some variables than other raters. *In terms of measurement theory, observed scores on a variable are reliable if the measurement errors arising from the differences between raters make up only a minor portion of the observed score.* If the effect of these individual differences is sizable the researcher would conclude that the measurement procedure is *unreliable.*

To avoid unreliable observed scores, researchers can pursue two avenues. First, they can train raters or observers. Training procedures help standardize how raters judge and code the stimuli in question. Second, they can construct more specific rating items on rating scales, or change how raters use the items or scales.

An Example from the Urban Residential Environment

I have participated in several projects assessing physical and social features of street blocks in the urban residential environment. [e.g., 7, 8] We focused on a range of features such as litter, graffiti, extent of abandoned housing, number of people on the street, vacant lots on the street, and so on. Information on these features was not available from archival city records or census data, so we needed to visit the blocks and gather the information on-site. Rating forms were developed, and raters were trained. Pairs of raters traveled to each block. Each rater, once on the block, walked up and down the block and completed his or her rating form *independently*. The two raters on a block did not converse during the actual rating. When the forms were coded, we could examine how well the two raters agreed in their ratings of features on a block. We have been able to obtain high levels of inter-rater agreement across a wide range of variables.

Consumer Guide

For any variables that required ratings, judgments, or observations, measures of interobserver agreement should be reported. The appropriate statistic to assess degree of interobserver agreement will depend upon the level of measurement. For variables assessed at interval or ratio levels of measurement, the **intraclass correlation coefficient** is one widely used coefficient for interrater reliability. It reports the percentage overlap between scores based on one rater, and scores based on a second (or third or fourth) rater. [9] Inter-rater reliability is marginally acceptable if intraclass correlations exceed + .60; preferably they should be above + 70.

Ideally, two raters will rate *all* the cases studied on all the variables used. If they do, then your reliability coefficients will be comprehensive. There are research situations, however, where the researcher may not have the needed resources for a comprehensive assessment of interrater reliability. She may be forced to limit the ratings by pairs of raters to a subsample of the cases. If only a subsample of cases is rated by two judges, the subsample should be chosen at random. (See Chapter 10 on sampling for more details on the reasons behind random sampling.) In addition to being random, the subsample should be sizable, comprising at least 20 percent of the full sample.

Beware interrater reliabilities based on simple correlations or percentage agreement between two raters. Such statistics fail to control for agreement that may occur between two raters simply due to chance.

Reliability in Participant Observer Research

In participant observation, discussed in detail in Chapter 11, the researcher spends much time with participants in a setting. She attempts to make sense of the ongoing dynamics in a situation using terms meaningful to the participants. The researcher not only participates in ongoing settings, but also keeps extensive field notes about experiences and conversations. She then attempts to develop a theoretical framework to explain the connections between different features of the setting or settings.

A typical criticism of participant observation research is that it is *low on reliability*. This is a problem of interrater or interobserver reliability. "Problems of internal reliability in ethnographic studies raise the question of whether, within a single study, multiple observers will agree." [10] In ethnographic research interrater reliability reflects "the extent to which sets of meanings held by multiple observers are sufficiently congruent so that they describe phenomena in the same way and arrive at the same conclusions about them."

Ethnographic researchers have defended themselves against the claim that their studies have low reliability. They point out that they have available many tools and procedures to insure that results are as reliable as possible. [10, 11] Here are some of the steps participant observer researchers can take to assess and maximize reliability of their findings. [10]

- Use **low inference descriptors**. These are categories of inference used by ethnographers phrased in precise, concrete terminology. Low inference descriptors include verbatim transcripts of conversations or specific detailed narratives of occurrences. They provide a record of what happened, as precisely as it can be reconstructed.

- Use *multiple researchers*. If it is possible for more than one researcher to serve as a participant observer then reliability can be increased dramatically. Each researcher can constantly cross-check with the other on their accounts of what happened and what it might mean.

- Enlist **participant researchers**. The researcher can seek reactions to her narratives and analyses from those who are members of the setting. Each can be asked to view transcripts or react to analyses of events that have transpired.

- Seek *peer examinations*. Researchers can seek corroboration from researchers working in comparable settings. They may use presentations and analyses from fieldworkers in other settings. Or, if several comparable sites are being examined simultaneously, as occurred with the Northwestern Reactions to Crime project, findings from different settings can be integrated and consolidated, as Aaron Podolefsky did. [12] Finally, when the researcher seeks to publish findings in a journal or scholarly book, other researchers in the field examine the data and conclusions for flaws.

- *Mechanically recorded data* from tape recorders or photos or archives can be maintained as a record that can be checked by other researchers.

In sum, the qualitative researcher has available to her a variety of techniques to ensure high reliability of her scientific analyses. A priori, it is a mistake to assume that the reliability of qualitative research efforts will be lower than the reliability of more quantitatively oriented techniques.

SUMMARY OF MAIN POINTS

- Reliability is concerned with the replicability or consistency of findings.
- If several variables tap into and reflect the same general concept, indexes based on those variables will have a *high level of internal consistency*.
- If a measuring instrument yields almost the same score in two different testing sessions with a short interval between test sessions, scores resulting from the instrument have good *test-retest reliability*.
- If a rating task results in two or more observers rating several stimuli similarly, then the resulting outputs from the rating task have good *inter-rater reliability*.
- Ethnographic research does not necessarily produce results with low levels of reliability.
- Ethnographic researchers have available to them several tools with which they can assess and increase the reliability of their findings.

GLOSSARY OF KEY WORDS

Cronbach's alpha
intraclass correlation coefficient
low inference descriptors
participant researchers
split half reliability
test-retest reliability

REFERENCES

1. Campbell, D., Fiske, D. (1959) Convergent and discriminant validation by the multitrait-multimethod matrix. *Psychological Bulletin 56*, 81–105.

2. Thurstone, L. I. (1947) *Multiple factor analysis and the expansion of the vector model*, University of Chicago, Press, Chicago.

3. Hindelang, M. J., Hirschi, T., and Weis, J. G. (1981) *Measuring delinquency*, Sage, Beverly Hills, CA.

4. Hogan, R., DeSoto, C. B., and Solano, C. (1977) Traits, tests, and personality research. *American Psychologist 33*, 255–264.

5. Hindelang, M. J., Hirschi, T., and Weis, J. G. (1981) *Measuring delinquency*, Sage, Beverly Hills, CA, p. 79.

6. Farrington, D. P. (1986) Stepping stones to adult criminal careers. In Olweus, D., Block, J., and Yarrow, M. R. (eds.), *Development of antisocial and prosocial behavior*, Academic Press, New York, pp. 359–384.

7. Taylor, R. B., Shumaker, S. A., and Gottfredson, S. D. (1985) Neighborhood-level links between physical features and local sentiments: Deterioration, fear of crime, and confidence. *Journal of Architectural Planning and Research 2*, 261–275.

8. Perkins, D. D., Meeks, J. W., and Taylor, R. B. (1992) The Physical environment of street blocks and resident perceptions of crime and disorder: Implications for theory and measurement. *Journal of Environmental Psychology 12*, 21–34.

9. Shrout, P. E., and Fleiss, J. L. (1979) Intraclass correlations: Uses in assessing rater reliability. *Psychological Bulletin 86*, 420–428.

10. LeCompte, M. D., and Goetz, J. P. (1982) Problems of reliability and validity in ethnographic research. *Review of Educational Research 52*, 31–60.

11. Goetz, J. P., and LeCompte, M. D. (1981) Ethnographic research and the problem of data reduction. *Anthropology and Education Quarterly 12*, 51–70.

12. Podolefsky, A. (1983) *Case studies in community crime prevention*, Charles C. Thomas, Springfield, IL.

CHAPTER 8

INTERNAL VALIDITY

Put most simply, validity addresses the question: Am I measuring what I think I am measuring? [1]

OBJECTIVES

Sometimes criminal justice researchers use measures whose connection with concepts or other measures are not clear. They conduct validity assessments to learn about those connections.

In the last chapter you learned how researchers establish that their measures are reliable. A procedure is reliable if someone else using the same procedures in the same situation would produce outputs or scores that were nearly identical. Nonetheless, researchers need to know more than this about their measures if they want to convince others that their research is high quality.

ORGANIZING THE VALIDITY QUESTIONS

What Variable Do I Need to Worry About?

In Terms of Validity, Think of Three Classes of Measures   Remember that variables function as indicators of concepts. When you are thinking about validity of measures, you may divide variables into three broad categories: those whose validity has been established through extensive empirical work, those whose validity is simply not questioned by

most researchers, and those whose validity the researcher must establish.

Validity Has Been Established   There are some variables you might use in a research project whose ability to function as an indicator of a concept in a broad range of situations has already been established. For example, you might be conducting a survey of students' victimization experiences while on campus. The Department of Justice has funded extensive work on how to ask about different aspects of victimization experiences. This work, discussed in Chapter 12 on survey research, has documented that reports of victimization incidents provided by respondents in the National Crime Survey (NCS) connect closely with other sources of information about these incidents, such as police reports. Therefore, if in your own research you were to use measures and procedures similar to those used in the NCS, you would not need to establish the validity of the questions and procedures you use. The validity of these measures has already been established.

Validity Generally Accepted   You also need not worry about the validity of measures whose use as an indicator of a concept is widely accepted. People routinely report their age at their last birthday, and researchers allow that these responses are correct or close to correct most of the time. Prisons routinely report daily populations, the number of inmates currently in the facility. Again, researchers allow that the observed scores generated by prison administrators on this variable are largely correct most of the time.

Validity Not Established   It is the third class of measures of interest to us here: those variables and measurement procedures whose validity has not yet been established. If this is the case, we do not know what correct inferences we can make about our measures. The **process of establishing validity** is the process of learning what we can correctly infer from observed scores on a variable.

In our hypothetical community policing example, last discussed in Chapter 5, we discussed the variable "Satisfaction with Being a Community-Policing Officer." Officers trained for these duties reported how pleased they were with this assignment on a 10-point scale ranging from "Extremely Dissatisfied" to "Extremely Satisfied."

You might wonder: Do the observed scores for this variable reflect how pleased the officers *really* were? Did the scores reflect satisfaction? Or did they reflect another concept? You might think of several factors related to the variable itself, or to the assessment procedure, that could "disconnect" the observed scores from the intended concept, and thus make your inferences based on these scores incorrect. You want to know if you measured the intended concept.

For example, the testing situation may not have been anonymous. Participants, fearing loss of confidentiality, may have been concerned that their scores would be communicated to their supervisors. This may have led them to report more satisfaction than they felt. Thus everyone may have reported observed scores on satisfaction that were higher than their true scores.

Another possibility is that only those officers anxious about their job security may have been concerned about supervisor reactions to their reported satisfaction with the CPO role. Therefore, high scores on satisfaction may, across the entire group of officers, reflect two concepts: satisfaction and job insecurity. In sum, in assessment situations, features of the assessment procedure, or the variables themselves, may prevent the variable from functioning as an indicator of the intended concept.

A second source of concern may arise because you wished to make theoretical connections between the concept of satisfaction and other concepts. For example, when asked why does it matter if the officer is satisfied with the role of a community police officer, you might have said something like this: "I think if officers are more satisfied, they will do a better job. They will be more motivated to resolve residents' complaints, be more involved with the community, and generally be more effective." In short you connected CPO role satisfaction with different aspects of CPO job effectiveness. You expected effectiveness might be an outcome of high satisfaction levels.

But is your expectation warranted? Unless you have independent measures of effectiveness, and have observed strong positive correlations between satisfaction scores and effectiveness scores, you may not be justified in making such connections. The process of validating measures involves collecting information so you can see if your proposed connections between different concepts are justified.

Validity Asks About Two Kinds of Questions

Establishing the validity of a measure involves many questions. These can be reduced to two types of questions (see Figure 8.1). [2, 3] One type asks about *practical* matters: "What can be inferred about other behavior?" [3] It is "**validity for decision making**." [2, p. 204] These validity questions ask about connections between the variable in question and other important behaviors or outputs. Asking if satisfaction with the CPO role leads to more effective community policing represents this type of question. A second type asks about *scientific* matters: "What can be inferred about what is being measured by the test." [3] It is "**validity for understanding**." [2, p. 204] You want to know how accurately and completely the observed scores represent the concept(s) to which they refer. Asking if the CPO satisfaction question measures job insecurity instead of, or in addition to, satisfaction exemplifies this type of question. We now examine each type of question, and its related validities.

VALIDITY FOR DECISION MAKING

Criterion-Related Validities

What Is a Criterion? A **criterion** is an outcome you seek to predict that meets three requirements. [4] First, it is "relevant to some important goal of the individual, the organization, or society" (p. 746). This **relevancy requirement** stipulates people agree that the goal in question is important, and that the measures used for gauging progress toward that goal are acceptable.

Criminal justice contains many important outcomes of broad interest to individuals, organizations, and the larger society: whether arrestees appear at trial; whether probationers complete their sentence without re-arrest; whether individuals, who have been previously arrested, get arrested a second or subsequent times; whether a defendant is convicted; and whether individuals are victimized, to name just a few. We would read-

If validity of measure used not yet established, or not widely accepted, you want to assess:

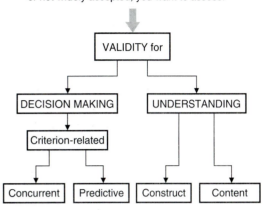

FIGURE 8.1
Taxonomy of Types of Validity Questions

ily agree that such goals, and increasing or decreasing scores on these goals as appropriate, are important for the criminal justice system and the larger society.

The second requirement is that the measure of the criterion used be *reliable*. [4] This **reliability requirement** specifies that the measure used should possess a high degree of reliability. If you were to measure the same variable at different periods of time, or with different raters, using methods that were roughly similar to one another, you should obtain comparable scores. For example, your criterion measure of drug use may rely on an analysis of hair samples. Unless the testing procedures could reliably produce scores from the hair samples, the variable could not be used as a criterion.

Usually the reliability with which you can measure a criterion limits the size of your validity coefficient. In most cases you are not able to obtain a validity coefficient that exceeds your reliability coefficient. But this limit depends upon the specific type of measure you use to gauge reliability, and may be exceeded in some cases. [4]

The third requirement is that your criterion measure must be **practical**: "available, plausible, and acceptable to those who will want to use it for decisions" (p. 746). For example, if you are trying to predict an offender's arrest history, researchers and policy makers alike would agree that it would be more acceptable, for decision-making purposes, to use actual arrest records rather than the individual's recall of his arrest history. [5, 6]

Choosing a Criterion For A Particular Measure May Vary in Difficulty   Choosing a criterion for a variable is sometimes difficult; sometimes easy. Consider our running example in community policing. You have obtained information from officers trained for community policing about their satisfaction with the job. You expect that this satisfaction will relate to actual job performance. But how specifically will you assess performance? You have many possibilities. Here are a few:

- You could survey all block leaders who have had contact with the CPOs, and ask them to rate each officer with whom they have worked on job effectiveness.
- You could follow officers while on duty and record aspects of officer behavior such as time spent with community residents, number of complaints investigated, number of establishments visited, and so on.
- You could obtain officer logs and code key items from those logs such as number of contacts initiated with other public agencies (e.g., sanitation to arrange trucks) to solve resident problems (e.g., trash filled lot).

Choosing a criterion is complicated by the fact that you do not know beforehand whether each of these possible items meets the relevance, reliability, and practicality requirements.

In sum, sometimes it will be clear to you what variable to choose as criterion for a vari-

able, and you will have a good idea beforehand whether the criterion meets the three requirements. Nevertheless, it also often happens that it is not clear to you which variable you should choose as a criterion; you do not know a priori how each possible criterion scores on the three requirements.

Criteria Can Have Many Facets   Sometimes a criterion can be captured with one variable. Racial disparity in prison sentence length served is a case in point. You examine the difference in average sentence length, for one type of crime, between (e.g.) Whites and African Americans. In other instances, however, a criterion may itself have several facets; it can be multidimensional. [4] In our community-policing example you want to prove that officer satisfaction with being a CPO is important because it relates to how effectively the officer carries out that role. To investigate effectiveness you might ask block leaders several questions about the CPOs with whom they have had contact. Yet when you create an index based on answers to all these different questions about effectiveness, you may find that all the different questions about effectiveness do not "hang together" and correlate highly with one another. They do not produce a sufficiently high coefficient alpha of internal consistency, or a sufficiently high split-half reliability coefficient. In short, there may be more than one dimension to the criterion you are investigating—effectiveness as revealed by leaders' answers to questions. This occurs often.

What Is the Time Frame?   You examine **criterion-related validities** when you wish to infer from an observed score on a variable a case's "most probable standing on another variable called a criterion." [7] You want to know if observed scores on the variable in hand can serve as an acceptable proxy for scores on the criterion variable. To investigate these validities you may correlate scores on the variable and the criterion and generate scatterplots, or you may cross-tabulate the items, generating cross-tabulation tables.[1] These examinations will generate **validity coefficients** stating how closely observed scores on the variable match observed scores on the criterion variable. For example, you may use block leader's overall effectiveness ratings of different community policing officers as a criterion for officer satisfaction with the CPO role. You create a scatterplot and find a strong positive correlation between the two variables (e.g., $r = .64$). This result would suggest you could use officer satisfaction scores as an acceptable proxy for effectiveness.

Concurrent You have observed scores on two variables: the variable of central interest, and the variable that will serve as a criterion for the variable of central interest. If you correlate scores on the variable of central interest and the variable serving as a criterion, and both variables refer to phenomena occurring in roughly the same period, then the correlation coefficient will be a **concurrent, criterion-related validity coefficient**. The central observed measure of interest, and the criterion variable, both refer to phenomena occurring at roughly the same time. So you are examining a *concurrent* criterion-related validity. For example, officer satisfaction with the CPO role, and block leaders' ratings of CPO effectiveness both may be gathered at roughly the same point in time (see Figure 8.2).

Predictive Alternatively, the criterion variable may refer to phenomena that will occur later. The behaviors, or attitudes, or attri-

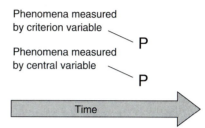

Concurrent, criterion-related validities: Both variables measure phenomena from same time frame

FIGURE 8.2

butes measured by the criterion variable occur *after* the attributes measured by the central variable of interest. You can use scores on the central variable of interest to *predict* scores on the criterion variable. In this instance you are assessing a **predictive, criterion-related validity coefficient**. For example, block leader's ratings of CPO effectiveness may be collected a year after you have asked officers to report their satisfaction with the CPO role (see Figure 8.3).

Predictive, criterion-related validity is a central concern in criminal justice research. (See Boxes 8.1 and 8.2.) Policy makers use information about an offender, criminal background, and current circumstances, to predict that person's future course of behavior. Successful prediction in these circumstances

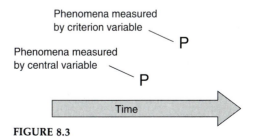

Predictive, criterion-related validities: Phenomena measured by criterion variable occur later than phenomena measured by central variable

FIGURE 8.3

---

[1] You may have to use a different procedure if one or both of your variables were measured at the ordinal level of measurement.

B O X 8.1

Predictive Validity
and Failure on Parole

Parole guidelines have been in use in the criminal justice system, in varying forms, since the 1920s. [8; see 9 for a review] Using the criminal history and characteristics of the convicted felon, the *risk prediction devices* attempt to predict the risk that the felon will fail on parole if released to parole supervision. The releasee may fail on parole by failing to abide by the parole guidelines, or by committing a new crime while on parole and being arrested for it. With such guidelines parole officials can release from prison those individuals likely to succeed on parole.

The parole guidelines used by the U.S. Parole Commission develop a total score, called a *Salient Factor Score*, based on the following items:

- offender's prior criminal convictions;
- offender's prior criminal commitments for longer than 30 days;
- age at time of the last offense;
- how long the offender was at liberty since the last confinement;
- whether the offender was on parole, probation, or escape status at the time of the instant offense; and
- whether the prisoner had a record of heroin dependence. [10; see also 11, 12]

Based on their scores on these items, the offenders are placed into one of four categories, where A represents the lowest risk of recidivism and D represents the highest risk of recidivism. The U.S. Parole Commission has verified that those who have higher scores on the Salient Factor Score are *less* likely to fail on parole. Figure 8.4 shows the predictive validity of the salient

factor score. Scholars have debated if such prediction instruments should play major roles in criminal justice policy making. [13]

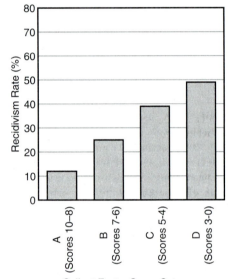

FIGURE 8.4

Data from the U.S. Parole Commission showed that those who have higher scores on the Salient Factor Score are *less* likely, in the future, to fail on parole. (*Source*: Hoffman, P. (no date). Predicting criminality. National Institute of Justice Crime File Study Guide. Washington, DC: National Institute of Justice.) *Note*: Recidivism was defined as "any new commitment of 60 days or more including a trip to prison for parole violation within a 2-year followup period." [14]

is critical to an efficient use of criminal justice resources, and minimal government intrusion into the lives of individuals.

Assumptions Behind Predictive Validity Studies The logic of predictive validation makes several assumptions about conditions during data collection. It only makes sense to expect that scores on your central variable of interest will predict scores on the criterion variable if these assumptions are met. See Table 8.1.

TABLE 8.1
Assumptions Behind Predictive Validation Studies

1. Conditions under which the predictive, criterion-related validity coefficients were obtained will remain after the study is completed; conditions will not change rapidly. "Rapidly changing conditions may limit the usefulness of a predictive study."

2. "The criterion possesses validity." The criterion measure chosen is appropriate and of high quality.

3. The cases in the predictive study are similar to the larger group of cases you wish to discuss.

4. The number of cases participating in the predictive validity study was adequate.

Source. American Psychological Association. (1974). *Standards for educational and psychological tests.* Washington, DC: American Psychological Association, p. 27.

VALIDITY FOR UNDERSTANDING

The remaining types of validity you can examine concern themselves with the scientific features of the measured variables. Whereas criterion-related validities underpin accurate, practical decision making, construct and content validities underpin accurate theorizing about relationships between variables and theoretical constructs. [2]

Content Validity

Questions of **content validity** are concerned with the relationship between the content of the variable used to generate observed scores, and the content of the domain that variable seeks to represent. These questions ask: "Have I covered all the bases?" In other words, you want to know if the observed scores on the variable of interest reflect the observed scores you would obtain had you used a different variable to measure the same domain of interest.

Content validity questions are perhaps clearest in cases where you are devising a test to measure an area of knowledge. If you are constructing a test of basic math skills, you will ask about addition, subtraction, multiplication, and division. You will be sure to ask about all four operations. The content of the items reflects the content of the larger domain.

In the last chapter we discussed the research on delinquency self-report scales conducted by Hindelang, Hirschi, and Weis. They used an inventory of 60+ different delinquency items in one version of the self-report form. Delinquency is reflected in many different types of behavior: status offenses, drug or alcohol use, violence toward others, vandalism, defying authority figures, larceny, and so on. Their self-report form possessed content validity to the extent that the items included tapped the different elements in the domain of delinquent behavior.

Defining Domain of Interest Assessing content validity requires two steps. First, you define the domain of interest: What is the population of items in which I am interested? In a test of math skills of a certain level, the performance domain is finite and unambiguous. Most would agree on the important topics to be covered. With delinquency, the total set of behaviors is less well defined.

People may be less likely to agree on the total set of relevant behaviors. People may disagree on whether truancy, or talking back to a parent, should be defined as delinquent behaviors. The domain is less objectively defined. Thus, the domains measured by variables may range from clear-cut to vague.

Domain of interest

Finite, unambiguous ⟷ Less objectively defined

Nevertheless, whatever its clarity, the first step in addressing content validity is to define as clearly as possible the domain of interest.

Sampling from Each Part of the Domain   In the second step you explain how you sampled or selected particular items from the domain of interest. You want to make the case that the particular items selected adequately represent the entire domain of items. You will learn more about sampling in Chapter 10. You want the final items in your measure to represent fully the possible items in each segment of the domain of interest (see Figure 8.5).

Face Validity   Some methods texts discuss **face validity**. The idea here is that you can get an impression of content validity simply by examining the assessment procedure and the items included. Thus, according to these texts, you could make inferences about the content validity of a delinquency self-report form simply by examining the items themselves, and deciding if they appear relevant to delinquent behaviors.

Face validity, however, is *not necessarily related to content validity*, or any other type of validity. [15] An item, or a portion of an assessment procedure, may appear relevant to the intended concept, but not be so. You gauge content validity by deciding how thoroughly and carefully the researcher completed a specific set of operations—defining

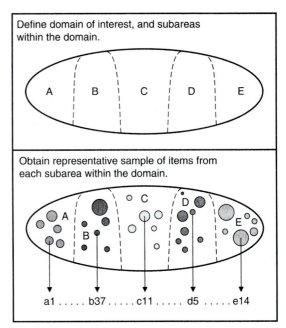

FIGURE 8.5
Establishing content validity requires two steps. First (top panel) you define the domain of interest, and the subareas within the domain. The domain may not be clear-cut. Second (bottom panel) you select representative items from each subarea within the domain.

the domain and its subareas adequately, and sampling properly from subareas of the domain. Judgments of face validity may be *unrelated* to any important validity information.

Construct Validity: Figuring Out the Meaning of the Measure

Construct validity applies when the investigator wants a measure of a characteristic which is deemed important by somebody but for which there is no already available indicator. The entity being validated is a series of measurement operations [2, p. 203].

From a theoretical vantage point **construct validity** represents the most important validity question. The process of construct validation asks: "Does the measure I am using of a particular concept actually reflect the intended concept? Or, does it reflect another related concept? Or does it reflect the intended concept *and* something else?" In short, the process of construct validation is concerned with establishing the *meaning* of the measure being investigated. [16] Whenever you evaluate observed scores on a variable with reference to a specified construct, i.e., whenever you accept a set of observed scores as an indicator of a concept, you are implying that the variable already has construct validity.

The process of establishing construct validity for a variable may be required for two reasons. [17] First, for any single observable variable there may be no single *primary* observable criterion against which it can be validated. Unless you can establish the meaning of scores on the variable through a concurrent or predictive criterion-related validity study, you *do* want to know about the construct validity of the observed scores.

Questions put to arrestees about recent drug use, therefore, may not need to have their construct validity examined. You would simply see how observed scores on these questions correlated with urinalysis or assays of hair samples testing for drug usage. If the concurrent criterion-related validity coefficients were strong and positive, you need not worry further about construct validity.

There is a second reason to investigate construct validity. For any observable variable chosen to reflect or tap a concept, one can always ask: Is the observable variable *in fact* a valid indicator of the underlying construct in question and *only* that underlying construct?

Evidence of Construct Validity Accumulates Slowly In contrast to evidence of criterion-related validity, evidence of the construct validity of a measure accumulates over a series of results. [18] To judge that a specific measure has construct validity, you want to see that it correlates strongly with other measures of the intended concept, and that it does *not* correlate with measures of separate concepts. [19] You do not judge the construct validity of a measure based on one single result; you look for a pattern of results.

The Steps in the Process Let's go back to our measure of officer satisfaction with the CPO role. You want to convince yourself that the measure *does* reflect the intended concept. You do *not* want it to reflect unrelated concepts such as general satisfaction with being a police officer, feelings of job insecurity, psychological well-being, or sociability. You want it to reflect the intended concept and just the intended concept.

Hypotheses About Connections Between Measures and Concepts The first step in your examination of construct validity is to predict connections between the intended concept and observed scores on the variable of interest. You may approach this in a *deductive* fashion, following Einstein's logic of scientific inquiry, or in an *inductive* fashion, following Holmes's logic. The process of construct validation should, ideally, include both inductive and deductive components. [2]

If you proceed deductively, observed scores on the variable reflecting your theoretical construct represent your independent variable, and observed scores on different variables serve as your dependent variables. Given your understanding of the construct in your theory, you make hypotheses about a range of variables. For example, you might hypothesize that officers more satisfied with the CPO role will be more involved with the local citizenry; they might contact more citizens during a week, or attend a greater number of community meetings during a month.

Your hypothesis suggests empirical associations to look for. This aspect of construct validation is similar to standard theory validation through hypothesis testing.

Construct validation is distinct from hypothesis testing, however, when you proceed inductively. You start by examining how scores on the variable of interest correlate, or do not correlate, with other variables. Before making explicit hypotheses about what construct your observed scores on the variable of interest represent, you would examine the pattern of correlations among different variables. In short, you may and should do a certain amount of inductive "fishing around" for empirical relationships, and after this exploration begin to offer hypotheses about what concept you think the specific variable reflects. [2]

For example, besides your measure of satisfaction with the CPO role, you may have the following additional variables:

- *Efficiency ratings*, completed by supervisory officers, of the officers assigned to CPO duty. These ratings were completed before officers received the CPO assignment.
- *Trainer ratings* of officer interest. Trainers who conducted the CPO workshops completed ratings of the officers' level of interest in the workshop material.
- *Workshop performance scores*. At the conclusion of the CPO training workshop officers completed a final examination that in-

cluded written exams and role-playing exercises.

You examine the correlations between these variables and your central measure of interest, satisfaction with the CPO role. You observe the correlations shown in Table 8.2.

You see that satisfaction with the CPO role does correlate strongly with how well the officers did during CPO training ($r_{13} = .67$; $r_{14} = .71$). Yet the CPO satisfaction variable does not correlate strongly with overall efficiency ratings completed by supervisors before the training began ($r_{12} = .20$). So it does not seem that officers more satisfied with the CPO role are just the better officers.

Gather Data and Analyze   Once you have examined some actual correlations between variables, and developed hypotheses about the meaning of the variable of interest, you collect data to test explicitly these hypotheses. For example, after the officers have been working for a few months, you could contact block leaders and get them to rate officers. You could examine officer logs to see how many community meetings they have attended, or the number of different community groups they have contacted. Once you have the data in hand, you analyze it, and modify your hypotheses as needed. You might find the correlations shown in Table 8.3.

TABLE 8.2

Correlations Between Satisfaction with CPO Role and Other Variables

Variable	1	2	3	4
1 Satisfaction with CPO role	1.00			
2 Efficiency ratings	.20	1.00		
3 Trainer ratings	.67	.31	1.00	
4 Workshop performance scores	.71	.18	.61	1.00

Note: Author-generated correlations for 100 officers.

T A B L E 8.3

**Correlations Between Satisfaction with CPO Role
and Additional Measures of CPO Performance**

Variable	1	2	3	4
1 Satisfaction with CPO role	1.00			
2 N of Community Groups Contacted	.52	1.00		
3 N of Community Meetings Attended	.64	.58	1.00	
4 Effectiveness ratings by block leaders	− .03	.09	.13	1.00

Note: Author-generated correlations for 100 officers. Data for variables collected after first 3 months of officers' CPO assignment.

It appears that officer satisfaction does relate to CPO activity, as reflected in number of meetings attended (r_{13} = .64) and number of local groups contacted (r_{12} = .52). It does not correlate, however, with local leaders' perceptions of officer effectiveness (r_{14} = − .03). This pattern of results leads to further questions.

Successive Verification In the third step of construct validation you address the questions raised as a result of your initial hypothesis testing. You modify, elaborate, or eliminate your hypotheses as needed, gathering the appropriate data along the way. The correlations shown in Table 8.3 imply that officer satisfaction as a CPO does correlate with level of CPO activity. This makes sense, given what concept you think your satisfaction measure is reflecting. Officers more satisfied with being a CPO will work harder at it, and put more energy into the assignment. This energy translates into more group contacts and more meeting attendance.

At the same time the data in Table 8.3 raise questions. You had hoped that more satisfied community-policing officers also would be more effective at community policing. Yet the low correlations between block leaders' perceptions of CPO effectiveness, and officer satisfaction as a CPO, suggest your hypothesis may not be empirically supported (r_{14} = − .03). But before discarding the hypothesis, you might want to know more about the measure of effectiveness you have used. Do local leaders' perceptions of the effectiveness agree with the perceptions of the local citizenry? Are leaders' perceptions of effectiveness stable over time (high test-retest reliability), or are they variable? You also might wonder if it is possible that there are two general aspects of effectiveness, one reflected in contact and meeting activity, and the other reflected in local leaders' ratings. These questions can be answered only through additional research. Construct validation is often an *iterative* process. Eventually, after one or more iterations, you may be able to lay aside all or almost all plausible alternate explanations of the "meaning" of the measure used.

In short, the construct validation process leads to new suggestions about the variable in question and other related variables. These questions lead to suggestions for further research. Through this process you gain a better understanding of the usefulness of the variable in question as an indicator of the intended concept.

Construct Validity and Other Validities
Robert Hogan suggests that all validity investigations, whatever their form, are different aspects of construct validation, or different steps in the process of construct validation. [16] In other words, the results of investigations of criterion-related validities, or content validity, have implications for the meaning

the researcher attributes to the measure being investigated. Thus they too can be seen as part of the construct validation process.

SOME LAST POINTS

Validity Is Not Measured Directly

To answer validity questions, you examine the correlations between the observed scores on the central variable of interest, and observed scores on other variables. Remember: We cannot measure concepts; we can only measure indicators of concepts. As a result of examining these correlations between variables, you will conclude that the particular type of validity examined is adequate, marginal, or unsatisfactory. Validity is not itself directly measured. Rather, it is an inference or judgment that you make based on a collection of correlation coefficients. [3]

Validity Is Specific

Your investigations of validity are always grounded in a specific situation: particular cases produced observed scores on particular variables in a specific time and place. This does not mean that the same level of validity will obtain in another place, at another time, using different variables, or with different cases.

You may find, for example, that a bail guideline instrument has excellent predictive criterion-related validity for a rural sample of predominantly Hispanic arrestees in Arizona. [20] (See Box 8.2.) You may find that it correctly predicts, 75 percent of the time, whether an arrestee will fail to appear at trial due to absconding or rearrest, or if he will appear at trial. You should not, therefore, conclude that the same level of predictive, criterion-related validity would obtain for a very different sample, or for a different time. Five years hence your instrument may pre-

---

Bail Guidelines

Bail guidelines seek to predict, from the information available when a person is arrested, whether that individual, if released on bail, will fail to appear at trial due to absconding or rearrest. [20, 21, 22] John Goldkamp and other researchers have developed bail guidelines for several jurisdictions. The specific items used, and how they are weighted, vary slightly from jurisdiction to jurisdiction. He has found that items addressing the following types of issues predict the likelihood that arrestees would appear at trial: community ties, length of residence in the community, lack of prior criminal history, lack of juvenile history, employment, and no history of alcohol or drug abuse. [21] Current use of drugs appears to help slightly in predicting subsequent rearrest if released. [23]

---

dict less successfully for this population. And it may not produce the same level of prediction when used with an urban, predominantly white pool of arrestees in Troy, NY. In short, you should not conclude that the same level of predictive, criterion-related validity would obtain for a very different sample, or for a different time. Answers to other types of validity questions are similarly specific.

Thinking About the Validity of Studies

So far in this chapter you have focused solely on the idea of the validity of *measures*. Once a researcher has established the validity of the different measures she has used there is still an additional internal validity issue. She needs to establish that the conclusions she has drawn, based on the empirical connections she has observed, between the measures she has used, are *interpreted* correctly.

In other words, the researcher needs to ask herself: are there alternate explanations other than the ones I have proposed, that are tenable, that could explain the pattern of findings? To establish the validity of the *conclusions* of the study the researcher would need to convince the reader that other plausible explanations have been considered and rejected.

Every study contains potential sources of invalidity, or **threats to validity**. A threat to validity is a factor at work in an investigation to which the researcher has not attended; it forms the basis for a markedly different inter-pretation of results than the one forwarded by the researcher. Thus, in every study, the researcher needs to pay attention to potential threats to validity, and do her best to eliminate them. Only after they have been eliminated can she establish **conclusion validity**: that her conclusions based on her data are valid and cannot be undermined by plausible competing explanations of findings. The process for establishing this depends on the particular type of study and is discussed in Chapter 13 on experiments, quasi-experiments, and evaluation research.

SUMMARY OF MAIN POINTS

- Validity investigations examine the meaning of the specific variables used in a study.
- You worry about the validity of a specific measure if its validity has not yet been established, or is not widely accepted.
- Broadly speaking, there are two types of validity questions: validity for decision making, or practical validity questions; and validity for understanding, or scientific validity questions.
- A criterion is an outcome variable you seek to predict that meets the relevance, reliability, and practicality requirements.
- Criterion-related validities examine the relationship between scores on the central measure of interest and scores on a criterion.
- A criterion-related validity may be predictive or concurrent.
- Content validity questions examine the relationship between the content of the variable used and the content of the domain represented by the variable.
- Face validity may not be relevant to content validity, or any other types of validity.
- Construct validity investigations clarify connections between the central variable of interest, the intended concept, and other concepts.

SUGGESTED READING

Carmines, E. G., and Zeller, R. A. (1979). *Reliability and validity assessment*. Beverly Hills, CA: Sage. You will find this an excellent introductory volume. The authors discuss all the standard topics in a clear, concise, traditional fashion. Chapter 2 covers validity.

GLOSSARY OF KEY WORDS

conclusion validity
concurrent, criterion-related validity coefficient
construct validity
content validity
criterion
criterion-related validities
domain
face validity
predictive, criterion-related validity coefficient

process of establishing validity
relevancy requirement
reliability requirement
threats to validity
validity coefficients
validity for decision making
validity for understanding

REFERENCES

1. Baker, T. L. (1988) *Doing social research*, McGraw Hill, New York, p. 119.
2. Campbell, J. P. (1976) Psychometric theory. In Dunnette, M. D., (ed.) *Handbook of Industrial and organizational psychology*, Rand McNally, Chicago, pp. 185–222.
3. American Psychological Association. (1974) *Standards for educational and psychological tests*, American Psychological Association, Washington, DC, p. 25.
4. Smith, P. C. (1976) Behavior, results and organizational effectiveness: The problem of criteria. In Dunnette, M. D., (ed.) *Handbook of industrial and organizational psychology*, Rand McNally, Chicago, pp. 745–775.
5. Bridges, G. S. (1987) An empirical study of error in reports of crime and delinquency. In Wolfgang, M., Thornberry, T. and Figlio, R. *From boy to man: From delinquency to crime*, University of Chicago Press, Chicago, pp. 180–194.
6. Wyner, G. A. (1980) Response errors in self reported number of arrests. *Sociological Methods and Research 9*, 161–177.
7. American Psychological Association. (1974) *Standards for educational and psychological tests*, American Psychological Association, Washington, DC, p. 26.
8. Burgess, E. W. (1928) Factors determining success or failure on parole. In Bruce, A. A. (ed.) *The Workings of the indeterminate sentence law and the parole system in Illinois*, Illinois State Board of Parole, Springfield, IL.
9. Gottfredson, S. D., and Gottfredson, D. M. (1979) *Screening for risk: A Comparison of methods*, National Institute of Corrections, Washington, DC.
10. Hoffman, P. (1984) Screening for risk: A revised salient factor score. *Journal of Criminal Justice 11*, 539–547.
11. Morris, N., and Miller, M. (1985) Predictions of dangerousness. In Tonry, M., and Morris, N. (eds.), *Crime and justice: An Annual review of research*, Vol. 6, University of Chicago Press, Chicago.
12. Ohlin, L. E., and Duncan, O. D. (1949) The Efficiency of prediction in criminology. *American Journal of Sociology 54*.
13. Goldkamp, J. S. (1987) Prediction in the development of criminal justice policy. In Gottfredson, D., and Tonry, M. (eds.), *Crime and Justice: An Annual Review of Research*, University of Chicago Press, Chicago, pp. 103–150.
14. Hoffman, P. *Predicting criminality*, National Institute of Justice, Washington, DC, p. 2.
15. American Psychological Association. (1974) *Standards for educational and psychological tests*, American Psychological Association, Washington, DC, p. 29.
16. Hogan, R., and Nicholson, R. A. (1988) The Meaning of personality test scores. *American Psychologist 43*, 621–626.
17. Cronbach, L. J., and Meehl, P. E. (1955) Construct validity in personality tests. *Psychological Bulletin 52*, 281–302.
18. American Psychological Association. (1974) *Standards for educational and psychological tests*, American Psychological Association, Washington, DC, p. 30.
19. Cronbach, L. J. (1970) *Essentials of psychological testing*, Third ed., Harper and Row, New York, p. 144.
20. Goldkamp, J., and Gottfredson, M. (1983) *Judicial decision guidelines for bail: The Philadelphia experiment*, National Institute of Justice, Washington, DC.
21. Goldkamp, J. S. (1985) Danger and detention: A Second generation of bail reform. *Journal of Criminal Law and Criminology 76*, 1–74.
22. Goldkamp, J. S., Gottfredson, M. R., and Jones, P. R. Guidelines for bail and pretrial release in three urban courts. Volume II: The Implementation and evaluation of bail/pretrial release guidelines in Maricopa County Superior Court, Dade County Circuit Court and Bos-

ton Municipal Court. Draft report for grant 84-IJ-CX-0056 from the National Institute of Justice. Department of Criminal Justice, Temple University.

23. Goldkamp, J. S., Gottfredson, M. S., and Weiland, D. (1990) Pretrial drug testing and defendant risk. *Journal of Criminal Law and Criminology 81*, 585–652.

CHAPTER 9

EXTERNAL VALIDITY AND LINKING THE BENCHMARKS

Despite widespread misconceptions to the contrary, the rejection of a given null hypothesis gives us no basis for estimating the probability that a replication of the research will again result in rejecting that null hypothesis. [1]

OBJECTIVES

In the last two chapters you have examined two benchmarks of scientific quality—reliability and internal validity. In this chapter you will investigate the third benchmark of scientific quality: external validity. You will assess the logic and procedures social scientists follow to learn whether the results of a study apply to other settings, different times, or other populations. In the latter part of the chapter you will take up the relationship between the trio of benchmarks. You will see that researchers sometimes must make "trade-offs" between these three benchmarks of scientific quality.

Recall the scenario introduced in Chapter 1. A jurisdiction carried out a probation program of electronic monitoring with house arrest, aimed at serious offenders who would otherwise have gone to prison. You were called to evaluate the success of the program after fatal incidents involving felons sentenced to HCEM. You began compiling information about the success of your program. You start to get a picture of how the program is doing.

- About 40 percent of those who complete their HCEM sentence are *not* rearrested for another serious offense within the following 2 years; 60 percent *are* rearrested within that follow-up period.
- About 80 percent of those sentenced to a year or longer on HCEM complete the first 12 months of their sentence without a technical violation or a rearrest. If the offender sentenced to HCEM commits a technical violation or is arrested for another offense, he loses the "right" to be on HCEM and is sent to prison.
- Among those sentenced to 18 months or longer, about 72 percent complete that period on HCEM without a technical violation or a rearrest.

You are writing up these results. A report comes across your desk. Apparently a program similar to your HCEM program has been running for 4 years in a nearby state. You know some probation and court officers working in that state. In general terms, their organization is not that different from yours.

As you start to look at their numbers you become increasingly bewildered. The results of their program look noticeably different from the results of your program. Table 9.1 details some major differences. Focusing on those who complete the HCEM sanction, their program looks more successful at reducing recidivism than yours.

You begin to wonder. "If their program was relatively similar to ours, how could their results be so different? Could it be differences in the makeup of offenders assigned to the program?" You compile some statistics on the offenders assigned to your program. You compare them to the other program's mix of offenders. Table 9.1 shows the numbers. You conclude that the two populations receiving the program do not look that different. Mystified, you scratch your head and wonder:

"Why is it that their results do not apply to our situation? Shouldn't their results generalize to our situation?"

Your questions concern *external validity*, establishing *the generality* of results that emerge from a particular study. You expect that the evaluation of a program similar to yours, with a roughly comparable population, should yield similar findings. Yet it does not.

You probably can understand immediately why this would be of concern to both researchers and practitioners. The latter are always seeking new programs with demonstrated effectiveness. If a program has been successful once, policy makers usually think

T A B L E 9.1

Comparison of Two HCEM Programs for Serious Felons
Outcomes and Population Characteristics

Outcomes		
	Yours	**Theirs**
Percentage of those sentenced to HCEM for 12 months or longer who complete the first 12 months without a technical violation or an arrest for a new crime.	80%	55%
Percentage of those sentenced to HCEM for 18 months or longer who complete the first 18 months without a technical violation or an arrest for a new crime.	72%	50%
Of those who complete their HCEM sentence, percentage who are NOT rearrested for another serious offense within the first 2 years following the completion of their sentence.	40%	79%
Population Characteristics		
	Yours	**Theirs**
Average number of previous convictions	2.4	2.6
Average age at first arrest	16 years	17 years
Average age	24 years	23 years
Average educational level	7th grade	7th grade
Percentage African American	30%	38%
Percentage Hispanic	20%	27%

Note: Artificial data.

it has a good chance of being successful again. This allows for a "one size fits all" mode of policy adoption. Each jurisdiction need not reinvent policy options from scratch.

For researchers, generality is also important. They want to believe that results obtained at a certain time and place with certain participants will apply elsewhere. They want their findings to be more than history. If the processes described by a theory are general, the connections observed in one setting should apply elsewhere. Nonetheless, as has happened in our hypothetical scenario here, researchers often observe failures to replicate findings. There are a range of reasons why such failures occur.

ORGANIZATION

You will review the basic questions related to external validity, and why such validity is important for theoretical and practical reasons. Researchers can conduct research so that it is more likely the results will be generally applicable. Nonetheless, generality is never established unless a replication attempt is successfully carried out. Finally, you will deal with the relationship between the three benchmarks of scientific quality. In many studies, researchers are unable to maximize all three, but must "trade off" between different benchmarks.

EXTERNAL VALIDITY

A study has **external validity** if its results hold up across people, across settings, and across different times. You will acquaint yourself with each of these issues in turn.

A fourth aspect of external validity concerns generalizing results across alternate measures of causes and effects. [2] We will not address that here, since we discussed alternate measures in the chapter on reliability.

Do Results Apply Across People?

The Issue Defined One important validity question is whether results that were obtained with one group of people apply to other groups of people. This query reduces to two separate but related concerns. These are: whether the results apply to the population from which the study participants were selected, and whether the results apply to different populations.

Often researchers will define a specific population of interest to them for study. **Populations** include all individuals or cases of a certain type. The following would all be examples of populations:

All burglars convicted of burglary between January 1, 1990 and January 1, 1991 in the state of Missouri.

All prisoners who are inmates in the Delaware County (PA) prison on June 30, 1992.

All cases processed by the San Francisco District Attorney's office where the defendant entered a guilty plea during the calendar year 1991.

All residents living in the United States and aged 18 or older on September 1, 1993.

All businesses convicted of violating one or more environmental regulations in the state of Oregon during the calendar year 1994.

All speeches delivered in the Utah State House during the 1994-1995 legislative session that addressed one or more criminal justice issues.

Populations can be large—all those living in the US aged 18 or older—or small—all inmates on death row in your state as of today. But the important point is that the boundaries of the population are clear: You can tell which individuals and cases are within the population, and which are excluded.

Generalizing to a Population Researchers investigating a particular population often will select participants or cases in a way that justifies inferring that the results they obtain with their selected cases will apply *to* the population from which they were selected. The process of selecting cases to be studied from a larger population of cases is called **sampling**. You will encounter this topic in Chapter 10. A researcher using a standard sampling procedure selects participants or cases so that she knows, roughly, what the chances were that various members or types of members of the population would be selected for inclusion in the study.

To increase the likelihood that obtained results will apply *to* the population from which they were selected the researcher will follow these steps. She will define the population of cases as clearly as possible. She will follow appropriate sampling procedures, and she will select enough cases. If she follows these steps, and if certain statistical assumptions hold, then she can legitimately assume that the results obtained with the selected cases *also* apply to the larger population from which they were selected. In other words she can claim the results *generalize TO the population of interest*. In many studies this is an important first step in establishing external validity. (See Figure 9.1.)

Generalizing ACROSS Populations If a researcher has established that his findings apply *to* the population from which he sampled cases, then the next external validity question is whether the results also apply to *other* populations, i.e., *across* populations. For example the National Crime Survey informs us that violent crime victimization rates correlate

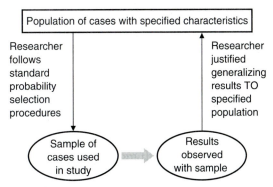

FIGURE 9.1
Steps in generalizing results TO a population.

negatively with age for adults [3, Table 9]. Older adults experience lower violent victimization rates than younger adults. We might want to know if the same relationship holds in the United Kingdom, or Estonia, or Zaire. Would the same relationship between age and violent victimization rate also hold *across* different populations? (See Figure 9.2.)

In the elaboration of the HCEM hypothetical running example discussed at the beginning of this chapter, you were confused. It looked like a result obtained with a similar population, in another jurisdiction, did not apply to your population of offenders sentenced to HCEM. You *expected* the results from the neighboring jurisdiction to apply *across populations*, i.e., to your program, because of program and population similarities. All else equal, you expect results to be more likely to generalize to different populations if those different populations of cases are more similar to the original population of cases studied. But often results do not generalize to a similar population of cases, as has happened in our scenario.

Do Results Apply Across Times?

A result from a study has external validity if it is something that can be repeated on differ-

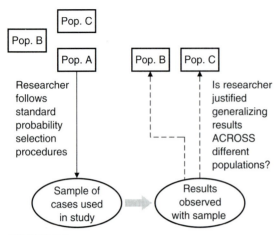

FIGURE 9.2
Steps in generalizing ACROSS populations.

ent occasions. If a certain result is obtained, can it be obtained *again* later?

From a practical as well as a theoretical perspective it is important to know if you can obtain a result on repeated occasions. Criminal justice managers want to know if they can rely on a "finding" before using it to make decisions and policies. Researchers interpret findings with theory, and presume that theory receives support at more than one point in time.

When you were looking at the results of the HCEM program for serious offenders in the neighboring state, you might think of some factors operating at the time that may have played a role in making the program so successful. Perhaps in the jurisdiction with the largest number of cases in the program, a judge who assigned many convicted felons to HCEM had earned a reputation as a severe judge. He may have often made a point of sending offenders on HCEM who failed to meet the program guidelines to one of the most violent, overcrowded prisons in the state to serve the remainder of their sentences. Yet you also know that there is now a new judge in that jurisdiction in the neighboring state, nowhere as strict as the former

judge, who is in charge of sentencing to HCEM. You might therefore expect that, were the study of offenders on HCEM to be repeated *now* in that neighboring state, the results would not show as much success.

Do Results Apply Across Settings?

The third aspect of external validity considers whether results obtain across different *settings*. It is possible that a certain program result could be obtained, and obtained repeatedly, with different program participants. For example, in the neighboring jurisdiction with the HCEM program for serious offenders, the program might operate successfully for several years with a variety of participants. It might be as successful 4 years later as when it began. It might work as well with burglars between the ages of 35 to 40 as it does with robbers aged 20 to 25. Nonetheless, such repeated successes over time and with different participants do *not* mean, necessarily, that the program also would be effective in *another setting*. Conceptually, the replication of a program or a study result in a different setting is an issue separate from the replication across populations and across times.

Of course, when a program is replicated in a different setting, the replication also usually involves different program participants and a different time than the original study or program. Therefore, to replicate a program or study result in a different setting is often the strongest form of external validity obtainable, and of greatest interest to policy makers. Box 9.1 describes efforts to replicate a policing experiment to reduce spousal assault.

REASONS *NOT* TO EXPECT EXTERNAL VALIDITY

Scientists often fail to replicate initial findings. There are some philosophical reasons

BOX 9.1

REPLICATING THE MINNEAPOLIS EXPERIMENTAL PROGRAM TO REDUCE SPOUSE BATTERING

Over the past few years criminal justice policy makers have shown a strong interest in the external validity of a Minneapolis policing experiment that reduced spousal assault. In that experiment police officers responding to spousal assault situations randomly selected one of three responses: jail the suspect for a brief time, order the suspect or the victim to leave the premises, or mediate between the two parties. Results from the study showed that arrest was more effective than other responses in deterring future violence. [4]

The results from the Minneapolis study have had a significant impact on policing practices across the country. [5, 6] This impact on policy has occurred despite a lack of information about the generalizability of the original Minneapolis findings.

Researchers have made several attempts to replicate these findings. [7, 8] The National Institute of Justice has funded six of these replication efforts to learn how generally effective such programs are. If such a program did have external validity, with different populations, and in different settings, it could be profitably used in a range of cities. Some replication efforts have failed to replicate the results of the original study.

suggesting why results should not generalize. See Box 9.2. In addition to these more metaphysical explanations for specificity of findings, several features of the research process may decrease the chances that findings may apply across populations, settings, and

times. Researchers call these reasons **threats to external validity**.

Features of the Research Process

Type I Error Statistics can contribute to failures to replicate a finding. The original study could have been statistically "incorrect." With all statistics there is a chance the researcher will conclude, based on statistical analyses of data, that a difference between two groups exists. The data may suggest less racial disparity in sentencing after vs. before new sentencing guidelines were put into effect, for example. Out there in the "real world," however, the difference may not exist. Statisticians call this a **Type I error**. In the original Minneapolis spouse battery experiment, researchers could have concluded, based on their data, that a difference existed between the arrest cases and the other cases, when such a difference did not exist in the "real world" (see Figure 9.3).

Typically, researchers will set the rate at which Type I errors occur at about 5 percent. That is, assuming certain conditions hold, 5 times out of 100 they will mistakenly conclude, based on analyses of their data, that a difference between treatments exists when it actually does not. Researchers in some situations may be justified in using a Type I error level that is higher or lower than this. The latter may be justified if the researcher is analyzing an extremely large dataset. The former may be justified for researchers who are in the initial phase of a research project, or seeking to maximize discovery.

Type II Error A replication attempt that fails to replicate the findings of an initial study may itself have an inadequate research design. In every statistical analysis there is a chance that a difference existing "out there" in the "real world" is not picked up by the researcher's statistical analysis. The analyses

BOX 9.2

PERHAPS WE SHOULD NOT EXPECT SO MUCH GENERALIZATION?

There has been considerable discussion over the last 20 years or so on how much we should expect results obtained once to replicate later or elsewhere. These discussions emerge from philosophy of science, conceptual critiques of behavioral sciences, and emerging theories in the natural sciences.

In the philosophy of social science, questions have arisen concerning the stability of behavioral processes. [9, 10] One viewpoint in this discussion describes a **transactional world view**. [11] It is grounded in the philosophies of Bentley, Dewey, and Pepper. Features of this perspective have direct implications for the issue of external validity.

For example, this perspective assumes that "change is inherent in the system and the study of its transformations is necessary to understand the phenomenon." [11] In other words, a priori, there is no rationale for expecting systems to stay stable. There is no reason for expecting that a hypothesis supported once in a certain location also will be supported later at another location. The researcher is examining two different systems.

Critiques of behavioral science have suggested we should not expect generality for a different but related reason. They argue that it is wrong-headed to look for generality of relationships that are inherently contextual. Gary Winkel, for example, argues that relationships between indicators of concepts must always be interpreted in that specific situation; to ignore the role of context in shaping those relationships amounts to decontextualizing the concepts and reducing their ecological validity, i.e., their correspondence to "real-world" processes. [12] He suggests we should focus on the context in which certain relationships occur, and not try to divorce the relationship between two indicators of concepts from the context in which that relationship appeared.

Chaos theory, a theoretical perspective originating in the natural sciences and now being embraced by some social scientists, also argues against expecting generalization. [13] This perspective assumes, for example, that simple systems can "breed complexity," and that certain processes may be sensitive to minute variations in surrounding conditions at the beginning of a sequence of events. Such an outlook argues strongly against expecting findings to generalize.

of the data failed to "notice" the difference that existed. Statisticians call this a **Type II error**.

Every quantitative investigation whose results are analyzed statistically possesses a particular Type II error level. The level is a feature of the study design. A well-designed study probably would have a Type II error level of no more than about 20 percent. [14] With a Type II error level of 20 percent the researcher has an 80 percent chance of capturing in the data analysis differences that

exist in the "real world." High Type II error levels result in many instances from including too few cases in a study.

Phenomena More Contextual than First Thought

Another possibility is that the original finding was more dependent on features of the research context than researchers initially thought. There are several philosophical reasons to expect this situation. See Box 9.2. The

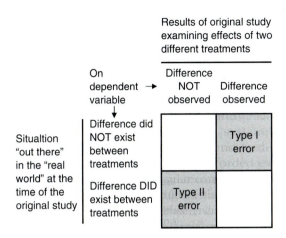

FIGURE 9.3   **Type I and Type II Errors.**

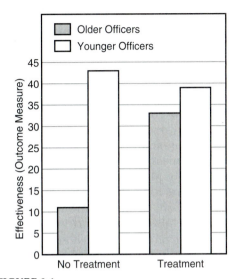

FIGURE 9.4
Author-generated example of a selection by treatment interaction in original study. Older but not younger officers benefit from the CPO training program. If a replication effort includes only younger officers, it will not observe an effect of the treatment on the outcome.

context-bound nature of a finding can spawn several threats to external validity. These threats can be thought of as *interactions* between an independent variable of interest and another characteristic of the research situation. (Interaction effects were discussed in Chapter 2.)

Depends on People   There might be an *interaction* between the qualities of the *populations* and the effectiveness of the program. Thus, the program may be more effective for one population than for another. Such a **treatment by selection interaction** would be a threat to the external validity of a study.

For example, an initial study finds that a training program for community policing may generally increase the effectiveness with which CPOs are perceived by local leaders. But the program may be effective only for older officers. It may have no influence on the effectiveness of younger CPOs. If a replication study includes only younger CPO officers, it will not find that the training program improves effectiveness (see Figure 9.4).

Depends on Time   There might be an interaction between treatment effectiveness and

the historical circumstances. What worked at a certain time no longer works, or vice versa, due to a change over time in other factors that influence the outcome of interest. For example, particularly effective trainers may leave a CPO training program; after their departure the program may be less successful, and participants in the program no longer display increased effectiveness. (See Figure 9.5.) Such a **history by treatment interaction** would be a threat to the external validity of the program results.

HOW IS EXTERNAL VALIDITY ESTABLISHED?

The results of a study, or evaluation, or program, are externally valid if they apply to different populations, different settings, and different times from those where the original work was completed. How do you *know* if the

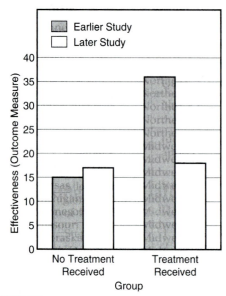

FIGURE 9.5
Author-generated example of a history by treatment interaction. After the departure of particularly effective trainer, the program no longer benefits participants.

results of a study or evaluation are externally valid? The answer to this question comes in two parts.

Steps That May Be Helpful

First, *a researcher can take several steps that lead you to EXPECT that the results of his study would have high external validity.* Although the exact steps involved vary depending upon the particular research tool being used, the following may be relevant in many situations.

- The researcher samples cases 'typical' for the topic being investigated. Anomalous or rarely occurring situations, or nontypical participants, will be avoided. For example, a researcher investigating police efficiency in big city police departments will not select a department where the police chief was indicted for embezzling, as happened in

Detroit in 1991. A researcher investigating prosecutorial plea bargaining practices would not find a typical district attorney's office in a city where the previous DA, in office for over 12 years, had just lost an election. You expect research based on non-typical participants or settings to have less external validity.

- The researcher will use generally accepted measuring procedures. They will have established construct validity and, as appropriate, acceptable criterion-related and construct validities. You expect the research based on novel methods to be less generalizable.
- The researcher could examine her findings separately for different subgroups within the study. She could find that the result "holds" for men as well as women, for Chicanos as well as Whites, and so on. If this was found, then she has completed an **internal replication** of results.

But Then Again Such Steps may NOT Be Helpful: External Validity is ALWAYS An Empirical Matter

Nonetheless, although there are several steps a researcher can take to lead readers to expect that her research will have external validity, how much external validity the results have is ALWAYS AN EMPIRICAL MATTER. As Jacob Cohen pointed out in the quotation at the beginning of the chapter, because you find something once, it does not mean you will find it again. I cannot overemphasize how important this point is. Until someone has completed a sound effort to replicate a study, we have no way of knowing the level of external validity of findings.

Even if a researcher takes several steps to "ensure" the results are externally valid, the goal might not be achieved. A study done with typical participants, tried and true methods, and in a typical situation may have less external validity than a study done with atypical participants, new methods, and in nontypical situations.

Consequently, it is patently unfair to criticize a study with remarks such as "The results probably have low external validity and would be unlikely to generalize." Results do not "probably" have low or high generalizability. They either *actually* have low or high external validity. Until the results of one or more sound efforts to assess empirically the external validity of a study are complete, external validity of the initial findings are unknown. *External validity can never be determined a priori.*

The above point suggests something you may find counterintuitive. When it comes to external validity, several little studies put together may be stronger than one big study. [15]

Consider the following situation. You have done a very small-scale study or a *pilot study*, and you have obtained a finding like the following: prior sensitivity training of police officers on community concerns results in more effective community policing. You seek to establish the external validity of this finding. Some policy makers at the federal level have funds available to explore external validity. There are two different ways you could structure such an effort. On the one hand you could design and support a large-scale, amply funded, multiyear research project involving a prestigious research team and several hundred officers from a large city police force. On the other hand you could support a handful of small replication efforts, done in three or four different cities, overseen by low-prestige researchers with small budgets. In this latter case, each effort would *not* involve a large number of participants. The question for you is this. Which design scenario, if both research strategies resulted in a replication of

the original finding, would more firmly establish the external validity of the finding?

Many think that the one big study will more firmly establish the external validity of the finding. Such a study probably would be well done. The quality or size of the study, however, is not relevant to the question of external validity. The latter, multistudy strategy would result in more firmly establishing external validity of the initial finding. If the multistudy strategy produced successful replications, it would have shown that, in different settings, with different participants, the same result appeared.

You are now familiar with the first "quirk" of external validity. There are several steps that a researcher can take to increase the external validity of study results. Those steps, however, may or may not result in findings with high external validity. The external validity of a study result cannot be determined a priori. It may be unrelated to the qualities of the original study. The only way that the external validity of a study result can be known is if another study carefully attempts to repeat the original study and succeeds.

Replications Are Rarities

At this point you may be thinking something like the following: "All right, if we want to know the external validity of a study finding, we repeat the study with another population, or in another setting, or at another time. We see how the results come out. Then we know if the original finding had external validity or not. No problem." Nonetheless, replication efforts are rare occurrences in the social sciences. There are several reasons for this state of affairs.

- Conducting a replication in the social sciences, with the exception of laboratory studies in psychology, can take months, or more likely years. Replication efforts represent a substantial time investment.

- Researchers trying to conduct a replication effort often have difficulty getting enough information about the original study procedures or materials. Original questionnaires or instruments get lost, and instructions about how to code the data are not easily retrieved. And, of course, people forget. These and other associated complexities make it difficult for researchers to conduct replication efforts.

- The payoffs are uncertain. If a replication effort is successfully completed, the researcher may have a difficult time getting it published. The editor and reviewers are likely to have a "ho-hum" response. [16] Journal editors like to devote scarce journal space to new, exciting research reports that significantly expand the field. If the replication effort is unsuccessful, publication may be even more difficult. Null findings, or findings of no difference, create problems in interpretation. (See below.)

- There are opportunity costs connected with attempting a replication effort. While researchers spend time and resources attempting to replicate another's findings, they are not spending time and resources on their own research. They are foreclosing other opportunities by trying to replicate another's results.

You Don't Know What to Infer From "Null" Findings of "No Difference"   A negative result—an attempt to replicate a finding that ends in failure—could have occurred for several different reasons. Researchers testing a hypothesis expect their results to show a "difference." For example, CPO effectiveness for officers receiving a special training program should be higher than the effectiveness of the officers not receiving the special training. But should the expected difference fail to emerge, it could be for a range of reasons.

The hypothesis may be incorrect. The study design may have been inadequate in some respect. Or it could be a result of Type II error. Since the researcher does not know the reason for the null finding, she is not allowed to interpret theoretically the pattern of no difference.

This conundrum bedeviled the researchers in the Omaha spouse battery replication study. They tried to match their study design and population to the original Minneapolis participants. Nevertheless, despite their care, there were several differences between the two studies. (See Table 9.2.)

> Although the two experiments are quite similar across most of the comparisons specified in Table [9-2], they differ on a few key points. Differences in the penalties resulting from court appearances associated with random assignment to arrest, differences in the areas of the cities covered by the experiments, differences in interview completion rates, and differences in outcomes measures and the way they were aggregated may affect the relevance of the two experiments for one another. [8]

Consequently, the researchers were not sure about the "cause" of the failure to replicate. Was it due to the differences between the two studies? Or was it because the original study was a fluke? As the Omaha researchers themselves noted: "Comparisons of the details of the two experiments reveal several significant differences. Whether these differences account for the differences in the findings of the two experiments *is uncertain*." [8; emphasis added]

Since negative findings are not easily interpreted, it is extremely difficult to show that a finding does *not* have external validity. The Omaha failure to replicate does not necessarily mean that the original Minneapolis findings have low external validity. The failure to replicate could be due to the differences between the two studies.

In sum, there are three possible classes of explanations for a replication failure. (1) The fault may be with the original study. (2) The fault may be with the replication attempt. (3) Or it could be that the phenomenon observed in the original study may not be as general a phenomenon as expected. Confronted with a replication failure, it is extremely difficult for researchers to know which of these three classes of explanation is applicable.

Replication and Holmes's Approach

The discussion so far has assumed Einstein's mode of inquiry. I have focused on learning if a research hypothesis tested in one situation applies to another.[1] If you follow Holmes's grounded theory approach, the reasons why you seek external validity are slightly different. The researcher developing grounded theory wants to develop hypotheses that fit the situation being examined and are meaningful to those involved in the situation. As part of this process the researcher is "drawn naturally into actively generating and verifying his hypotheses through comparisons of groups." [17]

This process of seeking out new situations to compare to the original one is called **theoretical sampling**. [18] Using the emerging theory, the researcher decides what "data to collect next and where to find them, in order to develop his theory as it emerges." The researcher needs to decide: "What groups or subgroups does one turn to next in data col-

lection? And for what theoretical purpose?" [19] In short the researcher seeks to gather new information about the relevant theory that has developed from the situations already studied.

The researcher pursuing discovery can achieve two things by examining data from different situations. First, he can refine, clarify, and amplify the key concepts and hypotheses in the developing theory. The second gain accrues over a longer period. The researcher, after repeated theoretical sampling, may be able to move beyond the discovery of **substantive theory** to the discovery of **formal theory**. [20] A theory developed to explain one aspect of social life—a substantive theory—can be developed into something more broadly applicable—a formal, general theory.

At different stages of a research project, you may adopt either Einstein's or Holmes's approach to replication. Most typically, Holmes's logic of inquiry is followed in the early stages of a research project. At this stage you may be more interested in examining how a correlation between two variables shifts as you change settings or populations. The differences you observe help you further elaborate your theory. Later, after you have formalized the additions to your theory, you may conduct a replication effort for the explicit purpose of learning if your hypotheses are or are not supported in a range of situations. At some point you will want to stick your neck out and say: "I am going to collect data in this new situation, and here is what I think will happen." In short, although you may begin by viewing your replication work as a process of discovery and theoretical sampling just to learn more about how things work, at some point you are likely to change to an explicit hypothesis-testing mode to learn about generality. Additional data from different situations is of strong interest for *both* Holmes's and Einstein's logic of scientific inquiry.

---

[1] Strictly speaking, the data do not suppport a research hypothesis. Rather they simply allow one to reject the null hypothesis that there is no difference in the two groups. This Fisherian legacy is still with us, because the data could support any one of several different alternate research hypotheses. The ability to reject the null hypothesis is not the same as being able to embrace your research hypothesis. [1]

TABLE 9.2
Role of Arrest in Domestic Assault
Comparison of Selected Characteristics in the
Minneapolis and Omaha Experiments

	Minneapolis Experiment	Omaha Replication
Relationship of Suspect to Victim		
Divorce or Separated Husband	3%	1%
Unmarried Lover/Boyfriend	45%	39%
Ex-lover/Boyfriend	—	9%
Current Husband	35%	42%
Wife/Girlfriend/Ex-girlfriend	2%	4%
Relative, Roommate, Other	15%	5%
Inclusiveness of the Experiments		
Total City Coverage	No[a]	Yes
Twenty-four Hour Coverage	Yes	No[b]
All Officers on Shift Involved	No[c]	Yes
Every Day	Yes	Yes
Police Information		
Number of Officers Eligible to Make Referrals	52	194
Concentration of Refusals		
3 Officers	28%	12%
Sampling Period (mo.)	16½	18
Sample sizes		
Mediate	92	115
Separate	108	106
Arrest	114	109
Total	314	330
Mean Number of Referrals per Month	18.5	18.3
Follow-up Period (mo.)	6	6[d]
Proportion of Cases Misapplied	17.8[e]	7.9
Interview Data		
Proportion of Initial Interviews Completed	62%	80%
Proportion of Interviews Completed after 6-month Follow-up	49%	73%
Face-to-face Interviews Only	No	Yes
Incentive Payments—All Interviews	No	Yes
Outcome Measures		
Official Arrest for Repeated Domestic Conflict of Any Sort	Yes	Yes
Official Complaint Reports Taken from Victims by Police Officers	Yes	Yes
Reports by Project Staff of Police Interventions for Repeated Domestic Conflict	Yes	No
Victim Reports of Episodes in Which She/He		
a. Was Actually Assaulted	Yes	Yes[f]
b. Was Threatened with Assault	Yes	No
c. Had Property Damage	Yes	No
d. Felt in Danger of Being Physically Hurt	No	Yes

	Minneapolis	Omaha
e. Was Pushed, Hit, or Hands Laid on Them	No	Yes
f. Was Physically Injured	No	Yes
g. Date of 1st, 2nd, 3rd Victim-reported Repeat Episodes with Injury	No	Yes
Proportion of Repeat Offenders Sentenced to Jail/Probation/Fines	2%	64%
Unemployment		
Victims	61%	50%
Suspects	60%	31%
Prior Assaults and Police Involvement		
Victims Assaulted by Suspect in Prior 6 Months	80%	52%[g]
Police Intervention in Domestic Dispute, Last 6 Months	60%	—
Victims Reporting the Police Ever Coming to Victim's Assistance Because the Suspect Was Hitting or Threatening Her/Him	—	64%
Couple in counseling program	27%	11%
Prior Arrests of Male Suspects		
Ever Arrested for Any Offense	59%	65%
Ever Arrested on Domestic Violence Statute	5%	—
Ever Arrested for Any Offense Against Victim	—	11%
Arrested for Any Offense Against Victims in Prior 6 Months	—	3%
Mean Age (yr.)		
Victims	30	31
Suspects	32	31

	Minneapolis		Omaha	
	Victims	**Suspects**	**Victims**	**Suspects**
Education				
> High School	43%	42%	34%	31%
High School Only	33%	36%	43%	50%
< High School	24%	22%	23%	19%
Ethnicity				
White	57%	45%	56%	50%
Black	23%	36%	37%	43%
Hispanic	—	—	3%	4%
Native American	18%	16%	4%	3%
Other	2%	3%	.3%	—

[a] Two precincts.

[b] 4 p.m. to midnight.

[c] Specifically trained domestic violence officers only.

[d] 12-month follow-up measures were also obtained in Omaha, but were not available for this report.

[e] Because of the variability between definitions of misapplication, care must be exercised in the interpretation of these proportions.

[f] Victim reports of assault were determined in Omaha on the basis of four measures (see d through g), each measure providing a different dimension of assault.

[g] Assault was determined in Omaha by victim reports of being physically hurt by suspects in the 6 months prior to the presenting offense.

Even when researchers plan a replication effort that closely matches the original study, differences are bound to occur. The Omaha police experiment was designed to replicate the Minneapolis experiment, yet numerous differences emerged. *Source:* Table 3. Dunford, F. W., Huizinga, D., and Elliott, D. S. (1990). The Role of arrest in domestic assault: The Omaha police experiment. *Criminology* 28 (2): 183-206.

Back to the HCEM Example Let's go back to the reprise of the running example of the HCEM program for serious offenders described at the beginning of the chapter. Here is one way you could use Holmes's approach to explore the differences between your HCEM program and the one in the neighboring state. You might wonder: "If I examine the neighboring program in closer detail, will I find clues to the higher success rate?"

You contact some friends of yours working in the program in the adjoining state. You obtain permission to visit and learn more about their program. You convince your supervisor that it might be worthwhile to learn more about their program first-hand.

When you arrive at the program you touch base with the head of probation and various assistants. You explain that you were impressed with the report of their program successes and wanted to find out more about it. After a morning of glad-handing folks, you and your acquaintance in the department begin to get down to business. She talks about the program philosophy and operating procedures, and the personnel training for those who are involved in monitoring HCEM. You visit the facility where the central monitoring computer connects to phone lines. You observe how probation officers can check on probationer whereabouts. Most of the probationers on HCEM must go to a job during daytime hours and call in from their job sites. But the probationers for the most part must be home on weekends and on evenings.

Since you are discovering the situation rather than testing a theory, you attend to all aspects of the situation. After a couple of days of visiting, "hanging around," and talking with program officers, you find striking several features of the situation.

First, the equipment used by the program is somewhat dated. The computers and hookup arrangements are not "state of the art" as they are in your state's program.

Further, the staff seem aware of this and willing to adjust. For example, if they know that there are certain problems with the machine verifying responses from program participants in certain parts of the state—due to phone line quality—every time a signal is *not* acknowledged from those counties, they will try to make a "voice" call as soon as they can to verify whether the "fail to respond" signal is correct.

Third, you notice that the agency has excellent relations with local sheriff's departments. For many departments the agency has obtained a "quick response" number, allowing them to patch in directly to the sheriff's department dispatcher and listen in when the officer assigned to check out a "failure to report" reports back.

Fourth, you find that the officers assigned to the program are proud of the fact that it is well run, with a good success rate. They make it clear they intend to keep it that way. You ask a couple of them how they intend to do that.

In confidential conversations program officers suggest that a probationer assigned to a program is most likely to commit a technical violation in the first week or two of the sanction. The likelihood of a probationer's "trying something" or "testing limits" is, the officers feel, highest during that period. Knowing this, the officers take steps to let the probationer know exactly what program limits are.

During the initial period the assigned officers may get the programmer on the system to increase the rate at which the computer calls the probationer's house asking for a "verify" signal, and to alter the times of calls to the probationer. (Very few of the probationers in the program are monitored continuously by the equipment.) The assigned officers watch the pattern of probationer responses to these signals closely to be sure there are no "failures to respond." They act on failures to respond extremely quickly. The officers also make several visits to probationers at both job sites and home. Thus, during the initial period, officers communicate to program participants a clear sense that the program (a) is vigilant, (b) intrusive, and (c) responds with alacrity.

The officers tell you that if a participant is weeded out of the program because of a technical violation it is most likely to occur in the first 2 weeks on HCEM. Program participants successfully completing the first 2 weeks of the program are therefore highly likely to complete the entire program. They are the more responsible, serious probationers who want the intermediate sanction to work, and are serious about avoiding imprisonment. (If you look back at Table 9.1, you will see that the percentage of participants who complete the first 12 months of sanctions in the neighboring state is much lower than in your program.)

Following this visit you return to your jurisdiction. You start reexamining some features of the HCEM program in your own state. You make mental comparisons between the operation of your program and the operation of the more successful program. You note several marked differences.

First, the equipment in your jurisdiction is definitely "state of the art." It is much more sophisticated in several ways than what you saw in the adjoining state. But there seems a 'downside' to the technological superiority.

In your program, probation officers assigned to the HCEM serious offender program are less personally involved in the day-to-day operations. They seem less vigorous about following up on "failures to respond," and less willing to initiate contact with local authorities to get help following up on potential violations. You think this more lackadaisical attitude may arise from the superior technological capacity of the program, leading the officers to think that matters will be taken care of without their personal involve-

ment. But you suspect it also may be due to "organizational climate" differences between your state's probation department and the department in the adjoining state.

Third, the program officers involved in your program seem to feel there is no need to be extra vigilant during the first 2 weeks a probationer is on HCEM. They do not request a higher frequency of calls to the home, nor do they conduct a larger number of onsite visits during the probationer's entry period into HCEM.

These thoughts lead you to develop concepts like "overreliance on technical equipment for program operation" and "sensitivity to time-varying demands for vigilance," and others. You are on the way to developing a grounded theory. Your impetus was a comparison between two seemingly similar programs with markedly different program results. Stated differently, your program's failure to replicate the results obtained in an adjoining jurisdiction with a similar population made a comparison between the two theoretically relevant, and led to a theoretically fruitful exploration of the differences.

RELATING THE BENCHMARKS

You've learned about internal validity (the proper interpretation of the measurements obtained); external validity (the generalizability of the results obtained); the reliability (the repeatability of the measurements obtained). At this point you may well think it is easy to conduct a high-quality study. You just take steps to ensure that your study scores high on each of the three benchmarks.

Yet, even with adequate resources and time, the job is not as easy as you might think. These three different aspects of scientific quality interconnect. To complete your understanding of scientific quality, you want to appreciate these connections.

Trade-offs Between Internal Validity and External Validity

To establish the internal validity *of a study* you need to establish that your interpretation of the pattern of results is correct. More specifically, you need to convince others that the cause-as-measured in a study did in fact cause the outcome-as-measured. Stated differently, you need to make a case that other factors (z) are not relevant to explaining the x → y relationship. (Recall the discussion of spurious correlation in Chapter 5.)

You can usually insure that a *study* will have high levels of internal validity by choosing and faithfully executing a study design that allows one to make causal inferences with confidence. You will learn more about these different study designs in Chapter 14.

An Example Suppose you were brought into the running example with community policing *before* the implementation of the foot patrolling. Suppose further that you were primarily concerned with conducting a study that would have high internal validity. Your main concern was to convince folks that such an initiative could *cause* a reduction in local crime.

If establishing causality was your main goal, you might opt for a study design that used **random assignment**. You might select a group of neighborhoods at random. For each selected neighborhood you toss a coin. "Heads" means the neighborhood receives the initiative; "tails" means the neighborhood continues to receive standard patrolling. What random assignment usually achieves, if used with a large enough sample, is a rough equivalence in the characteristics of those receiving the treatment, and those receiving the control condition. It creates an **initial probabilistic equivalence** between the two groups.

Since you will only be using a few neighborhoods you decide to make your random assignments more "efficient" by developing matched pairs of neighborhoods. In a **matched pair** each member of the pair is similar to the other on factors you think relate to your outcome variables. For example, you might match pairs of neighborhoods on racial composition, income level, and stability. Thus each locale can have a "control" community—a neighborhood that is similar to it on background characteristics but does not receive the treatment of interest.[2]

Naturally, the cooperation of the different community leaders is important. You schedule visits with the leader in each community that is a member of a matched pair, and you explain the upcoming study. You explain the reason for including control neighborhoods. You find out whether the local leaders will support the evaluation even if their locale is selected as a control rather than a treatment neighborhood.

Several neighborhood leaders refuse to go along and take their neighborhoods out of the study. They protest that they will not be used as "guinea pigs." They want the foot-patrolling officers in their communities *now* to deal with pressing problems. They do not "buy" your explanation that the benefits of these initiatives are not yet proven.

Leaders' refusal to participate cause you to "lose" several matched pairs of neighborhoods in which you had been quite interested: a pair of predominantly Hispanic neighborhoods, a pair of lower-income, predominantly White neighborhoods, two pairs of middle class predominantly African Amer-

---

[2] Your matching procedure will only be effective in enhancing internal validity if the variables on which you match your selected units do in fact connect empirically to your outcome.

ican neighborhoods, and others. The pool of neighborhoods available for random assignment to "treatment" or "control" status has been drastically reduced.

In short, you have opted for a more rigorous study design that permits you to be more confident of the internal validity of *study results*. Because of that rigid design, however, you have "lost" a range of potential locations from your study. Accordingly, you know less about the potential generalizability of your results to locations like those that were "lost." Thus, you may have sacrificed external validity to internal study validity.

Ecological Validity and Laboratory Experiments Laboratory experiments, popular in psychology, show most clearly the trade-off between internal validity of study results and potential external validity. Such studies take place in situations that have no counterpart in the "real world." They are likely to have low **ecological validity**. Research conducted in settings and with participants that are both highly similar to the ultimate situations and individuals of interest are likely to have *high* ecological validity. A study concerned with effects of imprisonment using college or high school students in a mock prison setting probably will have much lower ecological validity than a study with actual inmates in actual penal institutions.

The lab situation is unusual in several respects. The situation presents to the participant several **demand characteristics** that he is unlikely to encounter elsewhere. Demand characteristics are specific features of a situation that exert strong pressure on those in the situation to act in a specific way. A quasi-authority figure, the experimenter, is present. Participants often seek to please that person, and behave accordingly. If there are others in the situation, they are likely to be

strangers that the participant has not seen before and will not see again. Further, the participant's actions in the experiment are completely divorced from activities in the rest of his life. These conditions are peculiar to the lab situation. There is thus, a priori, little reason to expect that the processes explaining participants' behaviors in that situation will be applicable elsewhere. Of course, the expectation could be disconfirmed. (Remember: External validity is always an empirical matter.)

Researchers in areas such as psychology conduct lab experiments because, in the lab, they can control extraneous conditions and easily carry out the random assignment of participants to conditions. Such controls make it easier for them to establish that the condition or treatment-as-measured was solely responsible for the outcome-as-measured.

Nevertheless, because of their low ecological validity, and the concomitant uncertain relevance of lab results to situations outside the lab, we will not be discussing lab experiments further in this volume.

Which Type of Validity Do I Emphasize?

The above discussion illustrates only one of the potential trade-offs the researcher needs to consider. There are others. You could consider, for example, the trade-off between construct validity and external validity. To achieve a high level of construct validity for study measures, a researcher might opt to use several different measures of both independent and dependent variables. Collecting information using different methods, however, may be quite time-consuming. Consequently, certain respondents may opt out of the study. This may limit external validity.

Most criminal justice research orients toward matters that have considerable practical import. Practitioners and theorists want to know "What works?" Therefore the first and most important question about a study will be to establish its internal validity: is the cause or treatment-as-measured solely responsible for the effects-as-observed? We need to know exactly what it is that is working. [21]

The second most important benchmark will be potential generalizability. The criminal justice system deals with a range of offenders, jurisdictions, and organizational qualities. Policy makers will want to know if a treatment or program that works in one location or for one type of offender is also applicable to another location or another type of offender. The expansion of HCEM in the late 1980s represents an excellent case in point. Judges, initially, applied the sanction largely to individuals convicted of DUI or DWI (driving while under the influence; driving while intoxicated). Since then it has been expanded to a much broader range of offenders. Thus, from a criminal justice perspective probably the second most critical aspect of a study is its potential external validity.

Relationships Between Reliability and Validity of Measures

We have been focusing on the trade-offs involving scientific qualities of *studies*. Let's now consider more specifically the qualities of the *measures* that make up a study. We scrutinize the relationship between the *validity* of measures and the *reliability* of those same measures.

As you recall, if a measure is reliable the "output" of the measurement process is not heavily influenced by extraneous factors. If the same individual completes the same measure on several occasions close together in time, you will observe high test-retest reliability coefficients. But if the measure is not reliable, there will be sizable fluctuation in the readings and lower test-retest reliability coefficients.

Low reliabilities effectively limit the construct or criterion-related validity coefficients that can be obtained. Although there are exceptions, the reliability with which the indicators of the cause and the outcome are measured places a "ceiling" on the size of the validity coefficients that can be obtained linking the two measures. [22, 23]

An example may help clarify this point. Imagine you are researching delinquency self-report indexes and peer ratings of delinquents. You seek to develop a peer rating of delinquent and nondelinquent youths that correlates well with the delinquency self-report score of the person being rated, the target person.

Each target person completes a delinquency self-report scale. Scores on this scale could range from 0 to 50, with a higher score indicating more delinquency. Your group includes youths who have been adjudicated delinquent as well as those who have not. Self-reported delinquency scores for 12 of your study participants appear in Table 9.3, in the third column.

Each target person tells the researcher who his closest same-sex friend is. The researcher then contacts those individuals and asks them to rate the target person on a scale, ranging from 0 to 10. A higher score would show that the friend viewed the target person as *less* law abiding, i.e., more delinquent. These scores appear in the second column of Table 9.3. Subject numbers appear in the first column.

You correlate peer ratings and delinquency self-report scores. You obtain a concurrent

TABLE 9.3
Scores on Peer Rating of Delinquency, and
Delinquency Self-Report Scores
High Test-Retest Reliability Assumed for Peer Rating

Subject Number	Peer Rating	Delinquency Self-Report Score
1	8	39
2	3	20
3	5	30
4	7	35
5	6	32
6	6	37
7	7	42
8	7	28
9	3	15
10	2	18
11	4	40
12	5	30

criterion-related validity coefficient. It is a very substantial +.75. Your peer rating variable can predict 56 percent (.75²) of the differences in the delinquency self-report scores. The data points are shown in the scatterplot in Figure 9.6.

Imagine that the peer rating form used to produce the results shown in Table 9.2 is highly reliable. The researcher assessed test-retest reliability over a period of a few days and found it to be higher than .90.

But suppose that the peer rating procedure used was of *low* reliability. What would happen then? In the retest session a few days later the peer raters provided scores noticeably different from the first ratings. These new numbers appear in Table 9.4. The numbers in the "peer" column in Table 9.4 are two points higher or lower than the numbers in the same column in Table 9.3. I simulated random measurement error to represent low reliability by adding two to each even score and subtracting two from each odd score.

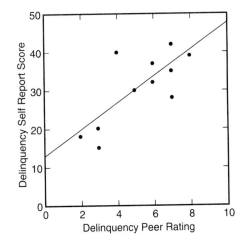

FIGURE 9.6
Correlation between delinquency self-report score and peer ratings of delinquency for 12 hypothetical participants. High test-retest reliability of the peer ratings assumed. $r = +.75$

This change results in a dramatically lower validity coefficient; it is now .31. The scatterplot of this correlation appears in Figure 9.7.

TABLE 9.4

**Scores on Peer Rating of Delinquency, and
Delinquency Self-Report Scores**
Low Test-Retest Reliability Assumed for Peer Rating

Subject Number	Peer Rating	Delinquency Self-Report Score
1	6	39
2	5	20
3	7	30
4	9	35
5	4	32
6	4	37
7	9	42
8	9	28
9	5	15
10	0	18
11	2	40
12	7	30

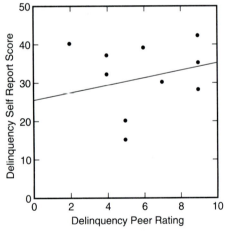

FIGURE 9.7
Correlation between delinquency self-report score and peer ratings of delinquency for 12 hypothetical participants. Low test-retest reliability of the peer ratings assumed. $r = +.31$

Peer ratings can now only predict 9.6 percent of the variation in delinquency self-report scores. This is a marked drop.

Measures of low reliability will yield low validity coefficients: it's as simple as that. In almost all situations, if a measure has a low reliability coefficient, it *cannot* have a high validity coefficient.[3]

---

[3] The relationship between the two types of coefficients can be stated more precisely. If *both* the validity coefficient and the reliability coefficient are expressed in terms of percentage of variance accounted for, the validity coefficient, except under special circumstances, cannot exceed the reliability coefficient.

SUMMARY OF MAIN POINTS

- External validity is concerned with the generality of a research finding.
- Both researchers and practitioners want a research finding to be general. Researchers seek generality as proof that their theory is broadly applicable. Practitioners want generality so that they can use research-based policies in other locations.
- There are three different aspects of generalizing: to different people, to different situations, and to different times.
- There are two different aspects of generalizing to different people. First the researcher seeks to generalize *to* the population from which the study participants were drawn. Second, the researcher seeks to generalize *across* different populations.
- If a researcher selects people from a well-defined population in a fashion that gave everyone an equal or known chance of being selected, readers are usually willing to assume that the results will apply *to* the population from which the participants were drawn.
- When it comes to predicting if a study's results are generalizable across populations, places and times, there are no guarantees. There is no way to learn, *beforehand*, if the results of a study will be generalizable. *External validity can only be established empirically* by subsequent research efforts.
- There are several reasons study results might not generalize. These reasons make up *threats to external validity.*
- Generalization is important if you are following Einstein's logic of scientific inquiry, or Holmes's.
- Researchers who seek to increase the internal validity of study conclusions may do so at the expense of other benchmarks of scientific quality.

- A rigorous study designed to increase internal validity of results may have lower external validity or lower ecological validity as a result.
- A study has ecological validity if the setting, measures, and participants involved are similar to the actual situation that is of central interest to the researcher or policy maker.
- Laboratory experiments are usually high on internal study validity but extremely low on ecological validity.
- Since criminal justice researchers focus on "what works," the most important benchmark of scientific quality for them to emphasize in their studies is the internal validity of study results.
- The second most important benchmark for them to stress, in general, is potential generalizability.
- The reliability of measures used places limits on the validity coefficients that may be obtained with those measures.

GLOSSARY OF KEY WORDS

cause
demand characteristics
ecological validity
external validity
formal theory
history by treatment interaction
initial probabilistic equivalence
internal replication
matched pair
populations
random assignment
sampling
substantive theory
theoretical sampling
threats to external validity

transactional world view
treatment by selection interaction
Type I error
Type II error

REFERENCE

1. Cohen, J. (1990) Things I have learned (so far). *American Psychologist 45*, 1304–1312.
2. Cook, T. D., and Campbell, D. T. (1979) *Quasi-experimentation*, Rand-McNally, Chicago, p. 37.
3. Bureau of Justice Statistics. (1990) *Criminal victimization in the United States, 1988*, US Department of Justice, Washington, DC (A National Crime Survey Report NCJ-122024).
4. Sherman, L. W., and Berk, R. A. (1984) The specified deterrent effects of arrest for domestic assault. *American Sociological Review 49*, 261–272.
5. Binder, A., and Meeker, J. W. (1988) Experiments as reforms. *Criminal Justice 16*, 347–358.
6. Sherman, L. W., and Cohn, E. G. (1989) The impact of research on legal policy: The Minneapolis domestic violence experiment. *Law and Society Review 23*, 117–144.
7. Berk, R. A., and Newton, P. J. (1985) Does arrest deter wife battery? An effort to replicate the findings of the Minneapolis spouse abuse experiment. *American Sociological Review 50*, 253–262.
8. Dunford, F. W., Huizinga, D., and Elliott, D. S. (1990) The Role of arrest in domestic assault: The Omaha police experiment. *Criminology 28*, 183–206.
9. Gergen, K. J. (1982) *Toward transformation in social knowledge*, Springer-Verlag, New York.
10. Rosnow, R. L. (1981) *Paradigms in transition: The methodology of social inquiry*, Oxford University Press, New York.
11. Altman, I., and Rogoff, B. (1987) World views in psychology: Trait, interactional, organ-ismic, and transactional perspectives. In Stokols, D., and Altman, I. (eds.), *Handbook of environmental psychology*, Vol. 1, Wiley Interscience, New York, pp. 7–40.
12. Winkel, G. H. (1987) Implications of environmental context for validity assessments. In Stokols, D., and Altman, I. (eds.), *Handbook of environmental psychology*, Vol. 2, Wiley Interscience, New York, pp. 71–98.
13. Gleick, J. (1987) *Chaos: Making a new science*, Penguin, New York.
14. Cohen, J. (1977) *Statistical power analysis for the behavioral sciences*, Second ed., Academic Press, New York.
15. Cook. T. D., and Campbell, D. T. (1979) *Quasi-experimentation*, Rand-McNally, Chicago.
16. Cook. T. D., and Campbell, D. T. (1979) *Quasi-experimentation*, Rand-McNally, Chicago, p. 234.
17. Glaser, B. G., and Strauss, A. L. (1967) *The discovery of grounded theory: Strategies for qualitative research*, Aldine, Chicago, p. 39.
18. Glaser, B. G., and Strauss, A. L. (1967) *The discovery of grounded theory: Strategies for qualitative research*, Aldine, Chicago, p. 45.
19. Glaser, B. G., and Strauss, A. L. (1967) *The discovery of grounded theory: Strategies for qualitative research*, Aldine, Chicago, p. 47.
20. Glaser, B. G., and Strauss, A. L. (1967) *The discovery of grounded theory: Strategies for qualitative research*, Aldine, Chicago, p. 79.
21. Cook. T. D., and Campbell, D. T. (1979) *Quasi-experimentation*, Rand-McNally, Chicago, p. 83.
22. Campbell, J. P. (1976) Psychometric theory. In Dunnette, M. D. (ed.), *Handbook of Industrial and organizational psychology*, Rand McNally, Chicago, pp. 185–222.
23. Cureton, E. E. (1967) Validity, reliability and baloney. In Jackson D. M., and Messick, D. (eds.), *Problems in human assessment*, McGraw Hill, New York, pp. 271–273.

PART FOUR

THE GALLERY OF RESEARCH TOOLS: DIFFERENT RESEARCH APPROACHES

Every researcher should be able to appreciate the potential value of all methods—though recognizing the inherent flaws of each. [1, p. 219]

In the following chapters you will learn about different methodologies used by criminal justice researchers. These chapters focus on how researchers use specific tools, or apply a method to a particular type of problem.

Previews

Chapter 10 introduces *sampling*. This is a process of systematically selecting units for study. Researchers sample systematically so that they can increase the external validity of their results *to* the population of units studied, and perhaps across populations. Although most clearly relevant to survey research, sampling procedures apply to nearly all other research approaches.

Chapter 11 presents *qualitative field research*. The investigator gets to know the participants in a setting over an extended period. The extended social interaction permits the researcher to analyze the setting and its participants. The researcher uses concepts native to the setting that make sense to its participants.

Chapter 12 describes *survey research*. It is perhaps one of the most widely used techniques in the social sciences. You will see how scientists construct questions, and questionnaires, and the different ways they can administer surveys. You also will learn about two nation-level victimization surveys: The National Crime Surveys (U.S.), and the British Crime Surveys (U.K.).

Chapter 13 reviews *true experiments*, *quasiexperiments* and *evaluation research*. In quasiexperiments researchers investigate the consequences of changes affecting some people or settings, but not others. True experiments are like quasiexperiments in many respects. In true experiments, however, researchers can "control" which people and settings experience a change, and which do not. With such procedures they can isolate more effectively the consequences of the change itself. Evaluation is a *purpose* of research and not a particular type of research tool. Evaluation researchers use a broad range of research tools. Typically, evaluation researchers want to know how a program or treatment was set up or put into place; they also want to know if it worked and if it didn't work, why not.

In Chapter 14 you will learn about *longitudinal research*, where groups of individuals are "followed" over time. Researchers collect information about participants describing them at two or more points in time. Many researchers currently favor longitudinal research as the best way to gain insight into the development of criminal behavior. [2] Such insights are essential to sound theorizing and policy making in criminal justice.

Chapter 15 considers a trio of research tools. *Content analysis* provides systematic procedures for examining written or spoken material. The techniques allow researchers to systematically measure variables indicating concepts. *Historical criminology* represents not a research tool, but a focus on a particular *type* of information. Such analyses inform about past trends in crime and criminal justice. With *unobtrusive measurement* researchers go to the setting of interest and collect information about setting characteristics that may not seem important to setting participants but may have theoretical or practical relevance. For example, they might read graffiti on subway walls, or note the location of junked cars. All three of these approaches are unobtrusive.

Chapter 16 describes two "special purpose" tools in criminal justice research. These tools are powerful, but less widely used than the methods described in the earlier chapters. *Meta-analysis* permits researchers to summarize what is known in an area based on past studies. Researchers can review a corpus of work and decide whether two variables are linked, and if so, the strength of the connection. *Simulations* allow researchers to model complex criminal justice processes and treatments. Microcomputer spreadsheet programs can be used to set up simple simulations.

Some Common Features In The Chapters

In each chapter in this section you will find sections addressing the same questions to each method:

- For what kinds of questions and situations is this method best suited?
- How applicable is this method to the two pathways of inquiry discussed: Einstein's and Holmes's logic of inquiry?

- What are the strengths and weaknesses of this method?
- What ethical issues are salient when this method is used?

Furthermore, in each chapter I will describe in some detail a few recent studies.

Why Do We Need Different Approaches?

You might be wondering: Do we really need all these different research approaches? Can't the field of criminal justice just settle down to a few tried-and-true techniques and stick with them?

It would not be wise for the field to settle into using just a small number of research techniques. The need for diversity in methodology emerges from the way knowledge accumulates in the social sciences. McGrath, Martin, and Kulka [1] suggest that research can be viewed as a *knowledge accrual process*. Two features of this process are important.

Research is probabilistic. Results of research never yield certainty; instead they suggest with increasing likelihood that something is the case (e.g., as A increases, B is more likely to increase).

Further, research is always *contingent*. What we have learned from a study is not independent of the means used in the study, or of the settings and cases examined. Consequently, "empirical information can gain credence only by accumulation of convergent results." [1, p. 213] It is never apparent what we "know" in an area or about a problem until we look at the results of a series of studies.

Consequently, by implication, we require "substantive findings derived from a diversity of methods of study" to have "knowledge" about an area of inquiry. [1, p. 213] If the same type of research tool is used repeatedly, researchers can never separate the *substantive* findings from the *methodologically bound* features of the results. Researchers shed most light on a problem when they attack it with different tools.

Different approaches, with varying flaws and strengths, illuminate different aspects of a problem. [1, p. 216] It is only after we have accumulated findings from a series of studies *that used diverse methodologies* that we can be certain that we really know something about an area.

Given the way knowledge accumulates in an area of inquiry, it will accumulate most quickly if researchers in the area use methods whose strengths and weaknesses complement rather than reproduce one another. The goal, over a series of studies, is to observe a convergence of findings from a diversity of research approaches. Thus, if the field of criminal justice research, as a whole, is to be competent, vital, and a source of insight, researchers as a collective must demonstrate competence in a variety of methods.

REFERENCES

1. McGrath, J. E., Martin, J., and Kulka, R. A. (1981). Some quasi-rules for making judgment calls in research. *American Behavioral Scientist,* 25, 211-224.

2. Farrington, D. P., Ohlin, L. E., and Wilson, J. Q. (1986) *Understanding and controlling crime: Toward a new research strategy.* New York: Springer-Verlag, p. v.

CHAPTER 10

SAMPLING

FOCUS

Sampling refers to a family of procedures used by researchers to select cases for study. If researchers sample cases systematically, they can justifiably generalize their results to the population from which they selected the cases. Sampling procedures are relevant to the entire gamut of tools used by the criminal justice researcher.

Criminal justice researchers examine cases. The cases can be just about anything: individuals, households, communities, organizations, cities, states, countries, legal cases, judges, court systems, speeches, newspaper articles, police departments, officials, log entries, and so on. The possibilities are almost endless. Regardless of the type of case examined, however, the researcher hopes to convince the reader that the results he has obtained apply not only to the particular cases he examined, but also to the larger population of cases from which he selected cases. In other words he wants to convince us that the results obtained with the examined cases generalize *to* the population of such cases

(Chapter 9). His ability to convince us that the results do apply to the larger population depends largely upon how he has selected his cases. **Sampling** refers to a family of procedures researchers use to select cases for study from a larger population of cases. In order to warrant such generalization, researchers must use **probability sampling procedures**—procedures directing how they systematically select cases from the population of cases. In this chapter you will investigate these different procedures. You will also take a look at **nonprobability sampling procedures**—procedures that may be more convenient but do not allow safe generalization to the population of interest. These procedures, and the concerns they address, are relevant not only to survey research, but also to all other tools used by criminal justice researchers.

In order to understand the logic linking samples to populations, you will explore material usually relegated to statistics. You will look into how populations of scores are distributed on variables, how means based on samples drawn from populations are distributed, and how the two are connected. We begin with this statistical background.[1]

POPULATIONS

A **population** of elements or cases refers to the **universe** of cases or elements of interest to the researcher. [1] For research purposes the population needs to be clearly defined in terms of four characteristics: (1) the content: what are the cases?; (2) the units: how are the cases grouped?; (3) the geographical extent of the cases; and (4) the temporal period. [1]

Defined populations are of two types. [2] In some cases they can be fully enumerated; you can know all the cases within the population. Examples include the population of books in your room at this time, the population of students attending the most recent class in your criminal justice research methods course, the population of coins in your pockets at the present time, all uniformed officers serving with the police department in your jurisdiction on December 1, 1993, or all offenders currently in the local jail.

In other cases populations can*not* be fully enumerated, or they cannot be completely enumerated without a superhuman effort. Although you can define them, they are more hypothetical: all persons in jail in the U.S. last Saturday; all women in the U.S. in 1990; all college students in Arkansas in 1994; or all victims of rape in 1993 in the United Kingdom.

SAMPLING CASES OR DOING A CENSUS?

Researchers must choose between doing a **census**—selecting all the cases in a popula-

tion for study—and sampling cases from the population and studying just those sampled cases. Perhaps the best-known census is the decennial census of the entire population of the United States, mandated by the Constitution and conducted by the Bureau of the Census every 10 years. In criminal justice the Bureau of Justice Statistics periodically conducts censuses of all local jails to determine the size of the population. [3]

Several factors influence researchers' decisions either to do a census and study a population of cases, or to sample from the population of cases and focus solely on the sampled cases. The size of the population is relevant. The larger the population, the more expensive it will be to do a census. The researcher will weigh cost in light of available resources, including the time available. Also relevant is the presence of a **sampling frame**: an accurate list of the cases in the population. The availability of a sampling frame drastically reduces the costs of sampling cases.

WHAT DO I LOSE FROM SAMPLING VS. DOING A CENSUS?

The advantage of doing a study of all units in a population is that you can know exactly certain **parameters** of that population. Parameters are proportions, averages, or ranges for a population on an attribute of interest. For example, in the case of the population of students in your criminal justice methods course, you might be interested in knowing the following parameters: the proportion of students who are seniors, the average age, or the average degree of liking for the textbook being used. If you were to ask all the students to complete a survey, and all students did so, the information from your survey can be used to state *exactly* how that population scores on the attributes of interest.

But in numerous situations researchers are unable to do a study with an entire population; they must sample units from the popu-

---

[1] If you have already had a course in statistics and understand such terms as *normal distributions, normal curve, z scores, mean, standard deviation, standard error,* and *confidence interval,* you may skip directly ahead to the material on sampling.

lation, and study the sampled units. Say that your criminal justice research methods class numbers 410 registered students, but you can afford to make only 25 copies of a survey. If you base your study on a probability sample (see below) rather than on a census of cases, and if certain other assumptions hold, you will not be able to know exactly how the population scores on one or more parameters. Nonetheless, you will be able to *estimate* population parameters with a known amount of precision.

In short, with a census you can say: the percentage of seniors in the defined population of all students in my CJ methods class is, e.g., 58 percent. With a probability sample, 25 completed surveys, and given certain statistical assumptions, you can still talk about this attribute, but in a less precise fashion. You can say:

the percentage of seniors in the defined population is 58%, + or − 19.3%.

You are stating an *estimate* of the population parameter. Surrounding that estimate is a **confidence band** or **confidence interval** of plus or minus 19 percent. That confidence interval is based on probability theory and sampling theory, to which you will turn momentarily. This estimate suggests, if you repeated the process of sampling 25 students in your class 100 times, given certain assumptions, 95 times out of 100 times the *actual* population parameter—percentage of seniors in the class—would fall within the range bounded by 38.7 percent and 77.3 percent.[2] This is an example of **parameter estimation**.

_____
[2] The example here does not fit one important assumption underlying statistical tests, namely, that numerous independent random samples could be obtained from the population. The example does not fit the assumption because of the small class size, i.e., small population size. But if I asked you to imagine a class size of 5,000, you would say I was not being realistic. Even though class sizes do seem to be increasing of late, they are not quite that large. Yet.

You might be upset that the range of the above estimate is too broad; it has a "spread" or confidence interval of almost 40 points. The spread or uncertainty in the prediction results from the size of the sample drawn, the nature of the probability sampling strategy, how certain you want to be about the location of the population parameter, and other factors. For example, if you obtained completed surveys from a random sample of 200 students, you could state your parameter estimate as follows: the percentage of seniors in the defined population is 58 percent, + or − 6.8 percent. In other words, were you to repeat this process 100 times, given certain assumptions, 95 times out of 100 times you are certain the *actual* population parameter— percentage of seniors in the class—would fall within the range bounded by 51.2 percent and 64.8 percent. The "spread" of your estimate has been reduced to about 13 percentage points.

Our ability to connect statistics from a sample, such as the percentage of seniors who completed a survey, with parameters in a population, such as the percentage of seniors in the class, hinges on statistical theory. In the next section you will investigate this material. You then will see how certain types of sampling procedures allow researchers to make these connections from samples to populations, and other types of sampling procedures do not.

STATISTICS AND PROBABILITY THEORY

Normal Distributions and The Normal Curve

In Chapter 5 you examined histograms: density plots displaying actual scores of a sample on a variable. Figure 10.1 shows the histogram of the variable Sociability for the 100 police officers receiving community policing

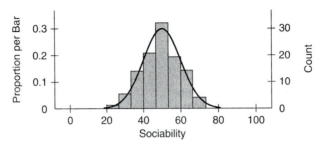

FIGURE 10.1

Histogram of scores for 100 CPOs on Sociability variable, with normal curve superimposed. *Source:* CPOSAT datafile.

training.[3] You can see that the scores taper off symmetrically on either side of the mean (48.1). You can also see that the most frequent scores are close to the mean or average score.[4]

Imagine now that you had scores on Sociability, not just from 100 police officers who had received training for community policing, but from an indefinitely large number of such officers. Imagine also that you can score the variable in a more precise fashion, resulting in bars in our histogram that are much "skinnier." Instead of a 10 different response categories, you have 1,000 or 10,000. If you were examining an indefinitely large number of cases, with extremely "skinny" bars in your histogram, the histogram would take on the form of a **normal curve**. [4] The curved line that you see on Figure 10.1 approximates the shape of that normal curve.

Normal curves are a family of curves that are:

- smooth, because the intervals are extremely narrow;

- bell-shaped in appearance, with more cases toward the middle than towards the ends;
- perfectly symmetrical, tapering away evenly at the left (lower scores) and at the right (higher scores); and
- based on an indefinitely large number of cases.

A normal curve exists for every distribution with a different mean and/or a different **standard deviation**.[5] (See Figure 10.2.) A standard deviation describes the "spread" or dispersion of scores in a distribution. The smaller the standard deviation, the more the scores cluster in the range close to the average; the larger the standard deviation, the more spread out the scores, and the fewer scores clustering close to the average.

---

[3] The data can be found on the workdisk in the files CPOSAT.WK1 or CPOSAT.DBF or CPOSAT.SYS

[4] Technically the mean or average is defined as:

$$\frac{\text{Sum of scores}}{\text{N of scores}}$$

[5] The formula for defining a standard deviation is as follows:

$$SD = \sqrt{((\Sigma\ (X - X_{average})^2)\ /\ N)}$$

where X = each individual score, $X_{average}$ = the mean, N = the number of cases in the sample.

If your variable represents nominal level measurement, and there are two possible response categories, the standard deviation is defined as:

$$SD = \sqrt{pq}$$

where p = the proportion of cases in the first category and q = the proportion of cases in the second category, and $p + q = 1.0$

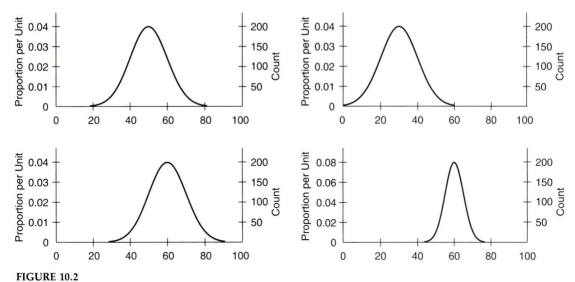

FIGURE 10.2
Top row shows two normal curves with different means and the same standard deviation. Bottom row shows two normal curves with the same means and different standard deviations.

Proportions of Cases = Area Under the Normal Curve

For distributions of scores that approximate the shape of a normal curve an important relationship exists between the mean and the standard deviation. No matter what the mean and standard deviation, if the distribution of scores approximates a normal distribution, a constant proportion of cases fall between the mean score and scores within one standard deviation of the mean; a constant proportion of cases also fall within two and three standard deviations of the mean. The area under the normal curve, which represents the portion of cases in that range, can be determined a priori if the scores in fact approximate a normal distribution. [5]

More specifically, in a normal distribution about 34 percent of the cases fall between the mean score on the variable and a standard deviation above the mean; 34 percent of the cases fall between the mean score and a standard deviation below the mean; 68 percent of the cases fall within one standard deviation

of the mean on either side; and 95 percent of the cases fall within *two* standard deviations of the mean on either side. See Figure 10.3.

Using Standardized Scores to Find Position Relative to Other Scores If you want to find out where a particular score exists in a distribution of scores, relative to other scores, you can use this relationship between areas under the normal curve, the mean and the standard deviation. You can create **normalized scores** (also called **standardized scores** or **z scores**) from raw scores. A Z score is created as follows:

$$Z = \frac{(\text{Raw score} - \text{Mean})}{\text{Standard deviation}}$$

For example, CASE 014 in the CPOSAT file scores 58 on Sociability. The mean is 48.16 and the sd = 9.94. The z score for this case on this variable is + .99 ((58 − 48.16)/9.94). Let's round this to +1.0. We know, therefore, since 50 percent of the cases score below the mean, and since 34 percent of the cases score

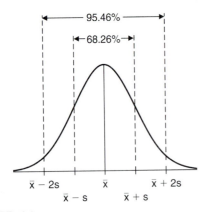

FIGURE 10.3
Areas under the normal curve. *Source:* Blalock, H. M., Jr. (1979). *Social statistics* (revised 2nd ed). New York: McGraw-Hill, Figure 7.7, p. 95.

between the mean and a standard deviation above the mean, that this score is higher than about (50% + 34%) 84 percent of the other scores. You can use Table 2 in Appendix A to translate between Z scores and areas under the normal curve, i.e., proportions of cases.

SAMPLING AND PROBABILITY THEORY

Sometimes Distributions of Scores Lean: Skewness

The variable we have examined above, scores on Sociability for CPOs, is distributed in an approximately normal fashion. If we superimpose a normal curve on the histogram, it approximates a normal distribution of scores except for being truncated at either end. (See Figure 10.1.) It is easy to imagine how, if you had lots of cases and "skinny" intervals, the histogram would approximate a normal distribution.

Sometimes, however, your histograms suggest a different story. The distribution can "lean" to the left, with many more scores at the lower end of the range for the variable,

and fewer cases at the upper end of the variable range. Figure 10.4 shows the histogram for a variable capturing *political views*. CPOs were asked to place themselves on a scale ranging from "Extremely Liberal in Politics," scored 1, to "Extremely Conservative in Politics," scored 10. Lower scores outnumber higher scores.

Distributions can also "lean" to the right, with higher scores predominating. If a distribution of scores leans in either direction you call it a **skewed** distribution of scores. If it is skewed, it is a **nonnormal distribution**. You cannot impose a symmetric, bell-shaped curve on the distribution of scores.

Random Samples from Skewed Distributions Are Normally Distributed

You decide to explore CPOs' political views further. But you want to examine only 10 cases. You decide to draw a simple random sample from the population. This type of sample will be defined later, but in such a sample each unit in the population has an equal chance of being selected, and a random selection procedure is used to independently

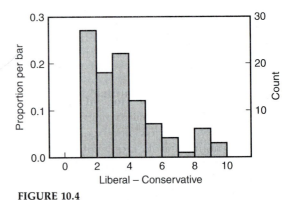

FIGURE 10.4
Example of a variable whose distribution is *non*normal. Histogram for Political Views for 100 CPOs. Note how the distribution is asymmetric and skewed. 1 = Extremely Liberal; 10 = Extremely Conservative. *Source:* CPOSAT datafile.

select each case. You might use a random number table (Appendix A, Table 1) to decide what cases to select into your sample. (See Box 10.1.) And, from that random sample, you can construct a **sample mean**, the average political views of those in the sample.

The mean score of cases in the sample represents one sample mean. You could then go back to your population and select a second simple random sample, and construct a second mean for this second sample. What you are starting to do is to construct a **distri-**

bution of sampling means. Each data point on this distribution is a mean of a sample.

If you had a large population of cases, and plotted means on a variable for a large number of random samples, you would find that the distribution of means approximated a normal distribution. This occurs even if the population of scores from which the samples were drawn is markedly non-normal. Given certain conditions, statistical theory tells us that means of random samples are always distributed normally regardless of the shape of the distribution for the population of scores. Figure 10.5 plots some of the means on this distribution of sampling means. The curved line represents a normal curve. As you can see the histogram of sample means begins to approximate a normal distribution.

Sampling Error

None of the sample means on Political Views falls exactly *at* the population mean for the 100 officers. Some means fall below the population mean. Some means fall above the population mean. Although it is possible for a

---

B O X 10.1

Using a Random Number Table

You can start anywhere in the table you want. Pick a starting point. Next, decide how many cases are in the population from which you are sampling. If you have 100 cases, then you are looking for three-digit numbers between 000 and 101. Start scanning three-digit numbers. You can go in any direction in the table you wish—left, right, up or down. Once you have started a scanning procedure, however, you must stick with that same procedure throughout. Further, once you have used a number, you cannot use any of the digits in that number again.

You might be scanning across a table with numbers like this:

10 09   73 25   33 91   49 91   45 23   80 32   17 90
05 01   45 11   76 20   82 66   95 41   84 96   28 52

Here are the cases you would sample:

10 09   73 25   33 91   49 91   45 23   <u>80 32</u>   17 90
<u>05 01</u>   45 11   76 20   <u>82 66</u>   95 41   84 96   28 52

You have sampled cases numbered: 100, 32, 5, 14, and 82 from these two rows of random numbers.

FIGURE 10.5
Samples of 10 cases each were randomly sampled from the 100 CPOs. The mean of each sample on the Political Views question was plotted. The means begin to approximate a normal distribution, even though scores on the variable itself are nonnormally distributed. *Source:* CPOSAT datafile.

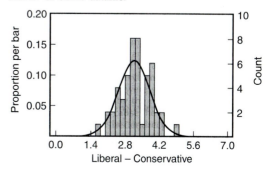

sample mean to fall exactly at the population mean, most of the time the sample means will be slightly "off." These discrepancies arise from **sampling error**. Sampling errors arise simply "by virtue of the fact that samples vary from one to the next." [6]

Here is an example. Put 100 pennies in a jar. With your eyes closed, reach in and randomly select and pull out 10 pennies. Calculate the average year from the date on these 10 coins. After you have calculated the average year, throw the 10 back in, stir all the pennies, and blindly select another 10. Calculate the average penny date again. Do this several times. You will see that the average dates for your samples vary. Assuming that you are doing the sampling in a perfectly random fashion, the variation arises simply from sampling error. If you were to begin drawing samples of 20, or 40, and knew the average date based on all the pennies, and plotted mean dates from these samples, you would see that the means from the larger samples cluster closer to the mean date on the population of coins.

Sampling error also applies to sample proportions as well as averages. In the CPO data file there are 22 women and 78 men. Draw several random samples of 10, and for each sample calculate the percentage of women. You will see that your sample means differ from but cluster around the population proportion of 22 percent women.

In sum, so far you have learned how statistical theory allows you to reliably predict that the mean scores for simple random samples drawn from a population of scores will always be distributed normally, even if the population of scores is skewed or nonnormally distributed. You have also learned that sample means or proportions will differ from the population mean, due to sampling error, but will in general cluster around the population mean score, or population proportion, on the variable of interest. Larger samples will yield sample means or proportions closer to the population mean or proportion.

The Sampling Distribution Describes the Population

When you draw a probability sample, where the chances of each element being put into your sample are known and are not zero [7], probability theory predicts some further features of the means of the samples drawn. Probability theory states that, under certain conditions, as the number of cases in each sample becomes large, the means of those samples approach the population mean. The mean of your sample means approximates the population mean.

In addition, probability theory also describes the "spread" or dispersion of the sample means. This spread is due, if certain conditions hold, to sampling error. The spread of the sample means or sample proportions is called the **standard error** of the means or proportions. The standard error tells you how large your sampling errors are. The larger your sampling error, the larger your standard error of sample means or proportions. We gauge how sizable our sampling errors are by calculating standard errors of our sample statistics such as means or proportions.

The standard errors are equivalent to the standard deviation of the sample divided by the square root of the sample size.

For a mean the standard error =

$$SD/\sqrt{N}$$

where N = the number of cases in the sample that are making up the sample mean.

For a proportion based on two response categories the standard error is equivalent to

$$\sqrt{p * q / N}$$

where p = proportion of cases in first category
q = the proportion of cases in the second category
p and q add to 1.00.

As you can see from these formulae, if you want to reduce your sampling error, you decrease your standard error by drawing larger samples. For example, you might draw a random sample of 5 CPOs from the file of 100. In your sample of 5 the proportion women might be 30 percent. The standard error associated with this sample proportion

$$SE = \sqrt{(.30 * .70)/5} = .20$$

If your sample on which the proportion was based was five times as large (n = 25) your standard error would be much smaller.

$$SE = \sqrt{(.30 * .70)/25} = .09$$

So if you are drawing larger samples your sampling errors, and therefore your standard errors of your means or proportions, will be smaller. Therefore, your sample means (or proportions) will in general be closer to the population mean (or proportion) for each variable of interest.

From the Sample to the Population

The standard error is a standard deviation of a sample proportion or a sample mean. In the case of the proportions of men vs. women CPOs, we know the sample proportions approach a normal distribution. And we know that the mean of sample proportions, if our samples are unbiased, will tend to cluster around the overall population proportion (22% women). Knowing all these we can estimate the population proportion precisely from our sample proportion. We can estimate a population parameter from our sample statistic.

Recall that in a normal distribution approximately 68 percent of the cases fall in a region from one standard deviation below the mean, to one standard deviation above the mean. About 95 percent of the cases fall in a region from two standard deviations below the mean to two standard deviations above the mean.[6]

Since the standard error is the standard deviation of the means, we can say if: certain assumptions hold, and you were to draw 100 random samples from the population, 95 out of 100 of those samples would yield a proportion within two standard errors of the population proportion. Thus you can say that you are 95 percent confident that the actual population proportion lies within the region bounded by (proportion + or − 2 SEs).[7] The same logic used here for sample proportions in relation to population proportions applies to sample means in relation to population means.

In short, with probability theory we can infer from a sample mean or a sample proportion that a population mean or a population proportion lies within a certain range of scores: sample mean (or proportion) + or − 2 SEs. We can also state how confident we are (95% or 95 times out of 100) that the population mean or proportion lies within that range of scores.

So far we have been discussing simple random samples, where every case in the population has an equal chance of being selected. It is called a **probability sample** because these chances of each element being selected are known. The same mathematics, with some modifications, apply to other types of

---

[6] To be technical, exactly 95 percent of the cases fall in the region from 1.96 standard deviations below the mean to 1.96 standard deviations above the mean. I round to 2 here for simplicity.
[7] You can select a different confidence level, such as 90%, 99% or 99.9%. For a different confidence level you select + or − a different number of standard errors.

samples, to be discussed below, where the probabilities of two different cases may not be equal. What is common to probability samples is that the chances of selection are known and calculable. With probability samples we can use probability theory to make precise estimates of the amount of sampling error. Therefore, if certain assumptions hold, we can precisely specify the region of scores where our overall population mean or overall population proportion can be found. You can*not* make sound estimates about the population, however, if you use nonprobability sampling procedures.

BIAS AND SAMPLING: NONPROBABILITY SAMPLING PROCEDURES

If you diligently carry through a probability sampling procedure and draw a probability sample from your population of cases, your sample of cases will represent an *un*biased subgroup of that larger population. The mean or proportion in your sample on a variable provides an unbiased estimate of the population mean or proportion. You will be exploring below a variety of different probability sampling procedures.

Probability sampling procedures contrast with **nonprobability sampling procedures**. These are also called **model sampling procedures**. A model sample is based on what you assume to be the case (a model) about the distributions of variables in the larger population. [8] There are several varieties. What they have in common are two features. (1) With a nonprobability sampling procedure you cannot use probability theory to make population estimates from sample means or proportions. Sampling error cannot be estimated. (2) With nonprobability sampling procedures you do not know how much bias you are introducing with your sampling procedures. You cannot be assured that your

sample means or proportions are *un*biased population estimates. The connections between the sample and the population are tenuous.

I am not saying that nonprobability sampling procedures are never appropriate. Sometimes they are. But you need to be aware that when you use these procedures you cannot make any legitimate inferences that go beyond the actual cases you have examined.

Varieties of Nonprobability Sampling Approaches

A haphazard or **convenience sample** would include anyone you can conveniently interview. If you were doing a needs assessment for the community-policing initiative discussed in the running example, you might be tempted to simply have interviewers walk the streets in the relevant neighborhoods and interview anyone they can about the matters of interest to you. These "person in the street" interviews, however, do not necessarily inform you about the population—all folks living in the neighborhoods. Why would you believe that the sample of people walking the streets in neighborhood N at a certain time of day, and who are willing to talk to an interviewer, would be representative of all residents in that neighborhood? It is the latter—the population—which is of interest.

Another type of nonprobability sample method requires that someone designate "typical" respondents or units. An expert might decide that a certain individual or household or organization or community is typical of a larger population. Such **purposive** or **judgmental sampling**, however, is also problematic. [9] Experts are unlikely to agree with one another on what constitutes a typical unit.

A third type of nonprobability sampling is simple **quota sampling**, where you interview people who fall into a particular category until you reach a specified number of respondents in that category. In the example being discussed here you might choose to interview any 10 renters and any 10 owners in each of the neighborhoods affected by the community policing initiative.

A fourth type of nonprobability sampling is **snowball sampling**. You use respondents to refer you to other potential respondents. You ask each new respondent for additional nominations, until there are no more new people being added to your list of respondents. This procedure can be extremely useful when you are seeking respondents who are rarities in the general population. For example, instead of interviewing residents in study neighborhoods, you may be interested in interviewing people who are informal leaders. Yet no lists of this population exist, making it difficult for you to locate these leaders. The most efficient means of contacting such persons might be through a snowball sampling technique. You locate a few informal leaders, and they refer you to others.

Limits of Nonprobability Samples

With nonprobability samples the connection is tenuous between the *sample* of people interviewed, and the *population* from which the sample was drawn. The researcher can argue that the sample represents the population. But the argument is valid only if the researcher correctly guesses the makeup of the population. Consequently, most of the time, these samples generate suspect parameter estimates. The amount of sample bias is usually unknown. The results emerging from nonprobability samples are, strictly speaking, applicable *only* to that sample that completed the survey.

PROBABILITY SAMPLES

Varieties of Probability Sampling

There are many different types of sampling designs you can use to obtain a probability sample. All of these designs represent elaborations on drawing a simple random sample (SRS). *In all types of probability sampling "there must be both some element of randomization and some sort of a complete listing."* [10] With probability sampling you can refer legitimately back to the population.

Simple Random Sampling All probability sampling designs can be viewed as variations on **simple random sampling** (SRS). [11] SRS is appropriate when you have an accurate list or **sampling frame** of the units in the population, and the size of the total population is not extremely large. The drawing for the state lottery in many states represents a familiar example of simple random sample. With SRS, here is how you proceed conceptually:

- A randomization procedure is used to select elements from a population.
- All elements are included for possible selection.
- All elements have an equal probability of being selected.
- The choice of one element to be included in the sample does not influence the chance that another element will be included in the sample; each choice is independent of the other choices. Therefore, any possible combination of elements in the final sample is possible.
- Once an element has been selected it is in the sample. The sampling is done at one stage.

Here is how the *mechanics* of drawing a SRS proceed:

- Assign each unit in the sampling frame a unique number.

- Use a randomization procedure to select a random sample of cases.
- Each time a random number is chosen that corresponds to the number of a unit on the list, choose that unit.

Suppose that you were interested in a project involving different states in the U.S. You do not want to do your study in all states, however, but just a few, say 10. In your study you view all states as equal; the fact that some states are larger than other states, or that some have higher crime than others, is not of interest. You could select a SRS by enumerating the states from 1 to 50. It does not matter how you order the states. That enumerated list is now your sampling frame. You could then go to a random number table and begin scanning for digits between 00 and 51. The first 10 numbers will tell you which states to include in your SRS. Table 10.1 provides an example of an SRS of 50 states. If n = the number of units you desire to select, and N = the number of units in the population, then the chance of any state being selected = $n/N = {}^{10}/_{50} = 20$ percent. This is your sampling proportion (20%) or sampling fraction ($^1/_5$).

Simple random samples are the "best" type of sampling design for many purposes. They are simple, efficient, and easy to implement under many circumstances. There are also many cases, however, where they are not feasible. Suppose you do not have available a list of the members of the population. Or suppose that the list is so long it would take an extremely long time to assign numbers to each element on the list. Or suppose your population is individuals but you only have information about households. It is for reasons like this that researchers have developed other kinds of sampling designs.

Other probability sampling methods can be viewed as modifications of simple random sampling procedures. Other methods make an either/or choice on five basic issues and combine those choices into an overall sampling design. [7] Let's discuss these five choices you need to make when settling on a sampling design.

Systematic Sampling vs. Random Sampling You might have a list of population units that is arrayed in a particular way. For example, the states listed in Table 10.2 have been sorted by the four geographic regions of the country (Northeast, South, Midwest, West). If you were to pick a simple random sample of states, there is a chance that your sample might *not* include any states from one of these four regions. In order to be sure that your selected units are spread out among the four areas, you might want to use systematic sampling. You also find systematic sampling useful when the sampling frame you are working with is extremely large, and completely enumerating all the units in the frame might be very time consuming.

In **systematic** or **interval sampling** units are selected from a list in such a way that the units selected are separated from one another by an interval. If you want to interval sample n units from a total of N available units, you:

- Define a sampling interval (i) where i = N/n.
- Pick a random start, using a random number table, between the number 0 and i + 1
- Select the unit whose number corresponds to the random start.
- Select every ith unit thereafter.

Table 10.2 provides the results of a systematic sample of states. The sampling interval was $^{50}/_{10}$ or 5. The **sampling fraction** or **sampling ratio** is the inverse of the sampling interval, and tells you the fraction of cases to be selected. ($SF = n/N = {}^{10}/_{50} = {}^1/_5$.) States are sorted by region and alphabetically within region, then enumerated from 1 to 50. From a random number table 3 was selected for a random start. The first selected state was Massachusetts. Then the sampling interval was added to the random start to obtain the

TABLE 10.1
Simple Random Sample of 50 States

Number	State	Random numbers used, in order	Selected states, in order corresponding to random number
1 AL	Alabama	84	
2 AK	Alaska	27	⟶ 1. NE
3 AZ	Arizona	55	
4 AR	Arkansas	69	
5 CA	California	28	⟶ 2. NV
6 CO	Colorado	17	⟶ 3. KY
7 CT	Connecticut	74	
8 DE	Delaware	23	⟶ 4. MN
9 FL	Florida	99	
10 GA	Georgia	31	⟶ 5. NM
11 HI	Hawaii	94	
12 ID	Idaho	72	
13 IL	Illinois	33	⟶ 6. NC
14 IN	Indiana	31	(already selected)
15 IA	Iowa	29	⟶ 7. NH
16 KS	Kansas	83	
17 KY	Kentucky	86	
18 LA	Louisiana	45	⟶ 8. VT
19 ME	Maine	65	
20 MD	Maryland	46	⟶ 9. VA
21 MA	Massachusetts	92	
22 MI	Michigan	20	⟶ 10. MD
23 MN	Minnesota		
24 MS	Mississippi		
25 MO	Missouri		
26 MT	Montana		
27 NE	Nebraska		
28 NV	Nevada		
29 NH	New Hampshire		
30 NJ	New Jersey		
31 NM	New Mexico		
32 NY	New York		
33 NC	North Carolina		
34 ND	North Dakota		
35 OH	Ohio		
36 OK	Oklahoma		
37 OR	Oregon		
38 PA	Pennsylvania		
39 RI	Rhode Island		
40 SC	South Carolina		
41 SD	South Dakota		
42 TN	Tennessee		
43 TX	Texas		
44 UT	Utah		
45 VT	Vermont		
46 VA	Virginia		
47 WA	Washington		
48 WV	West Virginia		
49 WI	Wisconsin		
50 WY	Wyoming		

Note: States sorted in alphabetical order. First column shows each state's number in the list. Sampled states are underlined. Column after states shows random numbers generated between (inclusive) 1 and 99. Next column shows, for numbers between 1 and 50 (inclusive) the corresponding state that was sampled, and the order selected.

Systematic Sample of 10 States from a Population of 50 States

State		Census Region		Enumeration Number	Sampled States
CT	Connecticut	Northeast	1	1	
ME	Maine	Northeast	1	2	
MA	Massachusetts	Northeast	1	3	1. RS Random Start
NH	New Hampshire	Northeast	1	4	
NJ	New Jersey	Northeast	1	5	
NY	New York	Northeast	1	6	
PA	Pennsylvania	Northeast	1	7	
RI	Rhode Island	Northeast	1	8	2. RS + 1 Sampling Interval (i * 1)
VT	Vermont	Northeast	1	9	
IL	Illinois	Midwest	2	10	
IN	Indiana	Midwest	2	11	
IA	Iowa	Midwest	2	12	
KS	Kansas	Midwest	2	13	3. RS + 2 Sampling Intervals (i * 2)
MI	Michigan	Midwest	2	14	
MN	Minnesota	Midwest	2	15	
MO	Missouri	Midwest	2	16	
NE	Nebraska	Midwest	2	17	
ND	North Dakota	Midwest	2	18	4. RS + 3 Sampling Intervals (i * 3)
OH	Ohio	Midwest	2	19	
SD	South Dakota	Midwest	2	20	
WI	Wisconsin	Midwest	2	21	
AL	Alabama	South	3	22	
AR	Arkansas	South	3	23	5. RS + 4 Sampling Intervals (i * 4)
DE	Delaware	South	3	24	
FL	Florida	South	3	25	
GA	Georgia	South	3	26	
KY	Kentucky	South	3	27	
LA	Louisiana	South	3	28	6. RS + 5 Sampling Intervals (i * 5)
MD	Maryland	South	3	29	
MS	Mississippi	South	3	30	
NC	North Carolina	South	3	31	
OK	Oklahoma	South	3	32	
SC	South Carolina	South	3	33	7. RS + 6 Sampling Intervals (i * 6)
TN	Tennessee	South	3	34	
TX	Texas	South	3	35	
VA	Virginia	South	3	36	
WV	West Virginia	South	3	37	
AK	Alaska	West	4	38	8. RS + 7 Sampling Intervals (i * 7)
AZ	Arizona	West	4	39	
CA	California	West	4	40	
CO	Colorado	West	4	41	
HI	Hawaii	West	4	42	
ID	Idaho	West	4	43	9. RS + 8 Sampling Intervals (i * 8)
MT	Montana	West	4	44	
NV	Nevada	West	4	45	
NM	New Mexico	West	4	46	
OR	Oregon	West	4	47	
UT	Utah	West	4	48	10. RS + 9 Sampling Intervals (i * 9)
WA	Washington	West	4	49	
WY	Wyoming	West	4	50	

Note: States have been sorted by region, and alphabetically within region. Sampling interval = N/n = $^{50}/_{10}$ = 5. Random number table was consulted to obtain random start between 0 and 6. The corresponding state was selected, and every ith state thereafter was also selected. Sampled states have been underlined.

second sampled state, Rhode Island. Then the sampling interval was added again, resulting in the selection of Kansas. The process was continued until 10 states were sampled. With systematic sampling you will always select exactly the number of cases desired.

As a result of the systematic sampling procedure the sampled cases reflect all four regions of the country. In the final sample you have two states from the Northeast, two from the Midwest, three from the South, and three from the West. You have succeeded in "spreading out" your sample across the regions.

Although systematic sampling is generally appropriate in the same types of situations as simple random sampling, there are two situations where you would want to avoid systematic sampling. (1) The lists from which you are extracting your sampled units have periodicities. You might have a list of neighborhood organization members arranged such that a leader name was followed by 10 non-leaders. If your interval was 10 and your random start was not 10, you would never sample a leader. [12] (2) The units you are sampling are times, and the list is arranged using a temporal dimension. [13]

Stratified Sampling vs. Unstratified Sampling   In the two examples above—SRS and systematic sampling—we have ordered the cases in the sampling frame before sampling, but we have not separated the different cases in the sampling frame into different groups. These represent examples of **unstratified sampling** procedures. If you organize cases in the sampling frame into different groups or **strata** (singular: **stratum**) and then sample *independently* from each of those groups, you can do **stratified sampling**.

Why? By grouping cases, and sampling from each of those groupings, you may be able to achieve a smaller sampling error than you would with a SRS or a systematic sample

using the same number of cases. In order to realize this gain in efficiency, however, you must organize the units in the sampling frame into groups that are relatively homogeneous on the outcome centrally relevant to your study. [10]

Proportional and Disproportional   One way to do stratified sampling is so that the sample sizes selected within each stratum are *proportional* to the fraction of the population within that group or stratum. You will scrutinize this type of stratification first, then go on to examine an example with disproportional sampling. In the latter case you select more or less from a group than would be warranted based on the group's contribution to the population.

Create Strata   You first divide units in your sampling frame into mutually exclusive and exhaustive groups (strata). Then, within each group or stratum, you select independent samples. You group cases into strata based on their scores on a **stratification variable**. This is a variable on which you already have information for your cases, and which you think correlates positively or negatively with the outcome of interest in your study.

Consider the following example. You have divided the 50 states into five strata, based on their percentage increase in the reported violent crime rate between 1985 and 1990. Percentage increase in the reported violent crime rate is your **stratification variable**. This variable represents a key aspect of the population of states, given the purposes of your study. For example, your dependent variable might be public support for increased prison construction. You expect that state scores on the stratifying variable, percentage increase in violent crime from 1985 to 1990, will correlate positively with support for prison construction.

The states in Table 10.3 have been sorted on this stratification variable. In the top stra-

TABLE 10.3
Choosing a Stratified Sample of States

Strata and States Within Strata	Violent Crime Rate 1985	Violent Crime Rate 1990	Violent Crime Rate Percent Change	Rank in Violent Crime Percent Increase	Random Numbers for Selection Within Strata
Highest					
Arkansas	298	532	78.6%	1	32 22 49 1 41 2 47 7 8 0 8 32
Illinois	553	967	74.9%	2	
Alabama	416	709	70.3%	3	
Indiana	284	474	66.9%	4	
Tennessee	402	670	66.8%	5	
Iowa	181	300	65.6%	6	
Georgia	457	756	65.5%	7	
Minnesota	191	306	60.3%	8	
South Carolina	617	977	58.3%	9	
North Carolina	410	624	52.1%	10	
Second Highest					
Nebraska	218	330	51.4%	11	44 21 9 28 10 27 12 18 26 16 5 31
Florida	827	1244	50.5%	12	
Missouri	477	715	50.0%	13	
Texas	512	761	48.7%	14	
Connecticut	375	554	47.7%	15	
Delaware	453	655	44.6%	16	
Louisiana	641	898	40.2%	17	
Wisconsin	191	265	38.6%	18	
Kansas	327	448	36.9%	19	
North Dakota	54	74	36.9%	20	
Third Highest					
South Dakota	120	163	35.7%	21	27 19 23 3 20 40 27 17 46 1 18 15
California	773	1045	35.2%	22	
Washington	372	502	34.8%	23	
Arizona	494	652	32.1%	24	
Oklahoma	423	548	29.4%	25	
New York	914	1181	29.2%	26	
Massachusetts	577	736	27.6%	27	
Ohio	398	506	27.2%	28	
Wyoming	237	301	27.2%	29	
Pennsylvania	343	431	25.7%	30	

tum are the 10 states that have increased the most, in the second stratum are the next 10 states with the highest percentage increases, and so on. You seek, for the purposes of your study, to include exactly 2 states from each of these groups.

Since you will choose an equal number of states from each stratum, and since the five strata are of equal size, you are doing propor-tional rather than disproportional stratified sampling. The number of cases sampled from each stratum is proportional to the propor-tion of the cases in that stratum.

You Reduce Between-Stratum Sampling Errors If you were to use SRS or systematic sam-pling you could not guarantee that you would extract exactly two states from each of

T A B L E 10.3 (*continued*)

Strata and States Within Strata	Violent Crime Rate 1985	Violent Crime Rate 1990	Violent Crime Rate Percent Change	Rank in Violent Crime Percent Increase	Random Numbers for Selection Within Strata
			Next to Lowest		
Rhode Island	355	432	21.7%	31	34 31 15 28 37 11 19 16 8 30 41 6
Mississippi	280	340	21.6%	32	
Kentucky	322	390	21.2%	33	
Virginia	293	351	19.7%	34	
New Jersey	553	648	17.1%	35	
Idaho	239	276	15.4%	36	
Maryland	807	919	13.9%	37	
New Mexico	687	780	13.6%	38	
Hawaii	252	281	11.5%	39	
Utah	256	284	10.9%	40	
			Lowest		
Colorado	476	526	10.5%	41	3 17 46 29 7 45 8 27 0 38 39 47
Michigan	717	790	10.2%	42	
New Hampshire	125	132	5.2%	43	
Oregon	488	507	3.9%	44	
West Virginia	172	169	−1.6%	45	
Vermont	133	127	−4.4%	46	
Nevada	655	601	−8.3%	47	
Maine	160	143	−10.5%	48	
Alaska	614	525	−14.6%	49	
Montana	213	159	−25.2%	50	

Note: 1990 figures from T. J. Flanagan and K. Maguire (Eds.) *Sourcebook of criminal justice statistics, 1991.* Washington, DC: U.S. DOJ. Table 3.129. 1985 figures from SYSTAT USDATA file. Rates are per 100,000 population. Violent crimes, include murder, forcible rape, robbery, and aggravated assault. Figures can be found on spreadsheet STATES.WK1 on the workdisk.

the five strata. From some strata you might sample 3, 1, or even 0 states. In short, with respect to the relative numbers of cases selected, you have sampling errors between strata. You are likely to oversample from some strata, and undersample from others.

With single stage cluster sampling, you are including every element within the sampled clusters. For example, you might be content analyzing newspaper stories about police officers killed in the line of duty. You cluster the stories by year. After selecting a year, you study every story within that cluster (year). But you are missing data from your nonsampled clusters, i.e., the years not selected.

As you can see from Table 10.3, you examine two-digit random numbers for each stratum, and choose the two states within each stratum corresponding to the first two random numbers encountered whose numbers match the cases enumerated within that stratum.

Within Each Stratum You May Use Any Probability Selection Procedure You Wish Within each stratum you may use any random sampling procedure you wish: SRS, systematic sampling, or PPS sampling (to be explained below), for example.

Only Stratify If You Can Create Homogeneous Groupings   It only makes sense to stratify if the groups of cases created by your stratification variable are, as a result of the stratification, somewhat homogeneous on your dependent variable. In short, with stratification you seek to create *homogeneous* groups of cases in each stratum. If you do not have the information necessary to organize the units in your sampling frame into groups that are somewhat homogeneous on the dependent variable, it does not make sense to stratify your sample.

In sum, to stratify your sample, you:

- Select a stratification variable that is related to the dependent variable of interest.
- Assign each element in the population to one and only one stratum. You seek to create strata that are as homogeneous as possible.
- Sample cases from *each* stratum, using the desired selection procedures.

Disproportional Sampling   You may be interested in manipulating your sampling fractions for different types of cases in your sampling frame. For example in your sample of 10 states you might want to include 6 states that were among the top 10 in percentage increase in reported violent crime from 1985 to 1990. You would **oversample** within that stratum, using a sampling fraction of $^6/_{10}$, to select 6 out of the 10 available. In the other four strata you would **undersample**, using a sampling fraction of $^1/_{10}$, to select 1 out of the 10 available in these four other groups.

Most typically researchers use disproportional sampling so that they can equalize the size of separate subpopulations and thus better compare them. If you are comparing men and women's fear of crime levels, those comparisons will be most efficient if your sample is 50 percent men and 50 percent women. If you are sampling students on a campus where women represent 67 percent of the population and men represent 33 percent of the population, and you want equal size samples, you will use a lower sampling fraction for men as compared to women. Here is how your sampling fractions would look if you sought a final sample of 100, were on a campus with 6,700 men and 3,300 women, and had cooperation from everyone in your sample.

Sex	Population size	Sampling fraction	Resulting sample size
Men	6,700	$^{50}/_{6700}$ (.007)	50
Women	3,300	$^{50}/_{3300}$ (.015)	50

If you have used disproportional sampling, and you seek to estimate a parameter for the entire *population*, you will need to **reweight** your sample so that each group is weighted in proportion to its share of the total population. In the example above you would need to weight men "up" and weight women "down." Researchers do this by assigning **case weights**. For example, men represent 67 percent of the population but only 50 percent of your sample. You would assign each male a case weight of 1.34 ($^{67}/_{50}$). You would assign each woman a case weight of .66 ($^{33}/_{50}$).

Element Sampling vs. Cluster Sampling
With a SRS or a systematic sample you directly sample the actual elements you will include in your study. There is no grouping of cases before sample selection. With stratified samples and cluster samples elements are grouped, and you first select groups.

With a stratified sample, units in the population are sorted into strata, based on scores on the stratification variable. You sample cases from *every* stratum. With cluster sampling the population is divided into a large number of groups or clusters. But you *sample* from *among* the clusters or groups. In other words, you include units from some clusters in your sample, but not from other clusters [14].

With cluster sampling most often you are not sampling elements directly; rather, you sample clusters of elements, and then, in a subsequent stage, you sample elements from within the cluster. This is a **multistage cluster sampling** procedure. If you sample a cluster, and then use *every* element within the chosen cluster, you have completed a **single stage cluster sampling** design.

Rationale Cluster samples are used extensively as a means of reducing research costs. Samples can be clustered on a geographical basis (precincts, neighborhoods, cities, states, etc.), an organizational basis (organizations, classes, identified groups), or some other basis. For example, if you were content analyzing newspaper crime reports, you might want to cluster the data by year and month within years.

Suppose you wanted to survey residents in a large city using door-to-door interviews. You could sample census tracts, and use those as your first-stage clusters. You could then sample blocks within sampled census tracts as your second-stage clusters. This would dramatically reduce the traveling costs associated with door-to-door surveying. You might interview every person within every household on the sampled blocks. Alternatively, you might continue with third-stage clusters, selecting households on the sampled blocks, and then proceed to sample individuals within households.

Cluster sampling is usually more economical than simple random samples, or systematic samples, and is especially appropriate in situations where no sampling frame for the entire population is available.

Cluster Heterogeneity Desired In stratified sampling you sought to create homogeneous strata, and you sampled from each created stratum. By contrast with cluster sampling, you are only sampling from *some* of the clusters. So in the first case (stratified) you are taking *some* from *each* group created. In the second case (clustered) you are only taking from *some* of the groups created.

With single stage cluster sampling, you are including every element within the sampled clusters. For example, you might be content analyzing newspaper stories about police officers killed in the line of duty. You cluster the stories by year. After selecting a year, you study every story within that cluster (year). But you are missing data from your nonsampled clusters, i.e., the years not selected.

Imagine further that the dependent variable of interest to you in this study is the degree of outrage expressed at the officer's death. Since you are including all the elements within each sampled cluster, there is no sampling error *within* clusters. Sampling error arises from *between* cluster differences. The stories in the year (cluster) you selected were different from the stories in the year (cluster) you did not sample.

Here's an example of how such errors can arise. You are examining just two randomly sampled years of stories. Coverage during one of those years was dominated by some unusually heinous officer deaths that occurred. Stories from that cluster will not be *representative* of the larger population of stories from the full period under investigation. If this is the case, your cluster sampling will have resulted in a large amount of sampling error because one of the clusters sampled was not typical of the population.

Consequently, with cluster sampling you desire clusters that are as *heterogeneous* as possible. You hope, especially if the number of first-stage clusters is small, that each cluster is a representative of the larger population of elements as possible. You also desire a large number of initial clusters.

TABLE 10.4
Cluster PPS Sample of 10 States

State	State Populations In 1990	Cumulative Population Before St.	Cumulative Population After St.	% Total Pop.	Random Start	RS + − SI
Connecticut	3,226,929	0	3,226,929	1.3%		
Maine	1,218,053	3,226,929	4,444,982	0.5%		
Massachusetts	5,928,331	4,444,982	10,373,313	2.4%		
New Hampshire	1,103,163	10,373,313	11,476,476	0.4%		
New Jersey	7,617,418	11,476,476	19,093,894	3.1%	13,911,296	
New York	17,626,586	19,093,894	36,720,480	7.2%		
Pennsylvania	11,784,434	36,720,480	48,504,914	4.8%		38,439,380
Rhode Island	988,609	48,504,914	49,493,523	0.4%		
Vermont	560,029	49,493,523	50,053,552	0.2%		
Illinois	11,325,247	50,053,552	61,378,799	4.6%		
Indiana	5,496,725	61,378,799	66,875,524	2.2%		62,967,464
Iowa	2,766,658	66,875,524	69,642,182	1.1%		
Kansas	2,467,845	69,642,182	71,110,027	1.0%		
Michigan	9,179,661	72,110,027	81,289,688	3.7%		
Minnesota	4,358,864	81,289,688	85,648,552	1.8%		
Missouri	5,079,385	85,648,552	90,727,937	2.1%		87,495,547
Nebraska	1,572,503	90,727,937	92,300,440	0.6%		
North Dakota	634,223	92,300,440	92,934,663	0.3%		
Ohio	10,777,514	92,934,663	103,712,177	4.4%		
South Dakota	693,294	103,712,177	104,405,471	0.3%		
Wisconsin	4,869,640	104,405,471	109,275,111	2.0%		
Alabama	3,984,384	109,275,111	113,259,495	1.6%		112,023,631
Arkansas	3,619,064	113,259,495	116,878,559	1.5%		
Delaware	658,031	116,878,559	117,536,590	0.3%		
Florida	12,774,603	117,536,590	130,311,193	5.2%		
Georgia	6,386,948	130,311,193	136,698,141	2.6%		136,551,715
Kentucky	3,665,220	136,698,141	140,363,361	1.5%		
Louisiana	4,180,831	140,363,361	144,544,192	1.7%		
Maryland	4,732,934	144,544,192	149,277,126	1.9%		

Taking Cluster Size into Account You can choose to give each cluster an equal chance of being selected. But in cases where the number of elements in the clusters differ, you may not want to give each cluster an equal chance of being selected. If there are more elements in some clusters than in others, you want to give those larger clusters a higher chance of being selected. In short, instead of *equal selection probabilities* for each cluster you may want each cluster's probability of selection to be *proportional to its size*, i.e., the number of elements within it. This is called **probability proportional to size** or **PPS sampling**.

If in cluster sampling you allow each cluster's chance of selection to be proportional to its size at each sampling stage, and sample accordingly within clusters, you will end up with a *self-weighting sample*. When you have completed all stages of sampling, the representation of different groups in your sample will be proportional to their representation in the total population. You will not need to reweight cases.

T A B L E 10.4 (*continued*)

State	State Populations In 1990	Cumulative Population Before St.	Cumulative Population After St.	% Total Pop.	Random Start	RS + − SI
Mississippi	2,534,814	149,277,126	151,811,940	1.0%		
North Carolina	6,552,927	151,811,940	158,364,867	2.7%		
Oklahoma	3,123,799	158,364,867	161,488,666	1.3%		161,079,799
South Carolina	3,407,389	161,488,666	164,896,055	1.4%		
Tennessee	4,822,134	164,896,055	169,718,189	2.0%		
Texas	16,824,665	169,718,189	186,542,854	6.9%		185,607,882
Virginia	6,127,680	186,542,854	192,670,534	2.5%		
West Virginia	1,782,958	192,670,534	194,453,492	0.7%		
Alaska	545,774	194,453,492	194,999,266	0.2%		
Arizona	2,337,395	194,999,266	197,336,661	1.0%		
California	29,279,015	197,336,661	226,615,676	11.9%		210,135,966
Colorado	3,272,460	226,615,676	229,888,136	1.3%		
Hawaii	1,095,237	229,888,136	230,983,373	0.4%		
Idaho	1,003,558	230,983,373	231,986,931	0.4%		
Montana	794,329	231,986,931	232,781,260	0.3%		
Nevada	1,193,285	232,781,260	233,974,545	0.5%		
New Mexico	1,490,381	233,974,545	235,464,926	0.6%		234,664,050
Oregon	2,828,214	235,464,926	238,293,140	1.2%		
Utah	1,711,117	238,293,140	240,004,257	0.7%		
Washington	4,826,675	240,004,257	244,830,932	2.0%		
Wyoming	449,905	244,830,932	245,280,837	0.2%		

Average contribution of state: Pop.: 2.0%   Sample: 3.7%
245,280,837   100.0%

For 10 States SI = 245,280,837 / 10 = 24,528,084
Random Start =   13,911,296

Note: States have been sorted by Census region, and within region alphabetically. Second column shows state population, based on 1990 Census estimates. The next two columns show cumulative population figures: before the state on the line is taken into account, and after it is taken into account. The difference between these two figures is that state's population. The next column indicates what percentage that state contributes to the total national population. Naturally, since there are 50 states, each state, on average, contributes 2 percent to the total population. The next column shows the random start, which falls within the interval for the New Jersey population. The next column shows the population figures for the random start plus 1, 2, 3, and so on sampling intervals. The average proportion of the national population contributed by the sampled states is 3.7 percent, since larger states were more likely to be sampled. Sampled states are underlined.

Table 10.4 provides an example. You want to interview people within 10 states. States are your clusters. You want your 10 states to be spread across the country, so you order them by geographic region, and plan to do systematic sampling. The size measure used for each state is its 1990 population. You select 10 clusters or states. Each state's chance of being selected is proportional to its population size.

Your sampling frame is based on each state's population. You calculate your sam-

pling interval (total population/n of desired cases). SI = 24,528,084. You choose a random start between 0 and your sampling interval. RS = 13,911,296. Your first cluster sampled is New Jersey, Pennsylvania is your second, and so on.

If you are PPS cluster sampling 10 states out of 50, your sample must include California. California contains almost 12 percent of the population for the entire country. Any cluster with more than 10 percent of the population must be selected, since you are PPS sampling and since your sampling fraction is $1/10$ or 10 percent.

The sampled clusters include three of the five largest population states: California, Texas, and Pennsylvania. This has occurred because larger states were more likely to be selected.

The steps involved in cluster sampling are:

- Assign each unit in the population to one and only one cluster.
- Determine or estimate the size of each cluster.
- If the sizes of the different clusters are comparable, you can randomly select clusters of elements or use interval sampling to select clusters.
- If the sizes of the clusters are different, use PPS sampling to select clusters with each cluster's chances of selection proportional to its size.
- Select units from within clusters (if needed; i.e., repeat above steps within clusters as needed).

Summing Up on Probability Sampling Decisions   In sum, when you construct a probability sample, you have five sets of choices to make. [15]

Do I Random Sample or Do I Use Systematic Sampling?   With a SRS, you do not need to organize the elements in the population in any order, although you do need to completely enumerate units in the sampling frames. With systematic sampling you will take every *i*th unit from a sampling frame that has been ordered on some attribute.

Do I Do Stratified Sampling or Unstratified Sampling?   In the former case you organize all the units in the population into homogeneous groups using a stratification variable that is theoretically important. You independently select units from *each* stratum. You are in effect constructing a sampling frame

within each stratum. Stratification reduces between-stratum sampling errors in terms of the relative number of cases selected. With unstratified sampling you select units from the entire population as one procedure.

Do I Element Sample or Do I Cluster Sample?   If you element sample, you directly select the units you will study. If you cluster sample you first select *some groups* of units for study, and then sample within clusters as needed. To keep sampling errors as small as possible, you seek to use clusters that are as heterogeneous as possible. Using samples that are clustered geographically, or on some other basis, may result in significant study savings.

Do I Use Equal Probabilities of Selection or Unequal Probabilities of Selection?   In the former case each unit in the population has an equal chance of being selected into your sample. Such procedures result in self-weighting samples. Assuming many conditions to hold, the frequencies with which certain types of respondents occur in your final sample correspond to the frequencies with which they occur in the general population. Thus, in this respect, your sample mean is a good estimate of your population mean. But there may be cases where you want different segments of the population to have *unequal* probabilities of being sampled. For example, you may want to have a sample that is 50 percent/50 percent on men/women, even though in the population studied the ratio is $3/2$. To use unequal probabilities of selection, you will need to first stratify your sample on the grouping available.

Do I Do Single-Stage Sampling or Multistage Sampling?   In the former case you do one level of sampling from the sampling frame, and after that procedure you have your units of study. In the latter case you make selections and selections within selections. For example, you might cluster sample census tracts, blocks within census tracts, and households within blocks. Multistage sampling is useful if a complete enumeration of all units in the population (e.g., households in the U.S.) is not available or is too large to conveniently use.

Combining Different Strategies Each of the five decisions can be made *independently*, so it is possible for you to *combine* different possibilities. You might want to do a citywide survey. You might decide that you want equal numbers of African Americans and Whites in a final sample for interviews (unequal selection). Therefore you group neighborhoods by racial composition, and sample equal numbers of predominantly African American and predominantly White neighborhoods (stratification). You choose neighborhoods, then blocks, and then households within blocks (multistage cluster sampling). Within each neighborhood you will choose blocks from a geographically ordered list in each neighborhood, using an interval selection procedure rather than a random selection of blocks.

SUMMARY OF MAIN POINTS

- You sample when you are unable to include in your study all the units of a population.
- Probability theory allows you to connect statistics that emerge from your sample, such as a mean or a proportion, with a population parameter.
- With probability sampling methods, you estimate population parameters with a certain degree of precision; you know the amount of sampling error.
- Certain distributions of scores can be mathematically described using normal curves.
- Standardized scores show the position of a score relative to other scores in the sample or population.
- Whenever you draw a representative random sample of cases from a population of cases, the resulting sample will not perfectly mirror the population due to sampling errors.
- Distributions of sampling means, where the samples are drawn using probability methods, are always normally distributed.
- With *non*probability sampling methods you cannot be sure that your resulting sample will yield unbiased estimates of population parameters.
- With probability sampling methods, as-

suming certain conditions hold, your resulting sample will yield unbiased estimates of population parameters.
- In a simple random sample all elements in the population have an equal chance of being selected, all selections are done with a randomization procedure, and all selections are independent.
- With a systematic sample you sort units in the sampling frame, find a random start, take the corresponding case, and take every *i*th unit thereafter where *i* is your sampling interval.
- With stratified sampling you sort units into homogeneous strata using a theoretically relevant stratification variable and probability sample within each stratum.
- With cluster sampling you group cases into heterogeneous clusters and probability sample *some* of the clusters.
- If the clusters differ on size you make each cluster's chances of selection equivalent to its population size.
- You may directly sample the final units for study in the first stage of sampling, or you may go through several stages of sampling in order to arrive at your final units.

SUGGESTED READINGS

If you want to learn more about sampling try Seymour Sudman's *Applied Sampling* (New York: Academic, 1976). It provides clear explanations of topics and numerous practical suggestions. The chapter "Small Scale Sampling with Limited Resources" may be of particular interest if you are planning a project. If you want to learn about the more advanced aspects of sampling, there is only one book to read: Leslie Kish's *Survey Sampling* (New York: Wiley, 1965). There is no other.

Finally, for the student who has everything: a book of random numbers. Rand Corporation "authored" *A Million Random Digits with 100,000 Normal Deviates* (Glencoe, IL: Free Press, 1955). Not a riveting read, and never on the *New York Times Bestseller List*, it is nonetheless a practical book if you need *a lot* of random numbers. For those scoffers who think the random number generators on their calculators or in their spreadsheet programs will do the trick: beware. It is actually very difficult to get a lot of really random numbers. Of course you may wonder: Does it matter?

KEY TERMS

case weights
census
confidence band
confidence interval
convenience sample
distribution of sampling means
interval sampling
judgmental sampling
model sampling
non-normal distribution
nonprobability sampling procedures
normal curve
normalized scores
oversample
parameter estimation
parameters
population

probability proportional to size (PPS) sampling
probability sample
probability sampling procedures
purposive sampling
quota sampling
reweighting cases
sample mean
sampling error
sampling fraction
sampling frame
sampling ratio
simple random sampling
single stage cluster sampling
skewed
snowball sampling
standard deviation
standard error
standardized scores
stratification variable
stratified sampling
stratum (pl: strata)
systematic sampling
undersample
universe
unstratified sampling
z scores

REFERENCES

1. Sudman, S. (1976) *Applied sampling*, Academic Press, New York, p. 56.
2. Baker, T. L. (1988) *Doing social research*, McGraw Hill, New York, p. 144.
3. Stephan, J. (1988) *Census of local jails 1988*, Bureau of Justice Statistics, Washington, DC.
4. Blalock, H. M. (1972) *Social statistics*, McGraw-Hill, New York.
5. Blalock, H. M. (1972) *Social statistics*, McGraw-Hill, New York, p. 95.
6. Blalock, H. M. (1972) *Social statistics*, McGraw-Hill, New York, p. 573.
7. Kish, L. (1965) *Survey sampling*, John Wiley, New York, p. 20.
8. Kish, L. (1965) *Survey sampling*, John Wiley, New York, p. 18.

9. Kish, L. (1965) *Survey sampling*, John Wiley, New York, p. 19.

10. Blalock, H. M. (1972) *Social statistics*, McGraw-Hill, New York, p. 560.

11. Sudman, S. (1976) *Applied sampling*, Academic Press, New York, p. 54.

12. Sudman, S. (1976) *Applied sampling*, Academic Press, New York, p. 56.

13. Sudman, S. (1976) *Applied sampling*, Academic Press, New York, p. 57.

14. Blalock, H. M. (1972) *Social statistics*, McGraw-Hill, New York, p. 567.

15. Kish, L. (1965) *Survey sampling*, John Wiley, New York.

CHAPTER 11

QUALITATIVE FIELD RESEARCH[1]

I wanted to observe and interact with girl gang members and to represent their own views of their situations. [1]

FOCUS

Qualitative field researchers allow participants in a setting to tell their stories in their own words. The procedures used provide outsiders with maximum insight into the situation.

Qualitative field research refers to a series of research techniques where the researcher has direct and sustained social interaction with participants in a particular setting. A researcher may "hang out" with and observe members of a setting or group for days, weeks, months, or years. She may ask participants in the setting to tell her their "life history," and tape record the story. She may informally question or interview a small or large number of participants in the setting. She may gather and examine a range of documents available describing various features of the setting or group. From the work an empirically supported conceptual analysis of setting dynamics will emerge.

Qualitative field research often relies heavily on **enthnography**. Terry Williams describes the basic activities and purposes of those who do ethnography.

An ethnographer tries to describe everyday behavior and rituals and, in the process, reveal hidden structures of power. As this technique requires the researcher to build a close relationship with those being studied, it is necessarily slow: days, sometimes weeks, may pass before the ethnographer can even begin to conduct an interview. These interviews are often open. . . . Ethnography also involves careful observation of individuals in their own social setting, and systematic recording of their action and speech. . . . But ethnographers also record far more subtle information, such as use of language, gestures, facial expressions, style of clothing; and must watch with care to capture exceptional episodes that can be particularly illuminating.

In this work the researcher is both an *observer* of activities as well as a *participant* in some activities. Thus, qualitative field research is also called **participant observation**. This definition of the techniques emphasizes that the researcher plays a dual role. Participant observation is a *broader* term for this area of research because the scope of activities car-

---

[1] Peter Jones provided particularly helpful comments on an earlier version of this chapter.

ried out by the participant observer may be broader than the range of activities carried out by the ethnographer.

> [Participant observation], in common parlance . . . refers to a characteristic blend or combination of methods and techniques that is employed in studying certain subject matter: primitive societies, deviant subcultures, complex organizations . . . social movements, communities, and informal groups . . . This characteristic blend of techniques . . . involves some amount of genuinely social interaction in the field with the subjects of the study, some direct observation of relevant events, some formal and a great deal of informal interviewing, some systematic counting, some collection of documents and artifacts, and open-endedness in the direction the study takes. [2]

These three different terms—*qualitative field work, ethnography,* and *participant-observation*—describe an overlapping set of research activities.

ORGANIZATION

The next section outlines the field research process. The next introduces you to three recent examples of qualitative field research: a teen cocaine gang, youth criminal involvement in three different neighborhoods in Brooklyn, and lower courts in two Massachusetts towns. I will describe each study's purposes, methods, and some of the major findings.

Next you will reconsider the running example with the HCEM program. You will walk through the steps that you might take if you wished to carry out a qualitative field study of the effects of HCEM on offenders serving time in the community. Good-quality qualitative field research is neither sloppy nor mysterious, but carefully follows a series of operations. Materials emerging from qualitative field research can be analyzed in different ways, and can be used for in Holmes's or

Einstein's mode of inquiry. You will see that researchers in this area have given careful thought to questions of scientific quality, and that there are several ways they can assess the reliability and validity of their data and conclusions. The chapter concludes with a look at ethical issues, costs, and benefits of this type of research.

THE FIELD RESEARCH PROCESS IN BRIEF

In brief, the field research process involves the following steps. First, you select a setting or group of settings that are theoretically or practically relevant to the questions you are pursuing. Second, you gain access to the settings of interest, negotiating with informal gatekeepers in these locations. If you will be working in an organization, you will negotiate with formal gatekeepers as well. Third, once you are in a setting, you begin to develop social ties with others in the setting, learning about the setting by listening and observing. You will religiously record observations, conversations, questions, reactions, and descriptions. You will put the material into field notes. As relationships develop with others in the setting and people begin to trust you, you will gain greater insight into the setting and the actions of its participants, and increasingly may become involved in the setting and its participants. Getting to know the people in a setting, and understanding the setting, may take months or even years. Fourth, you will eventually prepare to leave the field, apprising your acquaintances of your impending exit and wrapping up loose ends. Fifth, after leaving the setting, you will continue to analyze your field notes and write up findings based on those analyses. From your analyses will emerge what John Lofland calls "disciplined abstractions"— carefully constructed concepts developed from the material recorded while in the field that explain the behaviors and attitudes you observed there.

THREE RECENT EXAMPLES OF QUALITATIVE FIELD RESEARCH

Here are three examples of qualitative research on topics of central interest to criminal justice researchers: Why and how are teenagers in urban areas involved in drug dealing?; What is the relationship between employment opportunities and criminal involvement in urban neighborhoods?; and, Why do people take their personal problems to court, and how does their personal experience in court change their views about the law? In keeping with the spirit of ethnography I will allow these three researchers to tell their own stories in their own words, by quoting liberally from their books.

The Cocaine Kids

The Questions   Terry Williams wanted to know why kids get involved in cocaine dealing. "I wanted to find out about the kids who sold drugs. How did they get into the cocaine business, and how do they stay in it? How transient is their involvement—can they get out of the business? And where do they go if they do? What are the rewards for those who succeed?" [3]

The Approach   "The only way to find the answers to these questions was to follow the kids over time, and that is what I did. For more than four years, I asked questions and recorded answers without trying to find support for any particular thesis." [3] Terry Williams initially got into contact with the cocaine group he followed by being introduced to the leader, Max. He was "fourteen and already considered a 'comer' in the cocaine business." "I assumed we would talk and then go our separate ways: he trusted my

friend but he was shy; there was certainly no reason for him to talk with me about anything. . . . But there was something special about Max, and he became my friend and guide for nearly five years. I think we got along because I was an outsider and he had a story to tell, and he chose me to tell it to." [3]

For Terry Williams, Max was a **key informant**, someone who takes the researcher into his confidence, tells him what is going on in the setting, and may even tell him how to behave. He is a key source of information for the researcher about what is happening and why. Max introduced the researcher to the other members of the "crew." They in turn came to accept Williams. [4]

Recording what happened and what was said was important. "Clearly, detailed and descriptive field notes are essential in this approach, especially as the observer makes every attempt to accurately record the speech of those observed." [5]

At the same time, it was extremely difficult to record events or conversations as they were occurring. Tape recordings "would have been unintelligible—there are phones ringing, people coming and going, and often a more or less constant background of family arguments, babies crying, loud music and other disturbances." [5] Williams preferred not to take notes as conversations occurred because such note taking "warps discussion and inhibits the flow of words." He also mentions another, more personal reason for not taking notes as conversations occurred. "With guns openly visible and police raids a real possibility, I felt I had to keep my hands free, my eyes sharp, and my mind clear." [5]

Consequently, Williams "developed a method of jotting down key words and phrases immediately after each visit, and reconstructing conversations or a scene from those notes the next day. . . . It was not unusual to spend a day or more writing up an hour or two of field observations." [5] The resultant *field notes* became the key data source used to describe and analyze the setting and participants. (You will learn more about taking field notes later in the chapter.) The results were "six thick notebooks, including drawings and diagrams covering every nuance of the kids' operation—methods of production and packaging, forms of dealing and the flow of cash—and a great deal of material about the structure of dealing networks and the rituals of cocaine use." [5]

Williams's methodology represents a prototypical ethnographic approach: A lone researcher gets involved with a group and setting with which he was previously unfamiliar. He listens, observes, asks few questions, and scrupulously records.

Aside on Legality Williams's relationships with Max and other members of the "crew" raise important legal issues. When working with criminals a key question is how far you will go to fit in. Williams, for example, refused to ingest drugs, other than alcohol, or to carry any quantities of drugs while he was acquainted with Max and the other members of his crew. It is a misconception that to study criminals in natural settings one needs to become criminal oneself. [6] You are probably safer to be an overt "right square" and researcher instead of a phony deviant. [7] The researcher attempting to pass as a criminal or deviant runs the risk of winding up in some extremely uncomfortable situations.

Even though Williams did not participate in drug activities, he *did* observe them and he *did* fail to report them to the authorities. Many would conclude that Williams's failure to report was itself illegal. They would argue that his activities make Williams an accessory to criminal activity and subject to penalties including incarceration.

Conclusions Williams's work offers many insights into several aspects of the urban drug culture. He details the influences of arrest on those involved in dealing (pp. 103–104) and clarifies how ethnic factors (p. 51) and ecological factors such as abandoned housing patterns (p. 51) influence dealing operations. In many places his work addresses the question of the link between money, status and dealing. In dealing, the kids strive for status: they want to "get behind the scale" and arrange to distribute coke to other sellers.

The kids' attitudes toward the economic benefits of dealing are complex and deeply ambivalent. On the one hand, the possibility of earning serious money attracts them. They "are drawn to the underground economy because of the opportunities that exist there. The underground offers status and prestige—rewards they are unlikely to attain in the regular economy." [8] On the other hand they know that the idea of "getting ahead" is illusory (p. 55) and that the work is extremely dangerous. The teenagers who had "a stake in something" (p. 131) were likely to drop out of dealing. The shooting of a crew member appeared to play a role in several kids exiting the business. "All of the kids except Jake have also begun to live outside the underground; for them, I believe, the cocaine trade was only a stepping stone to the realities of surviving in the larger world." [9]

Getting Paid

The Questions Mercer Sullivan's book *Getting Paid* focuses on the relationship between economic opportunity and criminal involvement among inner city youth and young adults. Whereas Williams focuses on the lives of individuals, Sullivan takes a broader perspective. He carefully considers the influences of educational, employment, and criminal justice systems on neighborhoods, and how these factors influence individuals. "This book reexamines the questions of the relationships between criminality and employment opportunities through the analysis of comparative ethnographic data collected in three inner-city neighborhoods during the early 1980's." [10] Noting a current "tension" between social and individualistic explanations of crime and delinquency, Sullivan sought to "resolve that tension by examining variations in criminaltiy both within and between three neighborhood-based groups of young men." [11]

Thus, Sullivan sought to uncover how features of the locale, as well as differences between individuals, contributed to their criminal involvement. "By describing and comparing the criminal careers of young males as these careers develop within three specific community contexts, this book tries to overcome the hazards of assuming either atomized, autonomous individuals or monolithic, all-determining society." [12]

The Method Three different "high-risk" neighborhoods in Brooklyn—one Hispanic, one African American, and one predominantly White—were chosen for the project. Researchers sought to develop a clear picture of the relationship between employment opportunities, economic factors, and criminal activity in each of the three neighborhoods. The Vera Institute, with funding from a federal granting agency, ran the project.

Whereas Williams's project relied on one form of data—field notes based on observations and open-ended interviews—Sullivan relied on several different sources of data.

- Personal documents in the form of **life history interviews**. In a life history interview the respondent tells about his or her life and situation and the interviewer asks general questions; the interview is usually tape recorded. Such interviews will only be informative if there is a substantial degree of trust between the respondent and interviewer. It often takes a considerable amount of time to develop such a relationship. About a dozen young males in each neighborhood, who had been involved in both criminal activities and "straight" employment, provided the interviews.

> Establishing rapport was not easy in any of these neighborhoods; several months were consumed in making futile trips to social programs and schools and in driving and walking around the streets and eating lunches in local restaurants. During these first months, we had developed a very strict set of standards for disclosing the purpose of our work to prospective informants. We insisted that anyone cooperating with us be made aware not only that we were researchers but that we wanted to talk to youths who have been involved in income-oriented crime." (pp. 13–14)

- An ethnographer assigned to each neighborhood got to know residents in each locale. His purpose was twofold: to get to know and develop a trusting relationship with young males who could provide life histories, and to develop a detailed understanding about neighborhood views on work and crime.
- Researchers gathered official information about the neighborhoods, such as census data.

The process of establishing contact, albeit lengthy in each locale, also varied in each neighborhood. In La Barriada, the predominantly Puerto Rican neighborhood studied, the process went relatively smoothly. A local social worker introduced the assigned ethnographer to a young male who decided to trust him. The young male subsequently introduced the ethnographer to his friends. The local youths came in to the project offices and provided detailed life histories.

In the predominantly African American neighborhood studied, however, the contact process was much more lengthy. The author and the assigned ethnographer, over the course of a year, were unable to develop a trusting relationship with more than a couple of teens. After about a year contacts in the locale increased. Individuals returning from prison or youth homes provided taped interviews. Several teenagers, who had been suspicious earlier, decided to trust the researchers. In this locale the author also developed contacts with three older individuals involved in drugs at various levels.

In short, the time required to develop a detailed understanding of criminal involvement for profit in each locale took anywhere from several months to well over a year.

Conclusions Sullivan found differences in youth involvement in crime in each of the three neighborhoods. In the blue-collar, predominantly White neighborhood, sustained criminal involvement in crime-for-gain *on the streets* was not as widespread among local youth, as compared to the Hispanic or African American neighborhoods. Youth in the White neighborhood, through contacts, could get better jobs more easily. Not surprisingly, workplace theft was more common among youth in the White, blue-collar neighborhood.

In each neighborhood researchers observed a developmental sequence of criminal involvement as youths progressed from more

adolescent crimes such as street fighting to more serious, economically rewarding crimes. The sequence of involvement, as revealed in the Hispanic neighborhood, is shown in Table 11.1. Different patterns of sequential involvement in crime were observed in the other neighborhoods.

At the same time, the researchers also noted similarities among the youths in the different neighborhoods. Teens learned how to fight and use weapons at an early age; this experience was useful later and applied to economic crimes such as robbery. "Noneconomic adolescent violence in the form of street fighting provided early socialization into illegal behavior and the techniques of violence, which some individuals then went on to apply to systematic economic crime." [13]

Getting Justice and Getting Even

The Questions Sally Merry explored an elusive topic in *Getting Justice and Getting Even*. She focused on the "legal consciousness" that leads people to take their personal problems to court.

> The ways people understand and use the law I term their *legal consciousness*. Consciousness, as I am using the term, is the way people conceive

TABLE 11.1
Sequential Criminal Involvement Among Youth in La Barriada Revealed in *Getting Paid*

Age	Type of Criminal Involvement		
	Street Fighting	Burglary	Stealing Cars, Robbery
12–14	XXXXXXXX		
13–15		XXXXXXXX	
16 and Up			XXXXXXXX

Source: Adapted from Sullivan, M. *Getting paid.* Ithaca, NY: Cornell University Press.

of their 'natural' and normal way of doing things, their habitual patterns of talk and action, and their commonsense understanding of the world. [14]

She sought to "explore the legal consciousness of plaintiffs and to observe and report the way the parties, the mediators, and court officials talk about law, rights, property, problems, and cases." [15] Personal problems brought to court included such matters as an ex-girlfriend pursuing a restraining order against a former boyfriend, or a neighbor complaining about a troublesome and destructive dog.

The Method Merry pursued an ethnographic approach because she had "a desire to *present the perspective of people who use the courts* for help with their personal problems." [16; emphasis added] She was unhappy with earlier work on this topic that had used a large-scale survey approach. She cited three limitations of a survey-based approach to this topic. Such a tactic "flattens" our view of how "people understand and use the law," and does not provide a detailed understanding. Second, it forces individuals into a single consistent position on the topic rather than allowing them to entertain alternate viewpoints at different times. Third, it assumes that people's "stance toward law lies in the realm of the recognized and explicit, so that it can be elicited by questioning, rather than in more implicit assumptions about the nature of social relationships revealed in actions." [14]

The research project initially focused on two mediation programs connected with the lower courts in two Massachusetts towns, Salem and Cambridge, in the early 1980s, and on a parent/child mediation program in Cambridge receiving referrals from the juvenile courts. For each program researchers collected extensive data of different varieties. They completed detailed observations of proceedings; analyzed records; informally interviewed plaintiffs, defendants, and court personnel; and completed ethnographic and survey work in neighborhoods where plaintiffs resided. Sally Merry was assisted by a coinvestigator, Susan Silbey, and numerous research assistants. Neighborhood residents even helped in some data collection efforts.

Conclusions Several insights into the reasons for and consequences of going to court with personal problems emerge from Merry's analysis. For example, she argues that the increasing caseloads on the lower courts are *not* due to an increasing litigiousness of society in general, as some have proposed. Rather, "people turn to the courts as an alternative source of authority as they seek to escape the supervision of local political authorities and to avoid recourse to violence." [17]

Further, she asserts that going to court transforms participants' legal consciousness. They initially expect that their "rights" will be upheld. They find, however, that court personnel don't want to talk about rights. Instead of pursuing a *legal* or *moral* discourse, the court personnel want to talk about people getting along with one another, helping one another, duties to neighbors, and therapeutic interventions for those who need care. [18]

> Within settings defined as connected to the symbolic authority of the court, plaintiffs are routinely told that their problems are not legal or moral but therapeutic, that they concern only social relationships and the obligations inherent in these relationships. . . . Through this process, working-class plaintiffs are discouraged from using the court for their personal problems. [19]

Merry, using an ethnographic approach, gained a detailed understanding of what people expected to achieve by going to court, how the court responded to these expectations, and how the laypersons' views of courts were transformed by the experience.

How These Studies Exemplify Participant Observation

The three studies described above are different from one another in several ways. But in their *purposes* and *techniques* they are typical of participant observation studies. Let's explore a few of these differences and similarities.

Differences The studies differ in the number of data collection methods used. Williams relied solely on direct observation and informal interviewing. Sullivan relied on taped life histories, archival data, and direct observation. Merry relied on a broad range of data-gathering techniques, including informal interviews, structured surveys, and analyses of court documents. Her study clearly represents a **joint design** for field research. [20] It relied on a combination of research designs.

The studies differ in the scope of the settings investigated. Sullivan's and Merry's studies were **multisite investigations**. The multisite investigations compared and contrasted the dynamics occurring in different settings. Sullivan compared employment and crime dynamics in a Hispanic, African American, and White neighborhood. The contrast between the different study arenas contributed to the theoretical analysis of the crime—employment relationship. Merry assessed cases from a lower-income, more blue-collar town, and from a more affluent suburban town. By contrast, Williams worked with one group in one neighborhood and got to know

its members well. Multisite investigations, in general, tend to be *broader* in scope whereas single site investigations tend to have more *depth*, providing more detailed understanding.

Similarities *Purpose* All three studies exemplified the primary purposes of participant observation research:

1. *to hear people in their own terms describing their own situation.* The researcher does not ask people to use the research vocabulary of particular concepts or hypotheses. Instead, the researcher seeks to uncover the conceptual tools the participants themselves use to describe the situation. For example, Williams discusses the concept of "getting behind the scale:" working your way up in cocaine dealing so that you are packaging drugs and setting selling prices of sizable volumes of drugs.
2. *to gain a detailed understanding* or **verstehen** of the situation. In each of these studies researchers learned about the subjective interpretation of the situation held by the participant themselves. [2] The understanding the researcher develops is *systematic*, based on careful theoretical analysis of the material gathered from the setting(s).
3. *to convey a detailed description of the situation.* In each of these works the researcher communicates to readers a detailed, fully textured description of the situation being investigated. The researcher describes locations, participants, and actions.

Methods All three studies were also similar in the methodologies, involving:

1. direct behavioral observation of participants in 'natural' settings;

2. sustained genuine social interaction between members of the research team and the participants in the setting;

3. an open-endedness in study direction such that the analyses and data collection respond to the insights obtained.

THE STEPS IN CONDUCTING A QUALITATIVE FIELD PROJECT

In this section we will "walk through" the steps involved in carrying out a qualitative field research project. We will use the running example introduced in Chapter 1 on electronic monitoring with home confinement.

The Situation and the Questions

Recall that you are working in probation services in a southern state. Courts have taken to sentencing a large number of offenders to probation, where the conditions include HCEM. Due to a couple of attention-getting events involving probationers sentenced to HCEM, you were asked to investigate the safety and punitiveness of probation using HCEM.

Imagine now that you have completed the report requested by the Governor. Using official records, and comparing probationers sentenced to HCEM with similar "regular" probationers—from an earlier period—not sentenced to HCEM, you have uncovered some puzzling findings. For example, you have found that HCEM probationers tend to "outperform" regular probationers during the first 12 months on probation. See Figure 11.1. It shows the percentage of probationers studied, regular and HCEM, failing on probation by month. But as the figure also shows, during the second year of follow-up the picture reverses. The HCEM cohort starts losing probationers faster than the regular cohort. By the end of the follow-up period 86 percent

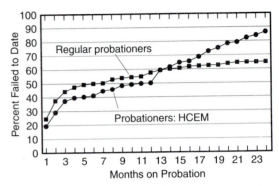

FIGURE 11.1
Artificial data. Figure shows the proportion of probationers failing by the length of time on probation. During the first year the probationers on HCEM do slightly better at staying on probation than do a matched cohort of "regular" probationers. But during the second year probationers on HCEM fail more than "regular" probationers.

of the HCEM cohort has failed on probation, whereas only 65 percent of the regular cohort has failed. Since each of these cohorts are large, these percentage differences are statistically significant. These and other puzzling findings, on which your official records and conversations with probation officers are unable to shed light, convince you that you need a more detailed understanding of the experiences of probationers sentenced to HCEM.

You discuss with your boss the possibility of taking 6 months off to study probation with HCEM using a participant-observation approach. Your progressive-minded boss, after listening to your arguments about the value such a study would have for statewide correctional policy, decides to go along with your idea *if* you can get funding for the research. You apply to a foundation and receive funding for a 6-month study that would support your travel to the field site, expenses there, and a salary for the study period.

You have told the foundation that you wished to understand how the probationers themselves view the effects of HCEM, and how the perceived effects of being on HCEM vary over time for the probationers.

Site Selection

Your first step is to select a *site* or *setting* where you will conduct your study. You have to make a *sampling decision* about the location where you will spend your time. [21] Several factors come into play in making this decision.

You want to be sure to select a site where you are a complete stranger, and where you do not have friends or acquaintances who are part of the setting. [22] The presence of friends or acquaintances may influence the research process in several ways. First, as an observer interpreting different situations and interactions, you may be more inclined to adopt the perspective of the participants to whom you are closest. Your interpretation of events may be biased by your social ties. Second, participants in a setting may react to the mere presence of an observer, doing or saying things they would not otherwise do or say. Researchers call such responses **reactivity**. Your connections with others in the setting may heighten the reactivity occurring due to your presence.

Another issue is representativeness. You want to select sites that are relatively typical of the phenomena being examined. For example, you do not want to spend time in a program that is implementing an extremely progressive probation with HCEM program, nor in one that is implementing the sanction in a regressive fashion.

You have examined several probation-with-HCEM programs around the country run by different jurisdictions, at the state, county, and city levels. You have made contacts with different probation agencies around the country as you seek out "typical" probation-with-HCEM programs. In addi-

tion, you have contacted many offender and prisoner rights groups. As a result of these discussions you have decided you would most like to study a program run by a county probation office outside a large city in Ohio.

As part of the site selection process you might want to begin keeping **field notes**. You can record your conversations with different people and organizations, your thoughts about the research enterprise, and your comments on, and emotional reactions to, what is happening. [23] (You'll be learning more about field notes below—what they are, how to take them, what to focus on, and how to analyze them.)

Access Routes

Now that you have chosen your site you need to gain access. When you are working in institutional or organizational settings, as in this example, you will need to gain permission from the **official gatekeepers**, the formal leaders of the setting. [24] You will need to tell them enough about your research purposes so that they know generally what you are doing and why. "The problem then is how to explain our purposes in a way that satisfies the gatekeeper and yet does not distort or unduly limit the nature of the study." [26]

Gaining permission from official gatekeepers can take time. It may involve contacting several different persons in the organization. Instead of allowing the situation to annoy you, however, you may benefit by collecting data during this period. Keep a careful record of what happened. View it as a chance to learn about the organization. "The best way to learn about the structure and hierarchy of an organization is to be handed around through it." [23]

Of course you may run into a setting where, after a time, it becomes clear that you have little chance of being cleared by the official gatekeepers. If, after a reasonable period, you think this is the case, you may need to select an alternate setting.

You go to the county probation office, talk with the head of probation services, the assistant director, and an administrative officer in the county supervisor's office. After numerous explanations and a couple of weeks they agree to allow you to hang around the setting and watch what is going on. You start spending time in the probation offices, talking with officers. You find that several probation officers are leery of your presence, particularly when they find out that their supervisor approved the project.

You also visit a couple of day centers run by the probation office. These day centers combine several services for probationers: postings about job opportunities, job counseling, and some employment training programs run by local companies. The day centers serve as a location where the probationer can meet with his or her probation officer. You sit in on some employment training sessions, talk with probation officers, and try to strike up conversations with probationers who are in the office. You find, however, that the probationers are not interested in speaking with you.

You learn after a bit that many probationers who use that center tend to "hang out" at a nearby bar, the Purple Poodle. So you decide to start spending time there. You get to know the barkeep and a couple of waitresses after a couple of weeks. One evening one of the waitresses introduces you to Fuzzy. He is a probationer serving his second HCEM sentence. He is also the informal leader of a group of probationers who use the bar. **He is an unofficial gatekeeper. If you want access to local probationers, you need his approval first. You tell him what you hope to find out. You tell him you are concerned that probation officials do not have enough of an**

understanding of the emotional and psychological effects of HCEM. You want to know more. He is extremely skeptical at first, but after some discussion and beer he says he will think about it. You see him again about a week later. He agrees to help you out and introduce you to some other probationers.

In short, in an organizational setting you will need to negotiate access with formal gatekeepers who control access to the setting. In a community setting you may need to locate and negotiate with informal leaders, who function as informal gatekeepers. The process of gaining access can be time-consuming but should be viewed as a time for learning, not just waiting. It may be necessary to gain access at multiple entry points in the setting, for example, to get the acceptance of line officers as well as supervisors. Table 11.2 summarizes some key issues in gaining access.

Building Field Relations

Now you are "in." You have begun to get to know persons in three different sites: the probation offices, the day center, and probationers at a local bar. Now you must *develop your field relations*: get people in the setting to trust you enough so they will speak with you frankly. [27, 28, 29] Unless you can get participants in the setting to trust you, their interactions will not be "natural." For your observations to be as valid as possible, and to keep participants' reactivity as low as possible, you need to minimize your presence in the setting. [30] There are several key elements to establishing field relations.

Being an Avid Listener: Learn the Argot
You want to listen constantly and talk little. People will say a lot if they think that others have an interest. In the initial stages avoid asking questions, even of a general nature,

TABLE 11.2
Issues in Gaining Access to Field Settings

Type of Setting	Gatekeeper	Multiple Points of Entry required?
Formal (e.g., an organization or a work setting or an institution)	*Official gatekeeper* must be convinced of project worth. Likely to be persons higher up in the status hierarchy. *Trust* not essential; gatekeeper must just be sufficiently assured that your project will not be a threat.	Yes, usually. (1) May have to convince several persons who have status in the organization. (2) To make contacts "lower down" in the organization, you will need to establish ties with *informal leaders*.
Informal (e.g., community setting)	*Unofficial gatekeeper* must be convinced of your sincerity. *Trust* essential. Once it is established, the unofficial gatekeeper will allow you to get to know others in the setting. May even serve as key informant.	Probably not. But you probably will have to establish access at every separate setting.

since you do not know how they will be interpreted. Pay particular attention to the nuances of language used by the participants in the setting. Try to decode special terms or **argot** used by members of the setting. These special terms may provide significant insight into how the participants view features of their situation. (Table 11.3 lists some argot used by the teens in the cocaine gang studied by Williams.) Avoid using these terms until you understand them well; their misuse may be mistaken for a condescending attitude.

Suspend Beliefs and Avoid Judging You do not want the participants in the setting to think that you disapprove or look down on their attitudes, actions, or beliefs. Participants will be extremely reluctant to share their intimate thoughts if they think that you

disapprove of them or their actions. Trust will develop only if they sense you are treating them as equals.

Be Prepared to Reciprocate Those with whom you have extensive contact in the field may request several favors of you. Anne Campbell studied the leaders of three girl gangs in New York City in the 1980s. She describes cooking chicken for one participant who was doing an errand. Another time she picked up Twinkies and beer for breakfast. [31] Eli Anderson in his case study of John Turner described helping him get a job, appearing in court for him, and lending him money. [32] Reciprocity involves sharing information with participants and doing favors for the participants in return for the information they are giving you and the time they are

TABLE 11.3

Argot Used by the Cocaine Kids

Beiging	chemically altering the cocaine so that it looks brownish, for those who think this indicates purity
Chalking	chemically altering the color of cocaine so it looks white, for those who think this indicates purity
Connect	(connection) a high-level supplier of drugs
Copman	drug dealer who has fallen from grace but still has access to high-level suppliers—can only get drugs for cash, not on consignment
Crimey	a friend who engages in illegal acts; a buddy, whether engaging in illegal acts or not
Fronting	taking drugs on consignment
Lines	a rough unit of measure used by dealers (a fraction of a gram); also the way cocaine is prepared for snorting
P.C.	part commission on a drug sale

(*Source. Cocaine Kids* (Excerpted from the Glossary), © 1992 by Terry Williams. Reprinted by permission of Addison-Wesley Publishing Company, Inc.)

spending with you. This give and take is an integral part of the relationship developed between the participant observer and some participants in the setting.

Develop Rapport with Participants; Try to Fit In; Do Not Obtrude   Dress as they dress; participate in the activities in which they are involved, if they ask you to join. Emphasize what you have in common with the setting participants. Play dumb; no one wants to talk to another person who already knows everything. [33]

In the criminal justice system the process of establishing rapport and trying to fit in may depend on the particular setting within the criminal justice system. For example, much interpersonal trust among police officers depends on **blackmail solidarity**: The officers have incriminating information on each other, and thus they trust each other. A breach of trust would free them to reveal the incriminating information. If a researcher is

working with police officers, they may push the researcher to engage in some officially proscribed activity, and not trust him or her until they possess this incriminating information. [34]

By contrast, trust among public prosecutors or defenders is often based more on a **clubhouse mentality**. The lawyers trust others who have the requisite credentials and contacts within their social networks. Influential external sponsorship is often important. [35]

Cultivate One or More Key Informants Qualitative field researchers who use a primarily ethnographic approach find it is important to develop a close relationship with one or more individuals in the setting who are well informed about setting activities, and willing to share that information with the researcher. Such a person is called a **key informant**: an informed participant in the setting who is willing and able to act as a *guide* during the course of your inquiry. He or she will help you "decode" events. The key informant will provide the needed background so that you can better interpret the situation. He or she also will play a key role in introducing you to other members of the setting, and vouching for you to them.

There are also disadvantages to relying heavily on key informants. (1) Their views of the setting may have particular biases. The researcher needs to consider carefully what those biases might be and how they might be influencing the information shared. (2) The key informant may not be informed about, or active in, the entire setting. His or her expertise may be limited to only a portion of the setting or its participants. (3) The researcher may develop an extremely close relationship with one or more key informants; this has been called the problem of **overrapport**. [36] An extremely close relationship may close off certain lines of inquiry in the setting that the researcher would have otherwise pursued. (4) The key informant may try to get the researcher to support his or her own position when conflicts emerge in the setting.

The potential liabilities inherent in relying on key informants can be overcome. The researcher learns to "sift" what the key informant says. She tries to "filter out" the content that may be due to the key informant's biases. If the key informant is only knowledgeable about a portion of the setting, the researcher can seek out another key informant to inform her about the rest of the setting. The researcher can make it clear that she is unable to take sides when conflicts emerge. With these and other tactics the potential disadvantages of relying on a key informant can be overcome by the field researcher.

Developing a solid relationship with one or more key informants is a key ingredient in furthering the aims of the field work. The advantages of relying on one or more key

informants usually far outweigh the potential disadvantages.

Keeping Field Notes

Let's say that, in the running example, you have done all of the above. Over the course of 3 months you have developed "working relationships" in each of the three settings of interest to you. You have gotten to know the workers in the probation offices, one of the day centers, and through your contacts at the bar you have gotten to know several probationers and ex-probationers. Many of these probationers are currently serving, or have previously served, a probation sentence where part of their time was on HCEM. You are dressing to fit in, listening carefully, trying to understand the argot, refraining from making judgments, and doing small favors for different people. For example, you have helped several probationers fill out applications for employment, and have even gone with a couple of them on job interviews to recommend them.

During this time you will be taking field notes. **Field notes** are the detailed recordings you make based on your observations and conversations in the field. Field notes play a pivotal role in ethnographic research. They are the raw data you analyze to develop concepts explaining events you have observed. They are extremely vital.[2]

---

[2] You might think that you could avoid the painstaking process of generating field notes by tape recording conversations and transcribing the tapes later. This may not be much of a saving and may cost you in data quality. Transcribing recordings is an extremely time-consuming process. Data quality may be affected because the machinery did not catch everything that was said, and the person with whom you were speaking may have been somewhat intimidated by the recorder. And of course a hidden recorder could cause the researcher serious problems and jeopardize his entire project, if it were discovered.

Time and Timing In many situations, particularly in the early stages of field research, you cannot take notes in the field. Instead you must remember what is occurring, and transcribe the information later. Sometimes you can note down key words or phrases after leaving the setting, and transcribe the information later into a detailed set of notes. Of course, you may be able to create some opportunities to jot a few notes while in the setting by, e.g., going to the bathroom or stepping outside for a smoke.

Even though you may enjoy interacting with participants in these three different settings, you should limit your time in the setting to the amount of activity you can record.

Observation without field notes is wasted. Take in only as much as you can transcribe. [37] It is not unusual for an hour or two of observation in a setting to require 6 or more hours for the creation of the field notes.

Recall You may think that it is extremely difficult to record activities and conversations with accuracy, but "novice observers will be amazed by the accuracy with which they can recall specific details through training, experience, and concentration." [38] With practice your ability to recollect will improve. Some hints for improving recall appear in Table 11.4.

T A B L E 11.4
Tips for Improving Recall for Field Notes

1. "Look for 'key words' in your subject's remarks." You do not need to remember a subject's conversation verbatim. But if you concentrate on important words used by your subject that will help you reconstruct the gist of the conversation.
2. "Concentrate on the first and last remarks in each conversation." This will help you reconstruct the direction the conversation took.
3. "Leave the setting as soon as you have observed as much as you can accurately remember."
4. "Record your notes as soon after the observation as possible."
5. "Don't talk to anyone about your observation until you have recorded your field notes." Such a conversation may bias or distort your recall.
6. "Draw a diagram of the physical layout of the setting and attempt to trace your movements through it."
7. "Once you have drawn the diagram and traced your movements, outline the specific events and conversations that occurred at each point in time before you record your field notes." This gives you an outline or structure around which to build your field notes.
8. "Pick up pieces of lost data after your initial recording session." Things you may have "missed" in your notes will come back to you later. When they do, incorporate them into your notes.

Source: Bogdan, R., and Taylor, S. J. (1975). *Introduction to qualitative research methods,* New York: Wiley, pp. 62–63.

But What Do I Record? [39] You may be tempted after an observation session just to write in your notebook "nothing happened." Whenever you are in the setting a *lot* happened.

Describe the Setting What was it like? Who was there? What were the appearances and locations of the different individuals? Over the course of your observations are there changes in the setting or in the number of participants? You want to be able to convey to your reader the essence of the setting and of the activities and actors there. [40]

Describe the Individuals. How do they dress? Dress conveys important social messages. (See Box 11.1.) Are there differences in how different individuals in the setting dress?

Describe the Interactions You Observe Who was talking to whom about what?

What Activities Took Place Organized activities occur within settings. [43, 44] What was going on? Who played what role in the activities? When did various activities begin and end?

Record Your Own Reactions and Comments In a separately labeled portion of every day's field notes, record your reactions, feelings, and interpretations of what you have seen or have heard. Why do you think Fuzzy said that to Larry? What is your explanation of why everyone was so nervous before the staff meeting?

If there are questions that you have about a person or an action or a comment, record your thoughts on how you might get this clarified. Should you be looking out especially for something? Should you try to talk to someone? Use the field notes as a medium where you can develop your plans for filling in gaps.

BOX 11.1

The Messages of Dress

Anne Campbell spent 6 months getting to know Connie, the 30-year-old leader of the Sandman Ladies, a girl gang attached to a male motorcycle gang. Dress was very important in the gang. They had strict rules about how to wear the club "colors"—patches sewed onto denim jackets with the sleeves cut off—who could and could not wear the club colors, and how the colors were handled. Connie dressed carefully and symbolically. "She is wearing a check blouse, jeans, and two belts, one with a demonic goat's head and the other apparently a chain from a BSA motorcycle. At the side of one belt is a small leather case that holds a knife. Connie always carries a flick knife and always in a visible place—as long as it is not a switchblade (which shoots the blade forward from the handle) and it is not concealed, the police will leave her alone." [41] "Connie runs back to the apartment to get her sunglasses. Last week she got beaten up." Until the swelling around her eyes goes down, "the sunglasses are compulsory wear . . . Over her blouse she wears a fur-lined leather jacket, a couple of sizes too big, and on top of that her patches. Sewn on her denim jacket are the full colors of the club: SANDMAN NYC LADIES." [42]

Record Things that Puzzle Even in what you might think of as very "normal" settings, you may observe oddities: anomalous or inexplicable activities or remarks. Make a note of these activities or remarks. They may point toward important aspects of setting functioning or interaction patterns.

The Role of Feedback in Note Quality Ask a person who is not familiar with the setting to go over your field notes after you have made entries for an observation session. That person may be able to pick up inconsistencies in your notes or may raise questions about the material that had not come to mind earlier.

Leaving the Field

At the end of your observation period you may want to start preparing to leave the field. This might involve several activities. If there are persons in the field with whom you feel you have developed a trusting relationship, you may want to schedule an extended interview with them to ask nagging questions you may have about what you have seen or have heard. Or you might want to get their reactions to some of your interpretations of what has happened. You might want to let setting participants know that you will be leaving, so that there is less of a sense of betrayal when you do depart. Be prepared to be grilled by the gatekeepers. They may wish to extort information from you before you leave. At this time it is probably important to arrange how you will share study findings with those in the field who are interested in your observations. [45]

Note that at different steps in the field research your level of involvement with setting participants has varied. It builds through the initial and middle stages, and declines at the end. As your involvement shifts, so too does your role. As you become more involved, you become more of a participant yourself in the setting, and less of an observer. At the end, as involvement decreases, you return to the role of being primarily an observer. (See Figure 11.2.)

Analysis

Analysis of the material you have gathered in the field—field notes, recordings of observations, results of structured interviews, personal documents, and archival documents—

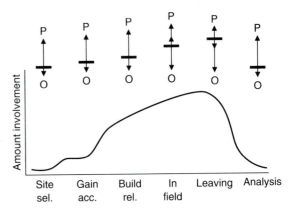

FIGURE 11.2
At different stages in the field process your level of involvement varies. As it varies, so too do the roles you play. You begin the process acting primarily as an observer (0). As the project progresses you act more like a participant (P). As you leave the field, involvement with setting participants declines, and you return to acting primarily as an observer.

will take place *throughout* your period in the field. One of the main advantages of qualitative field research is that there can be a constant interplay between your analysis of the dynamics you are observing, and the direction you choose for your data collection. As you will recall from Chapter 2, such an interplay is a key element in the grounded-theory or discovery-oriented mode of scientific inquiry. Nonetheless, after you complete the period of observation, you will pursue analysis more fervently. It often takes a researcher as long to analyze data as it did to collect it.

The purpose of analysis is to generate a plausible, empirically grounded and conceptually organized explanation of what has occurred in the settings investigated. To use John Lofland's term, you are developing **disciplined abstractions**. [46] More formally, the researcher makes the case through her data analysis that the hypotheses she favors are plausible. These hypotheses are likely to be **descriptive propositions**, not causal hypotheses of the simple "A causes B" variety. [47,

48] Descriptive propositions assert that a construct or variable is distributed in a certain way among members of a population. For example: "The negative impact of HCEM on self-esteem was more pronounced among younger as compared to older probationers."

Three Different Approaches to Analysis
Let's think of three different ways you could analyze your field notes. (This material comes largely from [49].) We will assume at the outset that your field notes are well organized. You have one file of field notes arranged sequentially. You also have all of your field notes indexed with key theoretical constructs you have developed during your study. For example, if you have a concept "reactance against the authority of the criminal justice system" or "quality of self image," you would have a folder for each concept. (*Reactance* is a psychological reaction against a condition of decreasing perceived behavioral freedom. The person attempts to reassert his autonomy.) Include in each folder all portions of your field notes that were exemplars of the concept.

Quasistatistics One approach allowing for the crude testing of provisional hypotheses is **quasistatistical analysis**. [50] There are two steps in such an analysis: *coding* and *analysis*.
Let's say your hypothesis is as follows:

the longer period of time a probationer serves on a sentence that includes HCEM, the more adversely his self-image is affected.

You will need to code *all* the information in your field notes that is relevant to these two concepts: time on probation with HCEM, and indicators of a derogatory self-image. For example, if you have a concept "derogatory self-image revealed in conversation," you would look through all of your field notes and tag each instance where a participant's conversation reflected an unfavorable self-

image. You also may decide that there are different aspects of this concept, such as "dismal work prospects due to personal inadequacies," "labeled by others as inherently untrustworthy due to stigma of having been convicted," and so on. (In essence this is a problem in *content analysis*, which will be discussed more fully in Chapter 15.)

Once you have the relevant parts of your field notes coded, you may need to standardize the measures, since you spoke to different probationers with differing frequencies. For example, you decide to standardize the counts of derogatory self-image references based on the number of substantial conversations you had with each person. So the standardized measure would be the proportion of substantial conversations you had with various probationers where they displayed a derogatory self-image. You will then need to code the time on probation with HCEM for each person with whom you conversed. This information you may have gathered in your conversations with probationers, or you may have obtained it through probation office files that a colleague allowed you to examine.[3]

Now you need to *analyze* the information, the second step in this approach. Say you have had substantial conversations over the 5 months you were in the field with 23 different probationers sentenced to HCEM as a condition of probation. You learn how long their sentence had run when they first began talking with you, and you cross-reference that to the percentage of conversations with seriously derogatory remarks about their self-

---

[3] The probation office files will probably be the most accurate source. Although some of the probationers you speak with may proffer accurate information, some may genuinely forget when they began their sentence, and others may distort the information for their own purposes. Of course other participants in the setting can be used to "check" on information provided, but unless such follow-up queries are carefully worded, participants in the setting may feel you are being too "snoopy."

image. Imagine that the results come out as in Figure 11.3. As you can see, it looks like probationers on HCEM feel noticeably more negative about themselves if they have been serving such a sentence for more than a year.

You may want to buttress this pattern you observed in your data with other information, because quasistatistics can only *partially* support your thesis. They do not take into account other factors that might explain the patterns you observe. Further, they derive from settings and observations that were not systematically selected. These limits aside, they can provide some support for your thesis.

Inspection for theory   If you were primarily interested in developing theory and concepts, you would take a different approach to your field notes. Instead of explicitly and laboriously coding the material, you would scan the material, and as you did so, you would modify your concepts and variables accordingly. Since the concepts and variables

FIGURE 11.3
Artificial data suggesting that, for probationers on HCEM, references to a negative self-image increases substantially during the second year of the sentence.

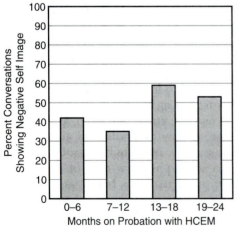

are constantly in flux it is difficult to code systematically the corpus of field notes. The researcher is "constantly redesigning and reintegrating his theoretical notions as he reviews his material." [49] You would progressively elaborate your concepts and the hypotheses interrelating them. The result is an elaborated theoretical structure. This approach is much more sensitive to the richness and texture in the data. With this approach, however, it is not possible, even in a provisional fashion, to test hypotheses.

Constant comparison[4,5]   This method combines the analytic approach of the first method and the theory development of the second method. [49, 51] The researcher engages in *joint* coding of the data and theoretical elaboration. The purpose is to generate theory more *systematically* than the second approach allows; "to aid the analyst in generating a theory that is integrated, consistent, plausible, close to the data—and at the same time is in a form clear enough to be readily, if only partially, operationalized for testing in quantitative research." [52] This analytic approach is most fruitful if pursued *while* the field work is ongoing. It allows you to focus the data collection in the field on the questions and propositions suggested by your developing theory. Since the theory guides the data col-

---

[4] Writers on this topic use the terms *categories* and *properties*. Instead I use the terms *concepts* and *variables*. I think this terminology is less confusing. I recognize that, when employing the constant comparative method, the resultant concepts may not be fully operationalized at all points in the research process.
[5] The method of constant comparison is somewhat similar to a fourth analytic method not described here: analytic induction. Analytic induction is different because it requires examination of all the available data, is couched at a more general level of analysis, and is thus further removed from the data. It allows provisional testing of hypotheses.

lection, this method can*not* be used for the provisional testing of hypotheses.

The approach requires four steps. First, you compare incidents applicable to each concept. For example, if you are working with the concepts "derogatory self-image," "despair about future prospects," and "reactions against the criminal justice system," you would examine the data in hand to decide whether the specific items recorded exemplify one of these particular concepts, and if so how. The cardinal rule of the constant comparative method is: *while coding an incident for a concept, you constantly compare that incident with other incidents also thought to reflect the same concept.* Those other incidents may come from other groups in the setting. For example, while coding a conversation with a probationer sentenced to HCEM for the concept "reactance against the criminal justice system," you would compare that incident to other incidents representing the same concept, even though those other incidents might come from "regular" probationers, probation officers, or staff in the day center.

Two other points about this step in the analysis. (1) You can examine different varieties of data in this step. You are not limited, as you are in the quasistatistics approach, to focusing on one data source at a time. You could examine incidents from your field notes, semistructured interviews with probation personnel, or reports on probationers, to gauge their applicability to your concept. (2) As this step begins to suggest specific *variables* or *indicators* of the concept in question, you should *stop and write a memo.* In your memo define your concept and the relevant variables. Provide a separate incident to illustrate each variable. Codify and clarify as best you can the theoretical notion you are developing. Categorical rules should be explicit and recorded in field notes or a coding man-

ual. The quality of the analysis emerging from your field notes will depend upon how systematically and reliably you categorize your observations.

In the second step you integrate the different concepts and their variables. For example, you might consider the different ways (indicators) that probationers show an adverse reaction to the criminal justice system: missing appointments, misinforming the probation officer, or tying up the phone system if they are on HCEM and are supposed to respond over the phone to check calls at random times. You might begin wondering if probationers who show one form of reactance also exhibit other forms of reactance. If so it would suggest the indicators reflect the same underlying concept. You might begin to think about how the degree of reactance relates to other concepts such as seriousness of criminal history, overall adjustment of the probationer, degree of derogatory self-image, or quality of the probationer–probation officer relationship.

Third, you start to limit the theory. You try to pare down your concepts and the dimensions of each concept to just the essentials. You seek *parsimony.* You also decide the *scope* of the theory: To what kinds of situations or individuals does it apply? What are its limits? The fourth and final stage is *writing theory.* With the field notes, concepts, and memos the theory should be transformed into an integrated written document without considerable difficulty. The result is a **substantive theory** that reflects and explains the dynamics in the settings examined. The theory also reflects the *diversity* in the data as well as its continuities. The resultant theory can be either descriptive, or it can contain causal hypotheses.

Table 11.5 summarizes and compares these three different approaches to develop-

T A B L E 11.5

Three Approaches to Analysis of Qualitative Field Data

	Method		
	Quasistatistics	**Inspecting for theory**	**Constant comparison**
Generates theory?	No	Yes	Yes
Systematically generates theory?	(does not apply)	No	Yes
Allows provisional testing of theory?	Yes	No	No
Steps	1. Define codes 2. Exhaustively code all incidents 3. Do quantitative analysis 4. Write results	1. Develop concepts 2. Inspect data for illustrative and generative purposes 3. Write theory	1. Compare incidents applicable to each concept. Compare each new incident to all other representatives as you go 2. Integrate concepts and variables 3. Limit theory 4. Write theory

ing and testing theory based on your field notes.

GENERAL ISSUES IN QUALITATIVE FIELD METHODS

Validity

The theories emerging from qualitative field methods generally rate high on *ecological validity*. They contain concepts and processes that make sense to, and emerge from, the actors in the setting. This approach can be high on *construct validity* if the researcher makes use of multiple indicators and ob-

serves the expected convergence. [50] Qualitative field studies may be high on *external validity* or *generalizability* if typical settings and participants are investigated, or if multiple sites are used. [53] Campbell, for example, in her analyses of the members of three girl gangs, cross-referenced their interviews with comments made by leaders of other girl gangs in New York City. [31]

Reliability

Qualitative field studies are often accused of possessing low reliability. [53] Detractors point out the following:

- Qualitative field studies examine situations that can never be exactly replicated. Williams, for example, observed reactions when Chili, a member of the crew, was shot.
- Researchers fail to detail exactly the research process.
- The ethnographic process is highly personalistic.

Nevertheless, it is quite possible for an ethnographic study to have high reliability. The following steps, which increase the reliability of findings, have been used in many studies: [53, 54]

- multiple ethnographers,
- sensitivity to the influence of the researchers' position in the settings investigated, [55]
- checks against possible contaminants of participant observation data,
- use of straightforward and precisely defined analytical constructs,
- and the collection of data of more than one type (e.g., archival analysis as well as ethnography).

Ethical Issues

We discussed earlier in the chapter the problems associated with observing illegal activities. An additional concern for field researchers is whether to remain covert as a researcher or be overt about this role. In Chapter 4 the issue of deception was examined. Scholars generally agree that, in a field situation, the researcher treats setting participants as collaborators. In order to preserve their autonomy only very minimal deception is allowable. Full disclosure early in the operation seems wisest. [See 56, Appendix]

Advantages

Qualitative field research relying heavily on ethnographic or participant observation techniques produces research brimming with in-sight into the settings investigated. The accompanying richness of texture produces compelling research findings. The researcher has the chance to unfold a convincing story about dynamics in the situations studied. Finally, the process of theory generation available to the researcher allows a close interplay between data collection, theory construction, and analysis. Consequently, the theory that emerges has several positive features. It uses terms sensible to those in the setting. It is clearly grounded in a particular setting.

Qualitative field methods are particularly suitable for situations where the available theory is sparse, or highly abstract and formal. They can maximize discovery and provide findings startling to theoreticians and policymakers alike. If you are devoted to Holmes's mode of scientific inquiry, qualitative field methods are your tool of choice. They provide more discovery than other methods.

Disadvantages

There are also some disadvantages to this type of research. First, it is extremely time-consuming. It takes at least several weeks and probably one to two years to complete the field work in a participant observation study. Many researchers may not be able to make such a time commitment. Note, however, that it is possible to *practice* qualitative field methods within a much shorter time frame.

Second, you may want to participate extensively in setting activities. As you increase your involvement in the setting (Figure 11.2), however, you may increase participants' reactivity to your presence. Your observations are increasingly likely to record reactions to your own presence and actions.

Third, to function effectively as a participant observer you need to overcome a number of psychological and interpersonal pitfalls.

- In situations people tend to focus attention on portions of the setting, or certain individuals. It may require effort to remain aware of events in the overall situation.
- As a new participant in a setting you are most likely to attract members of the setting who play marginal roles there. In order to gain an in-depth understanding of the situation, and to avoid being labeled by others as a marginal setting member, you will need to develop contacts beyond these marginal participants.
- Further, you will tend to agree with others in the setting whose views or temperament may be closest to your own. To avoid developing a biased perspective on the setting you will need to develop relationships with others in the setting who are different from yourself.

Fourth, these methods demand skill as well as time. You need to develop expertise at listening, flexibility in responding to situations, aptitude at reading the social environment, and a compulsiveness about recording field notes. Remember, though, that these are skills you can learn. They can be learned in classrooms and in field experiences. [57] There is no such thing as a born participant observer.

A fifth potential problem arises in that numerous scholars think qualitative field work cannot be high-quality scientific research. Many seminal studies in criminal justice have used participant-observation. Nonetheless, a significant number of my colleagues find such studies unacceptable. Outright rejection of carefully done qualitative field studies on the basis of alleged methodological problems (e.g., low reliability) is unwarranted.

Finally, if you want to follow Einstein's logic of scientific inquiry, do not embrace qualitative field methods. By and large they are unable to provide rigorous tests of causal hypotheses.

SUMMARY OF MAIN POINTS

- Qualitative field research involving sustained social interaction in natural settings between the researcher and setting participants is called ethnography or participant-observation.
- In participant-observation and ethnography the researcher plays dual roles: as an observer, and as a participant in the setting.
- A qualitative field study may rely on several data sources: direct observation, unstructured interviews, and analysis of official documents or personal documents such as taped life histories.
- In gaining access to a field site and participants the researcher needs to convince official gatekeepers and unofficial gatekeepers that the study will not threaten the setting or its participants.

- Once in the field the researcher begins to build relations with setting participants. The researcher fits in, shows interest, listens a lot, and asks few questions in the initial research stages.
- Researchers often rely on key informants who introduce them to others in the setting, tell the researcher about events he did not observe, and help the researcher decode events.
- Before entering the setting and while there, the researcher keeps field notes about events observed, conversations shared, and reactions to and interpretations of events. Events observed in the field that do not appear in field notes are useless for scientific purposes.

- Although some researchers tape record conversations in the field, or make notes while in the field, the preferred method is to make mental notes while in the field and produce field notes as soon after leaving the field as possible.
- Coding and analysis of field notes begins while the researcher is still in the field and extends for a considerable time afterwards.
- Analysis of field notes may lead the researcher to redirect his data collection efforts, thus influencing where or with whom he spends his time, or the questions he asks.
- Qualitative field studies are generally high on ecological and construct validity. There are several ways the qualitative field researcher can gauge and improve the reliability of his conclusions.
- Qualitative field research is especially suited to instances where the researcher seeks to *discover* information.
- Although qualitative field studies can be used to test hypotheses they cannot do so efficiently; hypothesis testing emerging from these studies is usually provisional.

RECOMMENDED READINGS

Several studies on *gangs* complement the Williams study (*The Cocaine Kids*) mentioned here. Joan Moore in *Homeboys* discusses three different Chicano gangs in the L.A. area and how they have changed over a several-decade period. [58; see also 59, 60] Anne Campbell in *The Girls in the Gang* discusses three leaders of girl gangs in New York City. [31] Her conclusions go against some arguments made by Freda Adler and others that women are getting more involved in crime because they are getting more liberated.

In the area of policing, Peter Manning's most recent book on 911 calls provides insight into police processing of emergency calls. [67]

If you're interested in *drugs* in the city, *The Cocaine Kids*, and *The Crack House*, both by Williams, are essential reading. [61, 62] Phillipe

Bourgois, who has also recently completed a book on the cocaine trade in Spanish Harlem, provides an interesting complement to Williams's work. [63, 64] Their conclusions are similar in several important respects.

For a comprehensive review of qualitative field research in criminal justice read George McCall's book *Observing the Law*. [65] Although somewhat dated, it provides a comprehensive listing of field studies in different areas (criminals, victims, police, courts, corrections, and so on). For a more general text on how to analyze qualitative data, see Miles and Huberman's *Analyzing Qualitative Data*. [66]

KEY TERMS

argot
blackmail solidarity
clubhouse mentality
descriptive propositions
disciplined abstractions
ethnography
field notes
joint design
key informant
life history interviews
multi-site investigations
official gatekeepers
over-rapport
participant observation
qualitative field research
quasi-statistical analysis
reactivity
substantive theory
unofficial gatekeepers
verstehen

REFERENCES

1. Campbell, A. (1979) *The girls in the gang: A report from New York City*, Basil Blackwell, New York, p. 1.
2. McCall, G. J., and Simmons, J. L. (1969) The Nature of participant observation. In McCall, G. J., and Simmons, J. L. (eds.), *Issues in partic-*

ipant observation, Addison Wesley, Reading, MA, pp. 1–50.

3. Williams, T, (1989) *The Cocaine Kids*, Addison Wesley, Reading, MA, p. 3.

4. McCall, G. J. (1978) *Observing the law: Field methods in the study of crime and the criminal justice system*, Free Press, New York, p. 102.

5. Williams, T. (1989) *The Cocaine kids*, Addison Wesley, Reading, MA, p. 3.

6. McCall, G. J. (1978) *Observing the law: Field methods in the study of crime and the criminal justice system*, Free Press, New York, p. 29.

7. McCall, G. J. (1978) *Observing the law: Field methods in the study of crime and the criminal justice system*, Free Press, New York, p. 44.

8. Williams, T. (1989) *The cocaine kids*, Addison Wesley, Reading, MA, p. 132.

9. Williams, T. (1989) *The cocaine kids*, Addison Wesley, Reading, MA, p. 131.

10. Sullivan, M. (1989) *Getting paid: Youth crime and work in the inner city*, Cornell University Press, Ithaca, NY, p. 2.

11. Sullivan, M. (1989) *Getting paid: Youth crime and work in the inner city*, Cornell University Press, Ithaca, NY, p. 8.

12. Sullivan, M. (1989) *Getting paid: Youth crime and work in the inner city*, Cornell University Press, Ithaca, NY, p. 10.

13. Sullivan, M. (1989) *Getting paid: Youth crime and work in the inner city*, Cornell University Press, Ithaca, NY, p. 113.

14. Merry, S. E. (1990) *Getting justice and getting even*, University of Chicago Press, Chicago, p. 5.

15. Merry, S. E. (1990) *Getting justice and getting even*, University of Chicago Press, Chicago, p. 1.

16. Merry, S. E. (1990) *Getting justice and getting even*, University of Chicago Press, Chicago.

17. Merry, S. E. (1990) *Getting justice and getting even*, University of Chicago Press, Chicago, p. 176.

18. Merry, S. E. (1990) *Getting justice and getting even*, University of Chicago Press, Chicago, p. 12.

19. Merry, S. E. (1990) *Getting justice and getting even*, University of Chicago Press, Chicago, p. 132.

20. McCall, G. J. (1978) *Observing the law: Field methods in the study of crime and the criminal justice system*, Free Press, New York, p. 13.

21. McCall, G. J. (1978) *Observing the law: Field methods in the study of crime and the criminal justice system*, Free Press, New York, p. 9.

22. Bogdan, R., and Taylor, S. (1975) *Introduction to qualitative research methods*, John Wiley and Sons, New York, p. 27.

23. Bogdan, R., and Taylor, S. (1975) *Introduction to qualitative research methods*, John Wiley and Sons, New York, p. 32.

24. Whyte, W. F. (1984) *Learning from the field: A Guide from experience*, Sage Publications, Newbury Park, Calif., p. 2.

25. Whyte, W. F. (1984) *Learning from the field: A guide from experience*, Sage Publications, Newbury Park, CA, p. 62.

26. Bogdan, R., and Taylor, S. (1975) *Introduction to qualitative research methods*, John Wiley and Sons, New York, p. 33.

27. Whyte, W. F. (1984) *Learning from the field: A Guide from experience*, Sage Publications, Newbury Park, CA, p. 76.

28. Kahn, R., and Mann, F. (1969) Developing research partnerships. In McCall, G. J., and Simmons, J. L. (eds.), *Issues in participant observation*, Addison Wesley, Reading MA, pp. 45–52.

29. McCall, G. J. (1978) *Observing the law: Field methods in the study of crime and the criminal justice system*, Free Press, New York, p. 14.

30. Bogdan, R., and Taylor, S. (1975) *Introduction to qualitative research methods*, John Wiley and Sons, New York, p. 47.

31. Campbell, A. (1979) *The girls in the gang: A report from New York City*, Basil Blackwell, New York.

32. Anderson E. (1992) The story of John Turner. In Peterson, G. E., and Harrell, A. (eds.), *Crime, drugs and social isolation: Barriers to urban opportunity*, Urban Institute Press, Washington, pp. 147–180.

33. Bogdan, R., and Taylor, S. (1975) *Introduction to qualitative research methods*, John Wiley and Sons, New York, p. 45.

34. McCall, G. J. (1978) *Observing the law: Field methods in the study of crime and the criminal justice system*, Free Press, New York, p. 89.

35. McCall, G. J. (1978) *Observing the law: Field

methods in the study of crime and the criminal justice system, Free Press, New York, p. 102.

36. Miller, S. M. (1969) The Participant observer and "over-rapport." In McCall, G. J., and Simmons, J. L. (eds.), *Issues in participant observation*, Addison-Wesley, Reading, MA, pp. 87–89.

37. Bogdan, R., and Taylor, S. (1975) *Introduction to qualitative research methods*, John Wiley and Sons, New York, p. 60.

38. Bogdan, R., and Taylor, S. (1975) *Introduction to qualitative research methods*, John Wiley and Sons, New York, p. 61.

39. Bogdan, R., and Taylor, S. (1975) *Introduction to qualitative research methods*, John Wiley and Sons, New York, p. 65.

40. Bogdan, R., and Taylor, S. (1975) *Introduction to qualitative research methods*, John Wiley and Sons, New York, p. 68.

41. Campbell, A. (1979) *The girls in the gang: A report from New York City*, Basil Blackwell, New York, p. 50.

42. Campbell, A. (1979) *The girls in the gang: A report from New York City*, Basil Blackwell, New York, p. 53.

43. Wicker, A. W. (1979) *Introduction to ecological psychology*, Brooks/Cole, Monterey, CA.

44. Wicker, A. W. (1987) Behavior settings reconsidered: Temporal stages, resources, internal dynamics, context. In Stokols, D., and Altman, I., (eds.), *Handbook of environmental psychology*, John Wiley and Sons, New York.

45. Whyte, W. F. (1984) *Learning from the field: A guide from experience*, Sage Publications, Newbury Park, CA, p. 200.

46. Lofland, J. (1974) Styles of reporting qualitative field research. *The American Sociologist 9*, 101–111.

47. McCall, G. J., and Simmons, J. L. (1969) The evaluation of hypotheses. In McCall, G. J., and Simmons, J. L. (eds.), *Issues in participant observation*, Addison-Wesley, Reading, MA, pp. 229–230.

48. Strauss, A., Schatzman, L., Bucher, R., Ehrlich, D., and Sabshin M., (1969) The Process of field work. In McCall, G. J., and Simmons, J. L. (eds.), *Issues in participant observation*, Addison-Wesley, Reading, MA, pp. 24–26.

49. Glaser, B. G. (1969) The constant comparative method of qualitative analysis. In McCall, G. J., and Simmons, J. L. (eds.), *Issues in participant observation*, Addison-Wesley, Reading, MA, pp. 216–228.

50. McCall, G. J. (1969) The problem of indicators in participant observation research. In McCall, G. J., and Simmons, J. L. (eds.), Addison-Wesley, Reading, MA, pp. 230–239.

51. Glaser, B. G., and Strauss, A. L. (1967) *The discovery of grounded theory: Strategies for qualitative research*, Aldine, Chicago, p. 101.

52. Glaser, B. G., and Strauss, A. L. (1967) *The discovery of grounded theory: Strategies for qualitative research*, Aldine, Chicago, p. 103.

53. LeCompte, M. D., and Goetz, J. P. (1982) Problems of reliability and validity in ethnographic research. *Review of Educational Research 52*, 31–60.

54. McCall, G. J. (1969) Data quality control in participant observation. In McCall, G. J., and Simmons, J. L. (eds.), *Issues in participant observation*, Addison-Wesley, Reading, MA, pp. 128–141.

55. Vidich, A. J. (1955) Participant observation and the collection and interpretation of data. *American Journal of Sociology 60*, 354–360.

56. Sullivan, M. (1989) *Getting paid: Youth crime and work in the inner city*, Cornell University Press, Ithaca, NY.

57. Lareau, A. (1987) Teaching qualitative methods: The Role of classroom activities. *Education and Urban Society 20*, 86–120.

58. Moore, J. W. (1978) *Homeboys: Gangs, drugs, and prison in the barrios of Los Angeles*, Temple University Press, Philadelphia.

59. Moore, J. W. (1985) Isolation and stigmatization in the development of an underclass: The case of chicano gangs in Los Angeles. *Social Problems 33*, 1–12.

60. Moore, J., Vigil, D., and Garcia, R. (1983) Residence and territoriality in Chicago gangs. *Social Problems 31*, 182–194.

61. Williams, T. (1989) *The cocaine kids*, Addison-Wesley, Reading, MA.

62. Williams, T. (1991) *The crack house*, Addison-Wesley, Reading, MA.

63. Bourgois, P. (1989) Just another night on crack

street. *New York Times Magazine* (12 November), 53, 60, 62, 64, 65, 94.

64. Bourgois, P. (1989) In search of Horatio Alger: Culture and ideology in the crack economy. *Contemporary Drug Problems 16*, 619–650.

65. McCall, G. J. (1978) *Observing the law: Field methods in the study of crime and the criminal justice system*, Free Press, New York.

66. Miles, M. B., and Huberman, A. M. (1984) *Qualitative data analysis: A sourcebook of new methods*, Sage, Beverly Hills, CA.

67. Manning, P. K. (1988) *Symbolic communication: Signifying calls and the police response*, MIT Press, Cambridge, MA.

CHAPTER 12

SURVEY RESEARCH

OBJECTIVES

In this chapter you examine several features of survey research: how to administer surveys, how to construct survey questions and answer formats, and the uses of survey research for Holmes's and Einstein's logic of inquiry.

ORGANIZATION

Surveys represent one of the most widely used social science tools. In this chapter you will explore different features of survey research. You first investigate the advantages and disadvantages of different interviewing modes: in-person, phone, and mail. You then examine some guidelines for constructing questions and response formats. You will learn about two of the largest surveys conducted in criminal justice: the National Crime Survey in the U.S., and the British Crime Survey in the United Kingdom. You will finish with a brief consideration of the uses of survey research for Holmes's and Einstein's logics of scientific inquiry, and some ethical issues surrounding survey research.

To provide some details for some of the related discussion, you will pursue the running example with community policing. Assume that you are conducting a survey in 24 different neighborhoods seeking to have the community policing initiative expanded to their areas. You want to construct a survey of households in each of these neighborhoods

in order to learn about current conditions in those locales, and attitudes toward policing. You hope to expand the initiative to locations that have problems to be addressed but also have residents who would be supportive of the proposed initiative.

HOW: IN-PERSON VS. TELEPHONE VS. MAIL INTERVIEWS

There are three modes for conducting interviews: by going to your designated respondents and interviewing them face to face; by calling them up and interviewing them over the phone; or by mailing them the interview and asking them to complete it and return it to you. Each approach has distinct advantages and disadvantages. The mode you select also has implications for *how* you ask questions in the survey.

In-Person

To conduct in-person or personal interviews you visit respondents and interview them, typically in their homes. "This was the mode of collection most frequently used throughout the formative years of survey research." [1]

There are important strengths to personal interviews. (1) The face-to-face contact between the interviewer and the respondent usually results in a situation that is involving for the respondent. People seem to prefer in-person to telephone interviews. [2] (2) The interviewer can use "props" during the interview, such as cue cards, to remind the respondent about possible answer categories he may use, or maps, or pictures. (3) People in general tend to be somewhat more cooperative about in-person as compared to telephone interviews. **Response rates**—the proportion of approached people who actually complete the interview—tend to be higher with in-person as compared to phone interviews. Further, (4) with a face-to-face interviewing situation, even if you are unable to obtain a completed interview, the interviewer can gather information about the household or respondent. An interviewer who has the door shut in his face can at least record information about the house or the street. Such information may prove useful later when comparing respondents and nonrespondents. Finally, (5) respondents are more willing to answer questions on sensitive topics in a face-to-face interviewing situation. [2]

Nevertheless, personal interviews also contain disadvantages. (1) The administration of interview schedules with large scale samples, such as a national poll, requires a sizable administrative infrastructure. Local field offices, and local supervisors, are needed to keep track of the sampling and the field efforts, as well as returned surveys.

(2) The "costs" of getting the interviewer to the interview site can be sizable. The costs include: the interviewer's time or salary while driving to and fro, and perhaps the salary of an escort if one is required; gasoline costs; and more time and expenditure if the interviewer needs to return to the site at a later time. Furthermore, in the last 20 years, as work and marriage patterns have resulted in fewer households with an adult home during the day, more return trips are required to complete personal interviews. By the late 1970s and early 1980s costs for sampling and data collection alone had risen as high as $100

per completed personal interview. [3] Currently, some survey researchers estimate that costs per completed in-person interview are at least $200 per case. [4]

(3) Finally, personal interviews of a large population often require that the researcher use multistage clustered samples. You select areas, then subareas within the sampled units, and so on. For some technical reasons, clustered samples produce population parameter estimates are less "efficient."[1]

Telephone Interviews

Telephone interviews have become increasingly popular in the last 40 years. They sport numerous advantages: fiscal, administrative, and quality related.

(1) Telephone interviews reduce data collection costs markedly. This is in part because the survey can be administered centrally. A national survey can be run from one office; there is no need for regional field offices. Such a setup dramatically lowers the "administrative overhead" associated with getting the surveys done. (2) In addition, since the interviews are all conducted out of central offices, supervisors can monitor the data collection process by listening in on interviews as they take place. Survey administrators can therefore be alerted much sooner to potential problems with the interview or particular interviewers. (3) The centralization also permits interviewing and data processing staff to work together more closely. Consequently they can closely track the overall survey effort. All of these advantages should result in a higher level of quality control.

---

[1] Although it depends on cluster heterogeneity, clustered samples generally have larger standard errors than do samples where the units are sampled independently. Thus with a clustered sample, as compared to a simple random sample or an interval sample, more cases are required to get a population parameter estimate with a comparable level of precision.

(4) In addition to the benefits from a more efficient administration of surveys, interviewer labor costs are reduced. Interviewers do not spend time traveling to survey sites. Additionally, **callbacks**—return trips or repeat calls to the person or location where an interview is desired but was not obtained on a prior attempt—are much less expensive.

(5) With telephone interviewing, researchers have more choices in how they sample. There is no need to cluster the sample, because there are no travel costs to the interview site.

(6) Telephone surveys can be combined with computer technology to speed up the processing of gathered information. The researcher can use *Computer Assisted Telephone Interviewing*, or CATI (see Picture 12.1). With such an arrangement the interviewer does not fill out a paper and pencil form while talking on the phone with the respondent. Rather he sits at a computer terminal where the survey questions are displayed. He directly enters the answers into the computer.

In addition to speeding up data processing, CATI also allows the researcher to easily vary question or response formats. For example the researcher might have a list of 20 scenarios but cannot ask all respondents to consider all of the scenarios. The computer can randomly select four scenarios for each respondent. This is less cumbersome than the process of printing up different versions of the questionnaire.

Finally, research indicates that CATI phone interviews are more standard than non-CATI phone interviews. With CATI, differences between interviewers have less influence on people's answers. [5] In short, phone interviews, particularly when combined with computer technology, allow greater efficiency, standardization, and researcher flexibility.

Before you run to the phones, however, bear in mind there are costs to telephone

PICTURE 12.1
Mr. Pat Baldasare, President, The Response Center, Inc., a Philadelphia-based survey research firm making extensive use of CATI techniques. With CATI they can conduct a high-quality, national-level survey within two to three days. (Bottom) Mr. Cedric Whitt, working on a computer-assisted interview at The Response Center. The screen shows the questions to be asked. He records the answers directly into the computer.

interviews. Here are some of the major problems you can run into doing phone interviews.

(1) With phone-based interviews you miss those households without phones. Estimates indicate about 9 percent to 10 percent of the U.S. population was without phones in 1980. The figure is probably higher in the 90s. [6]

You would not feel so badly about "missing" a portion of the U.S. population with your phone interviews if those missed were a random subgroup in the overall society. Alas, they are not. Households are *less* likely to have phone service if they have household heads who are *not* White and male; lower average age, income, and education levels; and a spouse absent. [7] Consequently, if you ignore people without phones you are likely to be *biasing* your sample compared to the entire population.

(2) Households with phones, particularly if they are upper-income households, may have answering machines. The machines make it more difficult to get through to the people living in the household. Household members are probably not going to return calls soliciting their participation in a survey.

(3) Even when you do get to people who have a phone and do get past their answering machine if they have one, however, they may be less willing to talk to you than they would be had they met you in person. Telephone interviews have a slightly higher nonresponse rate—about five percent higher in national surveys—as compared to personal interviews. [8] The **nonresponse rate** is the proportion of contacted cases where no interview was conducted. The response rate and the nonresponse rate sum to 100 percent of contacted cases.

Suppose you contact a female respondent who does have a phone, and she agrees to the interview. (4) The telephone interview holds the respondent's attention less well than an in-person interview. Respondents in a telephone situation are more likely to "break off" the interview before it is completed. About five percent of all telephone respondents did so in one national study, as compared to a negligible proportion in a comparable in-person interview. [9]

For the sake of argument let's say your respondent did *not* break off. She completes the interview. How would her responses have been different had she given you an in person interview? Researchers have found that the nature of the interviewer–respon-

dent interaction is different, in several ways, in telephone as compared to personal interviews. (5) Telephone interviews are more "fast-paced." Respondents give less complete answers to open-ended questions. (You will learn more about open- and closed-ended questions below.) (6) Telephone respondents will express more optimism about some topics, such as life satisfaction. (7) They are more reluctant to discuss personal matters. [10]

In sum, telephone interview situations appear to be qualitatively different from in-person interview situations, and this difference is reflected in different response patterns. (See Box 12.1.)

Mail Surveys

The third possibility is to *mail* a survey to respondents. Such a survey would be *self-administered*; respondents complete the questionnaire themselves without an interviewer being present.

The main advantage of mail surveys is the low cost. There are no interviewers whose wages and travel costs must be paid. There are no telephone calls to pay. No supervisors of the surveying operation are needed. After the survey has been mailed out, the only help you need is with processing data from returns. The only surveying cost is the printing and mailing of the questionnaires.

I hate to be repetitive but, again, there are costs. (1) You need to be able to define your population. You require access to a complete sampling frame of the population, preferably in the form of a mailing list, so you can draw your probability sample. If you do not have a complete listing of names and addresses, then the final sample you select may not be a representative cross-section of the population.

(2) If you have a list and can sample therefrom, you will need to work *extremely* hard on

B O X 12.1

RDD Telephone Interviews

No, RDD does *not* stand for *Recidivism Danger Detector*, or *Rodney's Demolition Derby*. It stands for *Random Digit Dial*. With this procedure telephone surveyors can contact households whose telephone numbers are unlisted.

The problem
Unlisted telephone numbers are a problem for researchers doing telephone interviews. In central cities and suburbs of Metropolitan Statistical Areas (MSAs—areas that are urban or suburbanized) up to 40 percent of telephones may not be listed. In rural areas the percentage of unlisted phones may be only about 5 percent. [7]

The solution
Researchers will have computers make up telephone numbers. The telephone numbers use prefixes in use in the local area, but a random number generator in the computer generates the last two or three or four digits. The interviewers then can call up households that have phones but do not have their numbers listed. These households would have been missed had the interviewers relied on published telephone directories or other lists. RDD techniques provide complete coverage of households with phones.

The costs of the solution
There are some drawbacks to RDD. (1) Most notably, the interviewers must work through a lot of numbers to get to working residential phones. Typically with RDD about 35 percent to 45 percent of the numbers generated are nonresidential or not working. Therefore the interviewer needs to make more calls for each completed interview. [11] You can reduce this problem to some extent by having the computer generate just the last two digits of the telephone numbers. This makes it more likely that you will be calling numbers actually in use. (2) If any of your sampling units are small geographically bounded units such as neighborhoods or blocks, it is difficult to get the numbers generated to exactly match these boundaries. (3) RDD interviews appear to have lower response rates than personal interviews. People are less willing to be interviewed when their number has been random digit dialed as compared to a situation where a surveyor shows up at their door. [12, 13] Some of these problems can be countered by combining telephone lists with RDD lists so that some selected residential numbers can receive an *advance letter* telling them about the upcoming survey. [11]

instructions and survey layout. Mail surveys require lucid instructions and flawless survey layout. If instructions are unclear or the survey is confusing in any way, you decrease the chances that people will answer it.

Even if you have a list and design the perfect survey, you may still have a problem getting people to answer it. (3) Traditionally, low response rates have vexed mail surveys. Over the course of the 20th century billions of uncompleted mail surveys have been filed in the round file. (See Figure 12.2.)

More recently, however, researchers such as Don Dillman have suggested that higher

response rates with mail surveys are possible. [14, 15, 16] He proposes several steps to improve mail survey response rates. Make contact with respondents before the survey. Follow up with them after they have received the survey, encouraging them to respond. Provide them with modest incentives for participating. Taking such steps reduces the "response gap" between self-administered interviews sent by mail and other types of interviews. Such steps also require more time and/or funds.

(4) Mail surveys do not represent effective tools for surveying the general population,

FIGURE 12.2
An example of two things: what can happen when you let people fill out surveys by themselves, and the "art" of interpreting survey results.

for the simple reason that people who cannot read are not going to complete the surveys. Illiteracy in the population is not random. It is more prevalent among those with fewer years of schooling. So you are "losing" a particular segment of the population, resulting in a biased sample of people completing your questionnaire.

(5) If people can read the mail survey, you still have a problem in that you have no control over which individual actually completes the survey. A survey sent to a household and intended for the "head of the household" may instead be filled out by the babysitter or a puckish middle-schooler. As a researcher you have difficulty determining who the respondent was.

With mail surveys you want to keep track of returns—how many completed returns come back in what period of time. The volume of returns over time is likely to build in a short period of time and then to fall rapidly. If you keep track of the rate over time at which completed interviews are being returned, you may be able to "time" your follow-up contacts in a way that is most efficient.

Since the response rate is such a concern with mail interviews, you might wonder *what* is an acceptable response rate. Babbie has suggested that a 50 percent response rate is adequate, 60 percent is good, and 70 percent is very good. [17] But he also points out that it is much more important to show that those who did respond are a representative cross-section of the sampled group than it is to have a high response rate.

Ideally, you would like to have meaningful information on those who did *not* respond. Background variables such as education, race, sex, age, and income would be helpful. You could then try and show that, on these variables, those who *did* respond were similar to those who did *not* respond. If the two groups were similar you could legitimately

analyze the results of a survey even if your response rate was extremely low (e.g., 10%).

So Which Mode of Administration Do I Use?

Do you feel like throwing up your hands? Yes, it is true that each method has its advantages and its disadvantages. But that does *not* mean that each mode of administration is equally preferable in all situations.

Mail surveys are especially preferable if you have very little money. Numerous Ph.D. dissertations in various social science fields have successfully used mail surveys. All you need is money for postage. In thinking of postage costs, be sure to keep in mind postage costs for advance letters telling people what is coming, and follow-up letters encouraging people to fill their survey out and send it back in. In a situation where respondents share membership in an organization or have some other common bond, you may be able to obtain a decent response rate with a survey, despite the results obtained by Joe's boss in *Jumpstart*. Of course you can only do mail surveys if you have access to a complete sample frame of the population from which you will be extracting your sample. Be warned however, that with a mail survey you are going to have to work *extremely* hard on questionnaire design and on your instructions.

Do *not* consider mail surveys if you have concerns about the literacy of substantial portions of your sample. For example, whereas a mail survey to a sample of students at a college seems feasible, a mail survey to a sample of urban residents, or a statewide sample, is probably not advisable.

Telephone surveys are attractive if your sampled respondents cover a wide geographical area, such as a county, state or country, *and* mailing lists of the population you want to cover are not available, or are prohibitively expensive. If you have the funds you can interview people by telephone from the red-wood forests to the Gulf Stream waters.

In person interviews are especially advisable in situations where the sampled units are small and geographically delimited (e.g., census blocks, city neighborhoods). I recommend them also for situations where you require relatively detailed responses from participants. If you have a lot of open-ended questions and will be relying on detailed answers to those questions, opt for in-person interviews.

There are numerous situations where you can use *either* in-person or telephone modes of administration. I have been involved in several studies that *combined* the two modes. First, interviewers tried to contact designated households using telephone contact procedures. If these failed, the interviewers moved to the field and sought information that would help them successfully complete a phone interview. They might find out from a neighbor the best times when someone was at home. They would then reattempt phone contact. If these efforts failed they would try and conduct an in-person interview in field.

BOX 12.2

When?

One issue we haven't discussed yet is *when* to conduct interviews. Studies have investigated the times of year, days of the week, and time of day when people are most easily contacted and most willing to be interviewed. The best times are between 6 and 7 pm on weekday evenings in the spring (March, April, and May). Months in the fall are second best. December is the worst month. Summer months are also not good times for completing interviews. [18]

WHAT: THE QUESTIONNAIRE

In this section you explore how to sequence topics in a survey, how to frame questions, and design response formats.

Preliminary

Preapproach Procedures Before you even begin to talk with the people you want to interview, you want to give them "advance information." You might want to send them a "preapproach" letter. The letter introduces the study to the respondents. In the letter you can tell them that they have been selected, explain the purpose of the interview, and give them a name and number to call if they have questions.

"Preapproach" procedures are a good idea regardless of the mode of administration you are using. If you are doing personal or telephone interviews, you want the introductory material to reach the sampled respondents or households before the interviewers call or arrive. With telephone interviews where you do not have an address, such as an RDD sample, you might want to make an "introductory" call where you introduce yourself, explain the study, and give people numbers to call if they have questions. [19] With mail interviews you can have the introductory letter arrive with the survey or actually be part of the beginning of the survey. Sometimes in mail surveys researchers will still send an advance letter to "prime" the respondent.

Screening A **screening procedure** may be required. In this procedure the correct respondent, called the designated respondent, is selected. Accurate screening is important so that respondent selection is done in a random fashion. If it is, the persons selected will be representative of the population.

Your screening procedure may involve identifying very special persons. For example you might screen a household to find out if anyone in that household has called the police department in the last 6 months. The screening procedure adds time to the total interviewing process but may be useful in selecting a certain number of cases with an attribute of interest.

Figure 12.3 provides an example of an actual screener.

Introduction Of course, even if advance materials have been sent to the respondent or advance calls have been made, before you begin an actual telephone or personal survey you will need to introduce the survey topic to the potential participant. You may need to complete the introduction twice—first with the initial contact person, and later with the designated respondent, after the screening procedure has been completed.

Often an introductory speech is prepared for interviewers to use. This standardizes the explanation of the project. All **contact persons**—the first person in the sampled unit with whom the interviewer makes contact—and **designated respondents**—those selected, using some random procedure, to be interviewed—receive consistent explanations of the project. If the introduction varied in different situations or across interviewers, that might influence participants' answers. Such influence would contribute to the total error in the survey. (See Box 12.3 on sources of error in surveys.)

Informed Consent You also need to get people's *permission* to conduct the interview (see Chapter 4). You may obtain consent in writing, or verbally. Variations in the amount of information you give respondents about the purposes of the survey does *not* influence their willingness to participate in and complete the interview. [26, 27]

The Questionnaire

The survey itself is the heart of the research effort. In designing it you consider three types of issues: the overall structure and flow of the items or the sequencing of the content, the structure of the individual items, and the response formats that will be used. Survey design is part science and part art form. I include here some "do's and don'ts," but these offer only rudimentary guidelines; other volumes can provide you with more detailed suggestions. [28, 29, 30] Good surveys are made, pilot tested, and revised—not born.

Pilot testing involves fielding a survey once it has been created so you can "work out the bugs." Although pilot tests can sometimes be extensive, in most situations you require only 25 to 50 completed interviews. You do not need to conduct the pilot study with a representative sample of people, although it is important that the pilot respondents be relatively similar to your final pool of respondents. Pilot testing, in addition to clarifying the weak points of a survey, can also be combined with the use of open-ended questions to develop response categories for questions.

Sequencing Items Ideally, the survey process resembles a structured discussion with one party asking questions, the other party answering, and the conversation moving in an orderly fashion from one topic to the next. It is important that the survey have structure. The interviewer covers one topic with a series of questions, then moves on to another topic. If the questionnaire "jumps around" too much, the respondent may tire more quickly, become confused, and/or break off the interview.

Start with Interesting Questions Construct initial questions that spark the respondent's in-

ADAPTIVE COPING WITH CRIME AND FEAR
SCREENER
VERSION 1/20

CASE # |__|__|—|__|__|__|—|__|__|

CASE # |__|__|

In order for me to determine the person in your household I have to speak with, I need to know how many household heads and spouses of household heads there are in your home.

Could you please give me, the first name, or initial, of each household head, or spouse of head, and their age, starting with the oldest.

ENUMERATION OF HEAD(S) AND SPOUSE(S) OF HEAD(S)

NUMBER	INITIALS/FIRST NAME	AGE
1.	*Max*	56
2.	*Maxine*	52
3.	*Barney*	41
4.	*Wilma*	39
5.		

CONSULT SELECTION TABLE:

# HEADS	SELECT #
1 1
2 1
3 1
4 4
5 2

- CIRCLE NUMBER UNDER # HEADS WHICH equals THE TOTAL NUMBER IN ENUMERATION LIST ABOVE

- CIRCLE NUMBER ON CORRESPONDING LINE IN SELECT COLUMN. THIS NUMBER IS R.

According to the research method being used by the University, I have to ask a few questions of (NAME or INITIAL).

A. Is that you?
- IF YES: BEGIN INTERVIEW

- IF NO, ASK: Can I please speak to (PERSON)

- IF PERSON IS AVAILABLE NOW, INTRODUCE STUDY AND INTERVIEW

- IF PERSON IS NOT AVAILABLE NOW, Could you please tell me the best time to contact (PERSON) (OBTAIN PHONE IF NOT ON LABEL.)

CONTACT: _____   PHONE: _____

FIGURE 12.3
An example of a typical screener form used in a household survey. In the top part of the form the interviewer enumerates heads of households and spouses of household heads, beginning with the oldest. This constructs the sampling frame for each household. Four heads or spouses of heads are listed. Then a selection table with random numbers inserted is consulted to determine the designated respondent. (In the actual study, different random selection tables appear on different screeners.) With four heads the table calls for selecting head #4, Wilma.

BOX 12.3

Errors in Surveys

Survey researchers are always concerned about "errors." These are not the kind of fielding errors made by shortstop Cal Ripken of the Baltimore Orioles during the 1990 season. (A total of only three, thank you.) When survey researchers refer to "errors," they are talking about factors in the surveying situation that result in respondents' "observed" answers deviating from their "true" answers. (Recall from our discussion in Chapter 6 that "Observed Score = True Score + Error.")

There are two general sources of errors in surveys: sampling and nonsampling. *Sampling errors*, as explained in Chapter 10, arise because samples drawn from a population will not match the population *exactly*. The means or proportions derived from the sample will deviate from the population means or proportions in predictable ways, if the sample is a probability sample and certain assumptions hold.

Nonsampling errors can come from five sources. [20, 21] *(1) Coverage* may be inadequate. The *sampling frame* may be inadequate or incomplete. Key portions of the population may be missed. *(2) Cooperation* may be low, resulting in a high nonresponse rate. As this rate increases, it becomes increasingly likely that nonrespondents will differ from respondents, and therefore that the surveyed individuals, and the nonrespondents, each represent biased subgroups of the total population. [22] The **nonrespondent bias** alters the resulting population parameter esti-

mate in ways that are hard to model. [23]

In the actual interviewing situation there are two sources of error. *(3)* Research has consistently revealed **interviewer effects**. Different interviewers obtain, on average, somewhat different answers to the same questions. These effects are usually linked to the interviewer's race, age, and experience, and are often "small" effects. [24] Effects of interviewer race may be substantial, however, when the questions being answered are race related. [25] Researchers may try to minimize such effects by matching interviewer and respondent on race.

There may be *(4)* **questionnaire effects** biasing the respondents' answers; effects of question phrasing, available answer categories, and answers to prior questions may all influence what the respondent finally says.

Finally, errors due to the *(5) mode of administration* shape responses. For example, people give less detailed answers in a phone as compared to face-to-face situation.

In sum:

$$\text{TOTAL SURVEY ERROR} =$$
$$\text{SAMPLING ERRORS} + \text{NONSAMPLING ERRORS}$$

$$\begin{array}{c} \text{NONSAMPLING} \\ \text{ERRORS} \end{array} = \begin{array}{c} \text{COVERAGE} \\ \text{ERRORS} \end{array} + \begin{array}{c} \text{COOPERATION} \\ \text{ERRORS} \end{array} +$$

$$\begin{array}{c} \text{INTERVIEWER} \\ \text{ERRORS} \end{array} + \begin{array}{c} \text{QUESTIONNAIRE} \\ \text{ERRORS} \end{array} + \begin{array}{c} \text{MODE} \\ \text{ERRORS} \end{array}$$

terest. At the same time the items should not be personal, complicated, or threatening. You want to draw the respondent into the interview, and give him a feeling that the experience might even be a little fun, and not boring and dull, as he had anticipated.

Group Similar Questions   If you have several questions on, e.g., respondents' attitudes to-

wards the police, you want to have him consider these queries as a group. Placing the items together makes it easier for him to focus on the topic. It may also facilitate your use of a common response format for a series of items. You'll get more information on answer formats below. You may also want to introduce each topic in the survey, as you get to it, with a couple of brief sentences.

Think about Effects of Sequencing That You Might Be Introducing People sometimes try to answer later questions so they are consistent with their answers to earlier ones. [31] Such effects can occur even when items are not close to one another in a questionnaire. [32] These are called **context effects**.

Consider this example. You ask a respondent a series of questions about the severity of various problems in the neighborhood. Later, you ask the respondent how effective the police have been at handling different kinds of problems in the neighborhood. The respondent might rate the police as less effective than he would have had he *not* already thought about the various neighborhood problems. If you think that there might be such context effects, pilot test different formats and see if they make a difference.

Save "Personal" Items for Last Many survey researchers will place questions they think the respondent unlikely to answer at the end of the interview. The logic is that some respondents might want to break off the interview because they are "offended" by personal questions. By placing these items at the end, you are assured that, if the personal questions do irritate respondents and lead them to break off the interview, they have already completed the bulk of the interview.

In addition, during the course of an interview the interviewer and the respondent may develop a modicum of trust and personal rapport. If this process does occur as the interview unfolds, respondents who would have refused to answer personal questions at the beginning of the survey may do so at the end.

Many surveys ask respondents to report their income level. In general purpose household surveys, this is an item that routinely has a high nonresponse rate.

Of course another way to deal with sensitive information in a survey is to use *ran-domized response techniques*. These are explained below in the section on validity (see Box 12.5).

Item Construction *Building vs. Borrowing* When you are building your questionnaire you have three choices: You can include in your questionnaire only items that have been used in other surveys; you can include in your questionnaire only items that you have constructed; or you can make up some of your own items and borrow some items.

I strongly advise borrowing some items from widely used surveys, *at least* for background items. If you use income, education, ethnicity, and occupation questions that come from other studies, you can compare your sample to the samples in those other studies.

You also might want to explore items specific to the purpose of your study that have been used in other studies. In the running example here you are interested in attitudes towards the police, and perception of neighborhood problems. These topics have been studied before. Your university probably belongs to the Inter-university Consortium for Political and Social Research (ICPSR). ICPSR is a place where major social and political survey files are archived. If your university belongs to ICPSR, you can get codebooks for any study on file at ICPSR. The codebooks include the actual survey questions asked, the response formats used, and the frequency distributions on the items. The number and range of studies archived there will astound you. [33]

But don't think that every good question about a topic has already been asked. And don't think that the questions perfectly suiting your purposes have already been formulated. One of the most fun parts of survey research is making up your own questions. You might choose to pay *no* attention to prior survey items on the topic of interest to you, and charge ahead formulating all your own questions. That's fine too. If you decide to make up items, I offer some general suggestions.

Use Clear, Simple Language In an interview situation respondents does not want to appear unknowledgeable. Therefore, if they do not understand some part of your question, they are unlikely to ask the interviewer to explain. To ask would be to admit ignorance. Instead respondents are likely to provide an answer even if they are not sure what the question is. People "volunteer . . . an opinion as a form of self-protection against being thought 'stupid' or 'uninformed.' " [34]

Therefore, you want to avoid technical terms or language that may not be easily understood by your respondents. Use the "grandmother test." If your grandmother would not understand the question, it is not simple enough. If you *must* use a technical term (e.g., probation, parole) then be sure to *define* it for the respondent at the beginning of the question.

Keep the Questions Short Longer questions are harder for respondents to understand. At the end of a long question they may not be sure exactly what the question *is*. And of course they won't ask. Furthermore, people get bored listening to a long question, leading them to break off the interview.

Ask Just One Thing Per Question My rule of thumb is *never* put *and* or *or* in a question. If you do, you are not sure how to interpret the answers that respondents do provide. Suppose I ask the following question:

> Is people dealing drugs in public and insulting people walking down the street a big problem, somewhat of a problem, or not a problem in your neighborhood?"

Suppose a male respondent says it is "somewhat of a problem." Does this mean that *both* public dealing and street hassles are somewhat of a problem? Or does it mean that one is a big problem and the other is not a problem, and he provided an "average" response? Or was he just thinking about one of these items when he provided his answer? Questions that ask about two things at once are called **double barreled questions**. Avoid at all costs. Separate each item into its own question.

Phrase the Questions in an Unbiased Fashion Avoid leading questions that suggest to respondents the answer they should give. Here is a leading question:

> Don't you think that the police officers in this city are, in general, totally incompetent?

Such a question reveals the viewpoint favored by the researcher. In interviews respondents are sensitive to the answer the researcher or interviewer "wants." Many will try to provide such an answer. Questions such as the above introduce a **response bias**—they suggest to the respondent that one response is favorable over another.

You should strive for a balanced presentation in your items. The question itself ought *not* suggest that any one response is preferred over any other response. For example:

> How would you rate the competence of the city police officers with whom you have had contact? Would you say that, in general, they were extremely incompetent, incompetent, somewhat incompetent, somewhat competent, competent, or extremely competent?

If You Are Asking about Retrospective Self-Report, Be as Specific and Recent as Possible Many surveyors ask people about things that they did in the past, or that happened in the past. The problem of forgetting becomes increasingly serious as the respondent is asked to recall events stretching over a longer period of time. One study asked high schoolers to report on drug use. [35] Respondents were asked about use over the past year, and over the past month. Rates based on the monthly reports were three times higher than rates based on the yearly recall!

When asking about retrospective self-report, you can improve accuracy by making the recall period for the question short and recent. Clearly specify the behavior asked about. Include "probes" (defined below) to help the respondent recall. We will return to the recall issue when we discuss the National Crime Survey.

Open- vs. Closed-Ended Questions   As survey research has progressed in this country, it has moved away from an emphasis on open-ended questions, where respondents are able to reply at length to a question, to an emphasis on closed-ended questions. [36] Of necessity this means that surveys are brief and somewhat superficial. Such a limitation is also inherent, because surveys cover broad populations. The coverage allows generalizations of results *to* populations. Surveys are ideally suited for investigations of "mass" societies.

Nonetheless, you may find when constructing a questionnaire, there are items you really would like to explore in an open-ended fashion. You might want details about incidents that have happened to a respondent. You may seek detailed information about attitudes or sentiments. Thus you may opt for including open-ended questions.

This is a perfectly acceptable practice, but bear in mind that open-ended questions entail costs. (1) They slow down the interview as the respondent replies, and the interviewer writes and summarizes. This leaves

less time for other items in the interview. (2) In mail surveys it may be difficult to decode written responses. (3) Open-ended responses must be coded or transcribed before being used. You, or the coders working for you, may find this a time-consuming process. (4) The coding of open-ended responses amounts to transforming open-ended questions into closed-ended ones, but with response categories generated by the participants rather than by you, the survey researcher. (5) With open-ended questions, in general, persons with fewer years of schooling will have less to say. These items, therefore, are biased in favor of those with higher education levels.

If, after having weighed the costs, you still want to include open-ended questions, do so. Open-ended questions will give you more insight than closed-ended ones. But you might also want to consider whether or not to explore a different methodology, such as participant observation, if exploration, discovery and insight are your major scientific goals.

Response Formats

How Many?   If you are designing your own questions, you must decide how many response categories to allow respondents. In cases where you have simple yes-or-no questions, this is not an issue. But in cases where you are eliciting information about attitudes, such as whether people agree or disagree with something, you have more options.

You may want to include several categories so that you can make fine distinctions between the attitudes of different people. Say, for example, you are asking residents if they would approve or disapprove of community police officers working in their neighborhood. (Of course this question would be preceded by a definition of a "community police officer," because you want all the respondents to have a common understanding of the term.)

At the simplest level you could ask people if they approve or disapprove of such a program. This response format allows you to separate people into two groups. But you may want to know more than that. You may want to distinguish residents who *strongly* approve of the idea from the residents who are only lukewarm in their approval. You need more response categories.

For most survey purposes four to five response categories are optimal. [37, 38] As the number of response options increases, so too does data quality and the external validity of responses offered. [37] In in-person and mail surveys people may be able to work with six or seven categories if the response format is consistent across a series of items. In telephone interviews you may want to limit many of your questions to response formats with three or four items. In telephone interviews respondents tire quickly of interviewers reading lists of response formats to them.

Do I Include a "Don't Know" Possibility? Interviewers will routinely probe if, when asked a question, the respondent says "I don't know" or "I'm not sure" or "I can't remember." A probe is a follow-up to the respondent, encouraging him or her to respond. If the respondent says, "I don't know," the interviewer might say something like, "Could you give me your best guess."

Although the interviewer may probe with reluctant respondents, you need to decide whether or not you want the interviewer, when reading the response options to the interviewee, to include, "Don't know."

There are two effects of interviewers telling respondents they can say, "Don't know." First, you end up with more people, overall, using the "Don't know" option. Second, people's answers to questions including the "Don't know option" appear to have higher external validity than answers to items where "Don't know" was *not* included as a specific option. [37]

When asking respondents about factual issues, researchers will routinely include a response category "Have not thought much about it." For example, if you are asking people if they approve or disapprove of plans to put more foot-patrolling officers on the city's streets, you want to separate those who are really not sure if they approve or disapprove of the idea, and would say "don't know," from those who did not even know the initiative was underway. The latter group rather than admitting that they did not know about the issue, can just say "Have not thought much about it."

Do I Include a Middle Option? Suppose you are asking respondents if they approve or disapprove of community police officers being deployed in their neighborhood. Say you have decided on six possible response options:

Strongly Dis- approve	Dis- approve	Dis- approve Slightly	Approve Slightly	Approve	Strongly Approve

What do you do with people whose tendencies to approve and disapprove are equal? There are some things they like about it, some things they don't like, and on the whole these two sets of items balance out.

You can include a middle category so your new response format would be as follows:

Strongly Disapprove	Disapprove	Disapprove Slightly	Neither Approve Nor Disapprove	Approve Slightly	Approve	Strongly Approve

Note that this middle category is different from a "Don't know" response. Here people are saying they do have an opinion, and that their opinion places them squarely in the middle on this matter.

Researchers have conducted several experiments on the effects of including middle categories in response formats. [39] Explicitly offering respondents a middle category results in more people saying they have a middle position on the issue. It also results in slight but significant decreases in the proportions of respondents offering "Don't know" responses. Explicitly including a middle category does not influence how respondents use the other response categories.

Ratings vs. Rankings   Let's say there are 10 different community problems in which you are interested. You want to know respondents' views on the relative seriousness of these different problems.

You have two options when presenting these concerns. You could use a common rating format for the series of items. For example, you might ask, "For each of these, tell me if it is a big problem, somewhat of a problem, or not a problem in your neighborhood at this time." Respondents use the same format for the different items. Once they get used to the response options, they can probably speedily answer the series of questions.

Table 12.1 provides a list of items asked using a common format from a survey I and my colleagues conducted in the early 1980s.

Another option is to ask people to *order* or *rank* the problems. They could indicate which problem is the most severe, the second most severe, and so on, until they come to the problem that is the least severe. (An ordering or ranking task is feasible with in-person or mail surveys, but probably less feasible in a telephone survey format.)

If you ask people to rank or order the data, they will probably take longer. Another disadvantage with ranking is that you end up with data measured at the ordinal level rather than the interval level. This restricts the operations you can perform on the data. Offsetting these inconveniences will be the more *differentiated* data you will obtain. The ranking task forces people to contrast the different items. Lower correlations between the different items result. [40] Thus if you have a series of items that is not too lengthy, are seriously interested in the differences between the items, and are not doing phone interviews, consider framing the questions as a ranking task.

Be Sure End Points Are Extreme   You want all of the response formats you provide to exhaust the range of possible responses. You do not want respondents to fall "outside" of

TABLE 12.1

**Example from A Phone Survey of List of Items
Using a Common Format**

Q. 22 Now I'm going to read a list of things that are problems for some
people in their neighborhoods. For each item I'd like you to tell me if it's a
big problem, somewhat of a problem, or not a problem in your neighborhood.

How about:

	BIG	SOME-WHAT	NOT	DK
A. Vandalism, like people breaking windows or spray painting build-ings?	2	1	0	9
B. Vacant housing?	2	1	0	9
C. People not keeping up their property?	2	1	0	9
D. People who bother other people when they walk down the street?	2	1	0	9
E. Litter and trash in the streets?	2	1	0	9
F. Vacant lots with trash?	2	1	0	9
G. Groups of teenagers hanging out?	2	1	0	9
H. The amount of noise in the area?	2	1	0	9
I. Bad elements moving in?	2	1	0	9
J. People fighting and arguing?	2	1	0	9
K. Crime?	2	1	0	9

the possible responses. Consider the following response format for a question about
whether respondents approve or disapprove
of community police officers being deployed
in their neighborhood:

Disapprove	Disapprove Slightly	Neither Approve Nor Disapprove	Approve Slightly	Approve

Respondents who approve *strongly* or who
disapprove *strongly* have no place to go. They
will be forced to use the "Approve" and
"Disapprove" categories. In your analysis
you will be unable to differentiate between
respondents who have moderately strong
opinions on the question vs. those who have
very strong opinions on the topic. You always want your "end" categories to include
the most extreme possible reports or opinions
possible.

After you have developed a response format, look at it critically. Ask yourself: Is there any range of opinion or reporting that is excluded? If there is, modify your format.

Be Sure the Response Options Are Balanced Respondents often can ferret out the answer they think the interviewer wants. Sometimes they will base their opinion on this perceived demand characteristics in the situation rather than their own opinions. Questions that are not phrased in an evenhanded way can generate such perceived demand. Response formats, likewise, should be balanced, with an equal number of categories on both sides of an opinion.

Suppose, when asking respondents in the 24 neighborhoods how they felt about community police officers being deployed in their community, you included the following response categories:

Disapprove	Neither Approve Nor Disapprove	Approve Somewhat	Approve	Strongly Approve

The format clearly directs more of the respondents' attention to "approving" responses, thus you are likely to get more approving than disapproving responses.

Avoid Vague Quantifiers When labeling different response options try and avoid vague quantifiers like *very* and *often*. Research has shown that vague quantifiers are interpreted differently in different contexts, making it difficult for the researcher to determine the exact meaning of these responses. [41] See Box 12.4.

Summary These few hints point out some of the more obvious pitfalls in designing answer categories or formats. They are no substitute for pilot testing your survey and making modifications based on your preliminary findings. For example, you may find, after carefully constructing a four-category response format, that, in a pilot test, 90 percent of your respondents use one response category, and another category is not used by any respondents. If the participants in your pilot study are similar to the final population you wish to survey, then you may wish to reconstruct your categories so they do a better job of "sorting" the respondents.

MAJOR NATIONAL VICTIMIZATION SURVEYS IN CRIMINAL JUSTICE

In this section you will learn about two major national surveys of victimization. The National Crime Survey (NCS) has been carried out in the United States on an ongoing basis since 1973. In the United Kingdom (England and Wales), the British Crime Survey (BCS) was conducted in 1982 and 1984.

The National Crime Survey

The NCS is a victimization survey. "In victimization surveys, representative samples are asked to report to survey interviewers any crimes that they have suffered during the reference period, typically the 6- or 12-month period preceding the interview." [42] Societal concern about the extent of disorder in the U.S., coupled with recognition that not all crimes are reported to the police, resulted in

BOX 12.4

How often?

The two figures show results from a survey in which respondents were asked how often they felt bored or excited. They were asked to use a four-point scale: "Never," "Not too often," "Pretty often," and "Very often." Later the researchers asked respondents how many times a day or a week they meant when they said, "Very often," or "Not too often" and so on. These reports were then converted into times per month. As you can see from the figures, "Pretty often" is closer to "Very often" than it is to "Not too often."

The lines extending up and down from each bar show the confidence intervals, and reflect how much people varied in their frequency estimates. As you can see, for both feeling states people disagreed more on what they meant by "Very often" than they did for the other two response categories.

But note also that, for "Not too often," people agreed much more closely on the frequency when they were describing boredom as compared to excitement. There appears to be substantial variability across individuals and contexts in the meaning assigned to these response categories.

So next time your friend Bill tells you that he sees police officers patrolling in his neighborhood "pretty often," don't be too sure you know what he means.

Source: Bradburn, N. M., & Miles C. (1989) Vague quantifiers. In E. Singer and S. Presser (Eds.). *Survey research methods.* Chicago: University of Chicago Press. Adapted from Table 1, p. 159.

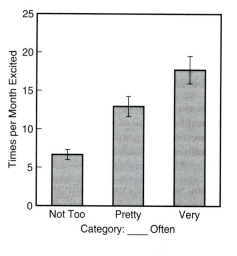

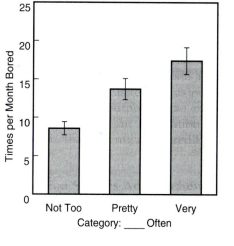

pilot national and city victimization surveys in the mid-1960s. The results of these early studies convinced policy makers to implement a national victimization survey. For example, a nationwide survey of 10,000 households in the continental U.S. indicated that the victimization rate for index crimes was more than twice the rate reported in the UCR. [43]

Pilot studies were carried out in 1970 and 1971. [44] These studies conducted *reverse record checks.* Interviewers followed up persons who had reported crimes to the police, and asked them about recent victimization experiences. Except for assaults, respondents recalled more than 70 percent of reported victimizations.

The NCS was implemented in 1972 by the Bureau of the Census. Initial results from the NCS puzzled researchers and policy makers. For example, those with more years of schooling reported being assaulted more frequently than those with fewer years of schooling. [45] These suspicions about class and culture biases in the survey culminated in a call for redesigning the NCS in 1976. [46] In 1979 a consortium of universities and private research firms began the evaluation and redesign effort. The Bureau of Justice Statistics started implementing these changes in 1986; all of the changes were to be implemented by 1992. The improvements involve extended efforts to "cue" respondents about crime incidents, a new definition of **series victimizations** (six or more incidents of the same type of crime happening to an individual), new questions about vandalism, and a move to a largely CATI system for interviews. [45, 47, 48] Table 12.2 summarizes the history of the NCS.

Sample   Victimization surveys require large samples because victimization is a rare event. [50] At any one time about 50,000 households are in the NCS sample. The survey uses a stratified, multistage, clustered sample of *addresses*. Researchers oversample areas high in reported crime.

Household members at an address are interviewed *every 6 months* for a period of up to 3 years in a *rotating panel design*. A household may therefore be contacted up to seven times over the 3-year period. At each household all household members aged 12 and up are asked about victimization incidents in the last 6 months.

Mode of Administration   As of 1992, plans call for completing the first and fifth interview using in-person procedures. Face-to-face contact will establish and maintain rapport. The other interviews (2nd, 3rd, 4th, 6th, 7th) are to be completed using CATI where possible. [47] Before 1980 about 20 percent of the interviews were completed by phone. Currently approximately 74 percent are conducted over the phone. [51]

Topics Covered   The interviewer obtains basic demographic information about each household member aged 12 and up (age, sex, marital status, race, education). Each person is asked if he or she has been the victim of one or more attempted or completed crimes in the last 6 months; he or she is asked about each type of crime separately. The crimes as defined (purse snatch/pickpocket, rape, robbery, assault, larceny, theft from a motor vehicle) differ somewhat from the UCR-defined crimes. For each incident recalled by a household member, he or she is asked a more detailed series of questions covering physical injury, economic loss, features of the offender, and notification of police and results. Respondents are also asked to report about household crimes such as burglary, larceny, and motor vehicle theft.

The British Crime Survey

History and Sample   In England and Wales, reported crime increased substantially in the 1960s and 1970s. Policy makers in the United Kingdom wished to estimate the total volume of crime, as compared to the volume of reported crime. In mid-1981 the Home Office —the UK's equivalent to our Interior/Justice/HEW departments—decided to go ahead with the national survey. Shortly thereafter it was decided to add Scotland to the survey.

TABLE 12.2

A Brief History of the National Crime Survey

1967	Victimization surveys reveal patterns of crime different from UCR patterns.
1970–1971	Law Enforcement Assistance Administration, and the Census, conduct pilot studies on victim survey methodology. Reverse record checks completed in Washington, Baltimore, and San Jose.
1972	National Sample Victimization Survey (later to become the NCS) is implemented; Bureau of Census interviews about 136,000 individuals in 60,000 *households*. National sample of 15,000 *businesses* also interviewed. (Business sample size later increased to 50,000 businesses; national business sample discontinued after 1977.)
1972–1975	Victimization surveys in 26 major cities. About 10,000 *households* with 22,000 eligible respondents in each city. Surveys of 1,000 to 5,000 *businesses* also conducted in each city.
1976	National Academy of Sciences panel criticizes NCS.
1979	Consortium of universities and private research firms, headed by the Bureau of Social Science Research, begins work on redesigning the NCS.
1981–1985	Tests of proposed changes in procedure to "screen" for victimization incidents. Resulted in improvement of 28 percent in victimization reporting.
1984	Fifteen percent cut in size of NCS sample due to costs of redesign efforts. New sampling procedure to "oversample" in high crime areas.
1986	Begin phasing in redesigned NCS; changes implemented that were "non-rate-affecting."
1990–1992	Final changes phased in: new procedure to "screen" for victimization incidents, vandalism and lifestyle items added, changed handling of series incidents, CATI introduced.

Sources: [45, 47, 48, 49]

The contract for the fieldwork was awarded to an independent research organization. [52]

Fieldwork for the first BCS was completed largely in February and March of 1982, with 90 percent of the interviews being completed during that period. A response rate of 80 percent was obtained. In England and Wales, 10,905 successful interviews were obtained. Another 5,031 were completed in Scotland, but have not been included in most analyses.

In 1984 the second BCS was carried out, and was restricted to just England and Wales. A total of 11,030 interviews were successfully completed.

Like the NCS, the BCS uses a multistage, stratified, clustered sample. Individuals aged 16 and over were sampled in the BCS, rather than addresses. The sampling plan is summarized in Table 12.3. Inner city areas were oversampled. The interviews were personal

TABLE 12.3
Sampling Plan for first British Crime Survey

I. England and Wales are divided into 552 parliamentary *constituencies*. Of these, 238 were sampled. Areas were stratified by type of area (e.g., inner city area). Within each stratum, each constituency's chance of being sampled was proportional to its population size (PPS sampling).

II. Within each constituency, either one ward or two polling districts were PPS sampled.

III. In each ward 60 addresses were drawn; in each polling district 30 addresses were drawn. A systematic random sampling procedure with a random start was used to ensure "spread" of sampled addresses across each locale.

IV. Within each household the interviewer tried to complete a survey with the elector whose name was linked with the address. In some situations a respondent was randomly chosen from among those household members aged 16 and over.

interviews. Three hundred and nine interviewers worked on the first BCS.

Topics Covered   There were three parts to the BCS survey. A *main questionnaire* collected background information and "screened" to determine if the respondent had been the victim of any crimes *in the preceding calendar year*. Each respondent who was a victim of a household or personal crime was asked to complete a *victim form* for each incident reported. A respondent could complete no more than four incident forms. Finally a *follow-up questionnaire* was used to gather information about lifestyles, police contacts, and fear of crime. It was completed by all respondents who completed the victim form, and by a randomly selected two-fifths of nonvictims. The follow-up questionnaire also asked about the respondent's *own* offending.

The second BCS, in addition to covering background characteristics, victimization incidents, and self-reported offending, also explored the following topics: views of the neighborhood, perceptions of local social and physical problems related to disorder, views on seriousness of various crimes, attitudes

toward punishing offenders and prison reform, and participation in neighborhood watch crime prevention programs.

Some Limits of Victimization Surveys

Victimization surveys represent an enormous improvement over reported crime statistics. They provide insight into the "dark figure" of unreported crime. [53] Changes in victimization levels will not reflect political forces, as changes in reported crime can. [54] Nevertheless, victimization surveys have important limitations. These are of two kinds: content related, and technical.

The content-related limitations of victimization surveys are due to omission. "Victimless" crimes such as drug use, prostitution, and white-collar crimes are not investigated. Critical criminologists feel that such omissions result in distorted views of criminal activity in society. In addition, large-scale victimization surveys such as the NCS and the BCS have limited coverage of the explanatory variables of interest to researchers trying to predict victimization. [45] Annual supplements to the NCS, and the second BCS, make efforts to overcome these constraints. But by definition, the volume of what can be included is limited.

The technical limitations of victimization surveys are several and have been widely investigated. [e.g., 50, 55] We have already alluded to some of these problems. **Forgetting** is a major problem. People are more likely to recall events occurring closer to the time they are asked to recall it.

Telescoping is another concern. "Telescoping is the tendency of the respondent to report events as occurring either earlier or later than they actually occurred." [56] People may *forward telescope* the victimization event, placing it within the reference period, when, in actuality, it happened prior to the reference period. They may also *backward telescope*. For example, a participant in the first BCS may place an incident that occurred in January of 1982 in December of 1981. (The reference period for the first BCS was all of 1981.) Researchers use techniques such as bounding to limit this form of response bias. Only information from second and subsequent interviews in the NCS are used for victimization estimates, because the reporting for each of these is *bounded* by the prior interview. Events that were reported from the second interview can be cross-checked against those reported in the first interview, the third can be cross-checked against the second, and so on.

There are other limitations as well. The main point is that victimization surveys are not flawless, and that researchers need to be aware of their limitations when using them for various purposes.

SURVEY RESEARCH IN THE GALLERY OF RESEARCH METHODS

Survey Research and the Logics of Scientific Inquiry

Einstein's Approach Survey methodology is *excellently suited* to the *Einsteinian* logic of

scientific inquiry if the following conditions hold:

1. You are sure that the predictor variable(s) (x or x_1, x_2..) are *causally prior* to the outcome variables (y or y_1, y_2..). For example, if the outcome is victimization experiences in the last 6 months, you are sure that the person's age, sex, race, education level, and family size preceded that experience.[2] If you are not sure about the proper causal ordering of your variables, you can use a panel design, interviewing the same persons at more than one point in time (See Chapter 14.)

2. In your survey you have adequate measures of potentially confounding or spuriously correlated variables, so that you can control for these sources of influence, unrelated to the predictor variable(s), on your outcome(s).[3]

3a. The outcome is an attitude or sentiment the reporting of which is not subject to significant amounts of response bias; or

3b. The outcome is a report of a behavior or an incident, by its very nature easily recalled, which has *recently* occurred, *and* the reporting of which is not likely to be subject to significant amounts of response bias.

As the conditions of your investigation deviate from one or more of the above conditions, the survey approach is likely to be less satisfactory for Einsteinian purposes.

Holmes's Approach Survey methodology is *moderately well suited* to the Holmesian purpose of discovery. Most surveys, of necessity, provide breadth (information about a range of individuals or situations) rather than depth (many details about particular individuals or situations). Therefore, they are not an

---

[2] Of course, there are situations where a victimization incident can change family size or marital status.

[3] See Chapter 5 for a discussion of spurious correlation.

appropriate medium for gaining a fine-grained description of particular people, institutions, practices, or places. A technique like participant observation or behavioral observation (Chapter 15) is probably better suited for providing specifics and texture.

Nonetheless, surveys can be profitably used to *explore* the *relationships between variables* in an open-ended fashion. Such exploration can play an important role in the process of theory development and elaboration. Surveys can be an excellent tool for discovering and clarifying theory based on observed empirical relationships. [57]

How would this work? Imagine that your need assessment survey of residents 18 years of age or over in the 24 neighborhoods being considered for the community policing initiative has been completed. In each neighborhood 30 randomly selected adults in sampled households on sampled blocks completed a phone or in-person interview.

When you started analyzing the results, you developed an index, from several survey items, measuring positive vs. negative attitudes toward local police officers. Those with high scores think the local police are highly efficient, sensitive to local needs, concerned about community problems, and working hard to bring crime and related problems under control. Those with low scores think the police are generally lazy, unconcerned about local issues, and only work on solving local crimes and disorder-related problems when there is strong central or local pressure to do so. You have operationalized an indicator of a concept, and now you want to see how scores on this indicator link with scores on other indicators included in your survey. Your goal is to gain a fuller picture of the differences associated with variation in this attitude toward the police.

You want to *discover* more about this concept, and to begin to generate a theory about it. You dichotomize scores on the pro- vs.

antipolice index, and start to *cross-tabulate* (Chapter 6) these dichotomized scores with any other items in the survey you wish. You are interested in other items in the survey on which pro- vs. antipolice respondents differ noticeably. You are discovering hypotheses for the purposes of generating—not testing—theory.

You need not be worried about whether or not your cross-tabulations are "statistically significant." This concern is not relevant. [58] You are just looking for noticeable differences between the two types of respondents.

Soon you will have piles of cross-tabulations. You start sifting through them, looking for patterns. You notice relationships such as the following. Those who are more supportive of the local police are more likely to be owners than renters, have lived at their current address for a shorter period of time, have a higher education level and are more likely to be employed, are less likely to have other family members living in the neighborhood, perceive disorder-related problems as more severe and are less likely to know someone who has been the victim of a street assault in the neighborhood in the last 6 months.

Once you have established these initial bivariate relationships, your next step is to see how these relationships hold up when you start to *control* for possible confounds. For example, you know that 17 of the 24 neighborhoods have gentrified significantly over the last decade, with upper-class, home-buying in-migrants replacing some poorer, rental households. When you look at the above bivariate relationships, you begin wondering if these are arising mainly from differences, in these gentrifying neighborhoods, between newer, better-to-do in-migrants vs. longer-term, less wealthy, residents. You code each of the neighborhoods as either "has gentrified noticeably over the last decade" vs. "has not," and reexamine the bivariate relationships in each type of neighborhood. You find that the relationships emerge more strongly when you are examining just the 17 gentrifying neighborhoods, and "wash out" when you are looking at the other 7 neighborhoods. In the 17 gentrifying neighborhoods, you would then go on to explore the impacts of other control variables (race, sex, age). You can see under what conditions the bivariate relationships weaken, and under what conditions they strengthen. You are now on your way to elaborating a theory about between-neighbor differences in attitudes toward local policing in gentrifying neighborhoods.

The open-ended, discovery-oriented analysis of survey data represents *theory generation*. To pursue the Einsteinian mode of inquiry and *test* the hypotheses you have developed, you will need data from another, separate survey, or another independent data source. But the important point here is that you can use survey data very profitably to explore relationships between variables, and to generate theory.

Survey Research and the Benchmarks of Scientific Quality

Validity   Many criminal justice researchers will have nothing to do with survey research. They think that what people say to a stranger they will never see again, about topics they rarely think about, in a very peculiar type of face-to-face or phone conversation, is generally unrelated to what those respondents do in the rest of their lives. In short, they think that survey items have low concurrent and predictive criterion-related validity coefficients. *Are these critics of survey research correct?*

If the critics are saying that people lie all the time, they are incorrect. But on the other hand, people don't tell the truth all the time either. You probably already knew that.

It looks like behaviors are truthfully reported on surveys to the extent that: (1) the behaviors and incidents are easily remembered; and (2) the reporting of the events is neither embarrassing nor subject to social desirability. People will underreport embarrassing or stigmatizing events, (e.g., being a child abuser) and will overreport something if it makes them look like a good citizen to do so (e.g., contributing to charity). [59]

If a question threatens the respondent's self-esteem, he is unlikely to answer truthfully. [60] But on a range of routine matters such as owning a car or house (97% accuracy), or owning a library card (86% correct), people report the actual state of affairs with a high degree of accuracy. [61]

Of special interest to criminal justice researchers are reports of victimization and offending. With regard to the former, you may recall that the reverse record check studies conducted in preparation for the NCS found that in the various pretests about 70 percent of reported victimizations were recalled during interviews.

More recently researchers have reexamined the process of matching up survey and police reports of victimization incidents. [62] They have observed that the proportion of incidents matched in a record check varied as a function of how closely they defined a *match*. Percentage of matches, in one study, varied from 14 percent to 100 percent, depending upon the rules used and whether human or machine coders were used. The criterion validity of victimization reporting depends on the matching procedures used. But perhaps more important to us here is the finding that victimization reports appear, generally, to have at least minimally acceptable criterion validity coefficients.

If we turn to offending, we also find that validity coefficients fluctuate. For self-reported delinquency [63] and self-reported arrests [64], survey procedures may provide criterion validity coefficients that are acceptable for some research purposes. Self-reported drug use among arrestee populations, however, does not appear to yield acceptable criterion validity coefficients when compared to urinalysis results, although results also appear to vary by drug. [65, 66, 67]

Techniques are becoming available, how-

ever, which make people *more* willing to report socially unacceptable behaviors such as drug use. *Randomized response techniques*, or RRT, provide *aggregate* level information about offending behaviors considered socially unacceptable. See Box 12.5.

B O X 12.5

Asking Those Hard-To-Ask-Questions *Without* Asking the Question: Randomized Response Techniques

By definition, criminal justice researchers are interested in a broad range of behaviors that are illegal: income tax evasion, drunk driving, stealing cars, violating the conditions of parole, embezzlement, drug use, and so on. Yet as we have discussed, research shows that in a survey situation people may be unwilling to admit to such behaviors. Randomized reponse techniques (RRT) allow the researcher to ask about illegal and deviant behaviors and obtain, under certain conditions, unbiased estimates of the frequencies of these behaviors in a population or subpopulation.

Here's how it works. Let's say you are interested in the proportion of college students who have driven while intoxicated (DWI) in the past month. You are conducting face-to-face interviews with a sample of respondents. Your interviewers define DWI for each respondent. But instead of your interviewers asking respondents the question directly, they give each respondent a randomization device, such as a coin. They ask the respondent to flip the coin. They tell the respondent *not* to tell them the results of the coin toss. But they instruct the respondent:

Say "YES" if *either* of the following is true: your coin came up heads, *or* you have driven while intoxicated in the last month.

The interviewer does not know, if the respondent says "yes," which question is being answered.

If this procedure was repeated with 100 respondents, you would expect 50 out of 100 to say "Yes" simply because their coin toss came up heads. Therefore, if you find that 65 percent of the respondents say "Yes" to this question, you know that the 15 percent above the expected 50 percent represents students who were DWI in the last month. Thus your DWI rate in the sample is 15 percent. [68] You can also compare subgroups such as men vs. women, upperclassmen vs. lowerclassmen and so on.

Generally, research indicates RRT *does* successfully eliminate or at least significantly reduce the bias due to underreporting of socially undesirable behaviors. [69, 70, 71, 72] RRT has been applied to a wide range of behaviors of interest to criminal justice researchers such as drug use, weapons possession by high school students, and white-collar crime, for example.

RRTs have associated costs. They require some extra explaining of the novel procedure, and carefully trained interviewers. And they are limited. They do not provide *individual* level reports of deviant or illegal behavior, but can only be used for group or subgroup estimates. Nonetheless they represent an extremely powerful survey tool for criminal justice researchers interested in parameter estimation of illegal or deviant behaviors among populations or population subgroups.

In sum, survey-based reports for a wide variety of activities and incidents appear to have acceptable criterion validity. Validity coefficients decrease as the social desirability or social opprobrium increases for certain responses. Reverse record check interviews suggest that reports of victimization incidents can have acceptable criterion validity. The size of the coefficient depends on how you define a match. With regard to offending or arrest the lessons appear to be twofold. (1) Overall, validity coefficients for survey reports of offending or arrest appear to be comparable to the validity coefficients obtained from other social science methodologies. (2) But, at the same time, there can be marked variations in the validity coefficients across different types of incidents or across different classes of respondents. As a researcher you want to consider the implications of these variations in framing your investigations and analyses.

Reliability Survey measures have perfectly acceptable levels of test-retest reliability, even when somewhat undesirable behaviors are being reported. For example, investigations of delinquency self-reports find very high coefficients when the test-retest interval is short, such as a few hours or days, and lower test-retest coefficients, of around .6, when the interval is longer, several weeks or months. [63] Survey measures based on internally consistent indices have greater test-retest reliability than measures based on single items or indices constructed of items that do not correlate highly with one another.

ETHICAL ISSUES

Ethical concerns are not paramount in most survey situations. The main concerns are reducing the burdensome nature of the surveying procedure, and preventing inadvertent disclosure of group or individual responses.

To deal with the first matter, interviewers schedule surveys at times least inconvenient to respondents. They stop without complaining if the respondent asks them to, even though the survey might not be completed. They do not force respondents to answer items they do not want to. They try to be generally considerate of the respondent in the interview situation.

To deal with the second concern, researchers will usually code interviews by subject number only. The respondent's name and address appear only on an informed consent form or a sample frame. If the items with the respondents' names and addresses are kept under lock and key, and ultimately destroyed, it is unlikely that others will find out exactly what certain people said in their interviews. In the NCS the Bureau of the Census masks identity of respondents so well it is impossible to determine in which state the interview was conducted.

Nonetheless, there are special ethical risks arising in some criminal justice surveys. A respondent who reports illegal or deviant behavior in a survey may be liable to subsequent prosecution. In these situations the researcher needs to be extremely candid with the respondent about the steps she will take to protect confidentiality. These issues were discussed in Chapter 4.

SUMMARY OF MAIN POINTS

- There are three different ways to conduct your survey: in person, by phone, or by mail. Each approach has its costs and benefits.

- There are two sources of errors in survey results: those that arise from sampling errors—the fact that only a small portion of the population is being interviewed and not the entire population—and those that arise from nonsampling errors.

- Nonsampling errors can arise from one or more of the following five sources: problems in coverage, problems in cooperation, nonrespondent bias, interviewer effects, and questionnaire effects.
- Contacts with potential respondents before the survey begins is an essential step in improving response rates.
- Key issues in questionnaire design include question content, response formats to be used by the respondent, and the sequencing of the items in the interview.
- Under certain conditions survey methodology is excellently suited to Einstein's mode of scientific inquiry, and moderately suited to Holmes's logic of inquiry.
- Surveys can be profitably used to generate grounded theory.
- External validity of many survey items is at least acceptable.
- Validity coefficients of survey items on offending and related incidents may vary from marginal to acceptable, depending upon several factors.
- Surveys items and indexes routinely yield acceptable test-retest reliability coefficients. Indexes tend to be somewhat more reliable than single items.

SUGGESTED READINGS

For a basic book on all aspects of survey research try Earl Babbie's *Survey Research Methods* (Belmont, CA: Wadsworth, 1973). It provides good, basic coverage of all aspects of sampling and survey methodology.

For helpful hints on how to design questionnaires try *Asking Questions* by Seymour Sudman and Norman Bradburn (San Francisco: Jossey-Bass, 1982).

If you are historically minded, you might enjoy Jean Converse's *Survey Research in the United States* (Berkeley: University of California Press, 1987). She describes the history of surveying in

this country from its origins at the end of the last century through 1960. Her discussions of the tension between practical survey researchers and academic researchers, and her speculations on where the field is headed, are thought-provoking. She provides a panorama of the development of this major field not found elsewhere.

KEY TERMS

callbacks
contact persons
context effects
designated respondents
double barreled questions
forgetting
interviewer effects
non-response rate
non-sampling errors
nonrespondent bias
pilot testing
questionnaire effects
response bias
response rates
reverse record checks
screening procedure
series victimizations
telescoping

REFERENCES

1. Garofalo, J., and Hendelang, M. J. (1977) *An Introduction to the National Crime Survey*, US Department of Justice, Washington, DC, p. 11.
2. Groves, R. M. (1989) Answers and questions in telephone and personal interview surveys. In *Survey research methods: A Reader* (Singer, E., and Presser, S., eds), pp. 208–223. Chicago: University of Chicago Press.
3. Groves, R. M., and Kahn, R. L. (1979) *Surveys by telephone: A National comparison with personal interviews*, Wiley, New York, p. 3.
4. LoSciuto, L., director for the Institute for Survey Research, Temple University. Personal communication, November 1992.
5. Groves, R. M., and Magilavy, L. J. (1989) Measuring and explaining interviewer effects in

centralized telephone surveys. In *Survey research methods: A Reader* (Singer, E., and Presser, S., eds), pp. 288–303. Chicago: University of Chicago Press. (survey research).

6. Groves, R. M., and Kahn, R. L. (1979) *Surveys by telephone: A National comparison with personal interviews*, Wiley, New York, p. 214.

7. Tull, D. S., and Albaum, G. S. (1989) Bias in random digit dialed surveys. In *Survey research methods: A Reader* (Singer, Ed., and Presser, S., eds), pp. 11–17. Chicago: University of Chicago Press.

8. Groves, R. M., and Kahn, R. L. (1979) *Surveys by telephone: A National comparison with personal interviews*, Wiley, New York, p. 219.

9. Groves, R. M., and Kahn, R. L. (1979) *Surveys by telephone: A National comparison with personal interviews*, Wiley, New York, p. 220.

10. Groves, R. M., and Kahn, R. L. (1979) *Surveys by telephone: A National comparison with personal interviews*, Wiley, New York, p. 222.

11. Traugott, M. W., Groves, R. M., and Lepkowski, J. M. (1989) Using dual frame designs to reduce nonresponse in telephone surveys. In *Survey research methods: A Reader* (Singer, E., and Presser, S., eds), pp. 79–98. Chicago: University of Chicago Press.

12. Groves, R. M., and Kahn, R. L. (1979) *Surveys by telephone: A National comparison with personal interviews*, Wiley, New York, p. 64.

13. Steeh, C. G. (1989) Trends in nonresponse rates, 1952–1979. In *Survey research methods: A Reader* (Singer, E., and Presser, S., eds), pp. 32–49. Chicago: University of Chicago Press.

14. Singer, E., and Presser, S. (1989) Mode of administration. In *Survey research methods: A Reader* (Singer, Ed., and Presser, S., eds), pp. 187–188. Chicago: University of Chicago Press.

15. Dillman, D. A. (1978) *Mail and telephone surveys: The Total design method*, Wiley, New York.

16. Armstrong, J. S. (1975) Monetary incentives in mail surveys. *Public Opinion Q.* 39, 111–116.

17. Babbie, E. (1989) *Practicing social research*, Fifth ed., Wadsworth, Monterey, p. 242.

18. Vigderhous, G. (1989) Scheduling telephone interviews: A Study of seasonal patterns. In *Survey research methods: A Reader* (Singer, E.,

and Presser, S., eds), pp. 69–78. Chicago: University of Chicago Press.

19. Groves, R. M., and Kahn, R. L. (1979) *Surveys by telephone: A National comparison with personal interviews*, Wiley, New York.

20. Anderson, R., Kasper, J., and Frankel, M. R. (1979) *Total survey error*, Jossey-Bass, San Francisco.

21. Singer, E., and Presser, S. (1989) Editor's introduction. In *Survey research methods: A Reader* (Singer, E., and Presser, S., eds), pp. 1–5. Chicago: University of Chicago Press.

22. Singer, E., and Presser, S. (1989) The Sample: Coverage and cooperation. In *Survey research methods: A Reader* (Singer, E., and Presser, S., eds), pp. 7–9. Chicago: University of Chicago Press.

23. Smith, T. W. (1989) The Hidden 25%: An Analysis of nonresponse on the 1980 General Social Survey. In *Survey research methods: A Reader* (Singer, E., and Presser, S., eds), pp. 50–68. Chicago: University of Chicago Press.

24. Singer, E., and Presser, S. (1989) The Interviewer. In *Survey research methods: A Reader* (Singer, E., and Presser, S., eds), pp. 245–246. Chicago: University of Chicago Press.

25. Schuman, H., and Converse, J. M. (1989) The Effects of black and white interviewers on black responses. In *Survey research methods: A Reader* (Singer, E., and Presser, S., eds), pp. 247–271. Chicago: University of Chicago Press.

26. Singer, E. (1978) Informed consent: Effect on response rate and response quality in social surveys. *American Sociological Review* 43, 144–162.

27. Singer, E., and Frankel, M. R. (1983) Informed consent procedures in telephone interviews. *American Sociological Review* 47, 416–426.

28. Converse, J. M., and Presser, S. (1986) *Survey questions: Handcrafting the standardized questionnaire*, Sage, Beverly Hills, CA.

29. Sudman, S., and Bradburn, N. M. (1982) *Asking questions: A Practical guide to questionnaire design*, Jossey-Bass, San Francisco.

30. Payne, S. (1951) *The Art of asking questions*, Princeton, NJ: Princeton University Press.

31. Sigelman, L. (1989) Question order effects of

presidential popularity. In *Survey research methods: A Reader* (Singer, E., and Presser, S., eds), pp. 142–150. Chicago: University of Chicago Press.

32. Schuman, H., Kalton, G., and Ludwig, J. (1989) Context and contiguity in survey questionnaires. In *Survey research methods: A Reader* (Singer, E., and Presser, S., eds), pp. 151–154. Chicago: University of Chicago Press.

33. Inter-university Consortium for Political and Social Research. (1991) *Guide to resources and services: 1991–1992*, ICPSR, Ann Arbor, MI.

34. Bishop, G. F., Oldenick, R. W., Tuchfarber, A. J., and Bennett, S. E. (1989) Pseudo-opinions on public affairs. In *Survey research methods: A Reader* (Singer, E., and Presser, S., eds), pp. 425–436. Chicago: University of Chicago Press.

35. Bachman, J. G., and O'Malley, P. M. (1989) When four months equal a year: Inconsistencies in student reports of drug use. In *Survey research methods: A Reader* (Singer, E., and Presser, S., eds), pp. 173–185. Chicago: University of Chicago Press.

36. Converse, J. M. (1987) *Survey research in the united states: Roots and emergence, 1890–1960*, University of California Press, Berkeley, CA, p. 413.

37. Andrews, F. M. (1989) Construct validity and error components of survey measures: A Structural modeling approach. In *Survey research methods: A Reader* (Singer, E., and Presser, S., eds), pp. 391–424. Chicago: University of Chicago Press.

38. Cox, E. P., III. (1980) The optimal number of response alternatives for a scale: A Review. *Journal of Marketing Research 17*, 407–422.

39. Presser, S., and Schuman, H. (1989) The Measurement of a middle position in attitude surveys. In *Survey research methods: A Reader* (Singer, E., and Presser, S., eds), pp. 108–123. Chicago: University of Chicago Press.

40. Alwin, D. F., and Krosnick, J. A. (1989) The Measurement of values in surveys: A Comparison of ratings and rankings. In *Survey research methods: A Reader* (Singer, E., and Presser, S., eds), pp. 124–141. Chicago: University of Chicago Press.

41. Bradburn, N. M., and Miles, C. (1989) Vague quantifiers. In *Survey research methods: A Reader* (Singer, E., and Presser, S., eds), pp. 155–164. Chicago: University of Chicago Press.

42. Garofalo, J., and Hindelang, M. J. (1977) *An Introduction to the National Crime Survey*, US Department of Justice, Washington, DC, p. 11.

43. Ennis, P. H. (1967) *Criminal victimization in the United States: A Report of a national survey.* (Field surveys II. President's Commission on Law Enforcement and the Administration of Justice.) US GPO, Washington, DC.

44. Lehnen, R. G., and Skogan, W. G., eds. (1981) *The National Crime Survey: Working papers (Volume I: Current and historical perspectives)*, US Department of Justice, Washington, DC.

45. Skogan, W. G (1990) The polls—a review: The National Crime Survey redesign. *Public Opinion Q. 54*, 256–272.

46. National Research Council. (1976) *Surveying crime*, National Academy of Sciences, Washington, DC.

47. Taylor, B. M. (1989) *New directions for the National Crime Survey*, Bureau of Justice Statistics, Washington, DC.

48. Whitaker, C. J. (1989) *The redesigned National Crime Survey: Selected new data*, Bureau of Justice Statistics, Washington, DC.

49. Garofalo, J., and Hindelang, M. J. (1977) *An Introduction to the National Crime Survey*, US Department of Justice, Washington, DC.

50. Skogan, W. G. (1981) *Issues in the measurement of victimization*, U.S. Government Printing Office, Washington, DC.

51. Bureau of Justice Statistics. (1991) *Criminal victimization in the United States, 1991*, U.S. Department of Justice, Washington, DC.

52. Hough, M., and Mayhew, P. (1983) *The British Crime Survey: First report*, Her Majesty's Stationery Office, London (Home Office Research Study No. 76), p. 4.

53. Biderman, A. D., and Reiss, A. J. (1967) On exploring the "dark figure" of crime. *Annals of the American Academy of Political and Social Science 439*, 1–15.

54. Black, D. J. (1970) Production of crime rates. *American Sociological Review 35*, 899–908.

55. Lehnen, R. G., and Skogan, W. G., eds. (1984) *The National Crime Survey: Working papers (Volume II: Methodological studies)*, US Department of Justice, Washington, DC.

56. Murphy, L. R., and Cowan, C. D. (1984) Effects of bounding on telescoping in the National Crime Survey. In *The National Crime Survey: Working papers (Volume II: Methodological Studies)* (Lehnen, R. G., and Skogan, W. G., eds), pp. 83–89. Washington, DC: Bureau of Justice Statistics.

57. Glaser, B. G., and Strauss, A. L. (1967) *The Discovery of grounded theory: Strategies for qualitative research*, Aldine, Chicago, p. 186.

58. Selvin, H. (1957) A Critique to tests of significance in survey research. *American Sociological Review 22*, 519–527.

59. Singer, E., and Presser, S. (1989) Validation. In *Survey research methods: A Reader* (Singer, E., and Presser, S., eds), pp. 325–326. Chicago: University of Chicago Press.

60. Bradburn, N., and Sudman, S. (1979) *Improving interview method and questionnaire design*, Jossey-Bass, San Francisco.

61. Parry, H. J., and Crossley, H. M. (1950) Validity of responses to survey questions. *Public Opinion Q. 14*, 61–80.

62. Miller, P. V., and Groves, R. M. (1989) Matching survey responses to official records: An Exploration of validity in victimization reporting. In *Survey research methods: A Reader* (Singer, E., and Presser, S., eds), pp. 356–370. Chicago: University of Chicago Press.

63. Hindelang, M. J., Hirschi, T., and Weis, J. G. (1981) *Measuring delinquency*, Sage, Beverly Hills, CA.

64. Wyner, G. A. (1980) Response errors in self reported number of arrests. *Sociological Methods and Research 9*, 161–177.

65. Mieczkowski, T., Barzeley, D., Gropper, B., and Wish, E. (1990) Tripartite concordance of self-reported cocaine use and three immunoassay techniques in an arrestee population. Paper presented at the annual meeting of the American Society of Criminology, November, Baltimore.

66. Wish, E. (no date) *Drug testing*, National Institute of Justice, Washington, DC.

67. Wish, E. D., and O'Neil, J. (1989) *Drug use forecasting: January to March 1989*, National Institute of Justice, Washington, DC.

68. Chadhuri, A., and Mukurjee, R. (1988) *Randomized response: Theory and techniques*, Dekker, New York, p. 4.

69. Zdep, S. M., Rhodes, I. N., Schwarz, R. M., and Kilkenny, M. J. (1989) The Validity of the randomized response technique. In *Survey research methods: A Reader* (Singer, E., and Presser, S., eds), pp. 385–390. Chicago: University of Chicago Press.

70. Warner, S. L. (1965) Randomized response: A Survey technique for eliminating evasive answer bias. *Journal of the American Statistical Association 60*, 63–69.

71. Zdep, S. M., and Rhodes, I. N. (1976) Making the randomized response technique work. *Public Opinion Q. 40*, 531–537.

72. Fox, J. A., and Tracy, P. E. (1986) *Randomized response: A Method for Sensitive Surveys*, Sage, Newbury Park, CA.

CHAPTER 13

QUASI-EXPERIMENTS, TRUE EXPERIMENTS, AND EVALUATION

FOCUS

Quasi-experiments permit researchers to observe how a change, or an experimental treatment program, affects a group of people. With true experiments, researchers can ensure that, initially, those receiving the experimental treatment are comparable, as a group, to those not receiving the treatment. They achieve this comparability through a process of random assignment. Quasi-experiments and true experiments represent designs excellently suited to the Einsteinian testing of causal hypotheses. Evaluation researchers may use these tools, or other tools, when they scientifically examine the consequences of a new program or policy.

ORGANIZATION

You examine three different types of research designs in this chapter: "weak" quasi-experimental designs, "strong" quasi-experimental designs, and "true" experimental designs.[1] You begin by exploring the important theoretical and practical differences among these three different classes of designs. You will

investigage threats to internal validity. These are factors interfering with the testing of causal hypotheses. You will investigate several specific research designs, and the strengths and weaknesses of each. You finish with a brief introduction to evaluation research. Evaluation is not a method but rather a purpose of research.

A WAY TO THINK ABOUT THE DIFFERENT RESEARCH DESIGNS

Common Elements

All experimental designs have several features in common. A change is introduced. The change either occurs "naturally" [1] or is introduced by an agent. The researcher wants to know what effect the change, called a **treatment**, has had, on some particular outcome. To measure the effects of the treatment she compares the outcome scores of the group receiving the "treatment" to some comparison group, or to the group itself before it received the treatment. "All experiments involve at least a treatment, an outcome measure, units of assignment, and some comparison from which change can be inferred and hopefully attributed to the treatment." [2]

---

[1] The experiments discussed here will always occur in the field; I do not discuss experiments performed in laboratory settings due to the low ecological validity of the latter.

Three Classes of Research Designs

At the same time there are important differences in experimental research designs. You will learn about three different classes of research designs in this chapter. These three classes of designs differ in two important ways: the *degree to which causal hypotheses can be rigorously tested, and the degree of difficulty in carrying out the design.* Stated differently, the designs vary in their suitability for Einsteinian inquiry, and in the difficulties surrounding their actual use. These latter **implementation difficulties** are the problems that arise, due to practical or political reasons, that may make it difficult to carry out a research effort, or put into place a program or policy.

When I refer to the "politics" of research, I allude to several features of a real-world, nonlaboratory research situation. You must get the different parties involved in the enterprise to agree to participate, and perhaps even to agree with one another. You must monitor the implementation—the putting into place—of the research design. You also need to attend to various aspects of data collection. You need to consider how different constituencies will react to different aspects of the research process, and the results. Although the intensity of the political climate surrounding a quasi-experiment or a true experiment can vary, you will always find these concerns present to some degree. The problems presented by such real-world efforts are not unlike some problems encountered in field research, where you negotiate with gatekeepers about gaining access to settings.

Figure 13.1 places the three classes of designs on these two dimensions. As you might expect, the two dimensions described above relate positively to one another. Those designs allowing you to test causal hypotheses with more rigor are the same designs that are more involved and politically difficult.

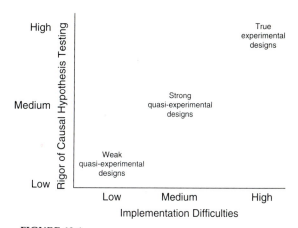

FIGURE 13.1

Designs used for quasi-experiments and true experiments can be classified into three groups: weak quasi-experiments, strong quasi-experiments, and true experiments. They differ in the amount of causal rigor they provide and the difficulties surrounding their use.

Weak Quasi-experimental Designs   In the far left and at the bottom appear designs providing the *least* causal influence, and posing the *least* implementation difficulties. These are **weak quasi-experimental designs**, also called **pre-experimental designs**. Designs in this class are relatively easy to do, albeit less informative than other designs. These designs:

- Include a group or groups of cases that receive an experimental treatment. These cases are the **experimental group**.
- They may or may not have a **control group** —cases that did not receive the experimental treatment.
- If a control group is present, researchers have probably done little to make the control group comparable to the experimental group.

Strong Quasi-experimental Designs   Appearing in the middle of the graph are those designs that generally provide *some* degree of causal inference, and *some* degree of implementation difficulties. These include **strong quasi-experimental designs**. These designs:

- Always include both an experimental group and a control group or a control period.
- Further, with these designs, researchers have taken steps to make the experimental and control groups more comparable to each other.

True Experimental Designs On the top right portion of the graph appear **true experimental designs**. These provide *substantial* causal inference and often create abundant implementation difficulties. These designs always:

- Include both experimental and control groups.
- Use random assignment procedures to assign cases to either experimental or control groups. It is this randomization procedure that make these designs "true" experiments.

Given the practical problems accompanying such designs, researchers have suggested they be used only if certain conditions are present. These conditions force the researcher to cross a "threshold" separating quasi-experimental from true experimental designs. Researchers differ on the exact location of the threshold. [3, 4, 5 vs. 6]

THREATS TO VALIDITY: ESTABLISHING AND GAUGING PLAUSIBLE IMPACTS

Defining Threats to Internal Validity

The classes of designs that are higher up and further to the right in Figure 13.1 can more adequately address plausible threats to internal validity. We can define threats to validity using terminology analogous to what you learned about classical measurement theory

(Chapter 6). Recall from that chapter the axiom of classical test theory:

Observed Score = True Score + Error

You can think of threats to internal validity (TIVs) in a similar fashion. Here, however, you are not concerned about an observed score. You are concerned with an *effect* of your independent variable—usually, a treatment. The results of your true experiment or your quasi-experiment provide an **estimate of the effect** of the treatment.

> The estimate of the effect is the size of the difference(s), on the outcome score(s), between your experimental treatment group(s), and your control group(s).

The estimate of the effect you observe, just like the observed score of classical test theory, has two portions:

ESTIMATE OF EFFECT = TRUE TREATMENT EFFECT + DISCREPANCY

What you observe in your data—the estimate of effect—is the sum of an unobserved "true" effect, and the discrepancy between the "true" and "observed" effect. [7] The **discrepancy** itself arises from all the different threats to internal validity (TIV) operative in the research design, and is simply *their* sum.

$$DISCREPANCY = TIV_1 + TIV_2 + TIV_3 + TIV_4 + TIV_5 + \ldots TIV_n$$

Thus you can define a **threat to internal validity** as

> anything that causes a discrepancy between a [true] treatment effect and its estimate. [7]

Conversely, whenever there is a discrepancy between true and observed treatment effects, it is because one or more threats to internal validity are influencing scores on the outcome variable(s).

Note two properties of these definitions. First, there is no directionality implied. An observed treatment effect may be larger or smaller than the true treatment effect. Second, there is no equality of size or sign implied across different threats to internal validity. Some may contribute substantially to the discrepancy. Others may contribute minimally. Some threats to internal validity may partially or completely offset other threats to internal validity.

Think of this everyday example. Imagine your department is currently offering two sections of a statistics course. In one section the instructor relies heavily on computers and computer labs. In the other section the instructor does not allow students to use anything more than a hand calculator. At the end of the semester you want to compare how much students in the two different classes know about statistics. You design a few simple questions to ask a sample of students from each class, creating an index of statistical knowledge. You reason that the noncomputer class students can serve as a control group for the students who took the computer-intensive class. The latter make up your experimental group.

The two groups differ in the type of statistics course they took. They also may differ in other ways as well, ways you do not know about. Here are some possibilities. (1) One class may have been scheduled for 8:30 am. The other may have been scheduled for noon. The more serious students may have signed up for the earlier class. (2) Or, students signing up for the noncomputer course may be more computer phobic than students signing up for the computer-based course.

In short, you do not know all the ways in which the two groups differ. These differences represent additional independent variables you have not measured. Furthermore, these differences may be as strongly related to the outcome as the independent variable in which you *are* interested: taking computer-based or non-computer-based statistics.

Imagine that, on your index tapping statistical expertise, the average score for students in the computer-instructed statistics course was 65. The average score for students in the non-computer-instructed statistics course was 85. Thus,

ESTIMATE OF EFFECT =
(experimental average − control average) =
−20

Your next step is to measure DISCREPANCY. Assume that you asked students in your survey about a host of other factors, threats to internal validity, that may have influenced your results. You asked how serious they were as students by asking them to report their GPA and average hours/week spent doing homework. You asked them to rate teacher effectiveness. You asked about prior knowledge of statistics, and so on. Using statistical techniques you then learned how much each of these TIVs influenced the outcome score. Adding up across all these different TIVs you may find that:

DISCREPANCY = −5.

You now know that:

−20 = TRUE TREATMENT
EFFECT + (−5).

Consequently, given the above equation you know that the *true* difference between the two groups on the outcome score was:

−15 = TRUE TREATMENT EFFECT

The noncomputer group outperformed the computer group by 15 points on your outcome index, after taking into account several threats to internal validity.

When Do I Go Looking for Threats to Internal Validity?

You may be spurred to investive action for either or both of the following reasons. First, you know that, with the research design you are using, one or more threats to internal validity could *plausibly* crop up. Based on what you know about the design, its limitations, and the context surrounding the research, you suspect that one or more threats could be at work. Second, based on what you know about the phenomena you are investigating, the treatment effect you observe does not look right. Other research suggests that your observed treatment effect should be larger or smaller than it is in your experiment or quasi-experiment. In almost every quasi-experiment or true experiment, *at least* one plausible threat will exist.

In many cases researchers will be unable to list all of the relevant TIVs. Further, they probably will be unable to measure all of the TIVs they suspect. They just do the best they can, trying to list all plausible threats, and then getting data for as many of them as feasible.

What Do I Do Once I Have Identified a Possible Threat to Internal Validity?

In the sections below you will read about the different threats to internal validity that can jeopardize the internal validity of your conclusions. If you are using a particular design, and it has one or more plausible threats to internal validity associated with it, you will try to measure each plausible threat.

You will use your data to learn two things if the TIV you suspect can be measured. First, does the TIV cause a difference, evident at the beginning of the study, or as the study progresses, between experimental (E) and control (C) groups? If it does cause a difference, how big is that difference? Second, and perhaps more importantly, how much of a discrepancy, on the outcome variables, between observed and true treatment effects does this difference plausibly cause? You want to assess initial group differences as well as the size of the discrepancy caused.

You consider both, because some initial group differences are *unlikely* to affect outcome scores. You may be doing a quasi-experiment on sentencing practices and find that your experimental and control groups differ substantially on average height. Your outcome is postrelease time free, before rearrest. Is it *plausible* that this group difference could have a substantial effect on an outcome such as time to rearrest? Although you might be able to develop some bizarre theses on why there could be such an effect, I think few would find it plausible.

On the other hand some initial group differences *could* plausibly influence outcomes. For example, your experimental and control groups in a sentencing quasiexperiment might differ significantly on seriousness of current conviction.[2] If this occurs, you would try to estimate how much impact the group difference had on outcome scores, and subtract that difference from the treatment effect you observe.

Figure 13.2 summarizes the steps in dealing with threats to internal validity.

DESIGNS PERMITTING MINIMAL CAUSAL INFERENCE: WEAK QUASI-EXPERIMENTAL DESIGNS[3]

We focus first on weak quasiexperimental designs permitting minimal causal inference, and posing minimal practical difficulties. Following the tradition of Tom Cook and Don Campbell, I will use a particular set of symbols to describe these different designs. Table

---

[2] I refer here to statistical significance of the difference, not just subjective estimates of significance.

[3] I will be covering only a handful of different quasi-experimental designs. Although many of them exist, space restrictions allow me to explain only some of the most common ones.

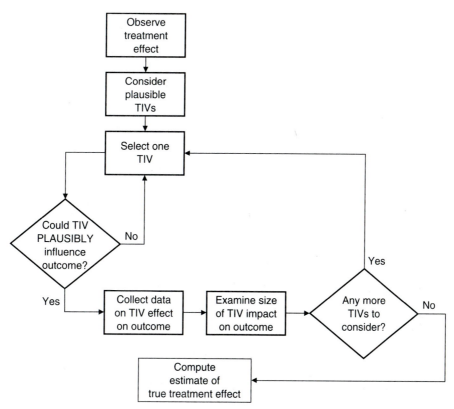

FIGURE 13.2
Steps for addressing plausible threats to internal validity.

13.1 explains the notation system used. [8, 9] I will explain how each design works, describe what you can learn from it, and detail some of its major limitations. I will explain how you could apply each design to the running example concerned with effects of sentencing guidelines. In the table the Os refer to the observations, and the Xs refer to the control condition or the experimental treatment.

One-Group Posttest-Only Design

Design You observe scores of cases receiving an experimental treatment on one outcome variable. The outcome is measured at one point in time, after the treatment has occurred. The measurement is a **posttest** observation. Graphically:

Xe O

For example, to return to our hypothetical running example with sentencing guidelines, you might decide to look at degree of racial disparity between the sentences given to White, African American, and Hispanic felons. You focus on felons convicted of similar offenses, and only on those receiving sentences of incarceration. You gather records for the period following the implementation of the sentencing guidelines.

You might find that there is a low degree of disparity between the sentences, in terms of length of prison term, across the three groups. The average prison term for Whites, Hispanics, and African Americans, for one class of offenses, might be closely compara-

TABLE 13.1

**Notation for Describing Quasiexperimental
and Field Experimental Designs**

Symbol	Stands For
O $O_1, O_2, O_3 \ldots$	Observation Series of Observations. Observations before a treatment are often called *pretest observations*; those occurring after are often called *posttest* observations.
Xc	Control or Standard Treatment, received by the control group
Xe	Experimental Treatment, received by the treatment group
$X_1, X_2, X_3 \ldots$ $X_A, X_B, X_C \ldots$	Different treatments that may occur sequentially. May also represent treatments of varying strength
O_1 Xc O_2 O_3 O_1 Xe O_2 O_3	*No line* separating the experimental treatment and control groups. Indicates *theoretical equivalence* created through random assignment.
O_1 Xc O_2 O_1 Xe O_2	*Wavy line* ( )indicates a difference in time cohorts; the control group was observed before the experimental group
O_1 Xe O_2 ---------------------------- O_1 Xe O_2 ---------------------------- O_1 Xe O_2	*Dashed line* (----) separates *nonequivalent* groups. The different groups could be in *different sites*. For example a treatment could be tried in three different cities. (Note also how the experimental treatment in the third city occurred later in time than the treatments in the other two cities.) Or the different groups could be nonequivalent for other reasons.

ble. You conclude that the implementation of the guidelines (Xe) has resulted in a low degree of racial disparity in sentencing.

Do not confuse this quasi-experimental design with a case study. [10] Ethnographic field researchers can use qualitative methods to develop detailed understandings of situational dynamics (Chapter 11). Such studies can provide considerable insight. The design described here is much more limited.

Limits   The major deficiency with this type of design is that you lack pretest observations. You do not know the state of affairs

before the experimental treatment—the new sentencing guidelines—was implemented. A low rate of racial disparity may have *preceded* the implementation of the guidelines. You have no grounds on which to base your conclusion that the implementation of the guidelines *caused* the currently observed low level of racial disparity.

Posttest-Only Design with Nonequivalent Groups

Design   You have available to you, beyond the posttest scores of those cases receiving the experimental treatment, the scores from another group of people, for the same period. Members of this *second* group did not experience the experimental treatment—sentencing under new sentencing guidelines. They continued to receive the standard treatment—sentencing without the new guidelines. Thus they can serve as a control group.

Graphically:

$$\frac{Xe}{Xc} \quad \frac{O_1}{O_1}$$

Box 13.1 provides details of an evaluation of an intensive supervision program that used a quasiexperimental design of this type.

BOX 13.1

Evaluating Intensive Supervision in New Jersey Quasiexperimentally

Over the past decade correctional and judicial authorities in many states have set up intensive supervision programs for probationers or parolees. These intermediate punishments, or punishments in the community, provide a higher level of public safety than "standard" probation or parole. They also free up valuable prison space for more deserving felons. For a review of these programs and their effectiveness see [11, 12].

New Jersey's intensive supervision program (ISP) is typical. Low-risk, nonviolent offenders who have already served 3 to 4 months in prison can be resentenced into ISP. Program participants meet or speak with their ISP officer daily. Officers conduct curfew checks, drug tests, and verify that the offender is keeping up with fines, or child support payments, or restitution. Participants must work, and as they progress through the program, supervision is reduced.

Evaluators compared the recidivism rates of a random sample of offenders sentenced to ISP with "a random sample of felons sentenced to prison for ISP-eligible crimes *before* the program was instituted." [13] From the comparison group they selected 132 cases that were closely similar to the ISP sample in terms of background characteristics and criminal records. Thus they attempted to increase the equivalence between the experimental (ISP) group (Xe) and the control group (Xc) by matching. The experimental design is like the posttest-only design with non-

equivalent groups, except that the two groups come from different periods. Graphically:

$$\begin{array}{c} Xc \quad O \\ \\ Xe \quad O \end{array}$$

Evaluators defined "success" as remaining conviction-free during the period following release from ISP or from prison.[4] They found that a significantly higher proportion of the experimental (ISP) as compared to the control group was successful (about 90% success vs. 80%). [13]

You might have some questions about these results. Was the higher success rate of ISP participants due to program participation, or due to their spending less time in prison? Also, the follow-up period for the control group started at an earlier point in time than the follow-up period for the experimental group. How might this have plausibly influenced the findings? How would you assess the size of these contributions to a discrepancy between observed treatment effect and true treatment effect?

Several evaluations of other ISP programs have used quasi-experimental designs similar to the one described here. For example Baird and Wagner evaluated the effects of Florida's community corrections program, the largest in the country. [14]

---

[4] A person who was arrested and not convicted would still be counted as a success.

How would you use such a design to examine the effects of the new sentencing guidelines on racial disparity? For example, you might find that, for up to 3 months after the sentencing guidelines were first introduced, offenders' lawyers could request that judges *not* use the guidelines in the sentencing process, but instead continue to use standard sentencing practices. So, during that 3-month period, you can examine the degree of racial disparity present among convicted African American, White, and Hispanic felons sentenced according to the guidelines (Xe). You can compare it to those sentenced using regular procedures (Xc).

You examine sentences for African Americans, Whites, and Hispanics within offense categories. You look at cases where sentencing occurred during this 3-month "phase-in" period. You control for different offense histories. You find the following for one important offense category:

	Sentence Length Differences	
	Sentenced Under Standard Sentencing during Period P (Xc)	Sentenced Under Phase in of New Sentencing during Period P (Xe)
Sentence length of incarcerated African Americans as compared to incarcerated Whites:	8% longer	3% longer
Sentence length of incarcerated Hispanics as compared to incarcerated Whites:	15% longer	5% longer

You measure sentence length in months of incarceration *sentenced*, not served. You conclude that the implementation of the guidelines caused a reduction in racial disparity in sentencing.

Limits   Your conclusion, however, may founder on a threat to internal validity called **selection or selection bias**. [15] The difference you observe may not be due to the experimental treatment. Instead it may arise from *preexisting dissimilarities between the members of the experimental and control groups.* Within the offense category examined here, White cases opting for sentencing under the new guidelines may have represented more serious felons, for example, than the White cases opting for standard sentencing practices. The lawyers in the former cases may have hoped that, under the new guidelines, their clients would be less likely to "get the book thrown at them."

If, within offense severity categories, there are differences in the cases of Whites receiving Xc and Whites receiving Xe, the resulting comparisons on racial disparity could be misleading.

Selection represents a potentially pervasive problem whenever you have nonequivalent groups. You should be especially concerned about this possible threat whenever units are allowed to *self-select* into an experimental vs. control condition.

One-Group Pretest-Posttest Design

Design You will find this design used often in criminal justice research. You collect information on an outcome before (**pretest scores**) and after (**posttest scores**) the units experience the experimental treatment. The pretest and posttest scores both come from the same group of cases—the experimental group.

This type of quasiexperimental design is better than the preceding two. You can observe if a change took place by comparing the before and after scores on the outcome variables of interest. The design provides you with a direct measure of the shift. Graphically:

$$Pretest \quad Posttest$$
$$O_1 \quad Xe \quad O_2$$

Say your state's code classifies felonies into five different levels of seriousness. Let's focus on cases sentenced within one level of seriousness for the 12 months preceding the implementation of the guidelines, and 12 months after. You separate the cases by race of offender.[5] Your results might look like this within one seriousness category:

	Sentence Length Differences	
	Before (O_1) (Pretest)	After (O_2) (Posttest)
Sentence length of incarcerated African Americans as compared to incarcerated Whites:	8% longer	4% longer
Sentence length of incarcerated Hispanics as compared to incarcerated Whites:	14% longer	13% longer

Limits You want to say that the implementation of the sentencing guidelines caused the reduction in racial disparity between White and African American cases. If you want to argue convincingly, however, you will need to address the following two potential threats to internal validity.

Perhaps most plausible is the threat to internal validity of **history**. An event other than the treatment, which took place between the pretest and the posttest, may have been responsible for the change observed. For example, the public debate surrounding the implementation of the sentencing guidelines may have sensitized many judges to racial factors in current sentencing practices, as it applied to African American offenders. Their heightened sensitivity to racial issues, not the implementation of the guidelines, may have been responsible for the more equitable sentencing of Whites and African Americans during the period.

A more subtle threat that might be at work is **statistical regression**. The threat arises because any process that continues over time experiences random, chance fluctuations. And, all else equal, scores far away from an average are likely to be followed by scores closer to the average.

A familiar example of this problem comes from baseball. A team may have a season batting average of .250. But the team does not hit .250 every month. One month they may hit .210, and the next month they may hit .255. If the owners install a new manager

---

[5] Although the race-offense category units are similar at O_1 and O_2, you will note that the *individual cases* will be different. The particular offenders whose sentences you measure at O_1 are unlikely to be measured again at O_2.

This design can also be applied, however, to instances where the same individuals are measured at O_1 and O_2. For example, you can measure the views of patrol officers toward community policing initiatives before (O_1) and after (O_2) they have participated in a special workshop (Xe) on the topic.

between the first and the second month, they might want to conclude that the managerial change caused the improved batting. The more likely explanation is that the average was "regressing" to its mean level. A month of below average batting, all else equal, is likely to be followed by a month when the average is *closer* to the season average.

In our sentencing example, within the offense category examined, the cases for which African American offenders were incarcerated may have been *more serious* during the year before the guidelines were set up, and *less serious* during the year after the guidelines were implemented. The reduced disparity between White and African American sentences may arise from the decreasing seriousness of offenses committed by African Americans, within the category of offenses examined here, rather than the implementation of guidelines. Differences like these in pretest vs. posttest crime seriousness within crime categories can arise from random fluctuations over time.

Designs in General and Particular Designs

Although the three designs described above *generally* provide minimal causal inference, cases can arise where the *particular* design is interpretable. You may encounter particular situations where the researcher, because of her familiarity with the context, or because of analyses she has completed, is able to dismiss the major potential threats to internal validity inherent in her quasi-experimental design.

DESIGNS PERMITTING A MODERATE DEGREE OF CAUSAL INFERENCE: STRONG QUASI-EXPERIMENTAL DESIGNS

We move now to the designs in the middle segment of the dimensions portrayed in Fig-

ure 13.1. The strong quasi-experimental designs can provide a fair degree of causal inference. They also can pose a modicum of implementation difficulties.

Untreated Control Group Design with Pretest and Posttest: With and Without Separate Pretest Samples

Design Social scientists frequently use this design. Box 13.2 details one example. You obtain pretest and posttest scores from an experimental group and a control group.

BOX 13.2

Community Crime Prevention in Chicago

Dennis Rosenbaum and his colleagues conducted a methodologically rigorous evaluation of a community crime prevention program in Chicago in the early 1980s. [16, 17] Neighborhood Watch groups were started on several blocks in each study neighborhood. Participants were interviewed at two points in time: before the intervention was implemented, and after. Also, simultaneously, researchers interviewed residents in *matched* (i.e., similar) control neighborhoods. (See below for more on matching.) The residents in the control neighborhoods did not receive the experimental treatment—implementation of a Neighborhood Watch program.

Investigators observed significant *increases* over time in the fear of crime levels of respondents in three of the four intervention areas, as compared to respondents in the matched control areas. In other words, many respondents organizing against crime experienced increasing fear levels as compared to matched respondents not organizing against crime. This was opposite to the researchers' expectations. Participation may have resensitized local residents to the local crime hazard. [18]

Scores from the same individuals may be obtained at O_1 (pretest) and O_2 (posttest). Graphically:

$$\frac{O_1 \quad Xe \quad O_2}{O_1 \quad Xc \quad O_2}$$

If you observe changes between the pretest and the posttest for the experimental treatment group, but no change or an opposite change in the control group, you can rule out the potential threats of history, selection, and statistical regression. A design somewhat like this also can be used with separate pretest samples; different individuals complete the pretest and posttest.

To apply this design to the sentencing guidelines example, imagine the following. Before the sentencing guidelines were implemented statewide, judges in a large city of over 500,000 (Metroville) agreed to use the guidelines on a trial basis for 6 months. Criminal justice officials hoped to learn from such a demonstration project about problems they might encounter when putting the guidelines into place statewide. You gather case and sentencing information for all convicted felons sentenced in this city. You concentrate on two sets of cases: those sentenced in the 6-month period *preceding* (O_1) the trial implementation of the guidelines, and those sentenced *during* (O_2) the 6-month trial implementation period. (Note here that your pretest groups have different cases in them than your posttest groups.)

Now you need a comparison group. Your fine state includes, besides Metroville, a second large city, Tallavannah. The two cities have about the same size population. Further, you find the judicial systems, crime problems, and population characteristics of the two cities roughly comparable. Therefore, using the same two periods (O_1 and O_2), you can collect information about sentences handed out in Tallavannah. You will want to focus on the same classes of cases in the two cities. You may even try to develop a set of matched cases in Tallavannah that, as a group, are closely comparable to the cases in Metroville for the corresponding period (cf. Box 13.1).

Your findings on sentence length, for one class of felonies, appear below. "+" means "higher."

	Sentence Length Differences			
	Experimental Metroville (Xe)		Control Tallavannah (Xc)	
	Pretest O_1	Posttest O_2	Pretest O_1	Posttest O_2
Sentences of African-Americans as compared to incarcerated Whites:	15% +	10% +	16% +	12% +
Sentences of Hispanics as compared to incarcerated Whites:	12% +	3% +	8% +	9% +

These numbers tell a story. The first two numbers in the first row show that racial disparity between White and African American sentences in Metroville, the site of the experimental implementation of the guidelines, decreased somewhat after implementation (15% + to 10% +). It looks like the treatment worked. But when we look at the last two numbers in the first row, we see that racial disparity between White and African American incarceration sentences decreased in the control site as well (16% + to 12% +)! Apparently between the pretest and the posttest, factors in these two cities, and perhaps statewide, led to reduced disparity between the sentences of these two groups. These factors may have arisen from historical, social, or political currents, or from statistical fluctuations.

The second row of numbers, comparing Hispanic and White sentences, tells a different story. The implementation of the guidelines significantly *reduced* disparity in Metroville (12% + to 3% +). During the same period in Tallavannah, disparity between White and Hispanic sentences *increased* slightly (8% + to 9% +). Therefore it appears the guidelines were effective in reducing racial disparity in sentencing between Hispanics and Whites for this class of felonies.

Limits This design is much stronger than the preceding quasi-experimental designs reviewed. You have a control site. You have pretest measures so you can directly assess changes. Nevertheless, you need to confront several potential threats to internal validity with this design.

Perhaps the most plausible threat to internal validity is **local history**, resulting from an interaction between *selection* and *history*. Historical forces may have been at work in the treatment site that were not at work in the control site, or vice versa. [19] For example, *local* political forces in Metroville may have increased judicial sensitivity to the sentencing of Hispanics. This change in the political-judicial climate, and not the implemented guidelines, may have resulted in the reduced disparity between White vs. Hispanic sentences in Metroville.

Since the example you constructed here centered on the implementation of a *pilot* project, designed for more widespread use at a subsequent time, I would like to mention two potential threats to the *external validity* of the

results observed here. The most likely threat is an **interaction between setting and treatment**. The site selected for the treatment, Metroville, was a site where the treatment worked for Hispanics. The treatment, however, may not work as effectively for Hispanics in different locations, such as other cities, rural areas, or other states.

Another plausible threat to external validity is an **interaction of history and treatment**. If the treatment worked in a particular historical context, spanning O_1 and O_2, this does not guarantee it will work in a different historical context. As always, generalizability is an empirical matter.

The major implementation difficulty you will experience with this type of design will be locating comparable comparison groups. You want a control group that is closely comparable, covering the pretest and posttest periods of the experimental group(s). You want the record keeping for the outcome variable to be closely comparable to the record keeping for the experimental group. And of course you need identical outcome variables.

Simple Interrupted Time Series

Design If you have access to archival records spanning a substantial period, and you know precisely the time a treatment began, you can apply a powerful quasi-experimental design known as **interrupted time series**. It requires *one* experimental group, and multiple observations for the period before and after the treatment implementation. *Multiple* usually means about 50 observation periods. In effect the observations from the period preceding the intervention serve as the comparison group.[6] So you need no separate control group. Graphically:

---

[6] You can also construct time series designs that have an additional control group, whose members do not receive the intervention. Then you can compare the experimental group's scores both to their preintervention scores and to the scores of the comparison group.

Pretest →   Posttest →

$O_1 O_2 O_3 O_4 O_6 \ldots Xe\ O_p\ O_{p+1}\ O_{p+2}\ O_{p+3}\ O_{p+4} \ldots O_n$

If you have available many observations for the period before and after the intervention begins, you can use statistical time series analyses to model the factors influencing the data. You can estimate the influences that long-term trends, due to regression or maturation, might have on the data. **Maturation** is a threat to internal validity present whenever you observe the same units over time. Units, such as organizations or individuals, age and mature. Changes between the pretest and posttest periods observed for individuals may be due to increasing experience, wisdom, cynicism or other factors. They may not be due to the experimental treatment.

With an interrupted time series you statistically model the factors that might be operating as TIVs, such as seasonal variations or other periodicities present in the data. These procedures allow you to focus on changes due to the treatment itself.

Conceptually, here is how the modeling works. It looks at the pretest observations, focusing on the factors influencing the numbers, such as seasonal variation. Figure 13.3 presents some artificial data on DUI rates for a large suburban county. As you can see, rates tend to go up in the summer and during the holiday season. There is also a gradual upward trend. The experimental treatment is a countywide crackdown on drunk driving. The statistics model how the DUI rates would have progressed had there been no change, and had pretest influences remained in effect (dashed line). The discrepancy between how the data would have progressed had there been no change, and the actual data, suggest an impact of the treatment on the outcome.

Box 13.3 describes the results of various interrupted time series analyses examining the effects of criminal justice reforms.

Returning to our running example, the data you would need to analyze the effects of

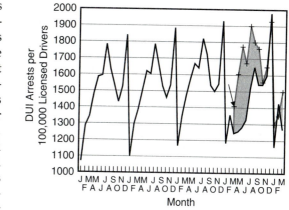

FIGURE 13.3

Effects of countywide drunk driving crackdown on monthly DUI arrest rates per 100,000 licensed drivers. Artificial data. Actual data shown in solid line. Data during the pretest period show peaks in the summer, and in December. Data also show increasing rates over the 3 years preceding the intervention. Arrow indicates the month the drunk driving crackdown began— March. Dashed series with crosses shows *expected* level of DUI arrests if the treatment had not taken place. It looks like the treatment "wore off" after several months. Shaded area represents the difference due to the treatment effect.

your state's new sentencing guidelines may be readily available from archival sources. Within offense categories you can develop monthly measures of sentence length, and sentence length disparity between racial groups, for the 3-year period before the guidelines were implemented statewide, and for 2 years after their implementation. You probably would want to develop separate time series for each class of offenses.

Limits Of course, as you may have guessed, although it surmounts some threats, interrupted time series analysts must attend to other potential threats to internal validity. You can model maturational, historical, and seasonal trends if the series is long enough. *History*, however, can still be a seri-

BOX 13.3

Interrupted Time Series
and Reform

Researchers have used interrupted time series analyses to gauge the consequences of a variety of criminal justice reforms. Here are three examples.

Community corrections

In 1978 Kansas initiated a community corrections act. The act sought to divert nonviolent, noncareer, prison-bound offenders, while maintaining public safety. By 1986 there were eight Kansas counties, including the four counties with the largest populations, taking part in the community corrections act. Intensive supervision made up the major program element in the diversionary program. Jones evaluated the effects of the program on monthly prison admissions in four of the eight counties. [20; see also 21] He observed significant decreases in one county following the intervention, a marginally significant decrease in a second county, and no clear evidence of a change in the other two counties modeled. (See Figure 13.4)

Reducing firearms violence.

Several researchers used interrupted time series analyses to examine the impacts of sentencing laws designed to reduce firearms violence. Deutsch and Alt investigated the effects of a state law passed in Massachusetts mandating a 1-year minimum sentence for anyone convicted of carrying a firearm without an appropriate license. [22] Following the passage of the law they observed decreases of around 20 percent in armed robberies and assaults in Boston. Analyses of mandatory sentencing practices designed to reduce firearms violence in other U.S. locations have produced more mixed results. [e.g., 23] Some of these analyses have shown that the

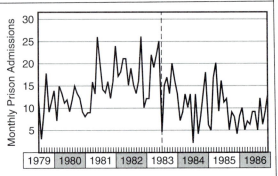

FIGURE 13.4
Interrupted time series analysis showed that, after the Community Corrections Act was implemented in Sedgwick County, Kansas, a significant decline in monthly "charge back" prison admissions occurred. "Charge-back" felons were those eligible for diversion from prison under the Act. *Source:* Jones, P. R. (1990). Community corrections in Kansas: Extending community-based corrections or widening the net? *Journal of Research in Crime and Delinquency 27:* 79-101. Figure 3.

criminal justice system responds to these reform efforts in unanticipated ways.

Drunk driving.

Numerous analyses have examined the effects of drunk driving laws on arrest rates for drunk driving. Many of these studies find short-term effects of "crackdowns" on the outcome of interest. [24]

Interrupted time series represent a powerful family of quasiexperimental designs. Although the analyses demand considerable expertise, they can expose complex and sometimes unanticipated consequences of reform efforts.

ous threat. [25] It is always possible that specific historical forces, influencing your outcome variable, came into play just at the time the experimental treatment began.

You can counter the threat of history in two ways. First, you can add a time series for a comparable control group that did not receive the intervention. If the experimental group changed following the intervention, and the control group did not, then history is a less plausible threat.[7] Second, you can gather from other sources, such as newspapers or regular interviews with local leaders, information on other events that could plausibly influence your outcomes. With this information you should be able to decide if particular forces were at work during the posttest period.

A second potential threat you will need to consider is *selection*. Because of the intervention the membership of the experimental group may change through **attrition**. Attrition occurs when cases or people leave an experimental or control group. Posttest group membership might then be different from pretest group membership. You are most likely to encounter this threat when membership in the group is voluntary, and individuals can opt out of being in the group.

A third potential threat, relevant only in some situations, is **instrumentation**. A change in the measuring instrument may occur between the pretest and the posttest. For example, the court system supplying you with records may have adopted a radically different record-keeping system just at the time policy makers implemented the experimental treatment. If the measuring instrument changes, or if measurement procedures change, differences you observe between pretest and posttest scores may not be due to

the experimental treatment. The differences could arise from these changes in procedures or instruments.

Given that the instrumentation threat may exist, you will always want to know the exact origins of your outcome measures. Who records what off what forms? Is the record keeping computerized? When did it become computerized? Have there been any changes in the computer system or programs? If significant changes have occurred, you will want to know the timing so that you can factor it into your modeling.

Three major *implementation difficulties* may occur with interrupted time series designs. First, you need records of the same variables, extending over a sufficiently long period. Sometimes you may encounter difficulties locating such records. They simply may not exist. Or the records may not be in a comparable format for the entire period. Second, once you have determined that the numbers exist, you need to ensure that the numbers are high enough so that they vary considerably. If the counts or scores are extremely low, you may encounter **floor effects**. When numbers start out very low during a pretest period, and you intend for the numbers to go lower as a result of an experimental treatment, it is hard for them to go lower during a posttest period. This is a problem, not only for time series analyses, but for all quasiexperimental and true experimental designs. Third, you need to know precisely when the experimental treatment took place. When did the pretest period end and when did the posttest period begin? Was the treatment suspended at all, or removed, during the posttest period?

In sum: (1) you need to obtain comparable data extending over time. (2) The data should fluctuate consistently above the lowest possible scores. (3) You need to know exactly when the experimental treatment was put into place, and for how long.

---

[7] Of course *local* history might still be a plausible threat.

CROSSING THE THRESHOLD FROM QUASI-EXPERIMENTS TO TRUE EXPERIMENTS

Our discussion moves now to the upper right section of Figure 13.1. True experiments can provide you with the highest levels of causal inference. Individuals or units are randomly assigned to receive the experimental treatment or to receive the standard, i.e., control treatment. Recent work has revealed that these designs also present the most serious implementation difficulties. When should one undertake a true experiment? When should one not?

Some criminal justice researchers see a low threshold separating quasi-experiments and true experiments. They think true experiments should be done often, because the scientific advantages of true experiments far outweigh the practical constraints. [6, abstract] Others recognize the serious problems related to running experiments. Dennis, for example, argues that experiments should be reserved *only* for major program initiatives with substantial and widespread significance for social policy. [3; see also 5] Dennis and Boruch suggest that all of the following conditions should be present before you commit yourself to pursuing a true experiment. [4]

1. There must be broad agreement that current practices need improvement.
2. Neither past research nor sound wisdom provides surety that the proposed program will achieve the intended goal.
3. Simpler, alternate research designs are inadequate for one reason or another.
4. The results, or lack of them, will prove relevant to social policy makers.
5. Both researchers and treatment providers who will distribute the program, must be satisfied that the implementation meets ethical standards.
6. To these five conditions I would add a sixth. [26] Your research or evaluation purposes center *solely* around testing a causal hypothesis.

TRUE EXPERIMENTS

Randomization

The central feature of true experiments is random assignment of cases to experimental or control conditions. With **random assignment** each case has an equal probability of being assigned to any condition. If there is one experimental condition and one control condition, each case has a 50 percent chance of being assigned to the experimental treatment. If there are two treatment conditions and one control condition, each case has a 33 percent chance of being assigned to each condition. A randomization procedure is used to assign cases to conditions, and each assignment is made independently of assignments of other cases.

Random assignment is different from random selection. In the latter case you are selecting a probability sample of cases from a population. In the former you are assigning cases that have already been selected to particular conditions. Random assignment procedures can occur after random selection procedures.

These random assignment procedures help eliminate several problems threatening the internal validity of study conclusions.

Advantages   After random assignment, the groups assigned to the different conditions are initially equivalent. [27] Although there will be differences due to sampling error, the groups, if large enough, are roughly equivalent to each other on any background measure you choose to assess. You have created **initial probabilistic equivalence**.

Randomization processes also provide two further advantages. If the treatment condition represents a scarce resource, and all cases are equally "needy," random assignment provides an equitable distribution plan. Finally, random assignment also creates the conditions for which many statistical models were designed. Nevertheless, these three benefits notwithstanding (initial probabilistic equivalence, equitable distribution of scarce resources, appropriate design for statistical models), there are problems that randomization does not solve, and some problems that it creates.

TIVs With Which You Still Must Contend
As noted earlier, attrition occurs in a quasi-experiment or a true experiment when participants in the study, for one reason or another, "drop out." The attrition process may operate differently in experimental and control groups. Members may leave an experimental group and a control group at different rates. Or different *types* of persons could leave the two different groups. Thus, two groups that were *initially* comparable may no longer be comparable at the end of the observation period due to **differential attrition**. The *initial* probabilistic equivalence created by random assignment does not guarantee *final* probabilistic equivalence.

As a true experiment or quasi-experiment progresses, there may be variations in the amount and type of treatment received, among the experimental group, or the control group. [3] In other words the experimental clients could experience **treatment dilution**, where every client in the experimental condition in a site does not receive the same treatment as every other client in the same condition in the same site.

Or there could be **treatment contamination or confounding**. Some clients in the control conditions could receive some of the experimental program elements. This situation would cloud the differences between the two groups.

Groups also could become less distinct due to **compensatory rivalry**. Service providers, or clients, finding out that they are in the control condition receiving no special treatments, may try to compensate and do better than they would have under other circumstances.

How to Cope: Lessons from the Rand Evaluation of 11 ISP Programs   Results recently became available from the "largest randomized experiment ever conducted in the field of American corrections." [28] Different sites implemented intensive supervision probation (ISP) programs with different program elements. High-risk probationers were randomly assigned to intensive supervision probation (Xe), or standard probation (Xc), in 11 sites across the country. Sites accepted clients for the experimental conditions from 1986 through 1990. A minimum of 150 clients were randomly assigned in each site. A team of researchers at RAND corporation, led by Joan Petersilia, conducted an evaluation effort. Reports from this effort illustrate the problems that can crop up with randomized field experiments. They also show how researchers can address some of these difficulties. [28, 29, 30]

Guaranteeing Truly Random Assignment   Reports from previous true experiments have suggested that randomization procedures can go awry if it is carried out by field personnel rather than researchers. [3] Participants may put pressure on field personnel to bend the assignment procedures. [e.g., 31] Also, after random assignment, field personnel—in this case, judges—can put pressure on the researchers to change the assignment. [32] They can seek to *override* the random assignment, placing a person initially assigned to one group in another group.

RAND researchers avoided these problems by doing the random assignment procedures themselves and allowing just a small number of overrides. Here is how the random assignment worked. Field personnel would call RAND with lists of ISP-eligible participants. RAND personnel would consult a random list of numbers. In any given call, based on the random numbers selected, half the cases would be assigned to the experimental condition and half would be assigned to the control condition. Deviations from random assignment—overrides—were allowed in each site, but only for emergencies, and only for up to 5 percent of the caseload in the site.

Researchers found that field personnel complained about the random assignment for some clients. They felt that they knew better what the best treatment was. Resistance waned, however, after the researchers explained at length to field personnel the importance of using randomization to learn "what works," and as the experiments progressed. Results suggest that the resistance to randomization can be overcome. Achieving this goal requires extensive contact between researchers and field personnel.

Randomize Late to Avoid Attrition after Assignment Researchers randomized "late" in the process. The randomization occurred after field personnel screened clients, and deemed them eligible. In the Marion County, Oregon, site, where the alternative to ISP was prison, offenders provided written informed consent, granting permission to the authorities to assign them randomly to ISP or prison.[8]

Maintaining Integrity of Treatment Condition, Avoiding Dilution Researchers used two strategies to avoid confounding treatment and control conditions in the RAND-evaluated ISP programs. First, they explained at

length to the relevant field officers how the experiment would only work if control and treatment cases were treated differently during the study. This also required that the control field officers not initiate any novel procedures, or introduce new program elements, during the experimental period. In addition, they sought to disguise control cases so that officers would not treat control cases serving in the experiment differently from other probationers. As a check on treatment and control integrity they focused data collection efforts on the program elements *received* by probationers. In other words they assessed the programs *as implemented*, not just *as designed*.

Other researchers have suggested that should contamination or treatment dilution occur, their effects can be monitored. If researchers have sufficient preexperimental data, they can statistically model the effects of treatment contamination. [3]

Summary Petersilia reached the following conclusions about doing large scale true experiments, based on the results of the 11 ISP evaluations. (1) Such experiments can be done and can be done well. (2) The random assignment by researchers was vital to the general successful implementation of the experiments. Resistance to random assignment by field personnel can be overcome. (3) Researchers should maintain extensive contact with field researchers to keep the experiments on track. (4) It was difficult for field personnel to take responsibility for data collection efforts. [28] Data collection efforts were most successful in sites where separate personnel took over data collection responsibilities.

THE MATCHING ALTERNATIVE

Researchers will sometimes argue that they can achieve initial probabilistic equivalence by using *matching* procedures. You can match

---

[8] Surprisingly, about 25 percent of the eligible group did not grant informed consent, because they preferred prison to ISP.

in one of two ways. You may try to match cases in the experimental group with cases in the control group on a case-by-case basis, or on a samplewide basis.

In the first approach, you compare each case in the treatment group to several non-treatment cases on several background characteristics. You select one nontreatment or control case that is comparable to the experimental case on all of the examined background characteristics.

In the second approach, you match the entire *sample*. You select for the control group the sample of cases that, *as a group*, match the treatment group of cases on the variables you have examined.

Matching is different from random assignment in two ways. (1) The researcher constructing matched pairs or matched samples centers attention on a few variables (e.g., x_a, x_b, x_c, x_d). Within each sample, or within each pair, he wants scores on each of those variables to be roughly equivalent. He may be able to achieve equivalence on *these* variables. Nevertheless, such an outcome does *not* guarantee equivalence on *other* variables (e.g., x_e, x_f, x_g, x_h).

Note that this procedure assumes the following: It assumes the researcher knows, theoretically, that x_a, x_b, x_c, and x_d are the important variables on which cases should be matched. It also assumes that data on these variables are available to him at the beginning of the research effort. In many research efforts these assumptions may not be warranted.

Not only does matching fail to guarantee initial probabilistic equivalence. (2) During the matching process the researcher may "lose" important parts of the sample. If he is developing matched pairs, for example, he will discard every case where there is not a *second* case scoring *similarly* to an already selected case on x_a, x_b, x_c, and x_d. Consequently, he may be focusing on a nonrepresentative sample of cases, thereby limiting

his ability to generalize his results to the population of interest.

EVALUATION RESEARCH

The RAND research on ISP programs you have just been reading about represents an example of *evaluation research or program evaluation*. Evaluation represents not a particular *type* of research, but a *purpose* of research.

> Evaluation research involves the use of social science methodologies to judge and to improve the planning, monitoring, effectiveness and efficiency of health, education, welfare, and other human service programs. [33]

Evaluation researchers can use any type of social science research tool they wish: content analysis, true experiments, quasiexperiments, surveys, computer simulations, and so on. In this section you will learn about the different types of evaluations, and the context surrounding evaluation research.

Evaluation researchers seek to provide information about programs that is scientifically sound. They use research tools that are as internally valid and as reliable as possible. Since their primary purpose is to evaluate something, however, an evaluation study must be more than scientifically credible. [34]

Evaluation Studies Address Several Different Concerns

Evaluations must consider the interests of the persons who have sponsored the program that is being evaluated, and the interests of the persons intended to benefit from the program. Many people have a "vested interest" in the results of an evaluation study. These individual **stakeholders** will be affected by the conclusions of the evaluation. In the sentencing guidelines example discussed in this chapter, stakeholders include the judiciary, prosecuting and defense attorneys, crime victims, the police, and the convicted individuals.

Typically, program sponsors have the largest "vested interest" in an evaluation study. The researchers usually will work with the program sponsors to develop many aspects of the program evaluation. Sponsors may suggest which type of client on which to focus, or the outcome variables of the most interest. Earlier in this chapter we were discussing an evaluation of the hypothetical sentencing guidelines. The different assessments of sentencing guidelines focused on changes in racial disparity in sentencing practices. You focused on this as an outcome of interest in large part because the sponsors of these guidelines hoped that the new procedures would reduce disparity. They had a stake, as did the convicted felons themselves, in seeing whether the new guidelines affected disparity.

Evaluation research is designed and conducted so that its results are as useful as they can be to policy makers, given the constraints under which the evaluation takes place. Policy makers need answers to specific questions from evaluation studies. You will learn below about the types of questions addressed by evaluation. If an evaluation study fails to address policy makers' concerns, the results will not be of interest to them. If, in your evaluation of the sentencing guidelines, you had reported to your boss and the governor how judges felt about the difficulties of implementing the new guidelines, and had failed to mention any effects of the new guidelines on sentencing practices and prison populations, your boss and the governor would have been disappointed. (You also probably would have been fired.)

Given the importance of addressing policy makers' concerns in evaluation studies, it is not unusual for stake holders, such as clients and policy makers, to work with evaluation researchers in designing evaluation studies. In the current example, you probably would have reported to your boss the outcome variables you intended to include after your initial assessment of available data. He would have informed the governor, who would have suggested changes as needed.

Of course, it can go less smoothly. It is not at all unusual in evaluation research for the scientists to disagree with other stake holders about how an evaluation should be conducted, or what it should include. Such differences of opinion follow from the large number of stake holders involved in an evaluation effort, and a surrounding atmosphere that is often politically charged.

Three Classes of Evaluation Studies

An evaluation study can focus on one or more of the following sets of issues: *program conceptualization and design, monitoring and accountability of program implementation,* or an *assessment of program utility.* [35] An evaluation covering all three of these sets of issues would be a **comprehensive evaluation study**. Typical questions of interest to researchers involved in these three different classes of evaluations appear in Table 13.2. Let's talk about each of these sets of concerns, and how they might be addressed in an evaluation of the new sentencing guidelines in our running scenario.

Program Conceptualization and Design: Before It Begins Evaluation research focusing on these issues asks about program *plans*. Researchers seek to analyze the ideas behind a program or a treatment *before* it starts. They want to know if the program plan clearly identifies the **target problem**—the social problem the program will address. For example, one target problem addressed by sentencing guidelines are racial disparities in sentencing practices. Researchers also want to know if the plan clearly identifies the **target population**—the individuals to whom the program will be delivered.

TABLE 13.2

Typical Questions for Three Different Types of Evaluations

Program Conceptualization and Design

* "What is the extent and distribution of the target problem, or population?"

* "Is the program designed in conformity with intended goals; is there a coherent rationale underlying it; and have the chances of successful delivery been maximized?"

* "What are projected or existing costs, and what is their relation to benefits and effectiveness?"

Program Monitoring Questions

* "Is the program reaching the specified target population or target area?"

* "Are the intervention efforts being conducted as specified in the program design?"

Program Utility Questions

* "Is the program effective in achieving its intended goals?"

* "Can the results of the program be explained by some alternate process that does not include the program?"

* What are the costs to deliver services and benefits to program participants?"

* "Is the program an efficient use of resources, compared with alternate uses of the resources?"

Source: From Rossi, P. H., and Freeman, H. E. (1985) *Evaluation: A Systematic Approach* (Third ed.). Beverly Hills, CA: Sage, pp. 39, 40, 45 and 46.

Beyond seeing if the plan specifies for what and for whom the program is intended, researchers also investigate how the program matches up with goals and theory. The goals of a program may have been stated in a piece of legislation or an announcement by a politician or policy maker. The researcher will try to judge if the proposed program looks like it can meet these goals.

An evaluation researcher also will ask if the designed program rests on sound theory or current wisdom. If a service delivery program takes account of current understanding of a social problem, it has a coherent rationale. If it ignores current understanding about a problem, it may be doomed to fail.

An interesting case in point is in the Department of Justice's "weed and seed" program. As of this writing (August 1992), DOJ is heavily supporting this approach to community crime and drug problems in urban areas. Programs using this approach seek to "weed out" drug-dealing, criminal elements in an urban neighborhood using targeted enforcement, police sweeps, and other police-based measures. The programs then try to "seed" prosocial behavior by sponsoring, e.g., after-school programs for youth. Some people feel that these programs contain serious flaws. The programs include no funds for drug-user rehabilitation. Further, they fail to consider what we currently *do* know about crime in communities and community crime careers. [e.g., 36] The enforcement activity, the critics charge, moves the criminal elements from neighborhood to neighborhood, but no serious changes in community crime careers result. Because the programs fail to build on what we know about crime in communities, many expect these programs to achieve only limited success.

Finally, evaluators concerned with conceptualization will examine proposed program costs in relation to proposed benefits or effectiveness. How much of a public "good," through increased public safety or decreased recidivism or decreased criminal justice processing costs, will be created for how many dollars? Researchers want to know how much it is going to cost to "do good." In our sentencing guidelines example, evaluators considering an implementation of guidelines would estimate the total costs associated with setting up the guidelines. They would gauge such matters as training costs, needed additional prison construction, new record-keeping systems, and so on. They would then try to calculate the cost per unit of "good" achieved. For every one percent reduction in racial disparity in sentencing for burglars, for example, what would the costs be?

Note that all these evaluation questions arise *before* the program begins. Ideally, such evaluations should take place before anything is put into place, thereby allowing planners to make needed changes before any implementation. It is not unusual, however, for design evaluations to take place well after a program begins.

What types of research tools will evaluators use at this stage? Researchers evaluating a program design may be likely to use computer simulations (see Chapter 16) as one of their research tools. These might be especially useful in projecting costs and benefits. They probably will rely on archival sources of information about the extent of the problem,

and the nature and extent of the target population. They may examine historical data and use surveys of involved personnel.

Program Monitoring: As the Program Unfolds As the program starts up, evaluators can examine program implementation and program delivery. **Program implementation** is the putting into place of different program elements. Each type of action in the program designed to create a "good" is a **program element**. **Program delivery** involves being sure that the intended recipients, the target population, receive the intended program elements.

At the implementation stage, personnel translate the program description into an actual service program. People are hired, procedures are developed, and the program gets ready for clients. In the sentencing guidelines example, implementation probably involved the following: working out agreements about how to score criminal histories and instant offenses; drawing up the actual sentencing grid and agreeing where to place the incarceration/nonincarceration line; training presentence investigators in how to produce information that could be easily translated into the sentencing grid; and training judges, prosecutors, and defense attorneys in the uses of the sentencing grid.

Programs Can Fail at the Implementation Stage This is a common occurrence. A program can be weakly or only partially implemented. [37, 38] Enough people may not be hired, personnel may be insufficiently trained, or political factors may block some initiatives.

A program also can fail at this stage simply because it fails to reach the intended people. All of the program elements may have been put into place, but those whom the program intends to serve simply stay away. A storefront drug rehabilitation program may have trained personnel all ready to go, but find no clients walking in through the door. The program has not been delivered.

If the evaluator discovers that there is a substantial gap between the program as planned and the program as implemented, then she will conclude that **implementation failure** has occurred. If this occurs, and if a program does not achieve intended results, policy makers should not blame the failure on the ideas, theory, and rationale that inspired the program in the first place. If implementation failure occurred, those ideas never got a chance to be tested.

Program Utility Evaluators concerned with program utility may focus on one or both of the following areas. They may ask: did the program receive its desired results? In doing so they are assessing **program effectiveness** or **program impact**. In the sentencing example earlier in the chapter, you looked at some quasi-experimental results suggesting that the guidelines had reduced some racial disparities in sentencing. These changes represent evidence of program impacts.

If the evaluators do establish that the program was effective, then they may go on to estimate the program's **efficiency**. A program's efficiency, or **cost-effectiveness** or **cost-efficiency**, reflects the ratio of program benefits to program costs. They want to know: what were the costs associated with each unit of positive program impact?

Gauging program efficiency can be a complex and sometimes imprecise task for an evaluation researcher. Think about the case of the sentencing guidelines example. Major program benefits may include decreased racial disparity in sentencing, increased incapacitation effects, and increased individual deterrence.

What would be the costs of implementing the sentencing guidelines? A sentencing commission was created to oversee the drafting and implementation of the guidelines.

Scientists were hired to create simulations depicting the effects of the new guidelines. Additional training of current court personnel was required. State officials also anticipated increased state prison populations and higher prison construction costs.

At this stage the evaluation researcher attempts to **monetize**, or assign a monetary value, to each cost and benefit associated with the program. Some researchers argue that many costs and benefits cannot be sensibly monetized. For example, what is the dollar value of a one percent reduction in racial disparity in sentencing for African American and White robbers? But if these inputs and outputs can be sensibly monetized, the researcher then calculates the ratio of costs to benefits. This helps policy makers and others gauge the efficiency of the program in relation to other alternatives.

Summary

Evaluation research is an extremely broad enterprise. The field has its own journals (e.g., *Evaluation Quarterly*), and its own professional association. Evaluation researchers use the tools you have been reading about in this volume to evaluate the success of a particular program, treatment, policy, or initiative.

QUASI-EXPERIMENTS, TRUE EXPERIMENTS, HOLMES, AND EINSTEIN

True experiments are *excellently* suited to Einstein's logic of inquiry in some respects. Random assignment reduces several threats to internal validity, and makes it easier for you to conclude that the treatment, the independent variable, *caused* the difference on the outcome scores you observe between the treatment and control groups. At the same time, they are *poorly* suited to Einstein's logic of inquiry because they are rarely theoretically driven. True experiments, in criminal justice, are most often done to assess a program option, not a theory-based hypothesis. It may be difficult for you to connect program options with relevant theory.

Quasi-experiments can be *moderately well* suited to Einstein's logic of inquiry. Efforts that are carefully done, and thoughtfully estimate impacts of plausible threats to internal validity, can allow you to make relatively confident causal statements.

In general, quasi-experiments and true ex-

periments are *poorly* suited to Holmes' logic of inquiry. In such projects it can be difficult for the researcher to modify data collection in light of theoretical insights emerging from analysis. Often all the data are collected before analyses begin. Further, given the high costs of many such projects, and the requirements for standardized data collection, it often can be difficult for the researcher to widen his net and collect additional information beyond that originally agreed upon.

SUMMARY OF MAIN POINTS

- Quasi-experiments compare a group that received an experimental treatment or a change with a nonequivalent group receiving a standard treatment or a control condition.
- True experiments compare the outcomes of two initially equivalent groups that have been assigned randomly to either one or more experimental conditions, or one or more control conditions.
- Quasi-experiments and true experiments serve mainly to test causal hypotheses, and establish that a difference between treatment and control groups on an outcome score was due to a treatment.
- Threats to validity cause the treatment effect observed to differ from the true treatment effect.
- Different plausible threats to internal validity accompany different designs.
- Once you have identified a plausible threat to internal validity, you attempt to estimate its impact using available or obtainable data.
- True experiments can provide stronger tests of causal hypotheses than quasi-experiments because they create initial probabilistic equivalence between the different randomly assigned groups.

- Many difficulties accompany the implementation of true experiments. With proper attention and effort, researchers can overcome many of these difficulties.
- Practical difficulties usually accompany large scale true experiments.
- Evaluation research focuses on the success or failure of a planned or implemented program of policy.
- In planning an evaluation study, researchers work closely with other interested stakeholders to design the study.
- Evaluation research may examine a program before it begins, as it gets underway, or after it has been running for a time.
- An evaluation addressing all three of these program phases is a comprehensive evaluation.

KEY TERMS

attrition
compensatory rivalry
comprehensive evaluation study
confounding
control group
cost-effectiveness
cost-efficiency
differential attrition

discrepancy
efficiency
estimate of the effect
experimental group
floor effects
history
implementation difficulties
implementation failure
initial probabilistic equivalence
instrumentation
interaction between setting and treatment
interaction of history and treatment
interrupted time series
local history
maturation
monetize
posttest scores
pre-experimental designs
pretest scores
program effectiveness
program impact
program delivery
program implementation
program element
random assignment
selection bias
selection
stakeholders
statistical regression
strong quasi-experimental designs
target population
target problem
threat to internal validity
treatment
treatment dilution
treatment contamination
true experimental designs
weak quasi-experimental designs

SUGGESTED READINGS

The "classics" on quasiexperimental design are two. Campbell, D. T., and Stanley, J. (1966). *Experimental and quasi-experimental designs for research.* Chicago: Rand McNally. Cook. T., and

Campbell, D. (1979). *Quasi-experimentation.* Chicago: Rand McNally.

For an excellent review of evaluation research see Weiss, C. H. (1972). *Evaluation research: Methods of assessing program effectiveness.* Englewood Cliffs, NJ: Prentice Hall.

REFERENCES

1. Campbell, D. T. (1969) Reforms as experiments. *American Psychologist 24,* 409–429
2. Cook, T. D., and Campbell, D. T. (1979) *Quasi-experimentation,* Rand-McNally, Chicago, p. 5
3. Dennis, M. L. (1990) Assessing the validity of randomized field experiments. *Evaluation Review 14,* 347–373
4. Dennis, M. L., and Boruch, R. F. (1989) Randomized experiments for planning and testing projects in developing countries: Threshold conditions. *Evaluation Review 13,* 292–309
5. Watson, K. F. (1986) Programs, experiments, and other evaluations: An Interview with Donald Campbell. *Canadian Journal of Program Evaluation 1,* 83–86
6. Farrington, D. P. (1983) Randomized experiments on crime and justice. In *Crime and justice: An annual review of research,* Vol. 4 (Tonry, M., and Morris, N., eds), pp. 257–308. Chicago: University of Chicago Press.
7. Reichardt, C. S., and Gollob, H. F. (1989) Ruling out threats to validity. *Evaluation Review 13,* 3–17
8. Cook, T. D., and Campbell, D. T. (1979) *Quasi-experimentation,* Rand-McNally, Chicago
9. Campbell, D. T. (1957) Factors relevant to the validity of experiments in social settings. *Psychological Bulletin 54,* 297–312
10. Cook, T. D., and Campbell, D. T. (1979) *Quasi-experimentation,* Rand-McNally, Chicago, p. 96
11. Byrne, J. M. (1986) The Control controversy: A Preliminary examination of intensive probation supervision programs in the United States. *Federal Probation 50,* 4–16
12. Byrne, J. M., Lurigio, A., and Baird, C. (1989) The Effectiveness of the new intensive supervision programs. *Research in Corrections 2,* 1–48
13. Pearson, F. S., and Harper, A. G. (1990) Contingent intermediate sentences: New Jersey's

intensive supervision program. *Crime & Delinquency 36*, 75–86

14. Baird, C. S., and Wagner, D. (1990) Measuring diversion: The Florida community control program. *Crime & Delinquency 36*, 112–125

15. Cook, T. D., and Campbell, D. T. (1979) *Quasi-experimentation*, Rand-McNally, Chicago, p. 53

16. Rosenbaum, D. (1988) A Critical eye on neighborhood watch: Does it reduce crime and fear? In *Communities and crime reduction* (Hope, T., and Shaw, M., eds), pp. 126–145. London: HMSO.

17. Rosenbaum, D., Lewis, D., and Szoc, J. (1986) Neighborhood-based crime prevention: Assessing the efficacy of community organizing in Chicago. In *Community crime prevention: Does it work?* (Rosenbaum, D., ed), pp. 109–136, Sage, Beverly Hills, CA.

18. Taylor, R. B., and Shumaker, S. A. (1990) Local crime as a natural hazard: Implications for understanding the relationship between disorder and fear of crime. *American Journal of Community Psychology 18*, 619–642

19. Cook, T. D., and Campbell, D. T. (1979) *Quasi-experimentation*, Rand-McNally, Chicago, p. 105

20. Jones, P. R. (1990) Community corrections in Kansas: Extending community-based corrections or widening the net? *Journal of Research in Crime and Delinquency 27*, 79–101

21. Jones, P. J. (1990) Expanding the use of non-custodial sentencing options: An Evaluation of the Kansas Community Corrections Act. *The Howard Journal of Criminal Justice 29*, 114–129

22. Deutsch, S. J., and Alt, F. B. (1977) The effect of Massachusetts' gun control law on gun-related crimes in the city of Boston. *Evaluation Quarterly 1*, 543–568

23. Loftin, C., Heumann, M., and McDowall, D. (1983) Mandatory sentencing and firearms violence: Evaluating an alternative to gun control. *Law and Society Review 17*, 288–317

24. Ross, H. L. (1982) *Deterring the drunk driver*, Lexington, Lexington, MA

25. Cirel, P., Evans, P., McGillis, D., and Whitcomb, D. (1977) *An exemplary project: Community Crime Prevention Project: Seattle, Washington*, U.S. Government Printing Office, Washington, DC, p. 211

26. Berkowitz, L., and Donnerstein, E. (1982) External validity is more than skin deep: Some answers to criticism of laboratory experiments. *American Psychologist 37*, 245–257

27. Cook, T. D., and Campbell, D. T. (1979) *Quasi-experimentation*, Rand-McNally, Chicago, p. 342

28. Petersilia, J. (1989) Implementing randomized experiments: Lessons from BJA's intensive supervision project. *Evaluation Review 13*, 435–458

29. Petersilia, J., and Turner, S. (1990) *Intensive supervision for high risk probationers: Findings from three California experiments*, Rand Corporation, Santa Monica, CA

30. Petersilia, J., and Turner, S. (1990) Comparing intensive and regular supervision for high-risk probationers: Early results from an experiment in California. *Crime & Delinquency 36*, 87–111

31. Ross, H. L. and Blumenthal, M. (1975) Some problems in experimentation in a legal setting. *The American Sociologist 10*, 150–155

32. Connor, R. F. (1977) Selecting a control group: An analysis of the randomization process in twelve social reform programs. *Evaluation Quarterly 1*, 194–244

33. Rossi, P. H., and Freeman, H. E. (1985) *Evaluation: A Systematic Approach*, Third ed., Sage, Beverly Hills, CA, p. 19

34. Cronbach, L. J. (1982) *Designing evaluations of educational and social programs*, Jossey-Bass, San Francisco

35. Rossi, P. H., and Freeman, H. E. (1985) *Evaluation: A Systematic Approach*, Third ed., Sage, Beverly Hills, CA

36. Reiss, A. J., Jr. (1986) Why are communities important in understanding crime? In *Crime and justice: A Review of research: Communities and crime*, Vol. 8 (Reiss, A. J., Jr., and Tonry, M., eds), pp. 1–34. Chicago: University of Chicago Press

37. Lattimore, P. K., Witte, A. D., and Baker, J. R. (1990) Experimental assessment of the effect of vocational training on youthful property offenders. *Evaluation Review 14*, 115–133

38. Pressman, J., and Wildavsky, A. (1984) *Implementation: How great expectations in Washington are dashed in Oakland*, Third ed., University of California Press, Berkeley, CA

CHAPTER 14

LONGITUDINAL AND CAREER RESEARCH

OBJECTIVES

Researchers use longitudinal studies to learn how people and society change over time. A particular type of longitudinal study, a prospective panel study, provides insight into the antecedents of delinquency and adult criminality, and the long-term consequences of criminal justice sanctions and programs. You will examine such studies and explore how they can be used to identify career criminals.

REVISIONS IN SENTENCING REFORM?

Let's return to the running example with sentencing reform. The sentencing guidelines are still in place. To set punishment levels, the guidelines evaluate the criminal history of an offender, as well as the seriousness of the instant offense. The guidelines used are not unlike those in Figure 14.1. It depicts the sentencing grid used by the Minnesota Sentencing Commission in the early 1980s. Nonetheless, your guidelines do not allow for the identification and incapacitation of career offenders *before* they have committed several crimes. The criminal history score on the sentencing grid takes into account the number and seriousness of the crimes committed *to date*, but does not address possible future crimes.

Despite these new sentencing practices, people express concern that the guidelines do not identify repeat offenders who are **career criminals**. A career criminal is an offender devoted to a criminal lifestyle, committing many crimes over the course of a criminal career. If committing street crimes, she is likely to come to the attention of the criminal justice system several times during this career.

Several politicians in the state legislature, and the governor, are pressuring the sentencing commission to revise the guidelines. They seek alterations to allow early identification of career offenders and mandate lengthy periods of incarceration for them. They argue that such changes would result in dramatically lower total criminal justice system costs. The expense of incarcerating the career offenders for a longer time would be more than offset by the savings achieved. The savings emerge because the system need not repeatedly rearrest and reprocess the same individuals.

Your boss wants you to learn if career criminals can be predicted. If two repeat offenders are being sentenced and one will go on to become a career criminal, can you relia-

Presumptive sentence lengths in months

Italicized numbers within the grid denote the range within which a judge may sentence without the sentence being deemed a departure. Offenders with nonimprisonment felony sentences are subject to jail time according to law.

Severity levels of conviction offense		Criminal history score						
		0	1	2	3	4	5	6 or more
Unauthorized use of motor vehicle Possession of Marijuana	I	12*	12*	12*	13	15	17	19 *18–20*
Theft related crimes ($250–$2500) Aggravated forgery ($250–$2500)	II	12*	12*	13	15	17	19	21 *20–22*
Theft crimes ($250–$2500)	III	12*	13	15	17	19 *18–20*	22 *21–23*	25 *24–26*
Nonresidential burglary Theft crimes (over $2500)	IV	12*	15	18	21	25 *24–26*	32 *30–34*	41 *37–45*
Residential burglary Simple robbery	V	18	23	27	30 *29–31*	38 *36–40*	46 *43–49*	54 *50–58*
Assault, 2nd degree	VI	21	26	30	34 *33–35*	44 *42–46*	54 *50–58*	65 *60–70*
Aggravated robbery	VII	24 *23–25*	32 *30–34*	41 *38–44*	49 *45–53*	65 *60–70*	81 *75–87*	97 *90–104*
Criminal sexual conduct, 1st degree Assault, 1st degree	VIII	43 *41–45*	54 *50–58*	65 *60–70*	76 *71–81*	95 *89–101*	113 *106–120*	132 *124–140*
Murder, 3rd degree Murder, 2nd degree (felony murder)	IX	105 *102–108*	119 *116–122*	127 *124–130*	149 *143–155*	176 *168–184*	205 *195–215*	230 *218–242*
Murder, 2nd degree (with intent)	X	120 *116–124*	140 *133–147*	162 *153–171*	203 *192–214*	243 *231–255*	284 *270–298*	324 *309–339*

1st degree murder is excluded from the guidelines by law and continues to have a mandatory life sentence.
*one year and one day

FIGURE 14.1

"The vertical dimension of the grid indicates the level of severity for the offense. The offenses listed in each category are the most frequently occurring offense(s) at each severity level. A measure of an offender's criminal history is provided with the horizontal dimension of the grid. The line running across the grid is the dispositional line—all cases that fall in cells below the dispositional line receive presumptive imprisonment sentences, and cases that fall in cells above the dispositional line receive presumptive non-imprisonment, unless a mandatory minimum sentence applies." (Knapp, 1984, p. 85) *Source:* Knapp, K. A. (1984). What sentencing reform in Minnesota has and has not accomplished. *Judicature 68*: 181-189. Figure 1.

bly and accurately predict which one that will be? If so, then the sentencing guidelines could be revised to allow the application of harsher sanctions to career criminals.[1]

The task you confront in this hypothetical scenario is central to effective criminal justice policy making. You seek to predict the effects of criminal justice actions on subsequent behavior of individuals.

ORGANIZATION

The tools used by researchers to address these questions are **longitudinal studies**. Longitudinal research refers to a broad range of research designs. All of these designs are

---

[1] For the moment we will ignore the host of policy, legal, financial, and political difficulties surrounding such an implemented policy.

similar in that cases are observed multiple times over a period spanning at least a couple of years. In the next section three types of longitudinal studies are introduced. You will then focus on the theoretical advantages and practical difficulties associated with one type of longitudinal study, a panel study. You will take stock of two major panel studies in criminal justice. You will then re-examine issues related to career research. Finally, you will examine some ethical issues particularly relevant to these research enterprises, uses of this research for Holmes's and Einstein's methods of scientific inquiry, and special issues relating to benchmarks of scientific quality.

VARIETIES OF LONGITUDINAL STUDIES

Traditionally, researchers identify three types of longitudinal studies. [1]

Trend

Trend studies examine how scores on one or more variables or indexes change over time in a general population. You have already seen several examples in the text of such studies. Figure 5.5 shows national trends in victimization rates over seventeen years. Figure 13.3 shows changes in DUI arrest rates in a hypothetical suburban county over several years. Such studies measure the same variable(s) at different points in time. *Different* cases are measured at different points in time. If your trend study is relying solely on surveys, it can also be called a **multiple wave design**. National polls conducted on a regular basis, such as the General Social Survey, represent multiple wave studies.

Cohort

By contrast **cohort studies** obtain measurements over time from cohorts. **Cohorts** are

groups of people who were born at the same time or who shared the same experience in a specified period. For example, new recruits entering a police academy at the same time make up a cohort. (For a list of European cohort studies see [2].) Several studies have used **birth cohorts**, following up the records of all individuals born in a certain location during a certain period. Perhaps the best-known birth cohort study in American criminal justice is Wolfgang's first Philadelphia cohort. [3, see also 4] Researchers gathered information on the juvenile records of all males born in Philadelphia during the year 1945 and who resided in the city from the ages of 10 to 18. Major cohort studies have been conducted in other U.S. cities as well, such as Racine (WI) [5, 6]. With cohort studies researchers can follow up the juvenile and criminal justice records of a large, representative population of individuals. Cohort studies represent the most typical type of longitudinal investigation of criminal careers. [7] The parameters of criminal careers can be recovered from cohort studies.

In the first Philadelphia cohort study researchers found that a small proportion of the birth cohort generated a large number of officially recorded delinquencies: 18 percent of the cohort, each of whom committed five or more recorded offenses, were responsible for 52 percent of officially recorded delinquent acts. See Table 14.1.

Most cohort studies are not able to obtain detailed survey or behavioral information from cohort members, because the cohort is too large, and the accompanying data collection would be too costly. Researchers rely upon official data, such as police or court records, as the principal and often exclusive source of information about criminal careers.

There are, however, some cohort studies that do obtain detailed information from sources beyond official records. A New Zealand study has combined a birth cohort design with extensive behavioral and psycho-

T A B L E 14.1

Delinquent Offenses by Delinquent Type in First
Philadelphia Cohort Study

Type of Delinquent	Offenders N	Offenders %	Offenses N	Offenses %
One-time offenders	1,613	46.4	1,613	15.8
Chronic offenders	627	18	5,305	51.9
Non-chronic recidivists	1,235	35.6	3,296	32.3
TOTAL	3,475	100	10,214	100

Source: Wolfgang, M., Figlio, R., and Sellin, T. (1972) *Delinquency in a birth cohort.*
Chicago: University of Chicago Press. Table 6.1, p. 89.

logical data collection from children as they grow. [8, 9]

Another example of an attempt to gain detailed information from a cohort comes in a follow-up study to the first Philadelphia cohort study. Wolfgang and his colleagues attempted to interview a random 10 percent of the members of the first Philadelphia birth cohort when the members of that cohort had reached 26 years of age. [4] They successfully interviewed 567 of the 975 comprising the 10 percent random sample. They also collected information from the FBI on recorded arrests when those individuals reached 30 years of age. Unfortunately the researchers discovered serious discrepancies between self-reported and officially recorded offense information. [10] The reliability and validity coefficients that resulted when they tried to match official and self-report data were dismally low. It is not clear how much of the discrepancy is due to respondent distortions or forgetting, and how much is due to inaccurate or distorted official record keeping.

When cohort studies in criminal justice focus on criminal careers, because of their design, they have several *methodological advantages*:

• Results from cohorts or representative samples derived from cohorts *describe the popula-*

tion, or can be legitimately generalized to the population.

• Prevalence rates and incidence rates for the population can be generated from the cohort information.

• Researchers need not rely upon respondent willingness to participate. Participants will not "drop out" because they do not wish to be studied.[2] The participating pool will not become biased due to attrition.

• Per-subject costs of studies can be low.

• Researchers can develop profiles depicting how individuals changed over time.

Simultaneously, cohort studies of criminal careers also possess several *methodological deficiencies* due to their structure:

• Quality of official record keeping may be highly uneven across jurisdictions, across agencies within a jurisdiction, or over an extended time. Therefore, offenses may be more detectable in some jurisdictions than in others, or if recorded by some agencies as compared to others, or at some times

---

[2] A related ethical question can be stated as follows: Are such studies unethical? People are being studied who have no knowledge of the study and have not consented to an examination of their files by researchers.

as compared to others. These over-time, cross-agency, or cross-jurisdiction differences create problems for researchers who want to compare results based on different data sources, or sources gathered over a long period.

- Information gathered by researchers lacks depth. They may have information on where persons lived, characteristics of their neighborhoods, and the nature and frequencies of their contacts with criminal justice agencies. But most cohort studies lack information on social, psychological, and life history variables.

Panel

The last type of longitudinal design is a **panel study**, where the *same* individuals or cases provide repeated measurements over an extended period of time. Two basic varieties of panel study exist: **retrospective** or **prospective**. (See Figure 14.2.) In the former case researchers ask participants or others who know participants to recall information about prior conditions, attitudes, feelings, or behaviors. They hope recalled information will help explain current behaviors. For example, researchers may interview parents of delinquents and nondelinquents, asking them to recall particular aspects of past child-rearing practices. Researchers generally agree that studies relying upon retrospective self-report are likely to be suspect for many reasons. "Retrospective data are notoriously unreliable." [11, p. 142] By contrast, if the panel study is prospective in design, researchers gather information about individuals *before* they become delinquent or criminal. *Current* information is gathered and used to predict the respondent's future behavior.

David Farrington, Lloyd Ohlin, and James Q. Wilson [12] have suggested that longitudinal panel studies should have the following characteristics:

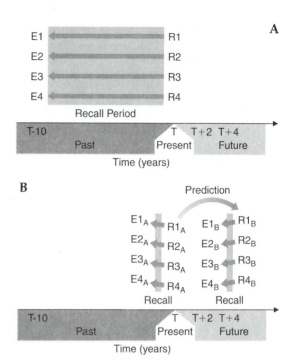

FIGURE 14.2

R = report; E = Event. Width of shaded area reflects length of recall period. **A.** With a retrospective panel study, the recall period between the actual event and the reporting of the event is likely to be several years. **B.** With a prospective panel study, the recall period is probably much shorter, more likely on the order of weeks or months. The shorter recall period will result in a more reliable data. If the data collection is repeated, reports from an earlier point in time (t = 0) can be used to predict reports from a later point in time (t = +4 years).

- They should be prospective in design.
- Researchers should interview subjects at least two different times.
- At least 5 years should elapse between the first and last interviews with the participants.
- The study should include at least a couple of hundred participants.
- The study should include information on delinquent or criminal behavior.

Obtaining such information is likely to require assessment of official criminal justice system records. At the time of their writing they enumerated 11 such studies that met these criteria and had been conducted in the United States.

REASONS FOR LONGITUDINAL PANEL STUDIES

Let's focus more specifically on longitudinal panel studies. What are the advantages of such studies?

Practical

Longitudinal study designs serve three practical or policy-related purposes in criminal justice.

1. They reveal the long-term effects of a treatment program. Since information is available from each individual in the study for several observations, individual behaviors and attitudes, measured after a treatment, can be contrasted with behaviors and attitudes from the period before the treatment.

2. They clarify long-term consequences of contacts with the criminal justice system, or of various pathways of criminal justice processing. You can examine the effects of various sanctions and processing outcomes by contrasting the behavior of individuals before and after they received the sanctions. *Understanding the impacts of criminal justice sanctions on subsequent offender behavior is perhaps one of the most important policy-relevant goals of criminal justice research.*

3. They can help criminal justice practitioners identify the individuals to whom sanctions or treatment can be directed for maximal impact, effectiveness, or cost-effectiveness. If longitudinal research designs allow practitioners, *ex ante* or beforehand, to identify career criminals reliably, to predict the ages when the career begins

B O X 14.1

Personality Precursors of Adolescent Drug Use: Policy Implications

---

An example of a longitudinal panel study results casting light on current policy comes from a study of 100+ male and female children assessed at regular intervals by teachers and observers between the ages of 3 and 14. Results showed that levels of adolescent drug use could be predicted from personality correlates a decade earlier. [13] The researchers, led by Jack Block, observed: "We find that early childhood characteristics are strongly related to adolescent personality characteristics, which, in turn, are related concomitantly to adolescent drug use." (p. 351) They conclude that current antidrug policy and education initiatives emphasizing the role of peer associations and sociological determinants of drug use are inadequate. "Peer groups may be decisive at the moment of choice regarding drug usage, but our results suggest that research must address the question of how adolescents come to belong to their particular peer groups in the first place. In any event, current social policies seeking to prevent drug use must be broadened." (p. 352)

---

and ends, as well as the persistence with which they pursue their careers, practitioners can incapacitate such criminals for the most active parts of their careers.

Theoretical

Causal Sequence Clarified   The major theoretical advantage to prospective longitudinal designs is that they provide clear temporal separations between predictor and outcome variables. Such separations assist in untangling webs of cause and effect. *The researcher knows what came before what.* Predictors measured at an earlier point in time cannot be the outcome of behaviors occurring and measured at a later point in time. Researchers can confidently model the later-measured behaviors or attitudes as outcomes of earlier-measured predictors.

Continuity of Behavior A second theoretical advantage comes from the insight these studies provide into the continuity of behavior. [14] Many intervention programs assume that troublesome behavior, among adults or juveniles, will be manifested continuously over time. Given this assumption, it is equally profitable for program intervention to occur at any number of different times. Prospective longitudinal studies allows researchers to learn if this assumption has empirical support.

To expand on this last point for a moment, research completed with young children has shown that stable individual differences in levels of aggression can be identified even when children are quite young. For example, the New Zealand birth cohort study mentioned above demonstrated that assessments of preschooler problems at 3 years of age allowed researchers to predict which children would have antisocial behavioral disorders at age 11. It did not allow the researchers, however, to predict delinquency status reliably at age 15. [8] Such findings are in line with more general findings on the stability of interpersonal differences in aggression. [15] See Figure 14.3.

Insight into Criminal Careers Third, and perhaps most importantly, longitudinal research can provide considerable insight into the course of criminal careers. "Longitudinal research can show when criminal careers begin, when they end, and how long they last." [16] Some researchers, however, question this advantage. They argue that we can learn all we need to about why people begin and

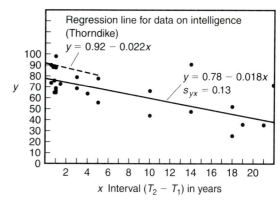

FIGURE 14.3

This figure plots the size of the correlation between two measures of aggression, taken at different times (vertical axis), and the length of time occurring between the two measures (horizontal axis). A solid line connects the data points. The line slopes downward from the left to the right, showing that, as more time elapses between the two measures of aggression, the lower the correlation between the two measures. Correlations taken within 3 years of one another range from around +.70 to greater than +.90. The dashed line at the top plots the same information for the trait of *intelligence*, based on 36 studies. The closeness of the dashed and solid lines suggests that aggression is nearly as stable a trait as intelligence. Results have also shown that the later the age of the first assessment, the more stable the individual differences in aggression over time. *Source:* Figure 2 from Olweus, D. (1979): Stability of aggressive reaction patterns in males: A Review. *Psychological Bulletin* (86): 852-875.

end criminal careers from cross-sectional research, where data is gathered from cases at one point in time. [e.g., 17 vs. 18]

Longitudinal Panel Studies, Cross-Sectional Studies, and the Causes of Changes in Behavior

The debate on the relative merits of longitudinal panel studies vs. cross-sectional studies arises largely from the particular strengths and weaknesses of each type of design. Each design provides a different perspective on the *types* of factors causing behavioral change.

Researchers generally classify influences, on behavior over time, as one of the following: period effects, cohort effects, and aging effects. Let's look into each of these in turn.

Aging Effects Aging effects refer to changes in behavior or attitudes that occur in an individual or a group, simply because those individuals or that group became older. [19] For example, Neal Shover has shown that attitudes toward criminal involvement among older property offenders who have been convicted, sentenced, and subsequently released are different from those of younger offenders. [20] To cite another example, the Adler's qualitative research with high-level smugglers showed that, as they aged and developed experience in the business, the lure of the trade diminished. [21]

The top panel in Figure 14.4 shows an aging effect on criminality in three different birth cohorts. Cohort 1 (C1) was born in 1907, Cohort 2 was born in 1917, and Cohort 3 (C3) was born in 1927. Within each cohort, the proportion incarcerated at each age increases to a high point in the late '20s or early '30s, and declines after that. These changes are due to the aging of each cohort. This effect of age on incarceration rate is similar for each cohort shown.

Cohort effects follow from membership of individuals in a group or cohort. It is one's membership in the group that influences one's attitudes or behaviors. For example, individuals born during the latter half of the baby boom, from 1960 through about 1970, may, throughout the course of their lives, experience more intense competition for jobs than those born in the first half of the baby boom, from 1945 through 1959. This might lead to higher rates of crime for the former birth cohort as compared to the latter birth cohort. This hypothesis of an effect of relative birth cohort size on property crime rates, la-

beled the **Easterlin hypothesis**, has gained empirical support. [22]

The middle panel of Figure 14.4 shows how a cohort effect may be added to an aging effect. The rate at which the third cohort (C3) was incarcerated was much higher than the incarceration rates for the previous two cohorts. The third cohort still showed an effect of age in incarceration rate, with the percentage imprisoned increasing until the late '20s or early '30s, and declining after that. But the beginning, peak, and ending incarceration rates for this third cohort were higher in comparison to Cohorts 1 and 2.

Period effects occur when particular historical periods have an impact on the likelihood that individuals will engage in certain behaviors or hold certain attitudes. For example, during the early 1970s as compared to the early 1960s, college students were more tolerant of drug use, and this in part explains the higher drug use rates among college students at that time. In the language of threats to validity (Chapter 13), these are impacts of history.

The bottom panel of Figure 14.4 shows how a period effect may override or modify an aging effect. For the three cohorts shown, incarceration rates were significantly lower during World War II. During this period the incarceration rates for each cohort, whatever the age of the cohort at that time, were significantly lower than would have been expected based simply on the aging effect.

For theoretical and practical reasons, researchers predicting delinquency or criminality, or the effects of criminal justice contacts on subsequent criminality, seek to unravel period, cohort, and aging effects. Consider this example. A state criminal justice system may be witnessing a dramatic increase in incarceration rates. If the increase is due largely to an age effect then it will "turn around" as the bulk of offenders in the state age out of prime incarceration years. But if

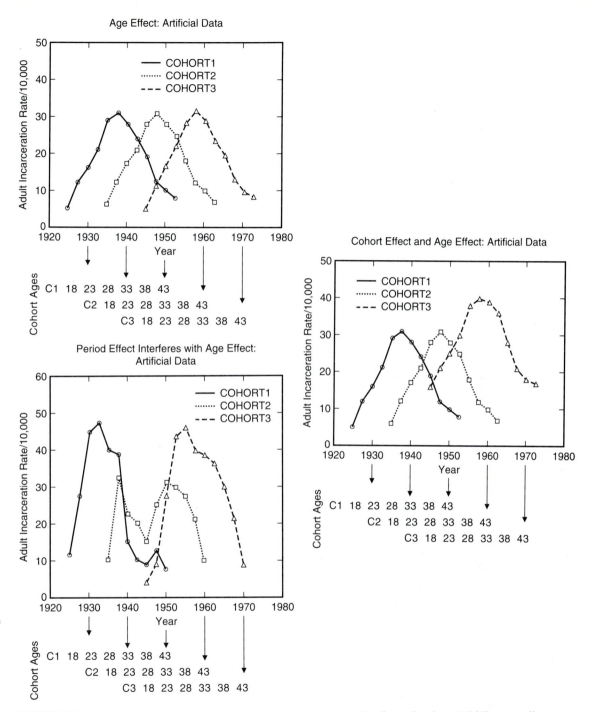

FIGURE 14.4

Each panel shows artificial yearly incarceration rates for three different birth cohorts. Cohort 1 (C1) was born in 1907, Cohort 2 (C2) was born in 1917, and Cohort 3 (C3) was born in 1927. **Top.** An effect of aging on incarceration for each cohort. **Middle.** Age effect modified by a cohort effect. Incarceration rates for C3 are higher. **Bottom.** Age effect modified by period effect. For all three cohorts, incarceration rates were low during the years of World War II.

the increase is due to a period effect, it may *not* turn around as the bulk of offenders age. Criminal justice planners would respond to the increase differently in these two instances.

The unraveling of these different effects is not so easy. *Most cross-sectional research designs confound—i.e., tangle up—aging and cohort effects.* For example, researchers may observe, based on data collected at one point in time, a connection between the age of persons in a sample and incarceration rates. The connection may arise from the different ages of the different groups in the sample. Or it may arise from the fact that people of different ages were born into different birth cohorts and had different experiences when they were younger. If people between 40 and 45 have a lower incarceration rate than persons between 30 and 35, is it because the first group is older? Or is it because the first group grew up in a different time with different opportunities and child rearing practices than the second group? No single cross-sectional research design can separate out aging and cohort effects.

If a longitudinal panel study includes more than one cohort, such as was shown in Figure 14.4, it *can* unravel the effects of aging vs. cohorts. Nonetheless, *most longitudinal surveys confound aging and period effects.* If you are following a cohort, and you find that, in a certain period, incarceration rates go up markedly, or go down markedly, you do not know if that is an age or a period effect. If you are following multiple cohorts, who are at different ages during the period in question (e.g., Figure 14.4, bottom), however, then you can separate out aging and period effects.

A LOOK AT TWO LONGITUDINAL PANEL STUDIES

In this section you will learn about two major longitudinal panel studies. For each study I will outline the major study characteristics and highlight key findings. This "close-up" should begin to give you an idea of the strengths, weaknesses, and demands inherent in these longitudinal studies.

Cambridge (U.K.) Study in Delinquent Development Since 1961, two British researchers, Donald West and David Farrington, have investigated the origins of delinquency. They have reported their results in four books, and in a number of journal articles and chapters. [e.g., 23, 24, 25, 26, 27, 28, 29, 30]

Structure The sample of boys investigated focused largely on birth cohorts living in a particular geographical area. Researchers recruited two cohorts of boys, and a small additional sample, born in the early 1950s. Most of the boys were enrolled in 1961–1962 in six state primary schools within a mile radius of a research office established in a working-class area of London. Of the 411 males, all but 12 were White. In toto the sample formed "overwhelmingly a traditional British white working class sample." [30, p. 137]

Figure 14.5 depicts the overall study design. The researchers collected many different types of data from many different sources. During the first 6 years of the study parents were surveyed by social workers. Teachers assessed participants when they were 8, 10, 12, and 14 years of age. Clinicians or social workers interviewed the participants several times over almost a 20-year span. In these interviews participants provided self-report information on delinquency and deviant involvement. Researchers scanned official records for information on delinquency when the participants were aged 10–17, and also obtained information on adult convictions.

Researchers attempted to interview all participants up until 18 years of age. After that,

Cambridge (U.K.) Study in Delinquent Development: London Year	Age of participants	Survey of parents by social workers	Teacher assessment	Collection of official police/ court data
1952–1954	Born			
1961–1962	8	XXX	XXX	
1962–1963	9	XXX		
1963–1964	10	XXX	XXX	
1964–1965	11	XXX		Criminal Records Office records repeatedly searched: offenses from Ages 10–17 recorded
1965–1966	12	XXX	XXX	
1966–1967	13	XXX		
1967–1968	14	XXX	XXX	
1968–1969	15			
1969–1970	16			
1970–1971	17			
1971–1972	18			
1972–1973	19			
1973–1974	20			
1974–1975	21			
1975–1976	22			
1976–1977	23			
1977–1978	24			
1978–1979	25			
1979–1980	oldest 25.5			

FIGURE 14.5

Design of Cambridge (UK) delinquency study. This figure does not show many interviews of participants by clinicians or social workers.

their interviews focused on selected subgroups of participants.

With its focus on family and school as well as the boy, high response rates, and its large number of observations over several years, this study is undoubtedly one of the best designed prospective longitudinal delinquency studies available.

Sample of Major Findings West identified five major background factors contributing to delinquency: "low family income, large family size, parental criminality, low intelligence and poor parental behavior." [31] Peer and teacher ratings of the boy's troublesomeness at an early age provided the best prediction of

juvenile convictions. [29] Such results underscore the general pattern that has emerged from studies on aggression. Aggressiveness seems a stable trait and predictive of future involvement in antisocial behavior. Figure 14.6 illustrates this continuity. [29, p. 373] At each age, behaviors from the earlier age period provide the best prediction of criminal behavior.

National Youth Survey (U.S.) *Structure* With major funding from several funding agencies, a national survey of youth was begun in the mid-1970s. Using a complex probability sample, researchers in late 1976 sampled 2,360 youths aged 11–17. In 1977 researchers successfully completed face-to-face interviews in the home with 1,725 youths, or 73 percent of the sample. Arrangements to ensure respondent privacy were made as needed. Teens answered questions on victimization, drug and alcohol use, and delinquent and criminal involvement. Teens were reinterviewed yearly in 1978 through 1981. In each survey, respondents provided information based on the *preceding* year. The sixth and seventh wave of surveys took place in 1984 and 1987.

In such multiple interview survey (panel) designs, **attrition** can be a problem. Attrition occurs in a survey when respondents interviewed in an earlier survey do not participate in a later interview. Researchers report, however, only a 13 percent loss in respondents over the first six waves of interviews. [32] Unfortunately, loss over the waves has been linked to social class. Urban African American youths were more likely to have been "lost" in later waves. [33] Overall, the researchers conclude that the sample remains representative over the first three surveys, despite these losses. [34]

At the time of the first interviews, researchers collected information on official delinquency for 80 percent of the sample. In the bulk of reported analyses, however, they rely

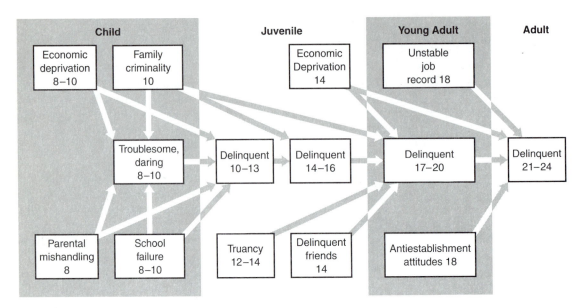

FIGURE 14.6

Influences on delinquency. Ages at which variables measured appear in boxes. *Source:* Farrington, D. P. (1986): Stepping stones to adult criminal careers. In *Development of antisocial and prosocial behavior*, edited by D. Olweus, J. Block, and M. R. Yarrow, 359–384. New York: Academic Press.

on self-reported criminal and delinquent behavior. Test-retest correlations based on interviews conducted 4 weeks apart revealed acceptable levels of test-retest reliability for those measures. Analyses also showed acceptable levels of internal consistency for the indexes constructed from these items. [35]

Figure 14.7 illustrates the structure of the NYS.

Sample of Major Findings   The NYS has been, and probably will continue to be, a source of major insights into the origins of delinquency and teen drug use. Findings to date have provided results with significant theoretical and practical implications.

One series of analyses conducted by Del Elliott and his colleagues examined the determinants of delinquency and drug use. [36] They found that, for both sexes, prior delinquency and involvement with delinquent peers best predicted self-reported deliquency

and self-reported drug use. Because the authors had available data over time, they could create a clear temporal ordering of the variables involved. In addition, the multiple assessments permitted researchers to replicate results, proving generalizability across times.

The availability of multiple waves permitted researchers to examine *delinquency careers*. [37] They defined four types of delinquents based on self-reported delinquent and criminal involvement: nondelinquents, exploratory delinquents, nonserious patterned delinquents, and serious patterned delinquents. (See Table 14.2.) They validated the typology against official arrest data.

A PLANNED LONGITUDINAL STUDY

At the time of this writing, pilot work is being conducted on a large accelerated longitudinal study on the origins of criminality. [38, 39] Researchers plan to follow each of seven

National Youth Survey (US)						
Year of Survey	Covering the Period	Median Age	Survey of Participants	Information on Household Collected from Other Family Members	Collection of Official Police Data	
1977	1976	13.87	XXX	XXX	XXX	
1978	1977	14.87	XXX		(Arrest data for 80%)	
1979	1978	15.86	XXX			
1980	1979	16.87	XXX			
1981	1980	17.81	XXX			
1982						
1983						
1984	1983	21	XXX			
1985						
1986						
1987	1986	24	XXX			

FIGURE 14.7
Data collection design for the National Youth Survey.

overlapping male cohorts for 9 years. They also will assess female cohorts. Each cohort has a different age at the time of initial data collection. The design will allow researchers to disentangle age, cohort, and period effects. Should this project receive funding and move forward, it may be one of the most important studies in human development ever completed.

CAREER RESEARCH

Career research seeks to understand the influences of criminal justice sanctions on the subsequent behavior of released felons. As such, it focuses on the connections between the fields of criminology and criminal justice. "The distinguishing characteristic of criminal career research is its concern with systematic changes in behavior over time as a result of cumulative criminal justice system contacts." [7, p. 322]

Researchers distinguish between career criminals and criminal careers. "A **criminal career** refers to the longitudinal sequence of offenses committed by an offender who has a detectable rate of offending during some period." [18, p. 2 emphasis added] Over a lifetime a criminal career may include one offense or many. A **career criminal** is a person who has a criminal career that includes a large number of detected offenses.

Origins, Limits, and Purposes

Career research relies upon the root metaphor of offending as a *vocational career*. The metaphor of a career emerged from criminological studies in the early part of this century, such as Sutherland's study *The Professional Thief*. [40] The career metaphor suggests that offending has a clear-cut beginning, proceeds through a series of developmental regularities, and ends at a particular "retirement" time. It also intimates that offenders may view their offending activities as a profession. Some qualitative work, particularly with burglars, supports the idea that offenders may view their crimes as "work." [e.g., 41, 42]

Simultaneously, research has revealed limits to this metaphor. Qualitative research with suburban burglars has shown that, although some of them do take a "professional" view toward committing burglaries, many do *not*. [43] Furthermore, although older offenders may view their crime careers differently than do younger offenders, in some careers criminals do not "retire." The Adlers's research with smugglers suggests that experienced felons oscillate between "straight" life and careers in the drug business, alternately pulled by the lures of one realm or another. [21]

The aptness of the career metaphor probably varies across crime types. It may be more fitting for burglars than for robbers. In addition, its suitability probably varies across in-

TABLE 14.2

Delinquent Typology Based on NYS

Nondelinquents	Youth engaging in fewer than 4 self-reported delinquent offenses and no UCR Part I offenses during any given calendar year
Exploratory delinquents	Youth engaging in 4 through 11 self-reported delinquent behaviors and no more than one UCR Part I offenses in any given year
Nonserious patterned delinquents	Youth engaging in 12 or more self-reported delinquent behaviors and no more than two UCR Part I offenses in any given calendar year
Serious patterned delinquents	Youth committing at least three UCR Part I offenses in a given year of assessment, irrespective of involvement in any other delinquent offenses during that same year

(*Source.* Dunford, F. W., and Elliott, D. S. (1984) Identifying career offenders using self-reported data. *Journal of Research in Crime and Delinquency* 21 (1), 57-86. Reprinted by permission of Sage Publications, Inc.)

dividuals. Some offenders may specialize in burglary, whereas others may do burglaries, robberies, and assaults.

Although we do not yet know the exact limits of the career metaphor when it is applied to adult offenders, we do know that this perspective brings into focus theoretical and policy issues central to criminal justice research and operations. On the theory side, the relevance of punishments for the goal of **individual deterrence** can be clearly framed within a career metaphor. Punishments meet the goal of individual deterrence when they convince the punished felon to retire permanently from a criminal career. Punishments meet the goal of **general deterrence** when they convince *other* offenders to retire permanently from their criminal careers, or when they convince nonoffenders not to embark upon a criminal career but, instead, to choose an alternate vocation.

On the policy side, the career perspective helps practitioners maximize **incapacitation effects**, preventing the largest possible number of crimes by imprisoning the appropri-

ate offenders. Incarceration, or closely supervised punishments served in the community, seek to prevent the maximum number of subsequent offenses possible using a sanction commensurate with the gravity of the instant offense and the dangerousness of the offender. To maximize incapacitative effects, practitioners strive to identify convicted offenders who are embarking upon, or already involved in, a criminal career. They then selectively incapacitate *them* for lengthy periods of time, or at least for as long as their career would have continued.[3] Such policies represent **selective incapacitation** strategies. In this way the sanction will result in preventing

---

[3] This view assumes that the crimes the criminal offender would have committed had she not been incarcerated will not be committed because she is not free to do them. For some crime types, such as drug dealing, this assumption may not be appropriate. A more appropriate metaphor might be the "temp help agency" metaphor. When an offender is incarcerated and removed from the temp help pool, this does not mean that workers are unavailable for a "job" (a crime). It just means that someone else in the available labor "pool" will take the "job."

the largest number of subsequent crimes against society. A felon in prison can commit crimes in the institution, but not in the larger society. Simultaneously, the societal costs of running prisons can be minimized if felons are not incarcerated past the time they would have "retired" from their life of crime. In short, with selective incapacitation strategies career offenders are identified and removed from society for the period they would have been criminally active.

Note, however, that the successful implementation of such a policy depends for its success on two methodological points. First, you must be able to distinguish, reliably and consistently, between *career offenders* and *noncareer offenders* at the *time of sentencing*. Second, you need the ability to predict, reliably, how long the offender's criminal career would have continued had she not been incarcerated for an extended period. From the incapacitation viewpoint, the sanction needs to continue only as long as there are offenses that would have been committed had the offender not been incarcerated, or under supervision.

Sentencing Guidelines and Career Criminals

Let us return to the problem with which we began the chapter. You have been asked to investigate the possibility of reliably identifying career criminals, i.e., those whose criminal career extends over a significant period and involves several recorded offenses. If such career criminals can be reliably identified, sentencing guidelines can be altered to selectively incapacitate them and prevent the occurrence of a large number of crimes. Here is an example of one way you could attack this problem.

You first decide to focus on burglars, since many burglars recidivate and many are not incarcerated for lengthy periods. You decide

that an offender will be labeled a career offender if he is arrested for three or more offenses within a 5-year period.

Predicting Criminal Careers 1991–1995 Based on Data Before 1990

Defining Career and Noncareer Criminals Assume that the current year is 1996. To see if you can predict career criminals who have been convicted of burglary, you examine records for burglars convicted in *calendar year 1990*. Many convicted burglars were sentenced to punishments in the community, or "straight" probation. Some were incarcerated. You locate 1,000 convicted burglars. For each of these you obtain information on subsequent arrests and conviction. All of those who were convicted of three or more felonies during the period (inclusive) 1991–1995 you label *career criminals*. All of those convicted of two, one, or no felonies during this period you label *noncareer criminals*. You do not care about the type or seriousness of the crimes for which the individuals were convicted. You care only about the frequency. You collect conviction information from the state and local courts.

Developing the Prediction Index. You now have two groups of offenders—those who went on to have a criminal career between 1990 and 1995, and those who did not. Using data based *only* on information that was available to you from official records *collected before sentencing in 1990*, you develop a prediction index to predict whether individual offenders would go on to become career criminals or noncareer criminals, controlling for amount of time they were incarcerated between 1990 and 1996. You might use items such as age of first arrest as a juvenile, number of juvenile arrests, employment status at time of arrest in 1990, marital status, total number of convictions, age at arrest in 1990, and so on. You correlate each predictor variable with the outcome: criminal career or no criminal career between 1990 and 1995. You are exploring the *predictive criterion validity coefficients* of each criminal history item.

You combine the individual variables that offer the best prediction into an index. You call this index a **career prediction index**. Each offender's score on the index reflects his criminal career before sentencing in 1990. This is your summary predictor variable.

The Actual Outcome   To see how well your career prediction index does, you separate scores on the index into "high" and "low" groups.[4] You cross-tabulate high vs. low scores on the prediction index with the actual outcome. Let's imagine the outcome appears as in Table 14.3.

Before attending to the cell frequencies within the table, examine the marginals. The proportion of burglars sentenced in 1990 manifesting a criminal career during period 1991 to 1995 was 70 percent ($^{700}/_{1000}$). This represents the **base rate** of the occurrence of criminal careers. The marginals at the right show the proportion *predicted* to be career criminals: 50 percent ($^{500}/_{1000}$). This represents the **selection ratio**.

What do we see when we examine the individual cells? Of those scoring "high" on the index, 90 percent ($^{450}/_{500}$) did show evidence of a subsequent criminal career. These represent the **valid positives** (VP: bottom right cell). Of those scoring low, 50 percent ($^{250}/_{500}$) did not manifest a criminal career. These represent the **valid negatives** (VN: top left cell). So overall your index correctly predicted 70 percent ((250 + 450)/1000) of the cases (VP + VN).

Your index failed, however, to predict correctly the outcomes for the other 300 individuals. Fifty who were predicted to manifest a criminal career given their high score on the prediction index, did not do so (**false positives**, bottom left cell). Half of those *not* predicted to have a criminal career did in fact do so (**false negatives**, top right cell).

Evaluating the Outcome: Costs of "False Negatives" vs. "False Positives"

So how good should you feel about your index? As you can see, it depends partially on whether you wish to minimize false negatives or false positives. Your false positives—those predicted to have a career who did not in fact have one—were only 10 percent of your high scores and only 5 percent of the total sample. These numbers sound acceptable. If you look at false negatives, however, the picture is less rosy. Half those predicted *not* to have a career had one; this represented 25 percent of the entire sample.

As a practitioner, when you weigh the relative "costs" of false negatives vs. false positives you will want to consider ethical and practical matters as well. Suppose you had used the prediction index at sentencing, and had adjusted incarceration length accordingly? You would have incarcerated for 5 years 50 individuals who would not have manifested active criminal careers during that period. Is this ethically correct? How can you justify the financial costs to society? At an estimated cost of $20,000 per inmate per year, you have squandered $5,000,000 of taxpayers's money. What about the 250 who were predicted not to manifest criminal careers, and received accordingly shorter sentences, but then went on to manifest criminal careers? What are the costs to society of those crimes committed? These represent tough issues that policymakers using tools like this need to address.

---

[4] How you choose the "cutpoint" between high and low scores is an important issue. For example, it changes your chances of finding false positives vs. false negatives.

T A B L E 14.3
Predicting Career Criminals with Career
Criminal Prediction Index:
Hypothetical Data

		No criminal career	Criminal career	
		1991–1995 **Actual outcome**		
Score on Career	Low	250 (VN)	250 (FN)	500 (50%)
Prediction Index (1990)	High	50 (FP)	450 (VP)	500 (50%)
		300 (30%)	700 (70%)	1000

Comparing Results to Random Results As a practitioner, besides weighing the costs of false positive and false negatives you want to consider how much your *prediction has improved over chance* with the use of the prediction device. Supposed you had just *guessed* about future criminality? How well would you have done? How do your results compare here to the results you would have obtained by chance? For more detail on these procedures, see the file RIOC.WP5 on the workdisk.

WEAKNESSES AND STRENGTHS OF LONGITUDINAL RESEARCH

Weaknesses

The Time Lag Problem and Generalizing Across Periods and Cohorts Developing predictive indexes illustrates one of the major practical problems with longitudinal research. The data collection requires the passage of a significant amount of time. Therefore, the conclusions you draw reflect the way things were in the past, and not necessarily the way things will be in the future. The results you obtain with longitudinal research may reflect largely *cohort-specific effects* or *period-specific effects*. If they do, then the generalizability of results to future periods is in question. But the possible lack of generalizability is especially crucial when longitudinal research has direct implications for policy issues such as selective incapacitation.

Commitment Longitudinal research requires an extraordinary commitment. Researchers must be willing to devote a substantial portion or perhaps most of their academic research careers to a project. The nature of the work makes it difficult for a researcher to generate large numbers of research articles in a short time. Given pressures on assistant and associate professors in academia to "publish or perish," devotion to a longitudinal project may be tantamount to professional suicide.

Perhaps more difficult than assuring investigator commitment is assuring *funder* commitment. It is extremely difficult for a longitudinal research project to receive ample, multiyear funding from an agency. Such difficulties hamper data collection and analytic strategies. [30]

Strengths

Clarify Temporal Orderings Perhaps the greatest theoretical strength of longitudinal research resides in its ability to temporally order variables. You know precisely which variable preceded which other variable. This knowledge proves crucial to researchers operating in Einstein's mode of inquiry. The clear temporal separation of variables permits clear tests of a causal rather than an associational logic.

Policy Relevance Longitudinal research may be more relevant to criminal justice policies than any other research tool. Policy makers need to know how criminal justice programs, sanctions, and contacts will influence individuals. Their central concern is with predictive validity: What will arrestees or inmates or probationers or parolees do? The research that most directly responds to this concern is longitudinal research.

LONGITUDINAL RESEARCH FOR HOLMES'S AND EINSTEIN'S PURPOSES

Longitudinal research is *excellently* suited for Einstein's mode of scientific inquiry: it represents one of the best available tools for testing causal hypotheses. Researchers can justifiably assert, if they proceed carefully, that they are testing hypotheses with a *causal* rather than an *associational* logic.

Longitudinal research is *moderately well suited* for Holmes's mode of scientific inquiry. Researchers can explore associational webs over time. For example, using the West and Farrington data, one could search for all correlates of 10-year-olds rated as "troublesome" by teachers. You could focus on

differences apparent when the group was aged 10. How were they different from those not rated as troublesome by teachers when they were 10? You also could explore the linkages between this variable and future characteristics of the youth, or criminal careers, or family background. What happened later to those who were rated as troublesome when they were 10? By looking for links across periods, as well as within periods, you can begin to generate powerful longitudinal theories.[5]

LONGITUDINAL RESEARCH AND BENCHMARKS OF SCIENTIFIC QUALITY

Longitudinal research, because of its nature, can score higher than other research techniques on benchmarks concerned with *predictive criterion validities*. It allows more time to elapse between the assessment of the predictor(s) and outcome(s). Consequently, the resulting validities *potentially*, can provide the researcher with insight into a future that is more distant than is the case with other research methods.

You could argue more generally that longitudinal research methods have the potential to provide more information to researchers on *construct validity* than do other research methods we have discussed so far. Recall the suggestion by psychologist Robert Hogan (Chapter 8) that all validity coefficients are really informing us about construct validity. The superior temporal reach of validity coefficients derived from longitudinal research

---

[5] Longitudinal research is not excellently suited to Holmes's purposes, because the researcher is constrained from collecting any data she wishes. Procedures such as content analysis and qualitative field methods give the researcher more opportunities than does longitudinal research to adjust data collection as she generates and elaborates concepts and theories.

therefore provides you with enhanced information on construct validity *over time*. Such information is not available with other methods.

Longitudinal methods may have a slight advantage over other research methods in the area of *reliability*. Because researchers collect data at multiple points in time, they can assess test-retest reliabilities. They also can examine inter-item consistency of indexes at more than one point in time. The specific advantage in assessing reliability provided by a particular study will depend in part on the length of the test-retest interval.

Turning to external validity, however, I would argue that longitudinal research *may* be at a slight *dis*advantage on this scientific benchmark. Longitudinal researchers are always assessing the way things *were*. Until particular longitudinal associations between variables replicate across periods and cohorts, one must remain skeptical. The linkages observed may emerge largely from cohort effects, or period effects, or both. You will not know if such linkages can be correctly applied to present cohorts in the present period unless researchers have conducted successful replication efforts across periods and cohorts. Bear in mind of course, as always—all together now—external validity is always an empirical matter. There are some things we just can't decide a priori.

SUMMARY OF MAIN POINTS

- There are three general types of longitudinal studies: trend, cohort, and panel.
- Trend studies examine how scores on one or more variables or indexes change over time in a general population.
- Cohort studies obtain measurements over time from cohorts. Cohorts are groups of people who were born at the same time or who shared the same experience in a specified period.
- In a panel study the *same* individuals or cases provide repeated measurements over an extended period of time.
- Prospective panel studies are superior to longitudinal studies based on retrospective recall.
- Prospective panel studies allow researchers to put variables in a clear temporal order, and to examine continuity of behaviors and attitudes over time.
- Aging effects refer to changes in behavior or attitudes that occur in an individual or a group, simply because those individuals or that group became older.

- Cohort effects follow from membership of individuals in a group or cohort. It is one's membership in the group that influences one's attitudes or behaviors.
- Period effects occur when particular historical periods have an impact on the likelihood that individuals will engage in certain behaviors or hold certain attitudes.
- If properly designed, prospective panel studies let researchers separate cohort, period, and aging effects.
- Longitudinal research may be the most practical of all criminal justice research methods. It informs policy makers about the consequences, over time, of criminal justice contacts, sanctions, and programs, on specific individuals.
- Prospective panel studies can be used to gauge the predictive criterion validity of different prediction indexes.

SUGGESTED READINGS

West and Farrington have written several volumes based on their London study: West's *Present conduct and future delinquency* (1969, Heinemann); West and Farrington's *Who becomes delinquent* (1974, Heinemann); and West and Farrington's *The Delinquent way of life* (Heinemann, 1977). Any one of these excellent volumes will provide you with a clear picture of the type of information generated from longitudinal studies.

If you want to read more about how researchers separate age, period, and cohort effects you may find Norval Glenn's *Cohort analysis* (1977, Sage Publications) of interest. He uses mostly political science examples, but the exposition is clear.

KEY TERMS

aging effects
attrition
base rate
birth cohorts
career prediction index
career criminals
cohort studies
cohort effects
cohorts
criminal career
Easterlin hypothesis
false positives
false negatives
general deterrence
incapacitation effects
individual (specific) deterrence
longitudinal studies
multiple wave design
panel study
period effects
prediction index
prospective
retrospective
selection ratio
selective incapacitation
trend studies
valid positives
valid negatives

REFERENCES

1. Elliott, D. S., Huizinga, D., and Ageton, S. S. (1985) *Explaining delinquency and drug use*, Sage, Beverly Hills, CA, p. 118
2. Mednick, S. A. (1981) Methods of prospective, longitudinal research. In *Prospective longitudinal research* (Mednick, S. A., and Baert, A. E., eds), pp. 11–15. New York: Oxford University Press
3. Wolfgang, M. E., Figlio, R. M., and Sellin, T. (1972) *Delinquency in a birth cohort*, University of Chicago Press, Chicago
4. Wolfgang, M. E., Thornberry, T. P., and Figlio, R. M. (1987) *From boy to man: From delinquency to crime*, University of Chicago Press, Chicago
5. Shannon, L. W. (1981) *The Relationship of juvenile delinquency and adult crime to the changing ecological structure of the city. (Preliminary Executive Report for National Institute of Justice Grant 79-NI-AX-0081)*, Iowa Urban Community Research Center, University of Iowa, Iowa City, Iowa
6. Shannon, L. W. (no date) *Assessing the relationship of adult criminal careers to juvenile careers*, Iowa Urban Community Research Center, University of Iowa, Iowa City (executive summary)
7. Petersilia, J. (1980) Career criminal research. In *Crime and justice: An Annual review of research*, Vol. 2 (Morris, N., and Tonry, M., eds), pp. 321–379. Chicago: University of Chicago Press.
8. White, J. E., Moffitt, T. E., Earls, F., Robins, L., and Silva, P. A. (1990) How early can we tell: Predictors of childhood conduct disorder and adolescent delinquency. *Criminology 28*, 507–527
9. Moffitt, T. E. (1990) Juvenile delinquency and attention deficit disorder: Boys' developmen-

tal trajectories from age 3 to age 15. *Child Development 61,* 893–910

10. Bridges, G. S. (1987) An Empirical study of error in reports of crime and delinquency. In *From boy to man: From delinquency to crime,* pp. 180–194. Chicago: University of Chicago Press

11. Widom, C. S. (1989) The intergenerational transmission of violence. In *Pathways to criminal violence* (Weiner, N. A., and Wolfgang, M. E., eds), pp. 137–201. Newbury Park, CA: Sage.

12. Farrington, D. P., Ohlin, L. E., and Wilson, J. Q. (1986) *Understanding and controlling crime,* Springer Verlag, New York, p. 27

13. Block, J., Block, J. H., and Keyes, S. (1988) Longitudinally foretelling drug usage in adolescence: Early childhood personality and environmental precursors. *Child Development 59,* 336–355

14. Farrington, D. P., Ohlin, L. E., and Wilson, J. Q. (1986) *Understanding and controlling crime,* Springer Verlag, New York, p. 98

15. Olweus, D. (1979) Stability of aggressive reaction patterns in males: A Review. *Psychological Bulletin 86,* 852–875

16. Farrington, D. P., Ohlin, L. E., and Wilson, J. Q. (1986) *Understanding and controlling crime,* Springer Verlag, New York, p. 26

17. Gottfredson, M. R., and Hirschi, T. (1986) The True value of lambda would appear to be zero: An Essay on career criminals, criminal careers, selective incapacitation, cohort studies, and related topics. *Criminology 24,* 213–233

18. Blumstein, A., Cohen, J., and Farrington, D. P. (1988) Criminal career research: Its value for criminology. *Criminology 26,* 1–35

19. Tonry, M., Ohlin, L. E., and Farrington, D. P. (1991) *Human development and criminal behavior,* Springer Verlag, New York, p. 31

20. Shover, N. (1983) The Later stages of ordinary property offender careers. *Social Problems 31,* 208–218

21. Adler, P. A., and Adler, P. (1983) Shifts and oscillations in deviant careers: The case of upper-level drug dealers and smugglers. *Social Problems 31,* 195–207

22. O'Brien, R. M. (1989) Relative cohort size and age-specific crime rates: An Age-period-relative cohort size model. *Criminology 27,* 57–78

23. West, D. J. (1969) *Present conduct and future delinquency,* Heinemann, London

24. West, D. J. (1982) *Delinquency: Its roots, careers, and prospects,* Heinemann, London.

25. West, D. J., and Farrington, D. P. (1973) *Who becomes delinquent,* Heinemann, London

26. West, D. J., and Farrington, D. P. (1977) *The Delinquent way of life,* Heinemann, London

27. Farrington, D. P. (1979) Longitudinal research on crime and delinquency. In *Crime and justice: An Annual review of research,* Vol. 1 (Morris, N., and Tonry, M., eds), pp. 289–348. Chicago: University of Chicago Press.

28. Farrington, D. P. (1983) Offending from 10 to 25 years of age. In *Prospective studies of crime and delinquency* (Van Dusen, K. T., and Mednick, S. A., eds), pp. 17–37. Boston: Kluwer-Nijhoff.

29. Farrington, D. P. (1986) Stepping stones to adult criminal careers. In *Development of antisocial and prosocial behavior* (Olweus, D., Block, J., and Yarrow, M. R., eds), pp. 359–384. New York: Academic Press.

30. Farrington, D. P., and West, D. J. (1981) The Cambridge study in delinquent development. In *Prospective longitudinal research* (Mednick, S. A., and Baert, A. E., eds), pp. 137–145. Oxford: Oxford University Press.

31. West, D. J., and Farrington, D. P. (1973) *Who becomes delinquent,* Heinemann, London, p. 190

32. Elliott, D. S., Huizinga, D., and Menard, S. (1989) *Multiple problem youth: Delinquency, substance use, and mental health problems,* Springer-Verlag, New York, p. 3

33. Elliott, D. S., Knowles, B., and Center, R. (1981) *The epidemiology of delinquent behavior and drug use among American adolescents. Project Report 14, The National Youth Survey,* Behavioral Research Institute, Boulder, CO

34. Elliott, D. S., Huizinga, D., and Ageton, S. S. (1985) *Explaining delinquency and drug use,* Sage, Beverly Hills, CA, p. 93

35. Elliott, D. S., Huiziniga, D., and Menard, S. (1989) *Multiple problem youth: Delinquency, substance use, and mental health problems*, Springer-Verlag, New York, p. 15

36. Elliott, D. S., Huizinga, D., and Ageton, S. S. (1985) *Explaining delinquency and drug use*, Sage, Beverly Hills, CA, p. 118

37. Dunford, F. W., and Elliott, D. S. (1984) Identifying career offenders using self-reported data. *Journal of Research in Crime and Delinquency 21*, 57–86

38. Farrington, D. P., Ohlin, L. E., and Wilson, J. Q. (1986) *Understanding and controlling crime*, Springer Verlag, New York

39. Tonry, M., Ohlin, L. E., and Farrington, D. P. (1991) *Human development and criminal behavior*, Springer Verlag, New York

40. Sutherland, E. (1937) *The Professional Thief*, University of Chicago Press, Chicago

41. David, P. R. (1974) *The world of the burglar*, University of New Mexico Press, Albuquerque

42. Letkemann, P. (1973) *Crime as work*, Prentice-Hall, Englewood Cliffs, NJ

43. Rengert, G., and Wasilchick, J. (1985) *Suburban burglary*, Charles C. Thomas, Springfield, IL

CHAPTER 15

UNOBTRUSIVE MEASURES

FOCUS

Criminal justice researchers observe behaviors and environments, counting and coding what they see. They code language to learn about the themes present in writing and speech. And they gather data from historical archives to learn about the way things were. All of these procedures represent unobtrusive measures, where the researcher does not come into direct contact with the cases studied.

UNOBTRUSIVE MEASURES: ON-SITE ASSESSMENT, CONTENT ANALYSIS, ARCHIVAL ANALYSIS, AND HISTORICAL CRIMINOLOGY

Almost all the research techniques you have learned about in Chapters 10–14 required some direct contact between the researcher and the individuals being studied. In this chapter you will investigate a range of procedures that do not require direct contact. **Unobtrusive** or **nonreactive** measures have two defining characteristics. [1; see also 2, 3] First, they do not require the cooperation of the respondent. The information can be gathered without the respondent necessarily knowing about it or assenting to it. Second, the data collection process does not in any

way contaminate or influence the response given. Such measures can be used as "stand-alone" variables, or to complement variables gathered from more traditional methodologies. [4]

All the techniques discussed follow the same overall research process.

- You decide on units of analysis and a sampling plan.
- You select the attributes of the units you will examine.
- You develop systematic procedures for creating variables to reflect the selected attributes, or for coding already available figures.
- You have observers, raters, or coders observe, rate, or code the items in question.
- You analyze the data produced.

Thus, in overall procedures, these research tools are similar to others you have already examined.

I have divided this broad grouping of tools into three families. You first will learn about **on-site assessment**. Raters or observers code behavioral or physical features of sampled cases. With **content analysis** you analyze linguistic messages such as speeches or newspaper articles. With **archival analysis** you analyze existing records to gain insight into the remote past. It represents the main tool used in historical criminology.

You will review each of these three types of unobtrusive measures below. After reviewing each type of assessment, you examine issues of scientific quality, and suitability for Einstein's and Holmes's modes of inquiry.

ON-SITE ASSESSMENT

Varieties

Physical Traces On-site assessments in criminal justice can focus on **physical traces**: physical evidence resulting from human behavior. These are of two types: measures of **accretion**, things that are added on as a result of human behavior; or measures of **erosion**, things that are worn away as a result of human activity. Accretion measures might include graffiti or trash in an urban residential environment. Box 15.1 describes an analysis of graffiti in a juvenile institution. (Also see [8].) Erosion measures might include wear patterns such as the frequency of window repairs at different school sites.

Site features You also can measure **site features** or **physical design**, recording features of the built environment. You can record features at a microlevel of analysis, such as the surveillance opportunities from a window to a sidewalk. I describe one such example below. Or, you can record features at a macrolevel of analysis. For example, you may look at how easy it is for traffic to move in to a neighborhood from main arteries, and correlate this feature with burglary rates. [5]

Behavioral Observation Thirdly, on-site assessment can observe human behavior, counting what kinds of people are found in what kinds of locations at what times. An

B O X 15-1

Graffiti in an Abandoned Juvenile Facility [6]

The Institute for Juvenile Guidance, in Massachusetts, was closed in 1970. It had served for many years as the most secure facility for juvenile males in the state. In 1983 two researchers, John Klofas and Charles Cutshall, sent assistants into the abandoned facility to record graffiti from 95 general population rooms. Recorders transcribed graffiti verbatim, and also noted the location of the items. Researchers transcribed a total of 2,765 graffiti. The items were then coded using content analysis.

Authors noted that inscriptions referring to the criminal justice system were most prevalent in the corridors where inmates would be located during the middle phases of their incarceration. This pattern suggests that "antagonism toward authority figures seems to be greatest in the middle phases of incarceration" (p. 369). Such a patterning provides support, using very different types of data, for Wheeler's thesis on **prisonization**. He suggested that the effects of becoming integrated into the institutional prison culture (i.e., becoming "prisonized") are most sizable during the middle phases of an inmate's career, and lower at the beginning and end of the time in the institution. [7]

example of **behavioral observation** comes from a study of 45 inmates in a prison dorm. [9] Researchers coded social contacts, nonverbal behaviors, and aggressive behaviors related to relative social position, or dominance. They found that more dominant social individuals in the group had greater access to more valued locations. For example, more dominant persons were more likely to be found closer to the television set. Behavioral analyses clarified setting dynamics.

An Example

Focus, Sample, and Units of Analysis Let me sketch out a physical assessment procedure we used in one study of physical features in the urban residential environment. We examined **defensible space features**, physical factors intended to separate public from private spaces, and to increase surveillance of public places like the street. We also examined physical upkeep and **territorial markers**, signs of personalization and investment in properties and grounds. [10, 11, 12] Our units of analysis were house structures. Baltimore, Maryland, was the study site. Using a multi-stage clustered sample we selected neighborhoods, blocks within neighborhoods, and households on blocks. In each sampled household we interviewed one adult member. We also took slides of the front and back of each interviewed house.

Developing Rating Scales and Training Raters We developed several bipolar rating scales. These appear in Table 15.1. Each of these were five-point scales. For each point along each scale, and the endpoints, we selected a typical slide. A few of these points are shown in Photo 15.1. We trained teams of research assistants to use the rating scales, providing them with detailed instructions. We selected a sample of slides, and pilot tested the scales. Raters reported on problems that occurred using the scales, and the scales were modified as needed. We finalized the scales and instructions. Pairs of raters then proceeded to independently rate slides of the fronts and backs of over 440 households.

Quality Checks We assessed interrater reliability by examining how well pairs of raters agreed with each other when rating the slides. We assessed construct validity by correlating ratings based on the slides with household member attitudes and perceptions as reported in the face-to-face interviews.

Some Areas in Criminal Justice Where On-Site Assessments Have Been Important

On-site assessments have played important roles in at least two areas of criminal justice research. **Environmental criminology** focuses on where offenders live and where offenses occur. Analysis of physical design has linked offense locations to many site- and area-level features. [13] This area of work has led to practical studies of **situational crime prevention**, where researchers try to design out crime by changing the physical environment. [14]

Behavioral observations have been important for examinations of police–citizen encounters. [e.g., 15, 16] By riding along with police officers and recording what happens, researchers have been able to identify the behaviors associated with effective policing.

CONTENT ANALYSIS

The Sentencing Guidelines Scenario

We return one last time to our running example with sentencing guidelines. A few months have passed. The governor for whom you were working was defeated in a tough reelection fight. A main issue in the campaign was the state's mandatory sentencing guidelines. Her opponent, now the governor, charged that the guidelines were bankrupting the state. It could afford, he argued, neither to house the increasing numbers of convicted felons sentenced to prison terms under the new guidelines, nor to pursue ambitious plans for prison construction. After his inauguration he introduced a bill calling for the repeal of the mandatory sentencing guidelines in the state and the abolition of the sentencing commission. After a rancorous, wide-ranging, sometimes ludicrous, occasionally eloquent debate, the legislature passed a law doing just this. You lost your job with the commission. You are making

PICTURE 15–1
Both pictures are from Baltimore (MD) and were taken in the summer of 1979. (Top) Front of a house on Oakland Avenue with the next to lowest score on real barriers. No fence or low bush or hedge restricts access from the sidewalk. Any guess on where the men are headed? (Bottom) Four proud residents on Old York Road, in Waverly, and the back of a house with the highest possible score on real barriers. There is a high fence and a closed gate. *Source.* Urbter Associates.

TABLE 15.1
Rating Scales: Real Barriers and Surveillance Opportunities

Real Barriers

There is a barrier that restricts and directs access from the sidewalk/alley (five-point scale)

Lowest score: There is no barrier, and no defined entry point from the public walkway onto the property

Highest score: There is a barrier more than 20″ in height with a controlled point of entry through the barrier

Surveillance Opportunities

From the house, there is an unobstructed view of you as you walk along the sidewalk immediately in front of the house/alley immediately behind the house. (five-point scale)

Lowest score: Little or no opportunities for someone in the house to see you

Highest score: You can be seen along all of the walkway from most viewpoints

ends meet working as a paralegal secretary by day and a pizza deliverer by night. You watch the movie *Mystic Pizza* when you're depressed.

You continue to be puzzled about, and interested in, what happened with the sentencing guidelines in your state. You cannot understand how a measure that was so broadly supported, forward-looking, and effective could be defeated. What were people thinking about when they initiated the program? What were they thinking about when they repealed the program?

You decide to investigate. You photocopy out of the public record all of the debate surrounding the initiation of the guidelines and commission, and their abolition. You want to focus on what people were saying in the legislature when the sentencing guidelines and commission were established, and when they were laid down. To answer your questions you will need to *analyze* the *content* of the materials you have gathered. You are ready to do a content analysis.

Definition and Data Types

Definitions of content analysis abound. [17, 18, 19] Holsti offers a fairly typical one:

> Content analysis is any technique for making inferences by objectively and systematically identifying specified characteristics of messages. [20]

Roberts offers a definition focusing on the application of statistical tools to the results of content analysis:

> Content analysis is the analysis of qualitative data for the purpose of making statistical inferences. [21]

The above definitions succinctly capture the essential elements of content analysis.

- Content analysis must be *objective*. It must be a procedure that more than one person can conduct, that someone can teach to others and that can be replicated.
- It also must be *systematic*. It requires codified procedures for examining, focusing on, and coding the content of messages.
- Content analysis is not concerned with the messages themselves; rather it focuses on *specified characteristics* of those messages. In terms of measurement theory, it focuses, not on the objects themselves, but on the attributes of those objects.
- It focuses on analyzing and *making statistical inferences*. It is not enough to count or tabulate certain characteristics of messages. Content analysis goes beyond this; it is not an accounting procedure, but a scientific one.
- And lastly, it is concerned with *messages*.

Content analysis procedures can be applied to a broad range of types of data. You can analyze any sources containing *streams of linguistic data*. [22] *Newspapers* or other *mass media* such as television and radio can be examined. For example, there have been many studies of crime news. Some highlights of this research appear in Box 15.2. You can analyze *official documents* such as speeches, transcripts, public records, or official correspondence. You could look at *personal documents* such as memoirs, personal letters, or memos, and perhaps compare them to official documents. You can examine *transcripts* of unstructured interviews; several researchers have analyzed their conversations with convicted felons to gain insight into the latter's views about crime. [23, 24] And finally, *social interactions* can be analyzed. Social psychologists have developed extensive coding schemes for analyzing verbal and nonverbal interactions in groups, for example. Anywhere you can find recorded words, you can apply content analysis.

Approaches to Content Analysis

At present there are three main approaches to content analysis. See Table 15.2. **Quantitative content analysis** focuses on the **manifest content** in texts, counting occurrences of specific words or phrases. This content is readily perceived, or obvious; it represents the "surface meaning of the text." [37] Such analyses can be aided by computers. The latter can keep count of words and phrases, and even display the context in which the words or phrases appear. For example, in a quantitative content analysis you might code a speech, simply counting how many times the word *equity* occurred.

If you have a dictionary, computers can produce and analyze the frequencies with which certain meanings occur. A **dictionary** links a number of words with a specific meaning. "The marriage of dictionaries with content analysis software thus provides a fast

BOX 15.2

Content Analyses and Crime News

Researchers have spent considerable effort over the last few decades analyzing the content of crime news and linking it with information about crime from other sources such as surveys, police statistics, and criminal justice system functioning. They have addressed several questions.

Is crime news distorted?
Yes. Studies routinely find that certain types of crimes are overreported. In the U.S. heinous and violent crimes are overreported compared to their actual frequency; in India corruption of public officials and disorders such as riots are overreported relative to their frequencies. [25, 26, 27, 28] The crime coverage in newspapers, as compared to that on television, may be closer to the actual frequencies of different crimes as reported to the police. [29] Crime coverage is also distorted in that it is excessive. Its reporting is disproportionate to its social significance. [30] But despite being excessive, it does not displace other news. When other kinds of stories (e.g., political) are breaking, crime news is shouldered aside. [30]

Crime news is not only distorted in terms of the types of crimes reported and their volume. It is also distorted in how it characterizes the locations and participants in crime. Papers may link race with crime more than is warranted. [27, 31] Some have even suggested that crime reporting in papers furthers a particular ideology. "The news fragments crime by abstracting it from legal priorities and by presenting violence as the indi-

vidual attributes of demographic categories. In this sense the routine news about serious crime is ideological." [31]

Does crime news influence criminal justice system officials?
It appears that it may. Analysis of the reporting of a "crime wave" in Colchester, England, in 1765, found that policing practices and penal policies were both influenced by the media coverage. [32] More recently an investigation of Milwaukee County during an 18-month period in the 1980s suggested that the amount of press coverage given to homicide cases influenced prosecutor decisions about whether or not to plea bargain the cases. [33]

Does crime reporting make residents more fearful of crime?
Yes, in some cases, although the nature of the relationship has not yet been fully clarified. One study linked the proportion of local, random, "sensational" stories with city fear levels. [34] A more rigorous study found that local homicide stories were positively linked to fear. People were less fearful, however, if there was *more* coverage in their papers on *nonlocal* stories. The researchers also observed that some were more fearful of the higher crime rate *because* it was given more coverage in the local paper. [35]

For a recent review of the portrayal of crime in the media see [36].

and convenient means of counting manifest expressions of words that fall into the meaning categories set out in one's dictionary." [38]

Of course, you want to proceed cautiously when making inferences *solely* from crude summary measures. They harbor potential problems. [39] For example, a legislator's

speech may be influenced by the *context* in which it was made, such as the preceding speech in the debate.

Another approach focuses more on meaning and underlying themes or **latent content**. This refers to the "deeper layers of meaning embedded in the document." [37] **Qualitative content analysis** "requires that coders

T A B L E 15.2
Three Approaches to Content Analysis

Approach	Focus	Computers?	Disadvantages
Quantitative	MANIFEST CONTENT: Frequency with which specified words and phrases appear in the material. (Can gather information on meanings of words and phrases under some conditions.)	CAN HELP. Can keep track of frequencies. Can show uses of key words or phrases in context. If dictionaries and software are used, can report frequencies of meanings.	1. Does not attend to *meanings* of words or phrases unless dictionaries and software used. 2. Grammatical content of messages ignored.
Qualitative	LATENT CONTENT: Trained raters, using codebooks, make judgements regarding the frequency with which certain themes occur.	Not used except for inputting data generated by the coders.	1. Time-consuming. 2. Labor intensive. 3. May be difficult to obtain high levels of inter-rater reliability. 4. Grammatical content of messages ignored.
Linguistic Content Analysis	LATENT CONTENT AND GRAMMAR: Meanings of words, and relations between meanings.	REQUIRED	Requires some background in linguistics.

make impressionistic judgements about the phenomena under investigation. Objectivity is maintained through rigorous sampling and training/supervising of coders." [38] For example, in a qualitative content analysis you might have coders read speeches and rate each speech on how strong the theme of equity was in each. From such coding you can develop **frequency indices**—reports on how often something occurs—**favorable vs. unfavorable indices**—showing if the remarks favor a topic—and **intensity indices**—reports on how intensely a view is expressed.

Experts have disagreed on the merits of latent vs. manifest coding. [40] It appears that there are advantages and disadvantages to each approach. [41] Manifest codes can be learned quickly by coders and are likely to yield higher levels of interrater reliability. They produce ratio-level measures, thereby

allowing powerful quantitative techniques to be applied. By contrast, with latent, thematic codes, recorder training is more laborious and time-consuming, levels of interrater reliability are likely to be lower, and measurement is likely to be at the ordinal level. Nevertheless, the resulting categories may be "closer" in spirit to the concepts the researcher wishes to assess; the produced variables may represent more satisfactory operationalizations of concepts. Perhaps the best approach, if practicable in the situation, is to have recorders do *both* manifest and latent coding. Most modern content analysts do this.

Blending elements of each of the above is **linguistic content analysis**. Phrases are coded into different linguistic categories. The result is a quantitative description of texts that not only classifies words into meaning categories, but also portrays the *relations between words*. [38] Since it allows researchers to consider grammar as well as words in their analyses, some researchers feel the approach superior to the preceding two. [38] For example, you might have a program examine speeches, observing what specific groups were mentioned as the object in prepositional phrases talking about "equity" and "fairness."

Steps in the Process[1]

Data Making The processes of *defining units*, *selecting units*, and *defining coding categories and procedures* are all involved in the larger task of **data making**: producing the elements you will analyze. Let's go through each of these processes.

Unitizing   "The first task of any empirical research is to decide what is to be observed, recorded, and thereafter considered a datum." [42] The process of defining your units of analysis is called **unitizing**.

For example, look at the material you have culled from the debates in the state legislature surrounding the implementation and abolition of mandatory sentencing guidelines. What is your unit of analysis: legislators? speeches? votes? paragraphs in a debate or in material read in to the record? Sentences? Words?

Content analysts typically attend to three levels of units. At the grossest level they want to define *units that are independent of one another*; these are called **sampling units**. They are free, intact entities, and there are no systematic relationships between them.

Consider your material from the public record of the debates. Are the separate words

in a speech or in material read in independent of one another? Certainly not. You might think likewise for sentences and paragraphs. How about whole speeches?

What a legislator says in a speech on one day on topic X is likely to be related to what she says the next day on topic X. How about using a legislator as a sampling unit? The different legislators, although affiliated with one party or another, are not systematically constrained by one another. So the population of sampling units that you want to begin with are all of the state legislators.

Next you must decide what are the units from which you will record information—the **recording units**. You cannot directly code up legislators; they are too large and too complex as units of description. You can, however, code up attributes of their speeches.

Your final decision on units is to decide on **context units**. The meaning of a word or sentence or paragraph or speech is codetermined by the context in which it appears as well as its content. In the material here, a speech vigorously decrying the costs of the mandatory sentencing guidelines can be given after 10 other similar speeches expressing the same views, or after 10 other speeches espousing opposite views. When coding the speech in question, you may want to take its context into account. A context unit is larger than the recording unit.

In defining all three of these types of units, you want to make decisions that will result in meaningful units, well suited to your research purposes, that can be efficiently and reliably identified. [43]

Sampling   Your first step is to draw your sample of legislators. You may use a SRS, an interval sampling procedure, a sample stratified by political party, or whatever best suits your needs.

You may need to do more than one level of sampling. If legislators gave many speeches,

---

[1] The steps described here follow Krippendorf.

you may need to sample speeches within legislators, simply to reduce your workload. As long as you use probability sampling procedures at all stages in the sampling, you will be justified in inferring back to your population of cases.

Recording   Now you come to the last step in data making: deciding what features of the data you want to code up and how to do it. You have selected your sample of legislators, and for each you have sampled speeches. Now you need to decide *who* will examine the material, *what* they will extract from the material, and *how* they will record their observations and reactions. In making these decisions you may wish to proceed as follows.

First, *familiarize yourself with the materials and the issues.* You may want to read some speeches that were not sampled to get a "feel" for the kinds of issues that crop up. You also may want to do outside reading on these issues to get a sense of important concerns.

Second, *establish initial coding categories.* What are the features that your recorders will be looking for in the texts they consider? You may want to include coding categories for both manifest and latent content. For coding of manifest content you will need to define a dictionary of words and/or phrases you want counted, and define the synonyms for each term. Your recorders can then examine the texts and tally up the frequencies with which the chosen words and phrases, and their defined synonyms, appear.

Coding of latent content requires analyzing the underlying themes or meanings behind words or phrases. For example, you might define themes such as the following based on your preliminary readings:

Taxpayers should not be burdened with any additional costs, no matter what the need.

Social goals such as equity or punishment proportional to the crime are less important than holding down taxpayer costs.

The sentencing guidelines have failed because they were not properly implemented or understood by the judges themselves.

Social goals, such as equity or punishment proportional to the crime, are more important than holding down taxpayer costs.

Mandatory sentencing guidelines have no deterrent effect on potential offenders, and thus no effect on the crime rate.

You would need to define each theme carefully, providing numerous and varied examples of each. Recorders could decide if each theme was present not at all, somewhat, or to a great degree in each speech examined. If you have the expertise, you also could pursue the third possibility mentioned at the beginning of the chapter: linguistic content analysis.

Third, you will need to select recorders and train them. All of the training and instructional materials, and procedures, should be standardized and written down so they can be replicated if need be. So you prepare your materials, coax two coworkers in your law office to assist you in this enterprise, with various promises (pizza discount coupons?) and go through training procedures.

As a result of the training you may find that you have to modify some of your definitions or procedures. For example, you may have to drop some latent codes because the recorders are unable to code text reliably for them. Or you may have to redefine your units. You may find that thematic codes can be reliably applied to *paragraphs* in speeches, but not to whole speeches.

Naturally, there will be some situations where you might want to use computers to do the actual recording. If your documents are already in machine-readable format, i.e.,

ASCII text format, or scannable, or short enough so that data entry will not take until the end of the century (what year is this, anyway?), you are in luck. You can use available software, instead of coders, for assessing manifest or latent content.

Continuing with the human coder scenario: you are ready to carry out the *recording* of data. You have 20 final manifest codes and 10 final latent codes. For each code or variable the recorder examines a paragraph and decides the extent to which it is present. For the manifest codes this is just a counting task. For each latent code more sophisticated judgement is required. A fourfold scale such as the following may be used [44]:

(1)	(2)	(3)	(4)
absent	barely ascertainable	present but not predominant	predominant

Data Reduction   The data are in. Your recorders have coded an average of 3.5 speeches for each of your 50 sampled legislators; all of the results of the coding have been entered onto code sheets and keypunched into a computer file. (Your recorders also never want to eat another pizza.) You now begin the process of examining how the different codes relate to one another, and how well coders agree with one another when using different codes. In this data reduction process you want to examine three matters:

1. Eliminate codes with unacceptably low interrater reliability. If recorders cannot agree on how to use a variable, it is not objective enough and should be dropped.
2. Examine how your variables interrelate in order to create summary indexes. If four variables reflecting the same concept correlate strongly with one another, add them up into an index. To standardize each variable you probably want to convert observed scores to z scores before creating the index.
3. Eliminate *redundant variables*. If scores from two variables correlate *too* highly with one another ($r > .90$) they both measure almost the same thing. If so you can eliminate one.

Analysis and Inference   The final steps are to analyze your data and make inferences.[2]

Estimates: How Often Did a Theme Occur?   You might be interested in making some estimates based on your data. For example, how often did the term *racial disparity* occur during the debates surrounding the passage of the sentencing guidelines, and the repeal of the sentencing guidelines?

Your results might show that this manifest content occurred more frequently in the debates surrounding the implementation of the guidelines (7.6 times/speech) than in the debates surrounding their abolition (5.3 times/speech)

To further explore the variables based on the manifest content, you might examine a sample of paragraphs where the key term occurs. You might find, for example, that in the second series of debates the term co-occurred often with *other* themes such "as fitting punishment" and "rationalizing the criminal justice system." Orators, however,

---

[2] I have skipped the step that Krippendorf calls developing "constructs for inference" (Chapter 9). It is primarily concerned with detailing how the data items you have coded are influenced by the surrounding context of the data items. This is not a necessary step.

often lumped these themes together as laudable goals that the state, unfortunately, could not afford. In other words, in the second series of debate the legislators paid "lip service" to the goal of equity. It was one of several worthwhile goals, goals they were prevented from pursuing because of current fiscal conditions.

Linking Themes As a second goal you might use your content analysis to explore *linkages* among constructs. For example, you might hypothesize that the levels of concern for fair, efficient criminal justice system functioning have a negative correlation with concerns about costs to taxpayers. You build two indexes. One combines several themes (latent codes) related to *fair, efficient criminal justice system processing*. The other combines several latent codes concerned with *costs and taxpayer burdens*. You construct an average score on each sampled legislator's sampled speech, for each index, during the two series of debates. You examine the correlations between these two themes across the speeches of all the legislators. You also decide to "break out" your results by party affiliation, since your reading in this area suggests it may be an important variable.

You find that speeches delivered by Democratic legislators during the implementation debates clearly showed the expected inverse relationship. (e.g., $r = -.76$). So too did the speeches delivered by the Republican legislators at this time ($r = -.62$). If the speech emphasized criminal justice system goals, it deemphasized costs.

In the debates surrounding the abolition of the sentencing guidelines matters looked the same for the Republicans. Their speeches still showed an inverse relation between the two themes ($r = -.58$). Matters were different, however, for speeches delivered by Democratic legislators. The expected inverse rela-

tionship has disappeared, and become slightly positive ($r = +.39$). These legislators delivered speeches that sometimes emphasized both themes, and sometimes emphasized neither. You wonder if, in this latter series of debates, the Democratic legislators were trying to show that they were sensitive to *both* socially laudable goals of improving criminal justice system functioning, *and* keeping down taxpayer costs.

Linking Content Analysis to Other Methods You also could look at the results of your content analysis as a means of *corroborating* parameter estimates or hypothesis tests deriving from other methodologies. In the hypothetical example here, you might have access to statewide surveys that also asked questions about the sentencing guidelines. Or, you may examine media coverage of the issues to see how it reported the issues during the periods surrounding the two debates. [e.g., 35]

Sidelight on Computers

In most social science fields, criminal justice included, computers have not been used extensively for sophisticated "word crunching" purposes. [45] Until recently the types of programs most widely used were of two varieties. "General Inquirer" programs, available since the 1960s, simply retrieved key words and displayed them. "Key Word In Context" (KWIC) programs allowed for analysis of the context in which key words appeared. [46, 47]

More recently there have been significant advances on two fronts. Computer programs that use "dictionaries" to link manifest content of words and phrases to meaning have improved significantly. In addition, programs for linguistic content analysis also have become more powerful. These latter programs start to make sense of the grammar inherent in text. [38, 48]

ARCHIVAL ANALYSIS AND HISTORICAL CRIMINOLOGY

Let me tell you about a jail. Inmates' wives and family members may come and stay for as long as they like. The family members must simply pay a modest fee. Even inmates' pets may come and stay! Authorities allow nonfamily visitors to enter any time of day or night. They can bring in beer, wine, or spirits if they wish. Inmates can order a wide variety of food. They pay for it, and it is brought. An alehouse in the jail is open until late at night. "Ladies of the street" may visit prisoners lacking female companionship. Prisoners maintain their own system of self-government. Officers in this system are elected by fellow inmates in free elections.

Does this sound like science fiction? Or like something that could only be true in an extremely progressive country? Read on.

This splendid facility also has a hellish side. Jailkeepers extort money from prisoners. The jail is chronically overcrowded. Designed to house 150 inmates comfortably, its population usually hovers above 275. Drunkenness is widespread. Brawling and fighting gets so out of hand the neighbors frequently complain about the commotion. The filth in many locations in the facility is truly appalling. Jail guards chronically steal incoming gifts intended for prisoners.

Sound barbaric?

The place? Newgate gaol [jail], the main jail in London, in the early 1700s. [49] This example of a major metropolitan jail over 250 years ago reveals stark contrasts with today's jails in the U.S. and the UK. Nonetheless, it also points toward continuities in some jail conditions over the past couple of centuries, such as overcrowding.

Historical criminologists analyze **archival material** and **historical documents** in order to learn about "the way things were" in criminal justice. Their purpose is always partly descriptive and exploratory. Researchers aspire to characterize how things were at a different time. But in addition, they explain, pointing out the factors leading to the situations observed. Therefore, they also make causal propositions and attempt to assess their validity.

Benefits of Historical Criminology

Lay Myths to Rest   Perhaps the most valuable consequence of historical research is that it helps us put aside persistent myths about the way things were. [50] By doing so it may render untenable some explanations for current phenomena, which rely upon these misconceptions. Consider some examples.

Frontier Traditions Explain Why We Are a Violent and Lawless People   "Popular wisdom says that generations of living on and conquering frontiers have made Americans a violent and lawless people. Popular wisdom is wrong." [51] McGrath investigated violence levels in two frontier mining towns in the 1800s. He found that although homicide levels were high, only willing combatants were usually involved in such incidents. Levels of robbery, burglary, larceny, rape, and juvenile crime were extremely low. Potential offenders were deterred from crime by the armed citizenry and the effectiveness of vigilante groups. The Wild West was not so wild.

Vigilantism Was a Frontier Tradition   Not so; vigilantism, indigenous to the United States, emerged well before the establishment of the frontier following the Civil War. It was present in places like South Carolina before the American Revolution. [52] Leaders of such groups were not marginal members of society. Often they were prominent business leaders.

Participants in Illegal Enterprises Enjoy Violence for Its Own Sake Historically, illegal entrepreneurs have sought to keep violence to a minimal level. Violence that did arise from these enterprises was spawned by the nature of the enterprise itself. [53] For example, with bootlegging in the 1920s, the product and transportation arrangements made hijacking a real possibility, against which entrepreneurs protected themselves. Further, the economics of liquor wholesaling itself spurred some violence. [54] Despite these "built-in" factors encouraging violence, leaders in these enterprises knew that violence was also bad for business. It drew newspaper attention to their activities and encouraged reform efforts. Therefore, they developed local, regional, and even international cooperative arrangements to check violence.

Provide Perspective on Current Situation
Besides laying to rest stubborn falsehoods about the past, historical research also can provide perspective on the current situation. It can show us how present dynamics and conditions are similar to, or different from, those of various past periods. We can view current features of crime and criminal justice functioning in a broader context. The work done by historical criminologists on homicide proves instructive in this regard.

Homicide Levels in Historical Context Over the past quarter century increasing homicide levels in the U.S. have worried the public and officials alike. These levels rose sharply from 1965 until about 1980. (See Figure 15.1) Many have complained about living in an increasingly violent society.

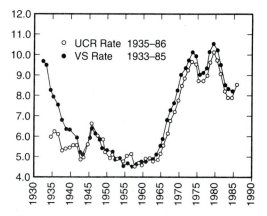

FIGURE 15.1
U.S. homicide rates, 1933–1986, per 100,000, from two sources The Vital Statistics are collected by the National Center for Health Statistics. The Uniform Crime Reports are collected by the FBI from local police departments. Vital Statistics figures are higher because they are based on the medical definition of *homicide*, "the intentional taking of another's life, while UCR uses the legal definition." Victims of police shootings are included in the VS figure but not the UCR figures. [55] *Source*. Zahn, M.A. (1989): Homicide in the twentieth century: Trends, types and causes. In: *Violence in America: The History of Crime*. Vol. 1. (Ed: Gurr, T.R.) Sage, Newbury Park, CA, pp. 216–234.

This dramatic upsurge in homicide rates, however, is not the first this country has seen. In the 1850s, and again after the Civil War, this country witnessed dramatic increases in homicides. [56, 57] Vital statistics data (Figure 15.1) also show that the homicide rate was high in the early 1930s and declined dramatically thereafter. In short there is historical precedent for the noticeable homicide increase witnessed between 1965 and 1980.

Turning to England, the evidence points toward long-term declines in homicide rates. Ted Gurr has argued that homicide rates in medieval England were *10 times higher* than the rates in modern England! [56] "The seemingly high rates of homicide in early nineteenth and late twentieth century London were actually very low when contrasted with the more distant historical period." [56] Over time, he has suggested, the change in homicide rates in England has formed a distended *U*, declining gradually for a long time, and then increasing slightly of late. See Figure 15.2.

Changes in the Nature of Homicide It is not only *levels* of homicide that have changed in the U.K. in the last several hundred years. The *nature* of homicides has also noticeably changed over that period. In medieval times homicides most often occurred among groups of acquaintances, growing out of quarrels among neighbors; bandits or robbers were charged in less than 20 percent of the instances. [56] It was a group affair resulting from brawling rather than one-on-one attacks. In 18th century England infanticide was the commonest form of homicide. [58] Excluding infanticide, most homicides were committed within the family.

In sum, the historical enterprise can show how current situations have precedence, and thus represent continuities with the past; it also can reveal how matters have changed over time.

Raise New Puzzles Lastly, historical research can raise new and puzzling questions. For example, if, historically in England and in this country, violence rates increase following a war, why is this necessarily the case? [59, 56] To take another example: Why did African American and White U.S. urban homicide rates progressively diverge starting in the late 1800s? [56] This type of research reveals features of history requiring explanation.

The Historical Method

Historical research is characterized by three features: attention to a period that is so dis-

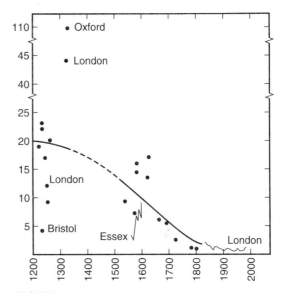

FIGURE 15.2
Homicide rates per 100,000 population in English counties and cities, 1200–1970. *Source*. Figure 1.2, p. 33. Gurr, T. R. (1989), Historical trends in violent crime: Europe and the United States. In: *Violence in America: The History of Crime*. Vol. 1. (Ed., Gurr, T. R.) Sage, Newbury Park, CA, pp. 21–54.

tant, archival materials are the main source of information; use of these archival materials; and careful interpretations of archival materials based on an understanding of the context in which the materials were generated.

Living Individuals Not Main Source Historical researchers rely upon **archives**— repositories of materials generated during the period under examination. These archives may be formal documents, or official records of proceedings, or they may be informal documents such as letters.

Criminal justice researchers have available to them many archival sources of information from different portions of the criminal justice system. *Court records* have been extensively examined for the purposes of understanding crime and violence levels in English locales since the 1500s. Records for a variety of courts, including assizes and manor courts, are available in some locales for that time. Historians have examined the number of people indicted for various crimes by these courts in different locales. [e.g., 60] *Institutional records* in England for places such as jails begin to be available later. Such records reveal the overcrowding, described at the beginning of the section, at Newgate jail in the early 18th century.

Police records in the U.S. present problems for the investigator who wishes to go back more than 50 years. "Municipal police forces in the 19th and early 20th centuries were too busy dealing with offenses to count them reliably, and no national agency was directed to collect comprehensive crime statistics until 1933 . . . moreover it took years after 1933 for the FBI to establish standard guidelines for classifying and counting offenses and to secure cooperation of thousands of local police forces." [56]

Information about crime is available from many sources *outside* the criminal justice system. In the U.S., historical researchers have relied heavily upon **newspaper accounts** of crime, and **coroner records**. Of course each of these has its limitations. The distortions of crime reporting discussed in the last box suggest important limitations of the former. Box 15.3 describes some problems with the latter.

Coming to the Archival Material With Perspective If you are a historical researcher you may rely heavily upon archived material from courts, coroners, or newspapers, but you do *not* take the material at face value. You *seek to understand the context in which that material was generated, and how that context influenced what was recorded.* [61] "Careful study of the sources and their historical and institutional context is necessary to identify and screen out the potentially misleading effects of these factors on long-term trends." [56] The historical researcher never takes the data at face value. By doing so he avoids **naive quantification**.

BOX 15.3

The Problems with Establishing How Someone Died

You probably think that coroner's records would be straightforward and reliable sources of information about how a person died, right? Think again.

The practices in a coroner's office affect what the coroner reports. In offices where the personnel were more qualified, investigations were more thorough. Marge Zahn details some problems confronting the historical criminologist hoping to rely on coroner's records.

For example the coroner, an appointed or elected official, is responsible for learning cause and/or manner of death. Coroners, in contrast to medical examiners, are not required to have medical training. In some places the only requirement for holding office is that they be of legal age to hold office. Early in this century, following late 19th century practice, a fee-for-service system among coroners directly affected their reporting of homicides. Coroners received a set fee for each death that they investigated and for which they established cause of death. The fee paid was the same no matter how much difficulty the case involved and the fee was, in cases of murder, often to be collected from the convicted offender. If, then, it was likely that the offender could not be found, as when a victim [was found] with a slit throat on the highway, or if the victim was an infant, these deaths were not likely to be reported as homicides but rather as a ruptured aorta, in the case of the slit throat, and suffocation for the infant. [55]

The Challenges
of the Historical Approach

Now that you have some sense of what historical criminologists are about, let's consider the special challenges posed by the materials they use, and how they meet these challenges. These challenges may pose threats to the conclusions researchers wish to draw.

The threat to validity most likely when examining data series extending over a long time, is **instrumentation**. [62] The nature of what the recording instrument counts changes over time. These **changes in recording practices** can be confused with actual changes in the volume or type of incident being recorded. The threat of instrumentation can arise for three different reasons.

The *categories* of the event itself may change. For example, during some periods of English history infanticide was classified as homicide; during other times it was recorded separately. [56] Vital statistics, before 1968, did not allow the classification "undetermined" if a coroner could not decide whether a death was due to accident or homicide. [55]

A related development is that the underlying legal *definition* also may change over time. For example, in English law there was no separate legal definition of manslaughter until the 16th century. [56]

There may be changes in *reporting practices*. For example, crime reporting in London changed significantly after a metropolitan police force was established in 1829. [63] Or, to take another example, as the 19th century progressed, coroners and police in both the U.S. and England became more adept at discriminating between death from unnatural causes, and death from homicide. Thus, more homicide cases came to their attention. [56]

There may be changes in **social tolerance** for various crimes. In the early part of this century, in some U.S. cities, public outrage over deaths due to autos led to drivers being prosecuted for homicide instead of vehicular manslaughter. [50] "As late as 1926, 23 trolley, truck and auto operators in Philadelphia were tried for murder in cases that would now be categorized as vehicular manslaughter." [56] Not surprisingly, Detroit, the city with the most cars in the 1910s, had the highest homicide rate in the late 1910s.

In addition to the threat of instrumentation, the scientific quality of many historical studies is threatened by the *fragmentary* nature of the data. All periods or all locations may not be covered by the archival material. [64] Consequently the researcher may not be warranted in generalizing her results *to* the population of interest. This is a particular problem with medieval studies of violent crime in England. [56] Records cover only some counties and some years. In the U.S., national crime data became available only after 1933, when the FBI began collecting information for the Uniform Crime Reports. UCR reports did not become reliable themselves until later in that decade.

Coping with the Challenges

How do historical researchers cope with these challenges? They respond in several ways. [56]

Focus on the Crimes Least Likely to Be Influenced by Changes in Reporting Practices, Social Tolerance, and Definitional Changes Historians of crime have concentrated largely on *homicide*. They don't do this because of a ghoulish character streak.

Homicide is the serious crime least likely to be influenced by the instrumentation changes discussed above. Definitions of this crime, and social tolerance of it, are both likely to vary less over a long period than would be the case for other crimes. Additionally, there are likely to be fewer variations in reporting practices.

This is not to say that homicide does not have instrumentation-related problems. The seriousness of these problems, however, is less than it is with other crimes.

Obtain Multiple Indicators of the Same Phenomenon from Different Sources In essence this is an effort to establish construct validity. If measures based on police records agree with measures based on independent, separate methods, such as coroner's records, then you have more confidence that, over time, the measures are reflecting variations in the same underlying concept. If the measures *diverge* over time, one of them may have been unduly influenced by instrumentation problems. Convergence between measures derived from different stages of criminal justice processing (e.g., indictments for homicide and executions for homicide) also would support construct validation efforts.

Box 15.4 details the efforts by one researcher to use multiple measures from two sources.

Look for Similar Trends in Different Sites. Historical researchers try to establish external validity of trends observed by attempting to replicate them in different cities or regions. For example, McGrath's work on frontier towns used information from two towns in different states. [51] Roger Lane examined homicide trends in both New York City and Philadelphia for the period 1899–1933. [50]

Of course, if divergent trends are noted in two locales, this does not necessarily cast doubt on the "reality" of either trend. It may

BOX 15.4

Coroners Records and Newspaper Reports

Eric Monkkonen examined homicides in New York City and other major U.S. cities during the latter half of the 19th century. [65] He reports in detail the results of trying to square newspaper reports with coroner records. Although coroners' records may be a reliable source of counts in the 20th century, they were not in the mid-19th century. Coroner records provided an undercounting of homicide because coroner's juries were likely to acquit, "on the basis of Victorian sentiment." [p. 96]

For the year 1865 Monkkonen counted homicides in New York City using the *New York Times Index*, and the coroner's reports. The *Times Index* reported 47, the Coroner's Report 56. He used name-by-name comparisons to find when both sources reported a case. He could match 35 cases. He concludes that the newspaper underreported homicides more than did the coroner's report; neither, however, was a reliable sole source of information about homicides in the city.

To do an individual case analysis, he resorted to reading the daily paper for 14 of the years between 1851 and 1869, and gathered information on 734 homicides. But even the paper, he recognizes, may have included some underreporting as crime news was displaced by war news.[3] The paper also may have displayed some bias, tending to report homicides of higher status persons while overlooking homicides of lower status persons.

---

[3] Note how this same pattern was revealed in analyses of modern day crime reporting. See Box 15.1.

simply mean that different trends took place in the different locales.

Look for Similar Trends with Linked Pairs of Offenses. You may have reasons to expect that two different offenses will vary together because there are similarities in the nature of the offenses, e.g., robberies and assaults, or homicides and assaults. If you observe similar trends for the pairs of offenses, you have evidence that the pattern has external validity at least across different types of crimes.

Again, a failure to observe parallel trends does *not* necessarily cast aspersions on either trend. The trends may diverge because of differences in the two types of offenses. For example, Neil Weiner and Marge Zahn constructed arrest *rates* for Philadelphia for the period 1857–1980. They verified that murder arrest rates and firearms violation arrest rates, over time, moved together after the turn of the century. The linkage reinforces the idea that availability of firearms in "emotionally volatile settings" contributes to homicides. [57, p. 116]

You can view efforts such as those described above, focusing on multiple sources or multiple crimes, as attempts to avoid naive quantification. [66] Researchers realize they must count the phenomena, but also recognize, for a host of reasons, that whatever counts they generate may be suspect. By taking the above steps, they can learn more about the limitations of their data and understand the context within which they were generated.

UNOBTRUSIVE MEASURES AND BENCHMARKS OF SCIENTIFIC QUALITY

In general, it is possible for all of the methods discussed in this chapter—on-site assessments, content analysis, and archival analysis—to generate variables with high reliability. Interrater or interobserver reliability is probably the most significant reliability is-

sue. Use of multiple raters, and/or multiple sites, and refinement of assessment procedures as needed, will result in acceptable quality. For archival analyses use of multiple sites, and/or multiple data sources may help establish external validity.

Construct validity is a key issue for all three of these tools. Multiple methods, assessments of correlations across items, and multiple operationalizations of a construct help establish construct validity.

Some of the methods discussed here have been faulted for low quality. In the case of content analysis, for example, some lament it has been wedged between qualitative and quantitative analysis into a "methodological ghetto." [41] This isolation has resulted in an underutilization of the methodology and low-quality studies. Nonetheless, the standards of scientific quality *can* be applied to content analysis studies. Such studies *can* have quite respectable "scores" on these benchmarks. [41] There are no inherent limits to the scientific quality of studies based on content analysis.

HOLMES AND EINSTEIN

On-site assessments and content analysis are well suited to Holmes's and Einstein's mode of inquiry; historical analysis is only moderately well suited to these purposes. All three sets of tools provide opportunities for discovery. Nevertheless, in this respect archival analysis is probably more limited than the other two because the data sources are more confining.

All three approaches can be used for serious hypothesis testing. Again, however, archival analysis is more restricted in this respect than the other two. Given the narrow range of materials with which historical criminologists must work, it can be extremely difficult for them to eliminate all possible confounding factors interfering with their central hypothesis of interest.

SUMMARY OF MAIN POINTS

- Unobtrusive measures allow researchers to study individuals without their knowledge and in a way that does not influence individuals.
- On-site assessments assess features of the physical and behavioral environment.
- Content analysis is used to analyze linguistic messages and make statistical inferences from those materials.
- Researchers analyze archival materials to understand how crime and criminal justice in the remote past were similar to, or different from, current-day dynamics.

ples. *Flex-Text-RES* counts and displays words and phrases (manifest content). It is available from Text Analysis Service Corporation (1221 Mamie Eisenhower, Boone, IA 50036). *The Ethnographer* displays text and phrases from field notes or other sources. It is available from Qualis Research Associates (PO Box 2240, Corvallis, OR 97339). *PLCA (Program for Linguistic Content Analysis)* analyzes meanings and grammar (latent content; linguistic content). It is available from MetaText, Inc. (1221 Mamie Eisenhower, Boone, IA 50036). All these programs run on IBM PCs with 512K or more RAM. Some require a hard disk.

SUGGESTED READINGS

You will find Robert Philip Weber's *Basic content analysis* (Sage, 1985) an excellent introduction to content analysis.

I recommend two volumes on the history of urban policing. Roger Lane's *Policing the city—Boston 1822–1885* provides a narrative history of the developments influencing the Boston Police Department. Eric Monkkonen's *Police in urban America 1860–1920* takes a more statistical approach. He examines arrest rates in 23 cities over the period. [67, 68] Both authors argue that there was a transformation in the role of policing in the latter part of the 19th century. Welfare-related functions became less important as crime control became more important. As Monkkonen puts it, there was a shift from class control to crime control.

AVAILABLE SOFTWARE FOR CONTENT ANALYSIS[4]

Several currently available programs provide analyses of linguistic data. Here are some exam-

KEY TERMS

accretion
archival material
archival analysis
archives
behavioral observation
changes in recording practices
content analysis
context units
data making
defensible space features
dictionary
environmental criminology
erosion
favorable vs. unfavorable indices
frequency indices
historical documents
instrumentation
intensity indices
latent content
linguistic content analysis
manifest content
naive quantification
nonreactive
on-site assessment
physical design
physical traces
prisonization

---

[4] The author and the publisher do not "recommend" these programs in any way. No warranty of these programs is expressed or implied. We do not guarantee that the information about these programs is completely correct.

qualitative content analysis
quantitative content analysis
recording units
sampling units
site features
situational crime prevention
social tolerance
territorial markers
unitizing
unobtrusive

REFERENCES

1. Webb, E., *et al.* (1966) *Unobtrusive measures*, McNally, Chicago.

2. Webb, E., Campbell, D., Schwartz, R., Sechrest, L., and Grove, J. B. (1981) *Nonreactive measures in the social sciences*, Houghton Mifflin, Boston

3. Sechrest, L., ed. (1979) *Unobtrusive measurement today*, Jossey-Bass, San Francisco

4. McGrath, J. E., Martin, J., and Kulka, R. A. (1981) Some quasi-rules for making judgement calls in research. *American Behavioral Scientist* 25, 211–255

5. White, G. F. (1990) Neighborhood permeability and burglary rates. *Justice Quarterly* 7, 57–68

6. Clofas, J., and Cutshall, C. (1985) Unobtrusive research methods in criminal justice: Using graffiti in the reconstruction of institutional cultures. *Journal of Research in Crime and Delinquency* 22, 355–373

7. Wheeler, S. (1961) Socialization in correctional communities. *American Sociological Review* 26, 697–712

8. Ley, D., and Cybriwsky, R. (1974) Urban graffiti as territorial markers. *Annals of the Association of American Geographers* 64, 491–505

9. Austin, W. T., and Bates, F. L. (1974) Ethological indicators of dominance and territory in a human captive population. *Social Forces* 52, 447–455

10. Taylor, R. B., Gottfredson, S. D., and Brower, S. N. (1980) The defensibility of defensible space. In *Understanding crime* (Hirschi, T., and Gottfredson, M., eds). Beverly Hills, CA: Sage

11. Taylor, R. B., Gottfredson, S. D., and Brower, S. (1984) Block crime and fear: Local social ties and territorial functioning. *Journal of Research in Crime and Delinquency 21*, 303–331

12. Taylor, R. B. (1988) *Human territorial functioning*, Cambridge University Press, Cambridge, UK

13. Brantingham, P. J., and Brantingham, P. L., eds. (1981) *Environmental criminology*, Sage, Beverly Hills, CA

14. Clarke, R. V., ed. (1992) *Situational crime prevention*, Harrow and Heston, Albany, NY

15. Reiss, A. J., Jr. (1971) *The Police and the public*, Yale University Press, New Haven, CT

16. Bayley, D. H., and Garofalo, J. (1989) The Management of violence by police patrol officers. *Criminology 27*, 1–23

17. Holsti, O. R. (1969) *Content analysis for the social sciences and humanities*, Addison-Wesley, Reading, MA

18. Krippendorff, K. (1980) *Content analysis*, Sage, Beverly Hills, CA

19. Holsti, O. R. (1968) *Content analysis*. In *Handbook of social psychology*, 2nd ed., Vol. II (Lindsey, G., and Aronson, E., eds), pp. 596–692. Reading, MA: Addison-Wesley

20. Holsti, O. R. (1969) *Content analysis for the social sciences and humanities*, Addison-Wesley, Reading, MA, p. 14

21. Roberts, C. W. (1991) Content analysis. Workshop presented at the annual meetings of the American Sociological Association, Cincinnati, OH, August.

22. Holsti, O. R. (1969) *Content analysis for the social sciences and humanities*, Addison-Wesley, Reading, MA, p. 42.

23. David, P. R. (1974) *The world of the burglar*, University of New Mexico Press, Albuquerque, NM

24. Letkemann, P. (1973) *Crime as work*, Prentice-Hall, Englewood Cliffs, NJ.

25. Priyadarsini, S. (1984) Crime news in the newspapers: A Case study in Tamil Nadu, India. *Deviant Behavior 5*, 313–326

26. Ditton, J., and Duffy, J. (1983) Bias in the newspaper reporting of crime news. *British Journal of Criminology 23*, 159–165

27. Smith, S. J. (1984) Crime in the news. *British Journal of Criminology 24*, 289–295

28. Davis, F. J. (1952) Crime news in Colorado newspapers. *American Journal of Sociology 57*, 325–330

29. Sheley, J. F. (1981) Crime, crime news and crime views. *Public Opinion Q. 45*, 492–506

30. Graber, D. A. (1979) Is crime news coverage excessive? *Journal of Communication 28*, 81–92

31. Humphries, D. (1981) Serious crime, news coverage, and ideology. *Crime & Delinquency 27*, 191–205

32. King, P. (1987) Newspaper reporting, prosecution practice and the perceptions of urban crime: The Colchester crime wave of 1765. *Continuity and Change 2*, 423–454

33. Pritchard, D. (1986) Homicide and bargained justice: The Agenda-setting effect of crime news on prosecutors. *Public Opinion Quarterly 50*, 143–159

34. Heath, L. (1984) Impact of newspaper crime reports on fear of crime: Multi-methodological examination. *Journal of Personality and Social Psychology 47*, 263–276

35. Liska, A. E., and Baccaglini, W. (1990) Feeling safe by comparison: Crime in the newspapers. *Social Problems 37*, 360–374

36. Garofalo, J. (1981) Crime and the mass media: A selective review of the research. *Journal of Research in Crime and Delinquency 18*, 319–349

37. Holsti, O. R. (1969) *Content analysis for the social sciences and humanities*, Addison-Wesley, Reading, MA, p. 12

38. Roberts, C. W. (1991) Linguistic content analysis. In *Verstehen and pragmatism: Essays in interpretive sociology* (Helle, H. J., ed.). Frankfurt: Peter Lang

39. Krippendorff, K. (1980) *Content analysis*, Sage, Beverly Hills, CA, p. 42.

40. Holsti, O. R. (1969) *Content analysis for the social sciences and humanities*, Addison-Wesley, Reading, MA, p. 13.

41. Woodrum, E. (1984) "Mainstreaming" content analysis in the social sciences: Methodological advantages, obstacles, and solutions. *Social Science Research 13*, 1–19

42. Krippendorff, K. (1980) *Content analysis*, Sage, Beverly Hills, CA, p. 57

43. Krippendorff, K. (1980) *Content analysis*, Sage, Beverly Hills, CA, p. 64

44. Krippendorff, K. (1980) *Content analysis*, Sage, Beverly Hills, CA, p. 96

45. Dennis, D. L. (1984) "Word crunching:" An Annotated bibliography on computers and qualitative data analysis. *Qualitative Sociology 7*, 148–156

46. Wood, M. (1984) Using key-word-in-context concordance programs for qualitative and quantitative social research. *Journal of Applied Behavioral Science 20*, 289–307

47. Stone, P. J. (1975) Report on the workshop on content analysis in the social sciences. *Social Science Information 14*, 107–111

48. Roberts, C. W. (1989) Other than counting words: A Linguistic approach to content analysis. *Social Forces 68*, 147–177

49. Sheehan, W. J. (1977) Finding solace in Eighteenth Century Newgate. In *Crime in England 1550–1800* (Cockburn, J. S., ed), pp. 229–245. Princeton, NJ: Princeton University Press.

50. Lane, R. (1989) On the Social meaning of homicide trends in America. In *Violence in America: The history of crime*, Vol. 1 (Gurr, T. R., ed), pp. 55–79. Newbury Park, CA: Sage.

51. McGrath, R. D. (1989) Violence and lawlessness on the western frontier. In *Violence in America: The History of Crime*, Vol. 1 (Gurr, T. R., ed), pp. 122–145. Newbury Park, CA: Sage.

52. Brown, R. M. (1979) The American vigilante tradition. In *Violence in America: Historical and Comparative perspectives*, Revised ed. (Graham, H. D., and Gurr, T. R., eds), pp. 153–185. Beverly Hills, CA: Sage.

53. Haller, M. H. (1990) Illegal enterprise: A Theoretical and historical interpretation. *Criminology 28*, 207–235

54. Haller, M. H. (1989) Bootlegging: The Business and politics of violence. In *Violence in America: The History of Crime*, Vol. 1 (Gurr, T. R., ed), pp. 146–162. Newbury Park, CA: Sage.

55. Zahn, M. A. (1989) Homicide in the twentieth century: Trends, types and causes. In *Violence in America: The History of Crime*, Vol. 1 (Gurr, T. R., ed), pp. 216–234. Newbury Park, CA: Sage.

56. Gurr, T. R. (1989) Historical trends in violent crime: Europe and the United States. In *Violence in America: The History of Crime*, Vol. 1 (Gurr, T. R., ed), pp. 21–54. Newbury Park, CA: Sage.

57. Weiner, N. A., and Zahn, M. A. (1989) Vio-

lence arrests in the city: The Philadelphia story, 1857–1980. In *Violence in America: The History of Crime*, Vol. 1 (Gurr, T. R., ed), pp. 102–121. Newbury Park, CA: Sage.

58. Emsley, C. (1987) *Crime and society in England, 1750–1900*, Longman, New York, p. 38

59. Emsley, C. (1987) *Crime and society in England, 1750–1900*, Longman, New York, p. 29

60. Cockburn, J. S. (1977) The Nature and incidence of crime in England 1559–1625: A Preliminary survey. In *Crime in England 1550–1800* (Cockburn, J. S., ed), pp. 49–71. Princeton University Press, Princeton, NJ.

61. Sharpe, J. A. (1984) *Crime in early modern England 1550–1750*, Longman, New York, p. 15

62. Cook, T. D., and Campbell, D. T. (1979) *Quasi-experimentation*, Rand-McNally, Chicago, p. 52

63. Emsley, C. (1987) *Crime and society in England, 1750–1900*, Longman, New York

64. Emsley, C. (1987) *Crime and society in England, 1750–1900*, Longman, New York, p. 26

65. Monkkonen, E. H. (1989) Diverging homicide rates: England and the United States, 1857–1950. In *Violence in America: The history of crime*, Vol. 1 (Gurr, T. R., ed), pp. 80–101. Newbury Park, CA: Sage.

66. Sharpe, J. A. (1984) *Crime in early modern England 1550–1750*, Longman, New York, p. 14

67. Monkkonen, E. H. (1981) *Police in urban America, 1860–1920*, Cambridge University Press, Cambridge, UK

68. Lane, R. (1967) *Policing the city: Boston 1822–1885*, Harvard University Press, Cambridge, MA

SOME NEWER APPROACHES IN CRIMINAL JUSTICE: META-ANALYSIS AND COMPUTER SIMULATIONS

FOCUS

In this chapter you focus on two new research tools: meta-analysis and computer simulations. Meta-analysis allows researchers to "add up" studies in an area. Computer simulations allow researchers to model real or imagined dynamic processes. Theorists and policy makers alike have strong interests in these tools.

In this chapter you find information about two "newer" approaches in criminal justice research. I label them "newer" for the following reason. Meta-analysis and simulations have drawn significant interest from criminal justice researchers in just the last 20 years.

The first tool you will examine is meta-analysis. If you have a series of studies on the same topic, you can systematically "add up" results across them to get a total estimate of findings. The second tool is computer simulations. With these simulations researchers and policy makers estimate how complex criminal justice processes work, and gauge the impact of policies before carrying them out.[1]

Although "newer," these two tools are accessible to a beginning researcher such as yourself. To do a meta-analysis, all you need is a handful of studies on a particular topic, and a hand calculator. To make a computer simulation, all you need is a microcomputer and a spreadsheet program. I strongly encourage you to get involved with these two techniques. You will become comfortable with them quickly. You also will appreciate, first-hand, the capabilities these techniques provide.

META-ANALYSIS

Meta-analysis and Other Approaches to Summarizing

Primary, Secondary, and Meta-Analysis Speaking generally, data analysis can be categorized into one of three types. [1] (1) In **primary data analysis** the researcher collects data and examines them for the first time. (2) In **secondary data analysis** the original researcher, or another researcher who has gained access to the data set, reanalyzes them. Secondary analysis is popular in criminal justice, political science, and sociology, because so many data sets are publicly available through the Inter-University Consortium for Political and Social Research. [2] (3)

---

[1] Social scientists, especially social psychologists, have been using human simulations for several decades. For example, they might ask college students to play the role of mock jurors, or high school students to play the part of prison guards. In this chapter, however, we deal only with *computer* simulations.

In **meta-analysis** you combine, add up, or aggregate results from several independent studies. You *integrate* the findings. You learn what they 'say' when you add up all the results. Psychologists were the first to develop meta-analytic procedures [3, 4]

Meta-Analysis Contrasted with Other Approaches to Summarizing   You might wonder: "Why get so fancy? Why not just read the different studies on a topic and summarize the weight of the evidence? In other words, why not just do a *literature review* on a problem of interest?"

A standard literature review summarizing the results of several studies has limitations. [5] The conclusions may reflect the quirks of the reviewer as much as the actual data in the studies themselves. In addition, such reviews often ignore the strength of the relationship between an independent variable (e.g., unemployment) and a dependent variable (e.g., crime). It is one thing to say whether a relationship exists, another to say how strong that link is. Finally, in such a review it is difficult for the reviewer to match exactly the weight of the evidence with the force of her conclusions. It is hard to make generalizations closely tailored to the features of the evidence.

You might reply: "If I cannot do a standard literature review, why not let me simply tally up the results of different studies? I can observe how many see a relationship and how many do not."

This approach is the **voting** or **ballot box approach** to summarizing research. You tally up how many studies "voted" "yes" on a question and how many "voted" "no."

Ted Chiricos [6] used this approach to summarize the results from 63 studies completed since 1960 that examined the relationship between unemployment and crime (U–C). (See Table 16.1.) When he considered simply the *directions* of the findings he found

the following. "[F]or all crimes combined the U–C relationship is three times more likely to be positive than negative" (75% vs. 25%) (p. 192). The number of studies finding that more unemployment went with more crime was three times larger than the number of studies saying that more unemployment was accompanied by less crime.

When he looked only at studies finding a statistically significant correlation—one that would not be expected by chance—the evidence was even more overwhelmingly in favor of a positive relationship between unemployment and crime. The number of studies finding a statistically significant positive relationship (more unemployment $\rightarrow$ more crime) was 31; the number finding a significant negative relationship (more unemployment $\rightarrow$ less crime) was 2. Further analyses showed that the strength of the unemployment–crime connection was *conditional*. In other words, it depended on other conditions such as the type of crime and the period.

The ballot box approach provides a method for summarizing the literature in an area that is more systematic than a standard literature review. Despite this improvement, it still does not answer an important question: How strong is the relationship between the independent variable and the dependent variable? To answer this question we turn to meta-analysis.

In short, meta-analysis, as compared to other summarizing approaches, provides for a statistical way to integrate results from different studies. The approach is more rigorous and objective than other techniques. [7][2]

---

[2] Other approaches to combining studies exist. Space precludes discussing them. For a discussion of clustering, see [8].

For an explanation of why we should *expect* results from different studies to disagree with each other, see [9].

TABLE 16.1

An Example of a Ballot-Box Approach to Summarizing Studies:

Unemployment and Crime

	N of Studies	% Positive/ % Negative	% Positive and Significant/ % Negative and Significant
All Crimes	288	75/25	31/02
Property Crimes	125	85/15	40/03
Violent Crimes	138	64/36	22/02

Note. Property crimes include burglary, larceny, auto theft, general and other property. Violent crimes include murder, robbery, rape, assault, and general violent.

Source. From Table 1, Chiricos, T. G. (1987). "Rates of crime and unemployment: An analysis of aggregate research evidence." *Social Problems* 34: 187–212.

The Mechanics of Meta-analysis

In this section you survey the actual steps involved in conducting a meta-analysis. I will link these steps with the procedures and results of a meta-analysis by Carol Garrett, investigating effects of residential treatments on adjudicated delinquents. [10]

Selecting Relevant Studies You first decide what studies you will include in your meta-analysis. You want to use clear and objective rules for deciding whether to include a study. At this stage you are defining a population of studies. As you learned in Chapter 10, populations must be adequately defined.

You want to decide if you will include just published studies, or unpublished studies as well. Since unpublished studies are more likely to contain null findings, this inclusion decision can have a significant impact on the conclusions of the meta-analysis. Most meta-analyses will strive to include sound, unpublished studies. [e.g., 11]

You want to specify a period, e.g., published since 1960, or published between 1960 and 1970. You want to specify the characteristics of independent and dependent variables for studies you will include. For example,

for studies you will include. For example, you might include all studies that have a treatment as an independent variable, and recidivism as a dependent variable. You can do meta-analyses with experimental or non-experimental studies, or both. You will want to specify characteristics of the people included in the study. For example, with delinquency you might be interested in studies with youth between the ages of 12 and 18. Garrett, in her meta-analysis, used the following criteria for inclusion:

(1) The study must have been completed between 1960 and 1983. (2) The treatment program must have been located in an institutional or community residential . . . setting. Diversion, parole, and probation programs were excluded. (3) Subjects must have been adjudicated juveniles . . . (4) The study design must have included some form of control procedure. [10, p. 289]

At this stage in the process you may be anxious you will find too few studies, or too many. Don't worry. Meta-analysis can be meaningfully conducted on as few as a half dozen studies. Some methods for combining probabilities work well with a few studies. [12] If you unearth such a large population of studies that a full-scale meta-analysis would take the next 5 years of your life, don't despair. You can reduce the number by probability sampling from the population.

Garrett found "126 studies that satisfied the criteria for inclusion in meta-analysis and were available within the time constraints of the study." [10, p. 290]

Select the Measure to Use   You want to describe the impact of the independent variable on the dependent variable. To do so, you will select a common statistical measure to use across studies. Several different measures are available. (See [13] for a discussion of these different methods.) They fall into one of two classes. One group focuses on levels of statistical significance across different studies. (See [12] for a brief discussion of these methods.) A second set addresses *magnitude of impact*— how sizable an effect did the independent variable have on the dependent variable? For a variety of reasons that have to do with the nature and limitations of statistical significance, the latter type of measure is preferable. These measures of impact assess **effect size**. [4]

The Mechanics of Effect Size (ES).   Garrett used the following measure of effect size:

$$ES = \frac{X_E - X_C}{SD_C}$$

where X_E = mean score of the experimental group on the dependent variable of interest.

X_C = mean score of the control group on the dependent variable of interest.

SD_C = standard deviation of the control group on the dependent variable of interest.[3]

---

[3] To obtain an unbiased estimate of the population effect size, you will want to use the denominator that relies on the pooled variance of *both* the experimental and control groups. See [14] for more details.

Example Calculation with Artificial Data   The following artificial data illustrate the construction of a measure of effect size for one study, using the formula used by Garrett.

Outcome = scores on an index measure of psychological adjustment. Scores can range from −3 (extremely poorly adjusted) to + 3 (extremely well adjusted)

Treatment group (n = 50) average score after treatment = + 0.50.

Randomly assigned control group (n = 50) average score at end of observation = − 0.50.

Standard deviation of control group scores on outcome scale = 1.2

$$ES = \frac{+0.50 - (-0.50)}{1.2} = +.83$$

Note that, had the experimental group and the control group had the *same* average score on the outcome:

$$ES = 0$$

Had the experimental group scored *worse* than the control group on the outcome:

$$ES < 0.$$

Interpreting ES   ES, a measure of treatment impact, can be interpreted in percentiles because it is in effect a standardized score or a z score. It is a measure of how many standard deviation units difference exists between the average person in the experimental group and the average person in the control group, on the outcome variable. Because of the properties of the normal curve (see Chapter 10), z scores show the proportions of a population falling above or below a particular score.

Therefore, if you observe an effect size of + .83 in a study, this can be translated into areas under the normal curve (See Appendix A), and can be interpreted as follows:

The 'average' person in the experimental group, with a 50th percentile score in that group on the outcome, had a score that was equivalent to a person scoring in the 80th percentile (.50 + .2967) in the control group.

Compute Common Measure Across Studies and Summarize

Garrett observed, across all studies, that the average effect size associated with the treatment, was +.37. In other words, across all studies the average—50th percentile—score on the outcome variable in the treatment groups was equivalent to the 64th percentile score on the outcome variable in the control group.

Variations and Elaborations in Summarizing

After you have computed a measure of independent variable impact, you can look systematically at subgroups of studies. Garrett, for example, classified studies into those that used "more rigorous" vs. "less rigorous" control procedures. She found that the average treatment effect size was larger in the less rigorous ($ES_{average}$ = .65) as compared to the more rigorous studies ($ES_{average}$ = .24). Sloppier studies had more optimistic findings. She also classified results based on type of outcome measure used. She found that treatments were less effective at influencing recidivism than they were at influencing outcomes such as psychological adjustment.

If you do classify studies into different groups, be sure that your classifications are reliable. Have a friend or coworker check on your classification decisions. You want to use rules that are as objective as possible for categorizing different studies. You might even want to assess the interrater reliability of how you and a friend classify studies.

Meta-Analysis, Significance, Policy, and Controversy

Meta-analyses can summarize an area of research systematically. But there are matters they can*not* resolve.

1. The results of a meta-analysis using measures of effect size do not tell you if the relationship between the independent variable and the dependent variable is statistically significant or not. [See 12, p. 192; 10, p. 304.] Effect size and statistical significance are not necessarily related to one another.

2. If you are examining studies where the independent variable represents a type of treatment program, meta-analyses can show if a treatment has resulted in a positive change on the outcome variable, and the size of that change. Nevertheless, they cannot tell you, or other policy makers, whether that treatment should therefore be carried out on a large-scale basis. Such a decision rests on social factors, policy considerations, and cost–benefit evaluations. [15]

3. Meta-analyses may not resolve controversies. (See Box 16.1.) Different researchers may set study inclusion limits differently, group studies differently, use different measures of effect size, or interpret the same measure of effect size differently.

Meta-analysis: Strengths and Weaknesses

The scientific "quality" of a meta-analysis depends on two factors. First, there is the quality of the studies you summarize. Studies may be low on internal validity, may use unreliable measures, or measures with poor criterion validity. If you only have access to low-quality studies in an area, there is nothing you can do to increase the "validity" of your meta-analysis.

If variations exist in the quality of the studies you are summarizing, there are steps you can take. You can classify studies based on study quality. Such a separation would allow you to report summary effect sizes separately for high- and low-quality studies. For example, Garrett separated studies with more rigorous designs, such as random assignment,

Correctional Treatment, Disagreement, and Meta-Analysis

Steven Lab and John Whitehead completed a meta-analysis of studies on the effects of juvenile correctional treatment. [16, 17] They looked at 50 studies published from 1975 to 1984, and grouped the studies by type of intervention. They concluded that few studies showed a strong relationship between treatment and outcome. "It appears that the earlier evaluations that claim that 'nothing works' are close to the conclusion to be drawn from the more recent evaluations of juvenile treatments." (Abstract)

D. A. Andrews and colleagues subsequently reanalyzed 45 of the 50 studies examined by Lab and Whitehead, and an additional 35 studies. [18] They argued that treatments would have an impact if they were *appropriate*. "[W]e predict that appropriate treatment—treatment that is delivered to higher risk cases, that targets criminogenic needs, and that is matched with the learning styles of offenders—will reduce recidivism" (p. 377). Using type of treatment as a vari-

able—they coded treatments as either criminal sanctions, appropriate, or inappropriate—they were able to predict the impact of treatment on outcome. In contrast to Lab and Whitehead's conclusion that little works, Andrews et al. concluded that appropriate treatment works. "[T]here is a reasonably solid clinical and research basis for political reaffirmation of rehabilitation." (p. 384)

Lab and Whitehead responded in a later piece. [19] They argued with Andrews's classifications of studies, calling it "utopian." They also tempered their original conclusion. "Our review of a particular set of studies showed that the majority were not effective, but some interventions were effective." (p. 414)

How does all this add up? Do not expect that the appearance of meta-analytic studies in an area of research will end or even dampen the controversies there. The analyses may just as well reinvigorate them.

from less rigorous designs. Of course, you want to be sure that the classification rules you use are objective and based on actual study characteristics. You also want them to be reliable, and repeatable with multiple raters.

The second relevant factor is how carefully *you* do the meta-analysis. If you have clear rules for study inclusion, search assiduously for the relevant studies, carefully record study features, and conscientiously calculate the needed statistics, your meta-analysis, *as implemented*, will be all that it can be.

In sum, the major weakness of meta-analysis is its dependence on the quality of the studies being summarized. Low quality studies may lower the validity of the findings generated from the meta-analysis. The main strength of the procedure is its systematic,

unbiased approach to studies, resulting in an objective, quantitative overview of work in an area.

Meta-analysis, Holmes, and Einstein

Meta-analysis is *excellently* suited to Einstein's mode of scientific inquiry. You can see if a hypothesis has support *over a range of different studies*. Support for a hypothesis over a range of studies, as shown by an average effect size significantly larger than 0, or by cumulated probabilities $< .05$, provides *empirical proof of external validity*.[4]

---

[4] To see if the average effect size is significantly different from 0, you need to compute confidence intervals for the effect size statistic. See [14].

Meta-analysis is *moderately well* suited to Holmes's mode of inquiry. You can use relationships observed between effect sizes, and study or population characteristics, to generate theories about why the independent variable has more of an impact on the dependent variable under some conditions as compared to others. Any study feature or population characteristic available to you across a range of studies can be correlated with measures of effect size. The relations you observe help to generate theory.

The limitations of meta-analysis for Holmesian purposes arise for two reasons. You are restricted to the features of studies and respondents reported by the original researchers. In addition, the situations and respondents "sampled" in the different studies may not correspond to the theoretical sampling strategy the Holmesian researcher might have followed.

SIMULATIONS AND MODELING

In this section we turn to a different tool: computer simulations and computer modeling of criminal justice processes. A **computer simulation** represents or models the behavior of a system on a computer. [20] "A computer simulation is a representation of a natural process with a computer program." [21] To help explain this abstract and sometimes complex research activity, we turn again to our running example concerned with foot-patrolling initiatives in particular urban neighborhoods.

A Hypothetical Example

The Foot Patrol Running Example One purpose of the foot patrol officers was to reduce the number of offenders active in the area, many of whom engaged in public drug dealing. The relevant community leaders have not only been pressuring the police de-

partment to begin this initiative in their own neighborhood. They also have demanded that the police department put in *enough* foot patrol officers to *eliminate* active offenders from their neighborhood. Your boss has asked you to estimate how many officers it would take to eliminate the large number of offenders currently presumed active in a target neighborhood.

Use a Simulation to Model a Process Over Time You explain to your boss you can use a computer simulation. It will estimate the kinds of influences varying numbers of foot patrol officers assigned to the locale would have on the offenders in the target neighborhood over time. If you make certain assumptions, the model can make specific predictions about the links between numbers of officers and numbers of active offenders. The simulation will model events, mimicking how the number of assigned officers and the number of active offenders in the locale might influence each other *over time*. Its projections result from the assumptions and calculations you build into the model.

For example, your simulation may expect that the main precinct officer could assign more officers to a particular neighborhood as the active offender population increased in that area. It also may expect that the main precinct officer could decrease the number of assigned officers as the number of active offenders in the locale waned.

Your boss, as usual, expresses amazement at how knowledgeable and capable you are. You scent a potential raise if you can "wow" him on this project.

You Can Use a Spreadsheet to Create the Simulation Computer **spreadsheets** can be used to create simulations. [22, 23] In a spreadsheet, you place data and formulas in cells, arranged according to rows, numbered 1, 2, 3, etc., and columns, labeled A, B, C, and so on. Formulas can refer to data in other cells, or to formulas in other cells. I have created a spreadsheet program that simulates the dynamics of interest. It is contained on the workdisk as a spreadsheet file SIM-ULAA.WK1. You can "run" the simulation using a spreadsheet program such as Lotus 1-2-3 or Excel. Instructions on running the spreadsheet appear in the file SIMULAA.TXT.

Assumptions in the Spreadsheet Simulation Used Here Simulations always contain assumptions about the way things operate. In the simulation described here are several assumptions.

- You start out with 50 foot patrol officers and 200 active offenders, including drug dealers, in the neighborhood.
- Patrol officers remain in the area only as long as the number of active offenders justifies their presence there. As the number of offenders declines, officers are withdrawn and the number of remaining officers in the locale decreases.
- There is constant, intrinsic pressure to 'export' officers out of the locale, and assign them to other locales.
- Officers have a certain success in capturing offenders or driving offenders out of the neighborhood.
- These two outcomes—capturing an offender, or deterring an offender from operating in the neighborhood—are treated as equivalent by the simulation.
- Offenders have a certain success in evading capture.
- The number of offenders in the locale, and the number of officers in the locale, change weekly.
- At the beginning of each new week, the number of foot patrol officers and the number of active offenders both depend solely on the numbers for the preceding week.

- There is no theoretical limit to the number of patrol officers that could be assigned to the locale.

The results of a simulation are only as realistic as its assumptions are. If you make improper assumptions, your simulation will not provide realistic results.

Results When you "run" the simulation you tell it to advance one week at a time. At each new week, it recalculates the numbers of offenders and officers in the locale based on its assumptions, and the numbers for the prior week. As you advance across weeks you can see how numbers of officers and offenders change in relation to each other.

Figure 16.1 shows the changes in assigned officers and active offenders in the neighborhood over a 52-week period. Officers increase in the locale (weeks 1–5), resulting in dramatic decreases in the number of active offenders. Numbers of assigned officers decrease also, but more slowly. Eventually, after large numbers of officers have been withdrawn, offenders start moving into the area again, or becoming active again (weeks 10–25). Officers increase as well, but only after the number of active offenders has started to increase dramatically. Finally, the high number of officers results in decreases in offenders. The cycle seen in weeks 1–26 repeats in weeks 27–52.

Comment Obviously the simulation depicted here has limitations:

- It oversimplifies complex processes. It assumes that very complex changes over time can be modeled with some simple mathematics.
- It depends upon several assumptions that may or may not be correct.
- It also leaves things out. It omits other factors shaping patrol allocation and offender

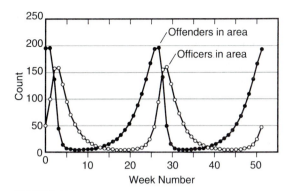

FIGURE 16.1

Results of a simulation of active offenders and assigned officers in a neighborhood. Each data point represents the levels of active offenders and assigned officers a week apart. *Source.* Results from spreadsheet SIMULAA.WKI. Spreadsheet dynamics loosely modeled after [22].

activity. You could, of course, modify the simulation to incorporate additional factors if you wished.

Nevertheless, albeit simple minded in many respects, the simulation is of interest. It reveals surprising results. For example, given the assumptions of the model, it takes many officers to reduce the active offender population to very low levels. Is the number of officers required to reduce the offender population larger than you would have thought? In addition, offender populations appear to "grow" faster than the number of assigned officers, a "finding" that seems reasonable given the nature of the criminal justice system. What other insights are suggested to *you* by the pattern of results?

The Purpose of Simulations

People use simulations for a range of purposes. You can use simulations for *theory-testing purposes.* [24] You define concepts, operationalize them with variables in the sim-

ulation, and define how they interact with other operationalized concepts. The procedure allows you to examine the consequences of a proposed hypothesis.[5] Based on the consequences you observe, you can make subsequent refinements in your theory. [26] You can then immediately examine the consequences of those refinements by rerunning the simulation.

Simultaneously, you can examine what effects changes in different system parameters would have on the outcome. You can imagine levels of an independent variable that are unlikely to occur in the real world. In the simulation above, for example, you could model what would happen if you started with 200 police officers assigned to the neighborhood. This ability to explore consequences of system parameters that are unlikely to occur in the real world represents an important advantage of simulations. [27]

Simulations also can be used for *policy evaluation.* The policy may focus on microscale or small-scale phenomena, such as the operations of a district court system [cf. 28], or macroscale or large-scale phenomena like the entire criminal justice system [29], or the entire U.S. economy. [30] The model may forecast future outcomes if a current situation continues, or if a new policy or program is put into place. (See Box 16.2)

A third general goal simulations serve is to *educate or rehabilitate.* Simulations allow individuals to role play how they might act in various situations. Through this role playing they can learn more about the situations and

---

[5] "Simulation may be able to assist in evaluating hypotheses, not in the sense that an experiment in the physical sciences can test a hypothesis, but in the sense of making plain the ramifications of a hypothesis. The value of specifying a hypothesis with sufficient clarity to be amenable to programming and of examining the consequences of that hypothesis should not be underestimated." [25]

B O X 16.2

Modeling and Minnesota Sentencing Guidelines

Minnesota criminal justice planners setting up determinate sentencing guidelines in the early 1980s developed a simulation forecasting the influence of the new guidelines on prison populations. [31, 32] The model depicted various pathways for offenders through the criminal justice system, and estimated probabilities for each pathway. (See Figure 16.2.) The model used data from 6,000 felony cases and examined sentencing length under the proposed sentencing guidelines. The simulation allowed policy makers to examine effects of the proposed guidelines on sentence disparities and racial makeup of the prison population. Planners constructed projections for a 5-year period. The model played an important role in the politics surrounding the implementation of the guidelines, because it was "plain vanilla" and decision makers had played key roles in its development. [33]

---

creases, a second may increase, and a third may decrease. For example, in the simulation above the number of foot patrol officers assigned to the locale depended upon the number of active offenders. As the latter climbed, so did the former; as the latter declined, so too did the former.

3. *Outcomes depend upon several conditions.* For example, the Minnesota Sentencing Guidelines simulation assumed that the final prison population was a result of several factors operating elsewhere in the system.

4. *The process requires random inputs.* The program does not fix 'scores' on the independent variables or inputs. The values result from random processes. Programmers can simulate random processes using **Monte Carlo Techniques**. [37] With such techniques programmers run a simulation many times, varying values on the input variables using specific types of distributions of random scores.

themselves. Resnick, for example, describes a therapeutic simulation for institutionalized delinquents. [35] Players face situations where they can act either prosocially or antisocially. The game involves more than just one player and a computer; certain choices require group discussion among the players.

When to Simulate

You might want to develop a simulation in any of the following situations: [36]

1. *The social process under investigation is complex*, with many actors or agents. In such involved situations outcomes cannot always be easily predicted.

2. *The processes you are examining change dynamically over time.* As one variable in-

Varieties of Simulations

Simulations come in many different varieties: [27, 38]

1. They may be **data-driven**, using actual data to set the values of the independent variables; or they may be **data-free**, setting initial levels of the independent variables based solely on theoretical considerations.

2. They may be **stochastic** or **probabilistic** simulations, relying on chance or Monte Carlo techniques to influence the scores of one or more variables in the simulation. Or they may be **nonstochastic** or **deterministic**, with scores on independent variables already set by the researcher. The above patrol officer simulation is an example of the latter. It allowed for no random variation in any of the variables or param-

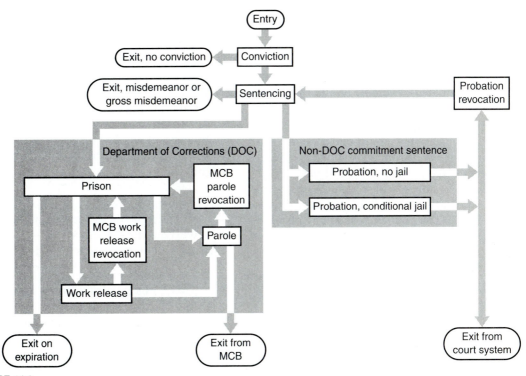

FIGURE 16.2
The flowchart used in the Minnesota Sentencing Guidelines simulation. "Using Minnesota Court data, branching probabilities were estimated to move felons through the system." [34] *Source.* Brent, E. E., Jr., and Anderson, R. E. (1990) *Computer applications in the social sciences.* New York: McGraw Hill. Figure 10.5, p. 198.

eters in the model. It could be changed into a stochastic model by introducing one or more random processes. For example, you could model random variations in the pressure to export foot patrol officers to other locations. This might correspond to real-world shifts in demand for patrol officers based on citywide variations in the crime rate.

3. Finally, simulations can model *discrete* or *continuous* phenomena. Many dynamic processes are also continuous. A process is continuous if there is no smallest possible discrete change on the variable because the variable is continuous (e.g.,

changes in temperature). It is possible, however, to approximate infinitesimally small changes with finite differences. [22]

Steps in Constructing a Simulation

There are four or three steps in simulation construction, depending on whether you use Holmes's mode of inquiry or Einstein's. In the Holmes mode of inquiry you make the following translations:

Real
World → Theory → Model → Program
Data   (Simulation)

In the Einstein mode of inquiry you make the following translations:

Theory → Model → Program
(Simulation)

Data   If your simulation is *data-driven*, you begin by collecting relevant data. Say you want to model the influences of increased prison construction on imprisonment rates at the state level. You would obtain state level information on prison bed capacity, and incarceration rate, over a period of years. Your simulation follows *Holmes's* mode of inquiry if you start with actual data; you are trying to infer causal dynamics from actual observations.

Alternatively, your simulation may be *theory-driven* rather than *data-driven*. If so, you need not consult actual data when formulating initial levels of variables, or in constructing links between variables. Here your simulation follows *Einstein's* mode of inquiry.

The above patrol officer simulation was largely data-free. You could make it data driven by deriving estimates of the number of offenders active in a neighborhood, the number of assigned foot patrol officers, and limits on the maximum number of foot patrol officers assignable to a neighborhood. You also could use data to set the values for the other system parameters, such as officer success in capturing or expelling active offenders.

Theory   The next step is to construct theory: state your concepts, operationalize them, and hypothesize how they connect to one another.

Following the Holmes method and using a data-driven simulation, you will be inferring concepts from the variables for which you have measures. You also will be developing hypotheses connecting variables based on the relations you have observed. Your theoretical statements should be causal and falsifiable. [39] They should reflect the actual relationships observed in the data.

You will be less encumbered if you are following the Einstein method. You will simply state your concepts, operationalize each, and specify how you expect them to relate to each other. For example, in the patrol simulation example, the theory says that the number of patrol officers imported into the neighborhood would be dependent upon the current number of active offenders in the neighborhood.

Model   Next you state your theory in a precise model. In the model you connect all variables with mathematical formulas. The patrol simulation above contains model statements such as the following:

This Week's Patrol Officer Count
in Neighborhood =
((Last Week's Patrol Officer Count) +
(Number of Patrol Officers Imported) −
(Number of Patrol Officers Exported))

Program   In the final step you develop the program. The computer program *is* the simulation. It is a *simulator* of the real world. Many simulation computer languages are available for creating simulation programs. (See [40] for a somewhat dated list of simulation languages.) You also can use simple spreadsheets for creating the program. [22] In the patrol simulation spreadsheet on the workdisk, the formulas appearing in the cells, and the initial settings in cells (e.g., initial number of patrol officers) make up the program.

Issues of Validity and Reliability

Now that your simulation is constructed, how can you learn if it is *valid*? A simulation has **simulation validity** if it *is similar in form to* *the system, which may be a real-world situation, it seeks to represent.* [39] Simulation validity represents a special type of *criterion validity*. The criterion is the system, which is often an actual data pattern, that you hope the simulation represents.

Components of Simulation Validity This overall simulation validity depends on three subtypes of validity. A data-driven simulation will be valid if *all* of the following are valid: the underlying theory, the underlying model, and the program. [39] If the theory correctly represents reality, the simulation has **theory validity**. If the model correctly represents the theory, the simulation has **model validity**. If the final program correctly represents the model, the simulation has **program validity**. If your simulation scores high on all three types of validity, then you can say the simulation itself is valid.

Sources of Error A simulation may *not* be valid because sources of error can enter at any step in the simulation building process. Thus, a more accurate description of building a data-driven simulation might be as follows, where E represents different sources of error introduced:

$$E_t \qquad E_m \qquad E_p$$

Real
World $\to$ Theory $\to$ Model $\to$ Program
Data $\qquad\qquad\qquad\qquad$ (Simulation)

Errors may enter through several avenues in the simulation construction process. [41, 42] There are three main types: errors in theory (E_t), errors in modeling (E_m), and errors in programming (E_p). Here are some examples:

- Your theory may leave out a key construct or process operative in the real world. (E_t).

- Your theory may *overfit* the data (E_t). That is, you may include variables that capture "noise" or random variation, mimicking every bump and wiggle in the data, rather than actual underlying dynamic processes. [41]
- Your model may leave out a key aspect of your theory (E_m). Your theory may specify that neighborhood characteristics influence a building's chances of becoming an arson target, for example, but your model may not include neighborhood characteristics. [43, 44]
- You make a programming error, and instead of adding two variables, as your model specifies, you multiply them (E_p). Programmers are human, too.

Assessing Validity

Theory-driven If your simulation is Einsteinian in nature and purely *theory-driven*, no precise technique for assessing its validity exists. No single set of data represents the best "benchmark" against which to "test" the simulation. You can, however, observe the following. Are the outputs produced by the simulation reasonable? Do they produce patterns that seem common-sensical? Would experts in the area find the results believable? Can any counterintuitive results be attributed to system dynamics, and not mistakes?

Data-driven If your simulation follows the Holmes mode of inquiry there are three strategies you can use to assess validity.

One approach is to see if the final simulation can reproduce the original data used to construct it. Worrall, for example, developed a simulation of the Adelaide (Australia) magistrate's court. She then validated the simulation by observing that it reproduced key features of court functioning such as number of adjournments and number of cases that went to trial. [28]

Figure 16.3 depicts this process of assessing **event history validity**. If event history validity is high—the simulation reproduces the data from which it was constructed—then you can conclude that model and program validity are high. If the reproduction effort is *not* successful, then either model validity, or program validity, or both, may be low. Event history validity does not allow you to assess theory validity, because you are going back to the same data you used to derive your theory.

A second approach requires splitting your original data into two random halves. (See Figure 16.4.) You develop your theory, model, and program using half the data. To establish validity, you assess how well your model produces the random half of the original data *not* used in your initial efforts. This approach is **split-sample cross-validation**. If it results in high simulation validity and can mimic the new data, then you know that theory, model and program validity are all high. If it results in low validity, one or more of these subtypes of validity may be low.

A third approach (**cross-validation**) is to develop the simulation based on one set of

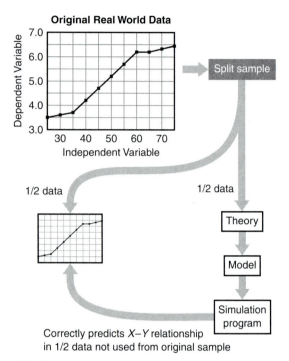

FIGURE 16.4
Split-sample cross-validation simultaneously tests theory, model, and program validity.

data, and then test the resulting simulation on a separate, independent source of data. (See Figure 16.5.) Again, if simulation validity is high, you have confirmed that theory, model, and program validity are all high. In this situation you are assessing the generalizability or *external validity* of the simulation, observing if it applies across different times, population, and places. Until you establish the external validity of a simulation, you should not assume it is present or absent.

How High Should Simulation Validity Be? How well should the data-driven simulation results "fit" real world data? Do I always need to worry about all three types of validity (theory, model, and program)? It depends on your purposes. The type and degree of val-

FIGURE 16.3
Event history validity simultaneously tests model and program validity. It cannot be used to test theory validity.

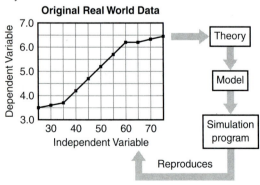

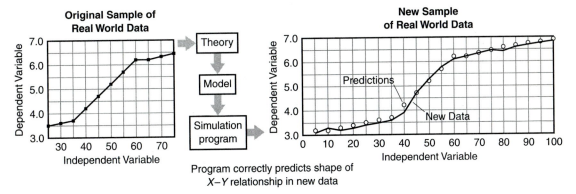

FIGURE 16.5
Cross-validation simultaneously tests theory, model, and program validity.

idity you require depend upon the type of problem you address. [39]

You may need an extremely high level of validity, for example, if you are modeling the costs and benefits of a planned policy. For such a purpose you may require that all three subtypes of validity be high.

But suppose you are constructing a simulation to reproduce historical trends linking violence and economics (cf. Chapter 15 on historical criminology)? If you know that the data you use as input are "noisy" and poorly measured, you may not require a high level of simulation validity. If you are never to apply the simulation to different historical circumstances, and different variables, you will not worry about theory validity.

Reliability Reliability is not an issue for deterministic or nonprobabilistic simulations. Each time you run the simulation you should obtain identical results.

With probabilistic simulations, however, results may vary. Each time you run the program, scores on the random input variables will change slightly. If you are developing a simulation of this variety, you will want to run it often. Then you can verify that the results are close to one another on successive runs.

Simulations, Einstein, and Holmes

Simulations are *well suited* to Einstein's mode of inquiry. They allow you to test simultaneously complex sets of causal hypotheses. Unfettered by data if you construct a data-free simulation, you can ask your simulation to 'imagine' how one variable would affect another under conditions unlikely to emerge in the real world. You can hypothesize what the effects would be on crime and imprisonment rates if all prison construction were stopped in the U.S. for 20 years. You could hypothesize what would happen to crime in Houston if the number of foot patrol officers was quadrupled in high drug sale areas in the city. Hypotheses such as these can be addressed with simulations, and tested. Bear in mind, however, this is not hypothesis testing in the usual sense, where you see if real data support your ideas. Instead, it is a systematic exploration of the *ramifications* or *consequences* of hypotheses. If I say things work like this, what happens?

Data-driven simulations are *moderately well suited* to Holmes's mode of inquiry. A data-driven simulation embodies a *grounded theory* that also has been *operationalized*. When you cross-validate the simulation, you learn whether your simulation is adequate. Limitations in the use of simulations for Holmesian purposes arise for two reasons. First, the data available to you may be limited. You may be interested in certain variables, but they may simply not be obtainable. Second, your ability to sample theoretically relevant, additional situations so as to clarify your theory is limited. The archival sources providing your in-formation constrain your explorations. Nonetheless, if your simulation *does* provide results that correspond closely to original or new data, at least you have established that the theory embodied in your simulation adequately represents *one* way that things *might* work.

SUMMARY OF MAIN POINTS

- In a meta-analysis, you "add up" the results from several different studies on a topic to obtain an overall picture of research in an area.
- Meta-analysis summarizes a group of studies more systematically than a standard literature review or a ballot box approach to summarizing research.
- Meta-analyses will not necessarily resolve disagreements in an area of research.
- A computer simulation models hypothetical or real-world processes, attempting to mimic them as closely as possible.
- Every computer simulation contains many assumptions about the way things operate; these assumptions may or may not be correct.
- Simulations can be used for testing theory, projecting future trends, estimating effects of new programs (policy evaluation), and education.
- A data-driven simulation is valid if it produces results that are similar in form to those appearing in the real world.
- Simulation validity represents a special type of criterion validity.
- If a simulation has high theory, model, and program validity, it will have high simulation validity.

SUGGESTED READINGS

Meta-analysis. I know of three introductory volumes. They are all readable, but require some background in statistics. The volume by Glass et al. is the most dated, published in 1981. [13] Wolf's is the most recent, published in 1986. [45] Rosenthal, who authored the third volume, has published most extensively in the area of meta-analysis and research methods. [46]

Simulations. If you want to know about the politics of modeling and simulations in the federal government, read *Datawars*. [30] See how decisions to use a simulation depend on far more than the qualities of the model.

KEY TERMS

ballot box approach
computer simulation
cross-validation
data-driven
data-free
deterministic
effect size
event history validity
meta-analysis
model validity
Monte Carlo techniques
nonstochastic
primary data analysis

probabilistic
program validity
secondary data analysis
simulation validity
split-sample cross-validation
spreadsheets
stochastic
theory validity
voting

REFERENCES

1. Glass, G. V. (1976) Primary, secondary, and meta-analysis research. *Educational Researcher 5*, 3–8

2. Inter-university Consortium for Political and Social Research. (1991) *Guide to resources and services: 1991–1992*, ICPSR, Ann Arbor, MI

3. Mosteller, F. M., and Bush, R. R. (1954) Selected quantitative techniques. In *Handbook of Social Psychology*, First ed., Vol. 1 (Lindzey, G., ed). Reading, MA: Addison Wesley.

4. Cohen, J. (1977) *Statistical power analysis for the behavioral sciences*, Second ed., Academic Press, New York

5. Cooper, H. M. (1979) Statistically combining independent studies: A Meta-analysis of sex differences in conformity research. *Journal of Personality and Social Psychology 37*, 131–146

6. Chiricos, T. G. (1987) Rates of crime and unemployment: An Analysis of aggregate research evidence. *Social Problems 34*, 187–212

7. Cooper, H. M., and Rosenthal, R. (1980) Statistical vs. traditional procedures for summarizing research findings. *Psychological Bulletin 87*, 442–449

8. Light, R. J., and Smith, P. V. (1971) Accumulating evidence: Procedures for resolving contradictions among different studies. *Harvard Educational Review 41*, 429–471

9. Taveggia, T. C. (1974) Resolving research controversy through empirical cumulation: Toward reliable sociological knowledge. *Sociological Methods and Research 2*, 395–407

10. Garrett, C. J. (1985) Effects of residential treatment on adjudicated delinquents: A Meta-analysis. *Journal of Research in Crime and Delinquency 22*, 287–308

11. Wells, L. E., and Rankin, J. H. (1991) Families and delinquency: A Meta-analysis of the impact of broken homes. *Social Problems 38*, 501–523

12. Rosenthal, R. (1978) Combining results of independent studies. *Psychological Bulletin 85*, 185–193

13. Glass, G. V., McGraw, B., and Smith, M. L. (1981) *Meta-analysis in social research*, Sage, Beverly Hills, CA

14. Hedges, L. V. (1982) Estimation of effect size from a series of independent experiments. *Psychological Bulletin 92*, 490–499

15. Rossi, P. H., and Freeman, H. E. (1985) *Evaluation: A Systematic approach*, Third ed., Sage, Beverly Hills, CA

16. Whitehead, J. T., and Lab, S. P. (1989) A Meta-analysis of juvenile correlational treatment. *Journal of Research in Crime and Delinquency 26*, 276–295

17. Lab, S. P., and Whitehead, J. T. (1988) An Analysis of juvenile correctional treatment. *Crime & Delinquency 34*, 60–85

18. Andrews, D. A., Zinger, I., Hoge, R. D., Bonta, J., Gendreau, P., and Cullen, F. T. (1990) Does correctional treatment work?: A Clinically relevant and psychologically informed meta-analysis. *Criminology 28*, 369–404

19. Lab, S. P., and Whitehead, J. T. (1990) From "nothing works" to "the appropriate works:" The Latest stop on the search for the secular grail. *Criminology 28*, 405–417

20. Little, A. (1984) Feigning reality. *BYTE 9*(March), 93

21. Brent, E. E., Jr., and Anderson, R. E. (1990) *Computer applications in the social sciences*, McGraw Hill, New York, p. 190

22. Matheny, A. (1984) Simulation with electronic spreadsheets. *BYTE 9*(March), 411–414

23. Miller, R. M., and Kelso, A. S., Jr. (1985) Analyzing government policies: Economic modeling with Lotus 1-2-3. *BYTE 10*(October), 199–211

24. Brent, E. E., Jr., and Anderson, R. E. (1990) *Computer applications in the social sciences*, McGraw Hill, New York, p. 188

25. Clune, T. (1985) Simulating society. *BYTE* *10*(October), 149

26. Coleman, J. S. (1989) Simulations games and development of social theory. *Simulation and games 20*, 144–164

27. Federico, P., and Figliozzi, P. W. (1981) Computer simulation of social systems. *Sociological Methods and Research 9*, 513–533

28. Worrall, J. (1982) A Computer simulation of a court of summary jurisdiction. *Australian and New Zealand Journal of Criminology 15*, 154–162

29. Blumstein, A., and Larson, R. (1969) Models of a total criminal justice system. *Operations Research 17*, 199–232.

30. Kraemer, K. L., Dickhoven, S., Tierney, S. F., and King, J. L. (1987) *Datawars: The Politics of modeling in federal policymaking*, Columbia University Press, New York

31. Knapp, K. A. (1986) Proactive policy analysis of Minnesota's prison populations. *Criminal Justice Policy Review 1*, 35–37

32. Brent, E. E., Jr., and Anderson, R. E. (1990) *Computer applications in the social sciences*, McGraw Hill, New York, p. 199

33. Brent, E. E., Jr., and Anderson, R. E. (1990) *Computer applications in the social sciences*, McGraw Hill, New York, p. 199

34. Brent, E. E., Jr., and Anderson, R. E. (1990) *Computer applications in the social sciences*, McGraw Hill, New York, p. 198

35. Resnick, H. (1987) Electronic technology and rehabilitation: A Computerized simulation for youthful offenders. *Simulation and Games 17*, 460–466

36. Brent, E. E., Jr., and Anderson, R. E. (1990) *Computer applications in the social sciences*, McGraw Hill, New York, p. 191

37. Hamilton, L. C. (1992) *Regression with graphics: A Second course in applied statistics.* Brooks/Cole, Pacific Grove, CA, pp. 304–312

38. Brent, E. E., Jr., and Anderson, R. E. (1990) *Computer applications in the social sciences*, McGraw Hill, New York

39. Stanislaw, H. (1986) Tests of computer simulation validity. *Simulation and games 17*, 173–191

40. Pratt, C. A. (1984) Going further. *BYTE* *9*(March), 204–207

41. Larimore, W. E., and Mehra, R. K. (1985) The Problem of overfitting data. *BYTE 10*(October), 167–180

42. Houston, T. R. (1985) Why models go wrong. *BYTE 10*(October), 151–164

43. Dillenbeck, B. (1985) Fighting fire with technology. *BYTE 10*(October), 249–251

44. Cook, R. (1985) Predicting arson. *BYTE 10*(October), 239–245

45. Wolf, F. (1986) *Meta-analysis: Quantitative methods for research synthesis*, Sage, Beverly Hills, CA

46. Rosenthal, R. (1984) *Meta-analytic procedures for social research*, Sage, Beverly Hills, CA

APPENDIX

TABLE 1
Random Numbers

10	09	73	25	33	76	52	01	35	86	34	67	35	48	76	80	95	90	91	17	39	29	27	49	45
37	54	20	48	05	64	89	47	42	96	24	80	52	40	37	20	63	61	04	02	00	82	29	16	65
08	42	26	89	53	19	64	50	93	03	23	20	90	25	60	15	95	33	47	64	35	08	03	36	06
99	01	90	25	29	09	37	67	07	15	38	31	13	11	65	88	67	67	43	97	04	43	62	76	59
12	80	79	99	70	80	15	73	61	47	64	03	23	66	53	98	95	11	68	77	12	17	17	68	33
66	06	57	47	17	34	07	27	68	50	36	69	73	61	70	65	81	33	98	85	11	19	92	91	70
31	06	01	08	05	45	57	18	24	06	35	30	34	26	14	86	79	90	74	39	23	40	30	97	32
85	26	97	76	02	02	05	16	56	92	68	66	57	48	18	73	05	38	52	47	18	62	38	85	79
63	57	33	21	35	05	32	54	70	48	90	55	35	75	48	28	46	82	87	09	83	49	12	56	24
73	79	64	57	53	03	52	96	47	78	35	80	83	42	82	60	93	52	03	44	35	27	38	84	35
98	52	01	77	67	14	90	56	86	07	22	10	94	05	58	60	97	09	34	33	50	50	07	39	98
11	80	50	54	31	39	80	82	77	32	50	72	56	82	48	29	40	52	42	01	52	77	56	78	51
83	45	29	96	34	06	28	89	80	83	13	74	67	00	78	18	47	54	06	10	68·	71	17	78	17
88	68	54	02	00	86	50	75	84	01	36	76	66	79	51	99	36	47	64	93	29	60	91	10	62
99	59	46	73	48	87	51	76	49	69	91	82	60	89	28	93	78	56	13	68	23	47	83	41	13
65	48	11	76	74	17	46	85	09	50	58	04	77	69	74	73	03	95	71	86	40	21	81	65	44
80	12	43	56	35	17	72	70	80	15	45	31	82	23	74	21	11	57	82	53	14	38	55	37	63
74	35	09	98	17	77	40	27	72	14	43	23	60	02	10	45	52	16	42	37	96	28	60	26	55
69	91	62	68	03	66	25	22	91	48	36	93	68	72	03	76	62	11	39	90	94	40	05	64	18
09	89	32	05	05	14	22	56	85	14	46	42	75	67	88	96	29	77	88	22	54	38	21	45	98
91	49	91	45	23	68	47	92	76	86	46	16	28	35	54	94	75	08	99	23	37	08	92	00	48
80	33	69	45	98	26	94	03	68	58	70	29	73	41	35	53	14	03	33	40	42	05	08	23	41
44	10	48	19	49	85	15	74	79	54	32	97	92	65	75	57	60	04	08	81	22	22	20	64	13
12	55	07	37	42	11	10	00	20	40	12	86	07	46	97	96	64	48	94	39	28	70	72	58	15
63	60	64	93	29	16	50	53	44	84	40	21	95	25	63	43	65	17	70	82	07	20	73	17	90
61	19	69	04	46	26	45	74	77	74	51	92	43	37	29	65	39	45	95	93	42	58	26	05	27
15	47	44	52	66	95	27	07	99	53	59	36	78	38	48	82	39	61	01	18	33	21	15	94	66
94	55	72	85	73	67	89	75	43	87	54	62	24	44	31	91	19	04	25	92	92	92	74	59	73
42	48	11	62	13	97	34	40	87	21	16	86	84	87	67	03	07	11	20	59	25	70	14	66	70
23	52	37	83	17	73	20	88	98	37	68	93	59	14	16	26	25	22	96	63	05	52	28	25	62
04	49	35	24	94	75	24	63	38	24	45	86	25	10	25	61	96	27	93	35	65	33	71	24	72
00	54	99	76	54	64	05	18	81	59	96	11	96	38	96	54	69	28	23	91	23	28	72	95	29
35	96	31	53	07	26	89	80	93	54	33	35	13	54	62	77	97	45	00	24	90	10	33	93	33
59	80	80	83	91	45	42	72	68	42	83	60	94	97	00	13	02	12	48	92	78	56	52	01	06
46	05	88	52	36	01	39	09	22	86	77	28	14	40	77	93	91	08	36	47	70	61	74	29	41
32	17	90	05	97	87	37	92	52	41	05	56	70	70	07	86	74	31	71	57	85	39	41	18	38
69	23	46	14	00	20	11	74	52	04	15	95	66	00	00	18	74	39	24	23	97	11	89	63	38
19	56	54	14	50	01	75	87	53	70	40	41	92	15	85	66	67	43	68	06	84	96	28	52	07
45	15	51	49	38	19	47	60	72	46	43	66	79	45	43	59	04	79	00	33	20	82	66	95	41
94	86	43	19	94	36	16	81	08	51	34	88	88	15	53	01	54	03	54	56	05	01	45	11	76

TABLE 1
Random Numbers *(Continued)*

98	08	62	48	26	45	24	02	84	04	44	99	90	88	96	39	09	47	34	07	35	44	13	18	80
33	18	51	62	32	41	94	15	09	49	89	43	54	85	81	88	69	54	19	94	37	54	87	30	43
80	95	10	04	06	96	38	27	07	74	20	15	12	33	87	25	01	62	52	98	94	62	46	11	71
79	75	24	91	40	71	96	12	82	96	69	86	10	25	91	74	85	22	05	39	00	38	75	95	79
18	63	33	25	37	98	14	50	65	71	81	01	02	46	74	05	45	56	14	27	77	93	89	19	36
74	02	94	39	02	77	55	73	22	70	97	79	01	71	19	52	52	75	80	21	80	81	45	17	48
54	17	84	56	11	80	99	33	71	43	05	33	51	29	69	56	12	71	92	55	36	04	09	03	24
11	66	44	98	83	52	07	98	48	27	59	38	17	15	39	09	97	33	34	40	88	46	12	33	56
48	32	47	79	28	31	24	96	47	10	02	29	53	68	70	32	30	75	75	46	15	02	00	99	94
69	07	49	41	38	87	63	79	19	76	35	58	40	44	01	10	51	82	16	15	01	84	87	69	38
09	18	82	00	97	32	82	53	95	27	04	22	08	63	04	83	38	98	73	74	64	27	85	80	44
90	04	58	54	97	51	98	15	06	54	94	93	88	19	97	91	87	07	61	50	68	47	66	46	59
73	18	95	02	07	47	67	72	52	69	62	29	06	44	64	27	12	46	70	18	41	36	18	27	60
75	76	87	64	90	20	97	18	17	49	90	42	91	22	72	95	37	50	58	71	93	82	34	31	78
54	01	64	40	56	66	28	13	10	03	00	68	22	73	98	20	71	45	32	95	07	70	61	78	13
08	35	86	99	10	78	54	24	27	85	13	66	15	88	73	04	61	89	75	53	31	22	30	84	20
28	30	60	32	64	81	33	31	05	91	40	51	00	78	93	32	60	46	04	75	94	11	90	18	40
53	84	08	62	33	81	59	41	36	28	51	21	59	02	90	28	46	66	87	95	77	76	22	07	91
91	75	75	37	41	61	61	36	22	69	50	26	39	02	12	55	78	17	65	14	83	48	34	70	55
89	41	59	26	94	00	39	75	83	91	12	60	71	76	46	48	94	97	23	06	94	54	13	74	08
77	51	30	38	20	86	83	42	99	01	68	41	48	27	74	51	90	81	39	80	72	89	35	55	07
19	50	23	71	74	69	97	92	02	88	55	21	02	97	73	74	28	77	52	51	65	34	46	74	15
21	81	85	93	13	93	27	88	17	57	05	68	67	31	56	07	08	28	50	46	31	85	33	84	52
51	47	46	64	99	68	10	72	36	21	94	04	99	13	45	42	83	60	91	91	08	00	74	54	49
99	55	96	83	31	62	53	52	41	70	69	77	71	28	30	74	81	97	81	42	43	86	07	28	34
33	71	34	80	07	93	58	47	28	69	51	92	66	47	21	58	30	32	98	22	93	17	49	39	72
85	27	48	68	93	11	30	32	92	70	28	83	43	41	37	73	51	59	04	00	71	14	84	36	43
84	13	38	96	40	44	03	55	21	66	73	85	27	00	91	61	22	26	05	61	62	82	71	84	23
56	73	21	62	34	17	39	59	61	31	10	12	39	16	22	85	49	65	75	60	81	60	41	88	80
65	13	85	68	06	87	64	88	52	61	34	31	36	58	61	45	87	52	10	69	85	64	44	72	77
38	00	10	21	76	81	71	91	17	11	71	60	29	29	37	74	21	96	40	49	65	58	44	96	98
37	40	29	63	97	01	30	47	75	86	56	27	11	00	86	47	32	46	26	05	40	03	03	74	38
97	12	54	03	48	87	08	33	14	17	21	81	53	92	50	75	23	76	20	47	15	50	12	95	78
21	82	64	11	34	47	14	33	40	72	64	63	88	59	02	49	13	90	64	41	03	85	65	45	52
73	13	54	27	42	95	71	90	90	35	85	79	47	42	96	08	78	98	81	56	64	69	11	92	02
07	63	87	79	29	03	06	11	80	72	96	20	74	41	56	23	82	19	95	38	04	71	36	69	94
60	52	88	34	41	07	95	41	98	14	59	17	52	06	95	05	53	35	21	39	61	21	20	64	55
83	59	63	56	55	06	95	89	29	83	05	12	80	97	19	77	43	35	37	83	92	30	15	04	98
10	85	06	27	46	99	59	91	05	07	13	49	90	63	19	53	07	57	18	39	06	41	01	93	62
39	82	09	89	52	43	62	26	31	47	64	42	18	08	14	43	80	00	93	51	31	02	47	31	67

TABLE 1
Random Numbers *(Continued)*

59	58	00	64	78	75	56	97	88	00	88	83	55	44	86	23	76	80	61	56	04	11	10	84	08
38	50	80	73	41	23	79	34	87	63	90	82	29	70	22	17	71	90	42	07	95	95	44	99	53
30	69	27	06	68	94	68	81	61	27	56	19	68	00	91	82	06	76	34	00	05	46	26	92	00
65	44	39	56	59	18	28	82	74	37	49	63	22	40	41	08	33	76	56	76	96	29	99	08	36
27	26	75	02	64	13	19	27	22	94	07	47	74	46	06	17	98	54	89	11	97	34	13	03	58
91	30	70	69	91	19	07	22	42	10	36	69	95	37	28	28	82	53	57	93	28	97	66	62	52
68	43	49	46	88	84	47	31	36	22	62	12	69	84	08	12	84	38	25	90	09	81	59	31	46
48	90	81	58	77	54	74	52	45	91	35	70	00	47	54	83	82	45	26	92	54	13	05	51	60
06	91	34	51	97	42	67	27	86	01	11	88	30	95	28	63	01	19	89	01	14	97	44	03	44
10	45	51	60	19	14	21	03	37	12	91	34	23	78	21	88	32	58	08	51	43	66	77	08	83
12	88	39	73	43	65	02	76	11	84	04	28	50	13	92	17	97	41	50	77	90	71	22	67	69
21	77	83	09	70	38	80	73	69	61	31	64	94	20	96	63	28	10	20	23	08	81	64	74	49
19	52	35	95	15	65	12	25	96	59	86	28	38	82	58	69	57	21	37	98	16	43	59	15	29
67	24	55	26	70	35	58	31	65	63	79	24	68	66	86	76	46	33	42	22	26	65	59	08	02
60	58	44	73	77	07	50	03	79	92	45	13	42	65	29	26	76	08	36	37	41	32	64	43	44
53	85	34	13	77	36	06	69	48	50	58	83	87	38	59	49	36	47	33	31	96	24	04	30	42
24	63	73	87	36	74	38	48	93	42	52	62	30	79	92	12	36	91	86	01	03	74	28	38	73
83	08	01	24	51	38	99	22	28	15	07	75	95	17	77	97	37	72	75	85	51	97	23	78	67
16	44	42	43	34	36	15	19	90	73	27	49	37	09	39	85	13	03	25	52	54	84	65	47	59
60	79	01	81	57	57	17	86	57	62	11	16	17	85	76	45	81	95	29	79	65	13	00	48	60
03	99	11	04	61	93	71	61	68	94	66	08	32	40	53	84	60	95	82	32	88	61	81	91	61
38	55	59	55	54	32	88	05	97	80	08	35	56	08	60	29	73	54	77	62	71	29	92	38	53
17	54	67	37	04	92	05	24	62	15	55	12	12	92	81	59	07	60	79	36	27	95	45	89	09
32	64	35	28	01	95	81	90	68	31	00	91	19	89	36	76	35	59	37	79	80	86	30	05	14
69	57	26	87	77	39	51	03	59	05	14	06	04	06	19	29	54	96	96	16	33	56	46	07	80
24	12	26	65	91	27	69	90	64	94	14	84	54	66	72	61	95	87	71	00	90	89	97	57	54
61	19	63	02	31	92	96	26	17	73	41	83	95	53	82	17	26	77	09	43	78	03	87	02	67
30	53	22	17	04	10	27	41	22	02	39	68	52	33	09	10	06	16	88	29	55	98	66	64	85
03	78	89	75	99	75	86	72	07	17	74	41	65	31	66	35	20	83	33	74	87	53	90	88	23
48	22	86	33	79	85	78	34	76	19	53	15	26	74	33	35	66	35	29	72	16	81	86	03	11
60	36	59	46	53	35	07	53	39	49	42	61	42	92	97	01	91	82	83	16	98	95	37	32	31
83	79	94	24	02	56	62	33	44	42	34	99	44	13	74	70	07	11	47	36	09	95	81	80	05
32	96	00	74	05	36	40	98	32	32	99	38	54	16	00	11	13	30	75	86	15	91	70	62	53
19	32	25	38	45	57	62	05	26	06	66	49	76	86	46	78	13	86	65	59	19	64	09	94	13
11	22	09	47	47	07	39	93	74	08	48	50	92	39	29	27	48	24	54	76	85	24	43	51	59
31	75	15	72	60	68	98	00	53	39	15	47	04	83	55	88	65	12	25	98	03	15	21	92	21
88	49	29	93	82	14	45	40	45	04	20	09	49	89	77	74	84	39	34	13	22	10	97	85	08
30	93	44	77	44	07	48	18	38	28	73	78	80	65	33	28	59	72	04	05	94	20	52	03	80
22	88	84	88	93	27	49	99	87	48	60	53	04	51	28	74	02	28	46	17	82	03	71	02	68
78	21	21	69	93	35	90	29	13	86	44	37	21	54	86	65	74	11	40	14	87	48	13	72	20

TABLE 1
Random Numbers (*Continued*)

41	84	98	45	47	46	85	05	23	26	34	67	75	83	00	74	91	06	43	45	19	32	58	15	49
46	35	23	30	49	69	24	89	34	60	45	30	50	75	21	61	31	83	18	55	14	41	37	09	51
11	08	79	62	94	14	01	33	17	92	59	74	76	72	77	76	50	33	45	13	39	66	37	75	44
52	70	10	83	37	56	30	38	73	15	16	52	06	96	76	11	65	49	98	93	02	18	16	81	61
57	27	53	68	98	81	30	44	85	85	68	65	22	73	76	92	85	25	58	66	88	44	80	35	84
20	85	77	31	56	70	28	42	43	26	79	37	59	52	20	01	15	96	32	67	10	62	24	83	91
15	63	38	49	24	90	41	59	36	14	33	52	12	66	65	55	82	34	76	41	86	22	53	17	04
92	69	44	82	97	39	90	40	21	15	59	58	94	90	67	66	82	14	15	75	49	76	70	40	37
77	61	31	90	19	88	15	20	00	80	20	55	49	14	09	96	27	74	82	57	50	81	69	76	16
38	68	83	24	86	45	13	46	35	45	59	40	47	20	59	43	94	75	16	80	43	85	25	96	93
25	16	30	18	89	70	01	41	50	21	41	29	06	73	12	71	85	71	59	57	68	97	11	14	03
65	25	10	76	29	37	23	93	32	95	05	87	00	11	19	92	78	42	63	40	18	47	76	56	22
36	81	54	36	25	18	63	73	75	09	82	44	49	90	05	04	92	17	37	01	14	70	79	39	97
64	39	71	16	92	05	32	78	21	62	20	24	78	17	59	45	19	72	53	32	83	74	52	25	67
04	51	52	56	24	95	09	66	79	46	48	46	08	55	58	15	19	11	87	82	16	93	03	33	61
83	76	16	08	73	43	25	38	41	45	60	83	32	59	83	01	29	14	13	49	20	36	80	71	26
14	38	70	63	45	80	85	40	92	79	43	52	90	63	18	38	38	47	47	61	41	19	63	74	80
51	32	19	22	46	80	08	87	70	74	88	72	25	67	36	66	16	44	94	31	66	91	93	16	78
72	47	20	00	08	80	89	01	80	02	94	81	33	19	00	54	15	58	34	36	35	35	25	41	31
05	46	65	53	06	93	12	81	84	64	74	45	79	05	61	72	84	81	18	34	79	98	26	84	16
39	52	87	24	84	82	47	42	55	93	48	54	53	52	47	18	61	91	36	74	18	61	11	92	41
81	61	61	87	11	53	34	24	42	76	75	12	21	17	24	74	62	77	37	07	58	31	91	59	97
07	58	61	61	20	82	64	12	28	20	92	90	41	31	41	32	39	21	97	63	61	19	96	79	40
90	76	70	42	35	13	57	41	72	00	69	90	26	37	42	78	46	42	25	01	18	62	79	08	72
40	18	82	81	93	29	59	38	86	27	94	97	21	15	98	62	09	53	67	87	00	44	15	89	97
34	41	48	21	57	86	88	75	50	87	19	15	20	00	23	12	30	28	07	83	32	62	46	86	91
63	43	97	53	63	44	98	91	68	22	36	02	40	09	67	76	37	84	10	05	65	96	17	34	88
67	04	90	90	70	93	39	94	55	47	94	45	87	42	84	05	04	14	98	07	20	28	83	40	60
79	49	50	41	46	52	16	29	02	86	54	15	83	42	43	46	97	83	54	82	59	36	29	59	38
91	70	43	05	52	04	73	72	10	31	75	05	19	30	29	47	66	56	43	82	99	78	29	34	78

TABLE 2
Areas Under the Normal Curve

Fractional parts of the total area (10,000) under the normal curve, corresponding to distances between the mean and ordinates which are Z standard-deviation units from the mean.

Z	.00	.01	.02	.03	.04	.05	.06	.07	.08	.09
0.0	0000	0040	0080	0120	0159	0199	0239	0279	0319	0359
0.1	0398	0438	0478	0517	0557	0596	0636	0675	0714	0753
0.2	0793	0832	0871	0910	0948	0987	1026	1064	1103	1141
0.3	1179	1217	1255	1293	1331	1368	1406	1443	1480	1517
0.4	1554	1591	1628	1664	1700	1736	1772	1808	1844	1879
0.5	1915	1950	1985	2019	2054	2088	2123	2157	2190	2224
0.6	2257	2291	2324	2357	2389	2422	2454	2486	2518	2549
0.7	2580	2612	2642	2673	2704	2734	2764	2794	2823	2852
0.8	2881	2910	2939	2967	2995	3023	3051	3078	3106	3133
0.9	3159	3186	3212	3238	3264	3289	3315	3340	3365	3389
1.0	3413	3438	3461	3485	3508	3531	3554	3577	3599	3621
1.1	3643	3665	3686	3718	3729	3749	3770	3790	3810	3830
1.2	3849	3869	3888	3907	3925	3944	3962	3980	3997	4015
1.3	4032	4049	4066	4083	4099	4115	4131	4147	4162	4177
1.4	4192	4207	4222	4236	4251	4265	4279	4292	4306	4319
1.5	4332	4345	4357	4370	4382	4394	4406	4418	4430	4441
1.6	4452	4463	4474	4485	4495	4505	4515	4525	4535	4545
1.7	4554	4564	4573	4582	4591	4599	4608	4616	4625	4633
1.8	4641	4649	4656	4664	4671	4678	4686	4693	4699	4706
1.9	4713	4719	4726	4732	4738	4744	4750	4758	4762	4767
2.0	4773	4778	4783	4788	4793	4798	4803	4808	4812	4817
2.1	4821	4826	4830	4834	4838	4842	4846	4850	4854	4857
2.2	4861	4865	4868	4871	4875	4878	4881	4884	4887	4890
2.3	4893	4896	4898	4901	4904	4906	4909	4911	4913	4916
2.4	4918	4920	4922	4925	4927	4929	4931	4932	4934	4936
2.5	4938	4940	4941	4943	4945	4946	4948	4949	4951	4952
2.6	4953	4955	4956	4957	4959	4960	4961	4962	4963	4964
2.7	4965	4966	4967	4968	4969	4970	4971	4972	4973	4974
2.8	4974	4975	4976	4977	4977	4978	4979	4980	4980	4981
2.9	4981	4982	4983	4984	4984	4984	4985	4985	4986	4986
3.0	4986.5	4987	4987	4988	4988	4988	4989	4989	4989	4990
3.1	4990.0	4991	4991	4991	4992	4992	4992	4992	4993	4993
3.2	4993.129									
3.3	4995.166									
3.4	4996.631									
3.5	4997.674									
3.6	4998.409									
3.7	4998.922									
3.8	4999.277									
3.9	4999.519									
4.0	4999.683									
4.5	4999.966									
5.0	4999.997133									

NAME INDEX

SUBJECT INDEX